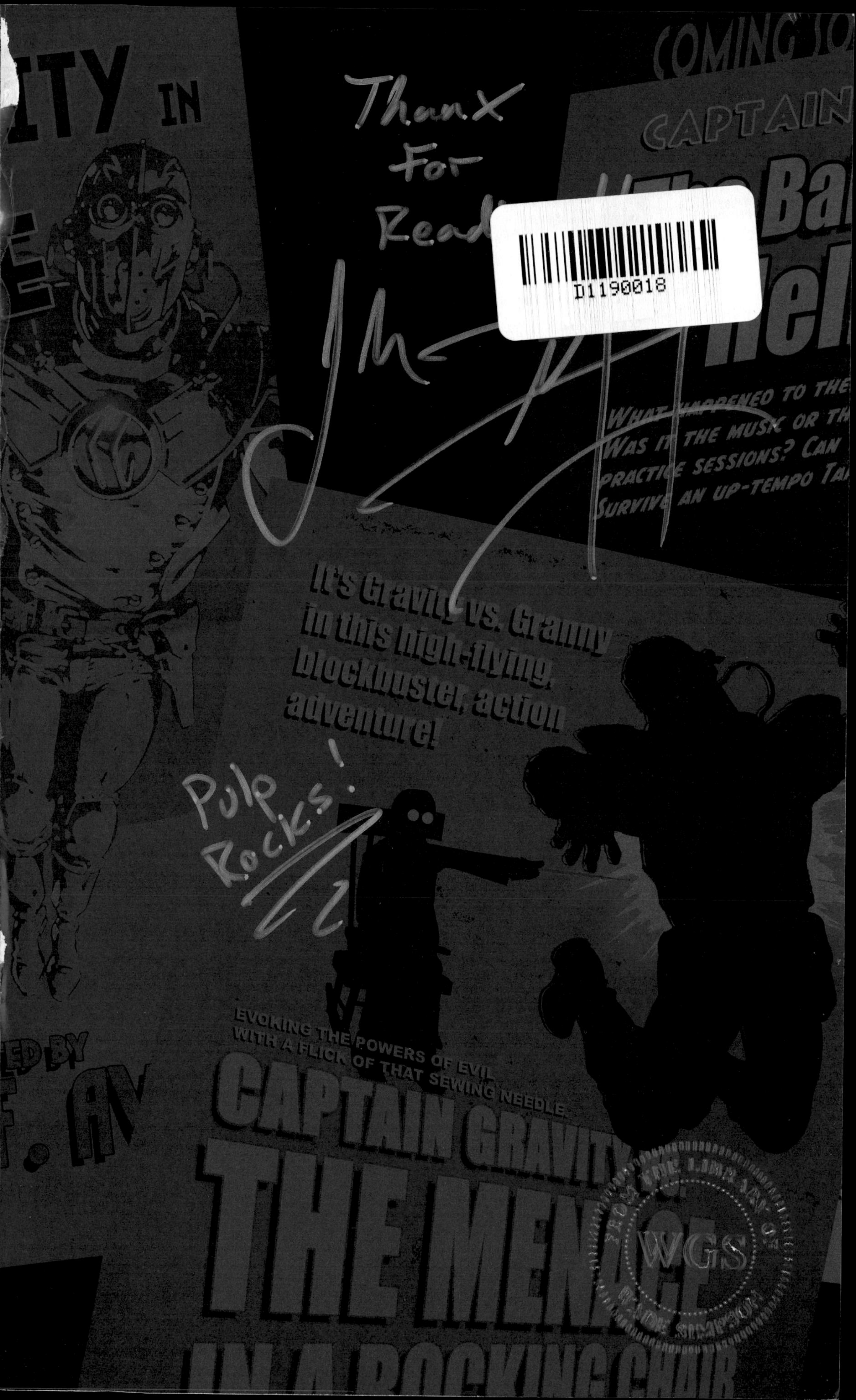

ITY IN
COMING SO
CAPTAIN
The Ba
Hel
WHAT HAPPENED TO THE
WAS IT THE MUSIC OR TH
PRACTICE SESSIONS? CAN
SURVIVE AN UP-TEMPO TA
It's Gravity vs. Granny in this high-flying, blockbuster, action adventure!
EVOKING THE POWERS OF EVIL WITH A FLICK OF THAT SEWING NEEDLE.
CAPTAIN GRAVITY
THE MENACE
IN A ROCKING CHAIR
Thanx For Read
Pulp Rocks!

A PENNY—FARTHING PRESS, INC. BOOK

penny
farthing
press™

CAPTAIN GRAVITY AND THE POWER OF THE VRIL GRAPHIC NOVEL
PUBLISHED BY PENNY-FARTHING PRESS, INC.
10370 RICHMOND AVENUE, SUITE 980
HOUSTON, TEXAS 77042
(713) 780-0300 OR (800) 926-2669
CORP@PFPRESS.COM
WWW.PFPRESS.COM

987654321

ISBN: 0-9719012-8-7

Printed in Canada

A PENNY-FARTHING PRESS PRODUCTION

CAPTAIN GRAVITY
AND THE POWER OF THE VRIL

WRITTEN BY JOSHUA DYSART • PENCILS BY SAL VELLUTO • INKS BY BOB ALMOND, JOE RUBENSTEIN & SAL VELLUTO • COLORS BY MIKE GARCIA • LETTERS BY RICHARD STARKINGS & COMICCRAFTS'S ALBERT DESCHESNE • COVER BY SAL VELLUTO & MIKE GARCIA

CREATED BY STEPHEN VRATTOS

PUBLISHER
Ken White, Jr.

SENIOR EDITOR
Michelle Nichols

EDITOR-IN-CHIEF
Marlaine Maddux

TALENT COORDINATOR
Courtney Huddleston

CREATIVE DIRECTOR
Trainor Houghton

GRAPHIC DESIGNER
Andre' McBride

ART DIRECTOR
Charles M. Hancock

OFFICE MANAGER
Pam Johnston

GERMAN CONSULTANT
Simone Spikes

**V. P. OF MARKETING AND
MEDIA COMMUNICATION**
Pamela Miltenberger

ACCOUNTS MANAGER
Selma Medina

penny
farthing
press™

LETTER FROM
THE EDITOR-IN-CHIEF

Dear *Captain Gravity* Readers,

Captain Gravity has always held a special place in the history and heart of Penny-Farthing Press. It was the very first comic book published by our company when we opened for business in 1998. Because our publisher, Ken White, had developed his love of the medium by reading Golden Age comics, he wanted our first endeavor (a four issue mini-series) to be an homage to that period. We sent out feelers to writers and other people in the industry and received several good story ideas. But, in the end, the *Captain Gravity* concept from Stephen Vrattos was the one that captured our imagination and was given the green light for development and publication. After the book was released, we immediately knew we had tapped into an under served reservoir of Golden Age fans. There was no doubt that we wanted to reprise the series down the road, we just didn't realize how difficult that would be. Ken had told us early on that he would only do it if we got the perfect story and the perfect creative team. Well, it has taken eight years to fulfill that criteria, but when we received an outstanding story proposal from Joshua Dysart, we knew we were on our way. We commissioned him to write a six issue mini-series while we began to assemble a creative team with all the special skills to make this story come to life. It was easier said than done. Eventually, after a few false starts, we brought together penciler Sal Velluto (his noir period art blew us away), Bob Almond (we told him to pull out the stops to reinforce Sal's pencils), and Mike Garcia's sophisticated colors that nostalgically help us remember the comics of that era but forcefully set the mood of this strong narrative. We all agree that, like music, these colors dramatically enhance our enjoyment of the story. Much effort and care has been put into this project and I think you will see it in the final product.

We are excited and optimistic about *Captain Gravity*, and we hope our readers will enjoy the story as much as we have.

Remember: NOBODY ESCAPES THE LAW OF GRAVITY!

Sincerely,
Marlaine Maddux

Penny-Farthing Press, Inc.
10370 Richmond Ave., Suite 980 • Houston, TX 77042 • 713.780.0300 • fax 713.780.4004 • www.pfpress.com

FIRST DAY COVE
首 日 封
20th January 1971

CAPTAIN GRAVITY™
And the POWER of the VRIL

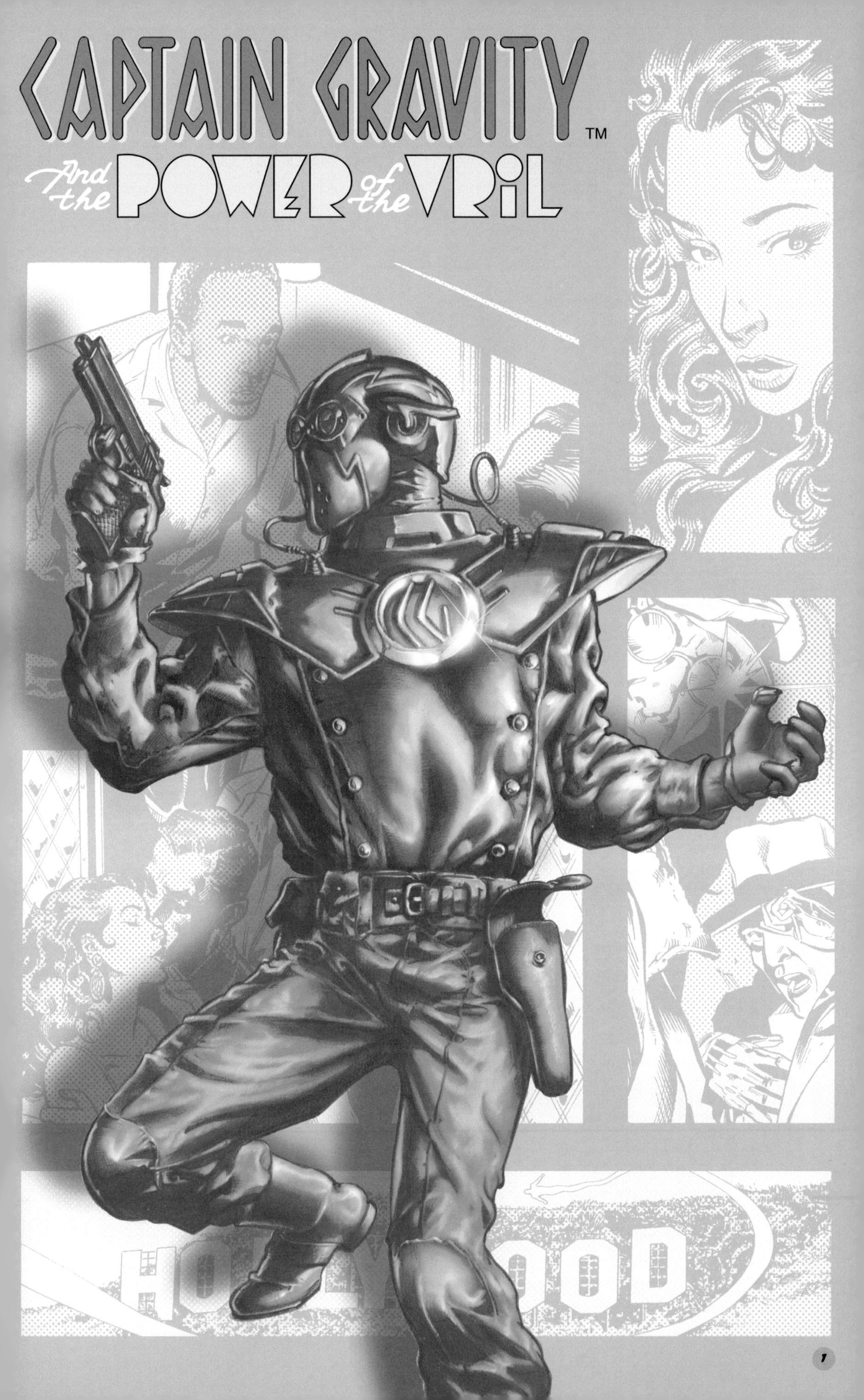

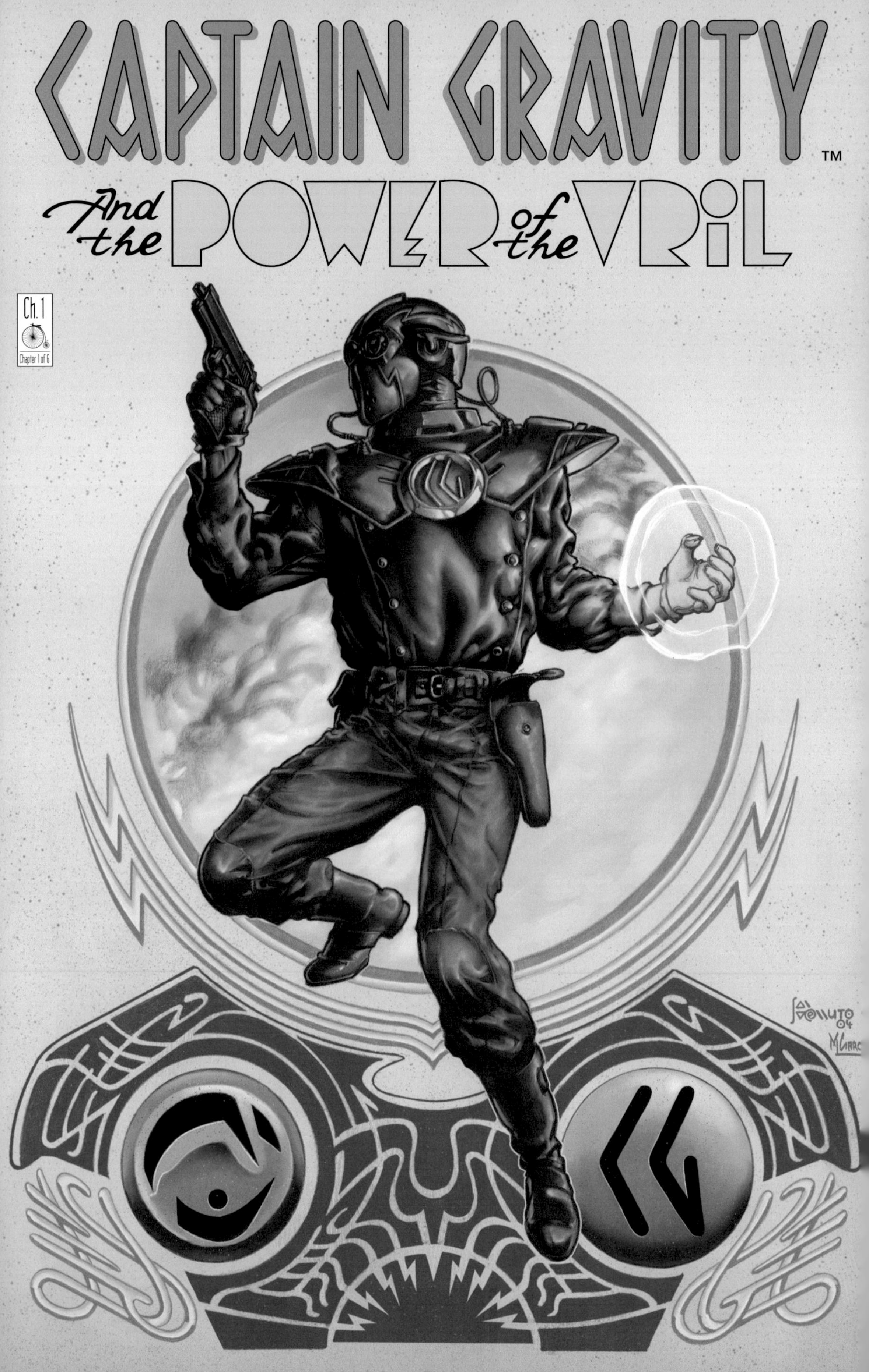
CAPTAIN GRAVITY™
And the POWER of the VRIL
Ch.1
Chapter 1 of 6

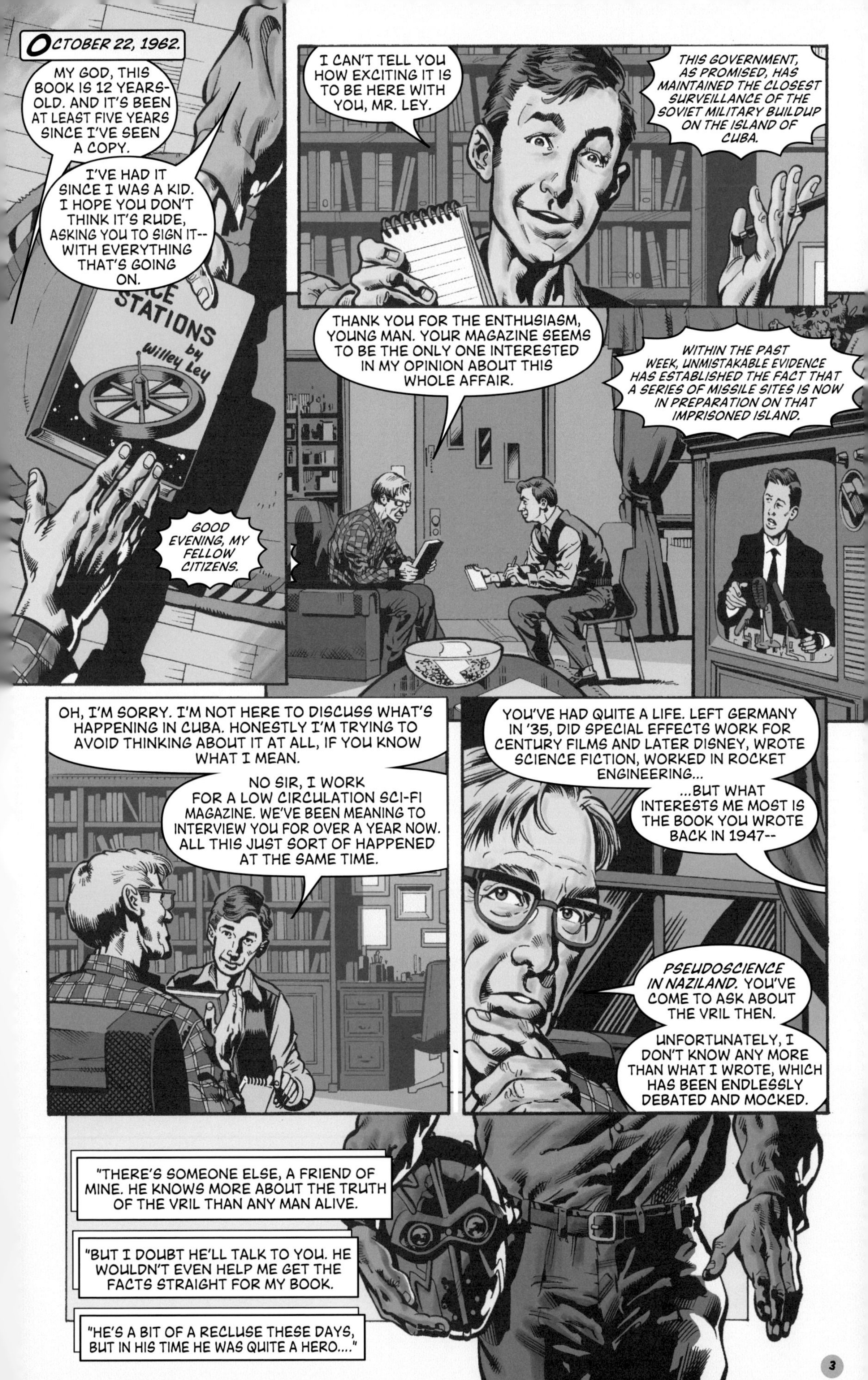
OCTOBER 22, 1962.
MY GOD, THIS BOOK IS 12 YEARS-OLD. AND IT'S BEEN AT LEAST FIVE YEARS SINCE I'VE SEEN A COPY.
I'VE HAD IT SINCE I WAS A KID. I HOPE YOU DON'T THINK IT'S RUDE, ASKING YOU TO SIGN IT-- WITH EVERYTHING THAT'S GOING ON.
STATIONS by Willey Ley
GOOD EVENING, MY FELLOW CITIZENS.
I CAN'T TELL YOU HOW EXCITING IT IS TO BE HERE WITH YOU, MR. LEY.
THIS GOVERNMENT, AS PROMISED, HAS MAINTAINED THE CLOSEST SURVEILLANCE OF THE SOVIET MILITARY BUILDUP ON THE ISLAND OF CUBA.
THANK YOU FOR THE ENTHUSIASM, YOUNG MAN. YOUR MAGAZINE SEEMS TO BE THE ONLY ONE INTERESTED IN MY OPINION ABOUT THIS WHOLE AFFAIR.
WITHIN THE PAST WEEK, UNMISTAKABLE EVIDENCE HAS ESTABLISHED THE FACT THAT A SERIES OF MISSILE SITES IS NOW IN PREPARATION ON THAT IMPRISONED ISLAND.
OH, I'M SORRY. I'M NOT HERE TO DISCUSS WHAT'S HAPPENING IN CUBA. HONESTLY I'M TRYING TO AVOID THINKING ABOUT IT AT ALL, IF YOU KNOW WHAT I MEAN.
NO SIR, I WORK FOR A LOW CIRCULATION SCI-FI MAGAZINE. WE'VE BEEN MEANING TO INTERVIEW YOU FOR OVER A YEAR NOW. ALL THIS JUST SORT OF HAPPENED AT THE SAME TIME.
YOU'VE HAD QUITE A LIFE. LEFT GERMANY IN '35, DID SPECIAL EFFECTS WORK FOR CENTURY FILMS AND LATER DISNEY, WROTE SCIENCE FICTION, WORKED IN ROCKET ENGINEERING...
...BUT WHAT INTERESTS ME MOST IS THE BOOK YOU WROTE BACK IN 1947--
PSEUDOSCIENCE IN NAZILAND. YOU'VE COME TO ASK ABOUT THE VRIL THEN.
UNFORTUNATELY, I DON'T KNOW ANY MORE THAN WHAT I WROTE, WHICH HAS BEEN ENDLESSLY DEBATED AND MOCKED.
"THERE'S SOMEONE ELSE, A FRIEND OF MINE. HE KNOWS MORE ABOUT THE TRUTH OF THE VRIL THAN ANY MAN ALIVE.
"BUT I DOUBT HE'LL TALK TO YOU. HE WOULDN'T EVEN HELP ME GET THE FACTS STRAIGHT FOR MY BOOK.
"HE'S A BIT OF A RECLUSE THESE DAYS, BUT IN HIS TIME HE WAS QUITE A HERO...."

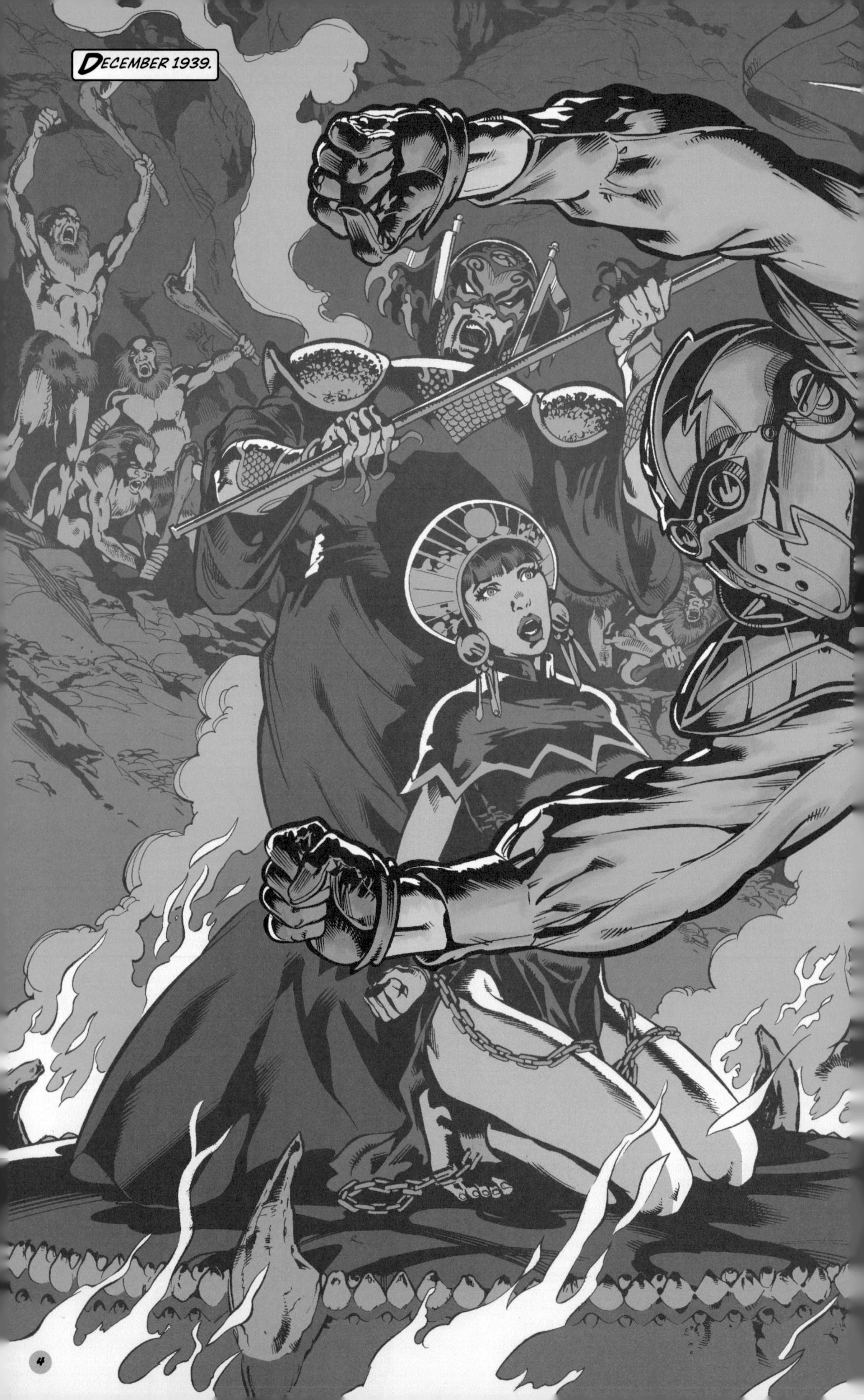
DECEMBER 1939.

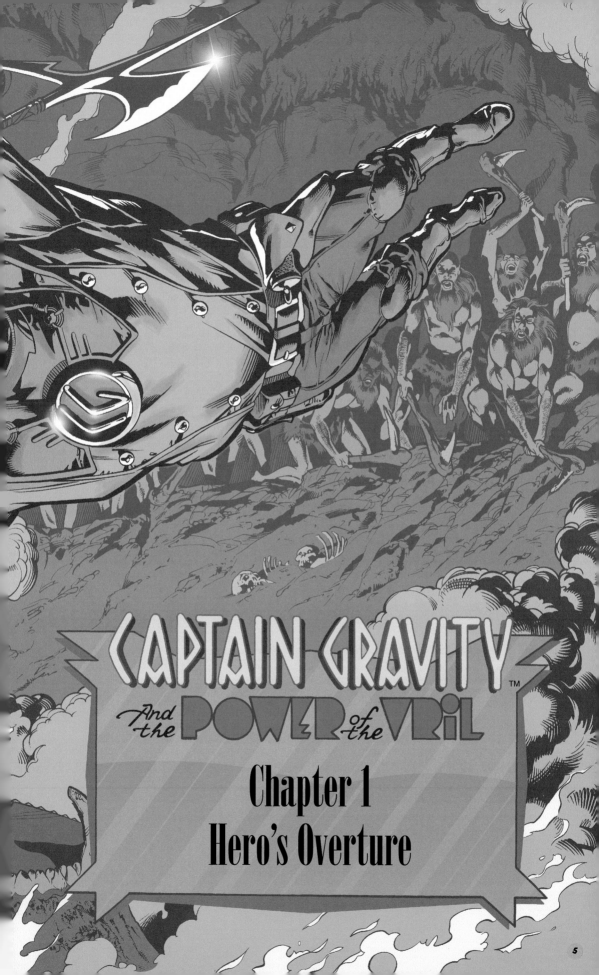

CAPTAIN GRAVITY
And the POWER of the VRIL

Chapter 1
Hero's Overture

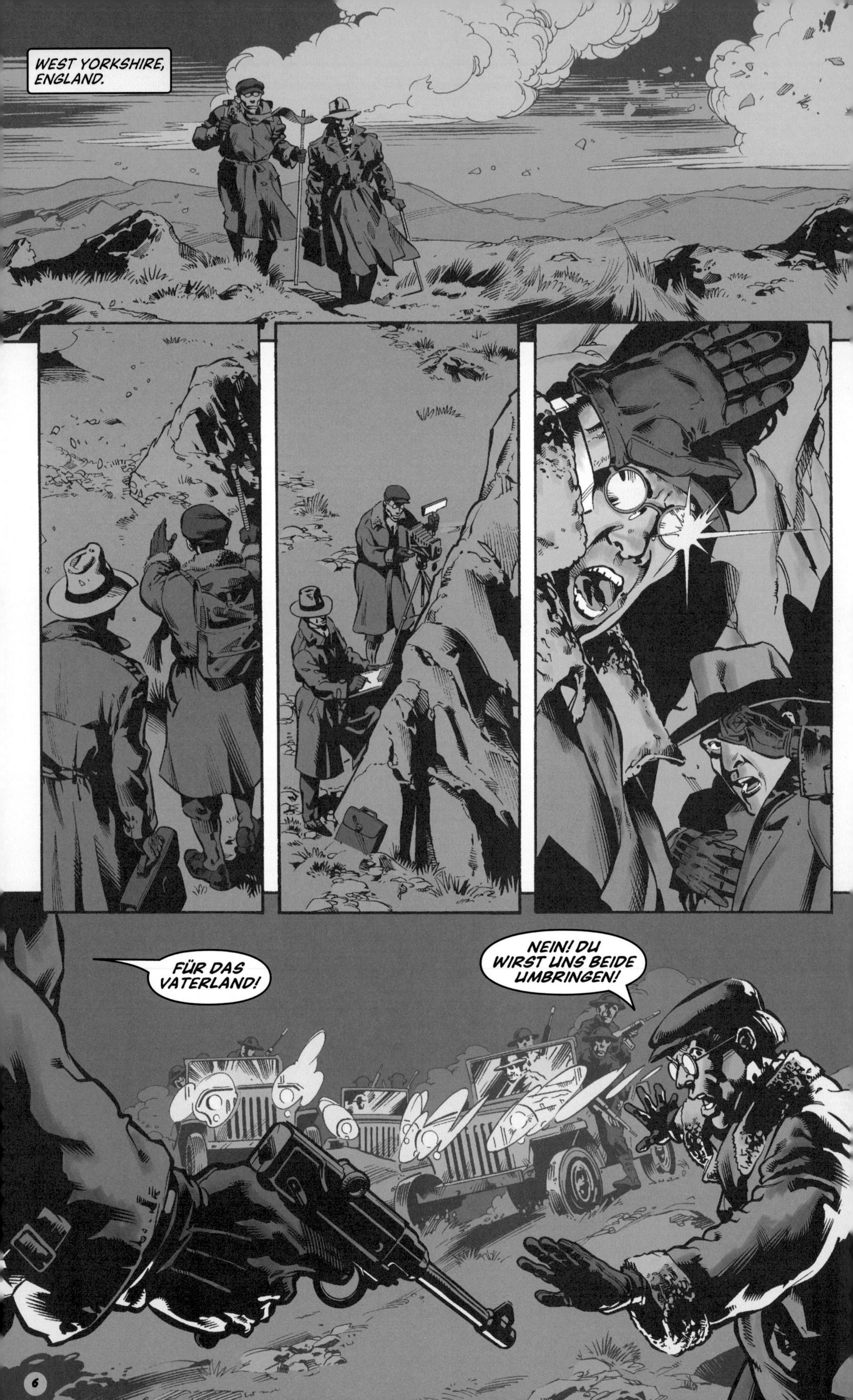
WEST YORKSHIRE, ENGLAND.
FÜR DAS VATERLAND!
NEIN! DU WIRST UNS BEIDE UMBRINGEN!

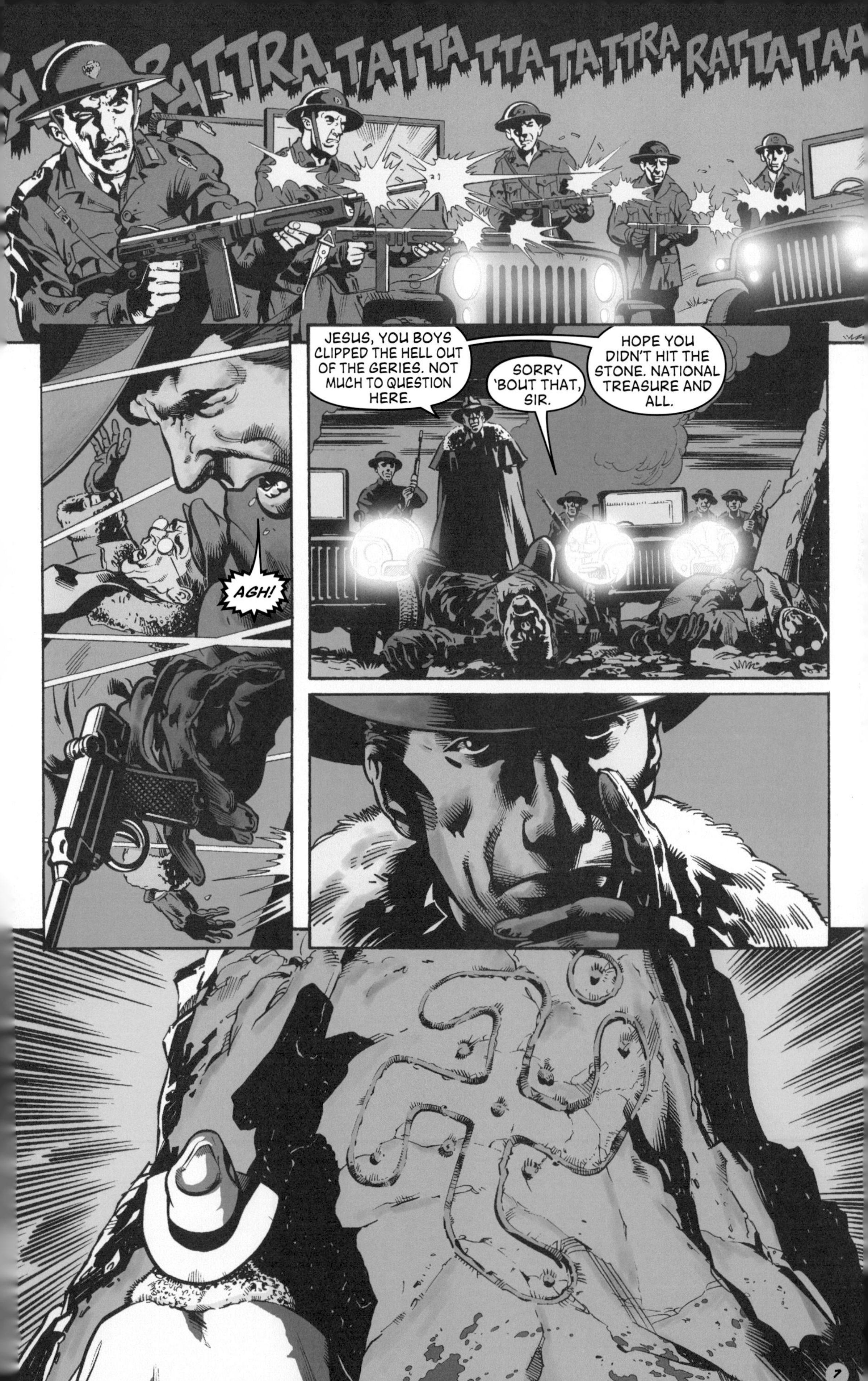
RATTRA TATTA TTA TATTRA RATTA TAA
AGH!
JESUS, YOU BOYS CLIPPED THE HELL OUT OF THE GERIES. NOT MUCH TO QUESTION HERE.
SORRY 'BOUT THAT, SIR.
HOPE YOU DIDN'T HIT THE STONE. NATIONAL TREASURE AND ALL.

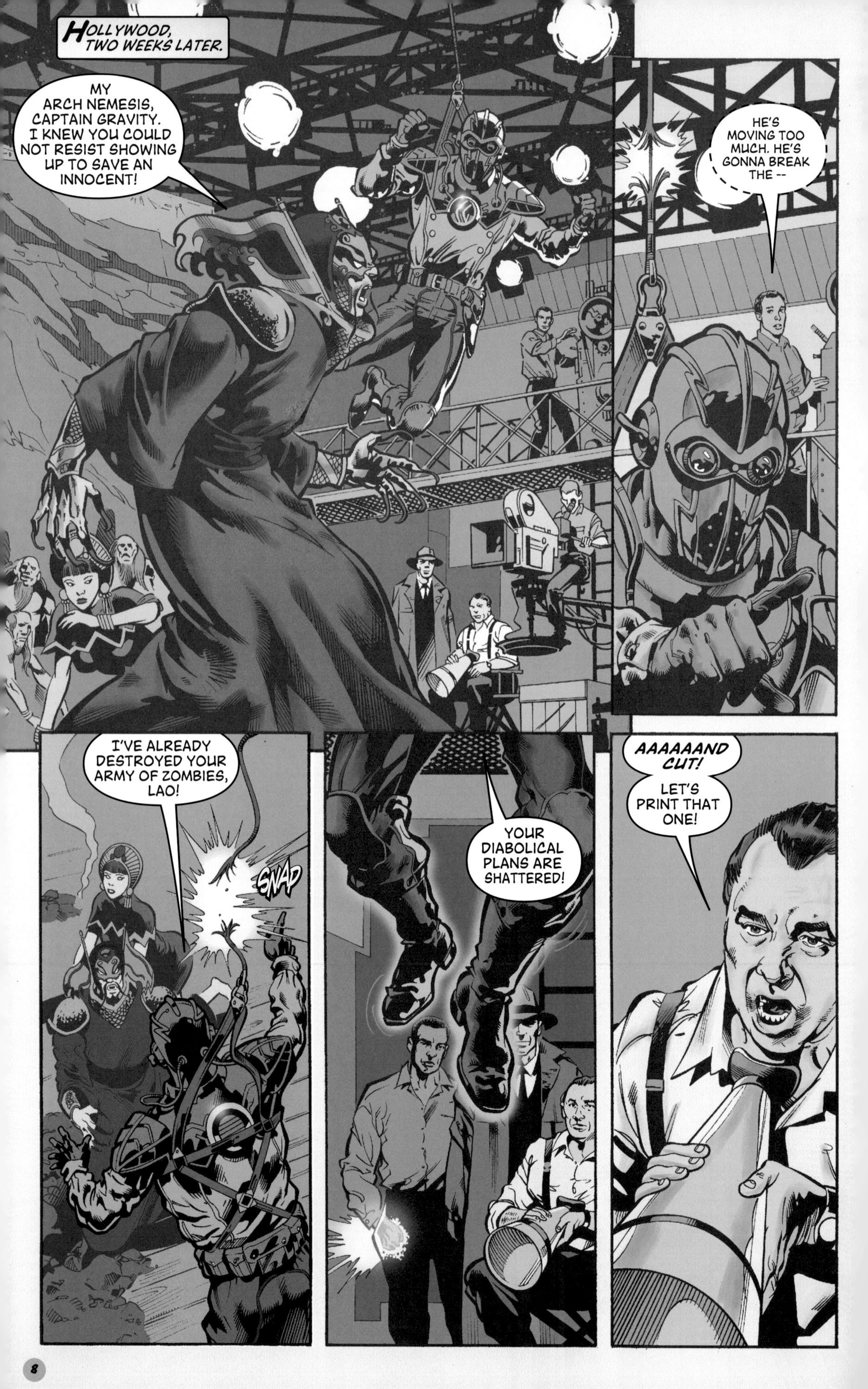
HOLLYWOOD, TWO WEEKS LATER.
MY ARCH NEMESIS, CAPTAIN GRAVITY. I KNEW YOU COULD NOT RESIST SHOWING UP TO SAVE AN INNOCENT!
HE'S MOVING TOO MUCH. HE'S GONNA BREAK THE --
I'VE ALREADY DESTROYED YOUR ARMY OF ZOMBIES, LAO!
SNAP
YOUR DIABOLICAL PLANS ARE SHATTERED!
AAAAAAND CUT!
LET'S PRINT THAT ONE!

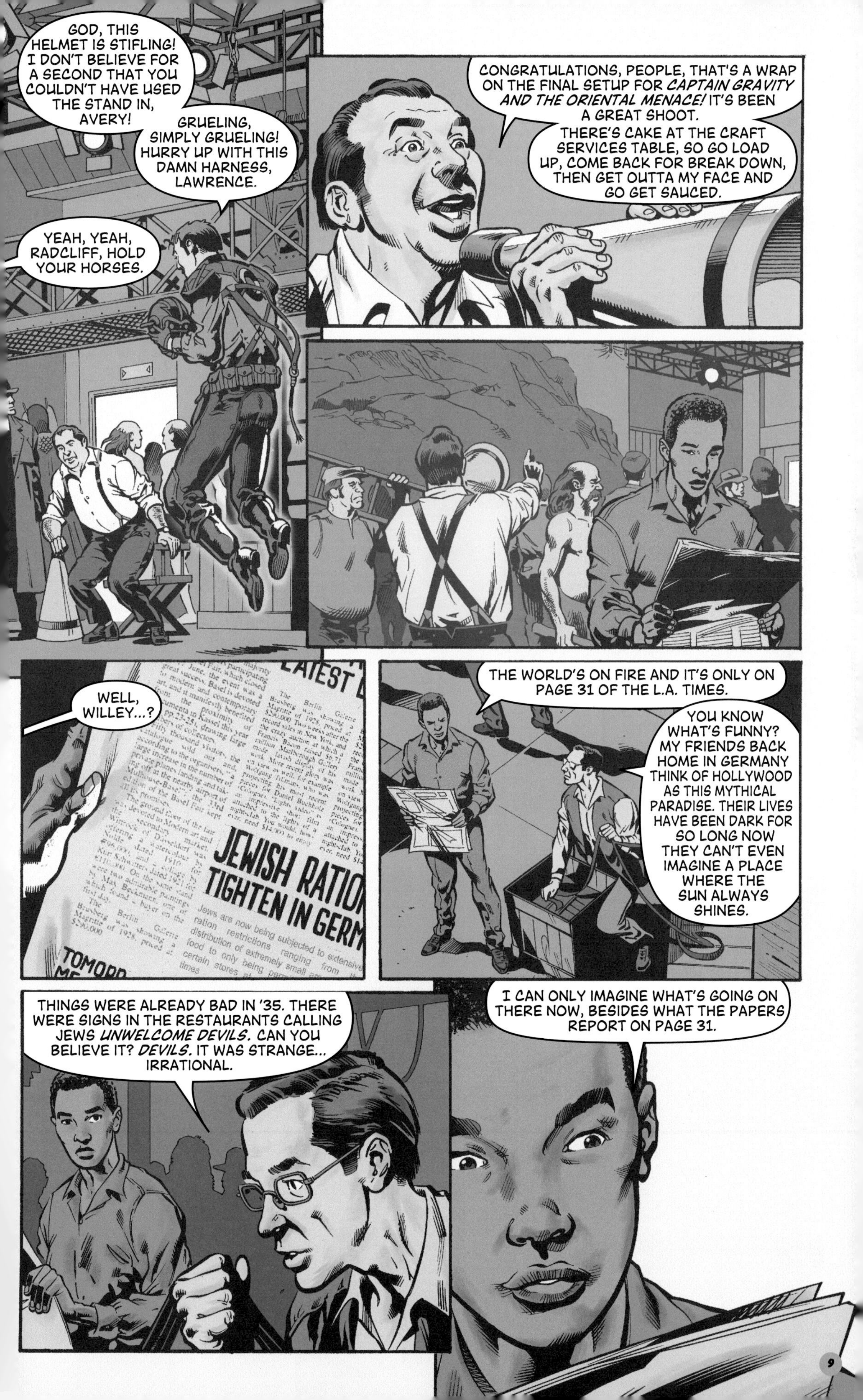
GOD, THIS HELMET IS STIFLING! I DON'T BELIEVE FOR A SECOND THAT YOU COULDN'T HAVE USED THE STAND IN, AVERY!
GRUELING, SIMPLY GRUELING! HURRY UP WITH THIS DAMN HARNESS, LAWRENCE.
YEAH, YEAH, RADCLIFF, HOLD YOUR HORSES.
CONGRATULATIONS, PEOPLE, THAT'S A WRAP ON THE FINAL SETUP FOR *CAPTAIN GRAVITY AND THE ORIENTAL MENACE!* IT'S BEEN A GREAT SHOOT.
THERE'S CAKE AT THE CRAFT SERVICES TABLE, SO GO LOAD UP, COME BACK FOR BREAK DOWN, THEN GET OUTTA MY FACE AND GO GET SAUCED.
WELL, WILLEY...?
THE WORLD'S ON FIRE AND IT'S ONLY ON PAGE 31 OF THE L.A. TIMES.
YOU KNOW WHAT'S FUNNY? MY FRIENDS BACK HOME IN GERMANY THINK OF HOLLYWOOD AS THIS MYTHICAL PARADISE. THEIR LIVES HAVE BEEN DARK FOR SO LONG NOW THEY CAN'T EVEN IMAGINE A PLACE WHERE THE SUN ALWAYS SHINES.
THINGS WERE ALREADY BAD IN '35. THERE WERE SIGNS IN THE RESTAURANTS CALLING JEWS *UNWELCOME DEVILS.* CAN YOU BELIEVE IT? *DEVILS.* IT WAS STRANGE... IRRATIONAL.
I CAN ONLY IMAGINE WHAT'S GOING ON THERE NOW, BESIDES WHAT THE PAPERS REPORT ON PAGE 31.

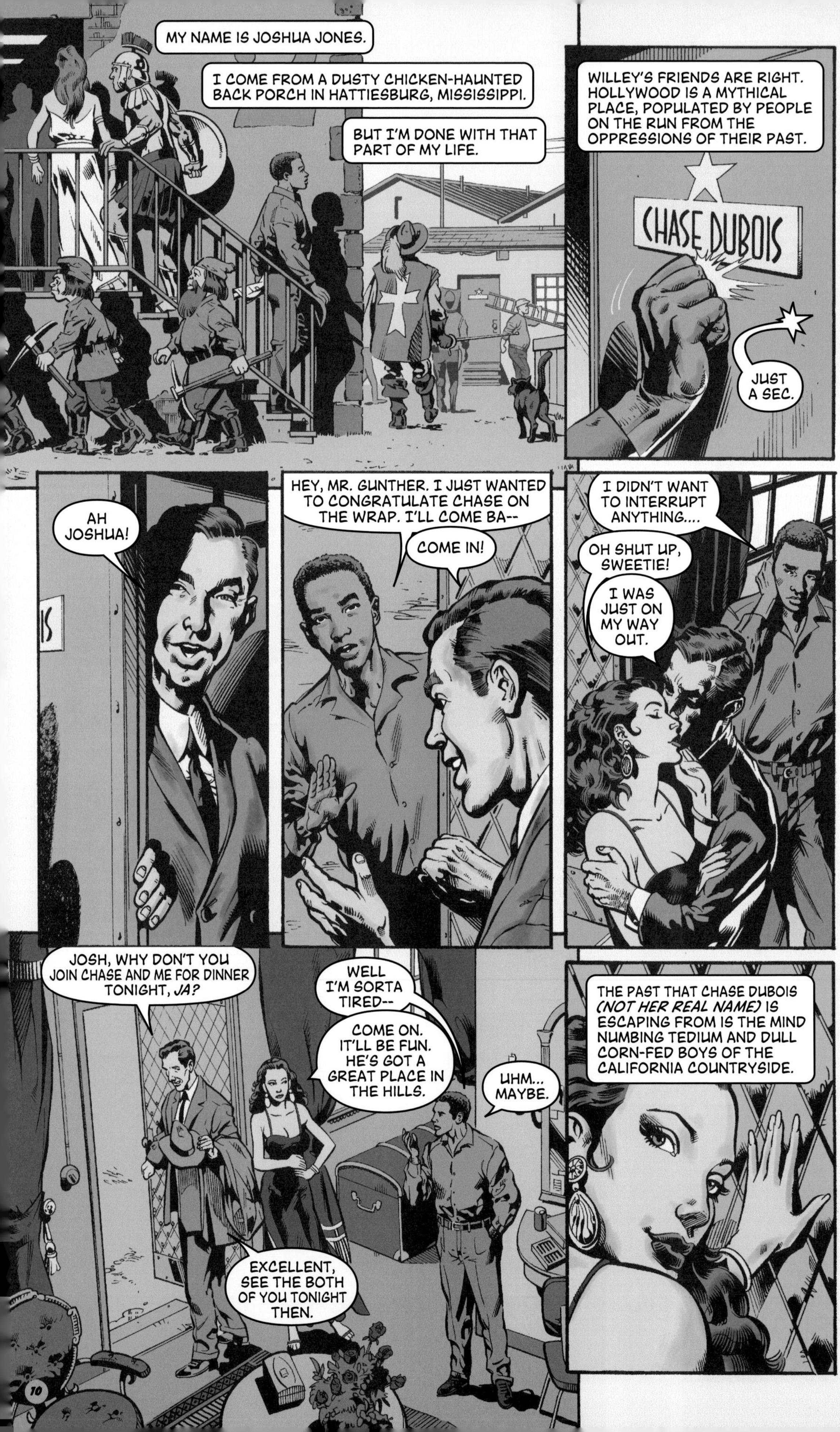
MY NAME IS JOSHUA JONES.
I COME FROM A DUSTY CHICKEN-HAUNTED BACK PORCH IN HATTIESBURG, MISSISSIPPI.
BUT I'M DONE WITH THAT PART OF MY LIFE.
WILLEY'S FRIENDS ARE RIGHT. HOLLYWOOD IS A MYTHICAL PLACE, POPULATED BY PEOPLE ON THE RUN FROM THE OPPRESSIONS OF THEIR PAST.
CHASE DUBOIS
JUST A SEC.
AH JOSHUA!
HEY, MR. GUNTHER. I JUST WANTED TO CONGRATULATE CHASE ON THE WRAP. I'LL COME BA--
COME IN!
I DIDN'T WANT TO INTERRUPT ANYTHING....
OH SHUT UP, SWEETIE!
I WAS JUST ON MY WAY OUT.
JOSH, WHY DON'T YOU JOIN CHASE AND ME FOR DINNER TONIGHT, *JA?*
WELL I'M SORTA TIRED--
COME ON. IT'LL BE FUN. HE'S GOT A GREAT PLACE IN THE HILLS.
UHM... MAYBE.
EXCELLENT, SEE THE BOTH OF YOU TONIGHT THEN.
THE PAST THAT CHASE DUBOIS *(NOT HER REAL NAME)* IS ESCAPING FROM IS THE MIND NUMBING TEDIUM AND DULL CORN-FED BOYS OF THE CALIFORNIA COUNTRYSIDE.

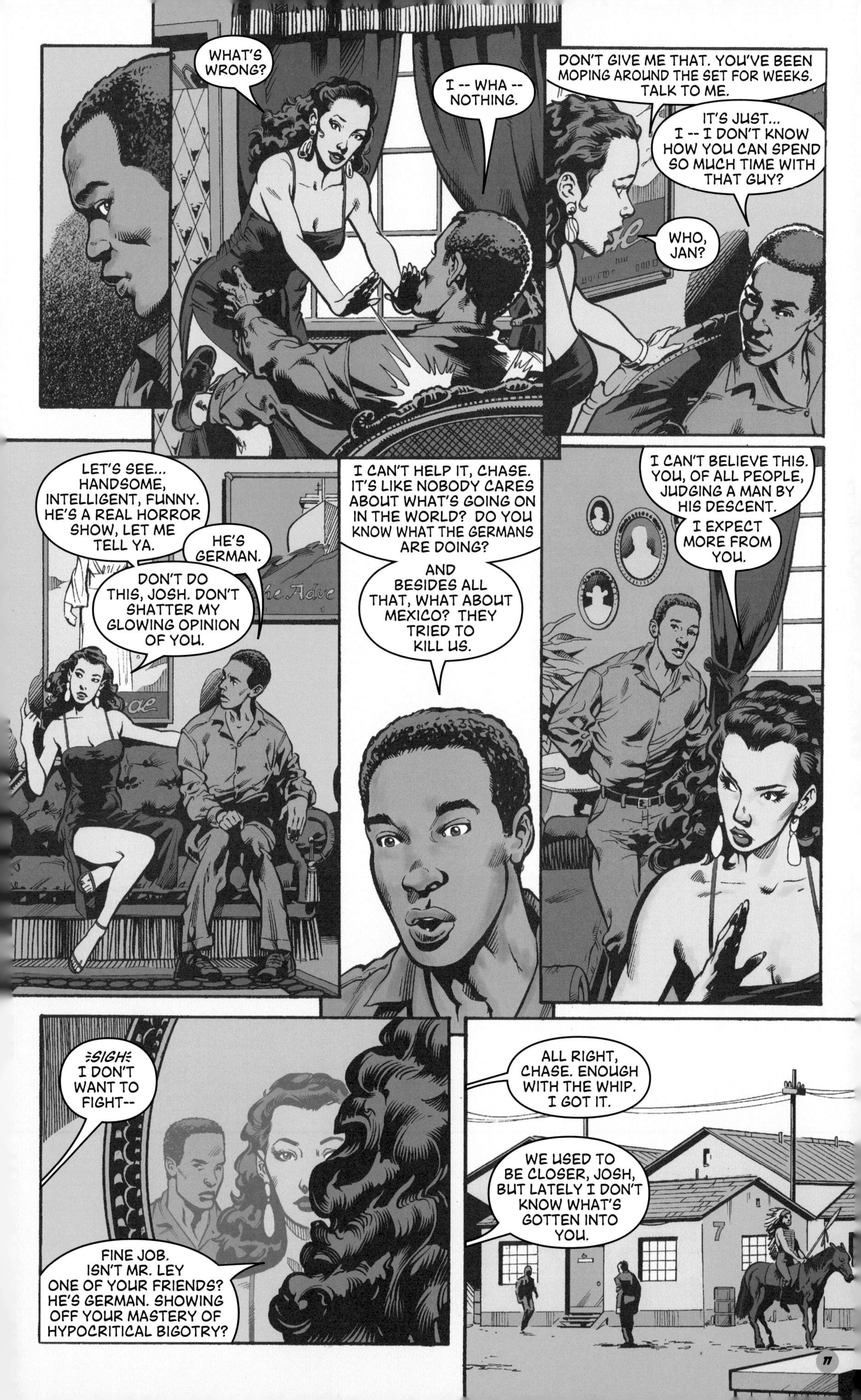
WHAT'S WRONG?
I -- WHA -- NOTHING.
DON'T GIVE ME THAT. YOU'VE BEEN MOPING AROUND THE SET FOR WEEKS. TALK TO ME.
IT'S JUST... I -- I DON'T KNOW HOW YOU CAN SPEND SO MUCH TIME WITH THAT GUY?
WHO, JAN?
LET'S SEE... HANDSOME, INTELLIGENT, FUNNY. HE'S A REAL HORROR SHOW, LET ME TELL YA.
HE'S GERMAN.
DON'T DO THIS, JOSH. DON'T SHATTER MY GLOWING OPINION OF YOU.
I CAN'T HELP IT, CHASE. IT'S LIKE NOBODY CARES ABOUT WHAT'S GOING ON IN THE WORLD? DO YOU KNOW WHAT THE GERMANS ARE DOING?
AND BESIDES ALL THAT, WHAT ABOUT MEXICO? THEY TRIED TO KILL US.
I CAN'T BELIEVE THIS. YOU, OF ALL PEOPLE, JUDGING A MAN BY HIS DESCENT.
I EXPECT MORE FROM YOU.
SIGH I DON'T WANT TO FIGHT--
FINE JOB. ISN'T MR. LEY ONE OF YOUR FRIENDS? HE'S GERMAN. SHOWING OFF YOUR MASTERY OF HYPOCRITICAL BIGOTRY?
ALL RIGHT, CHASE. ENOUGH WITH THE WHIP. I GOT IT.
WE USED TO BE CLOSER, JOSH, BUT LATELY I DON'T KNOW WHAT'S GOTTEN INTO YOU.
7

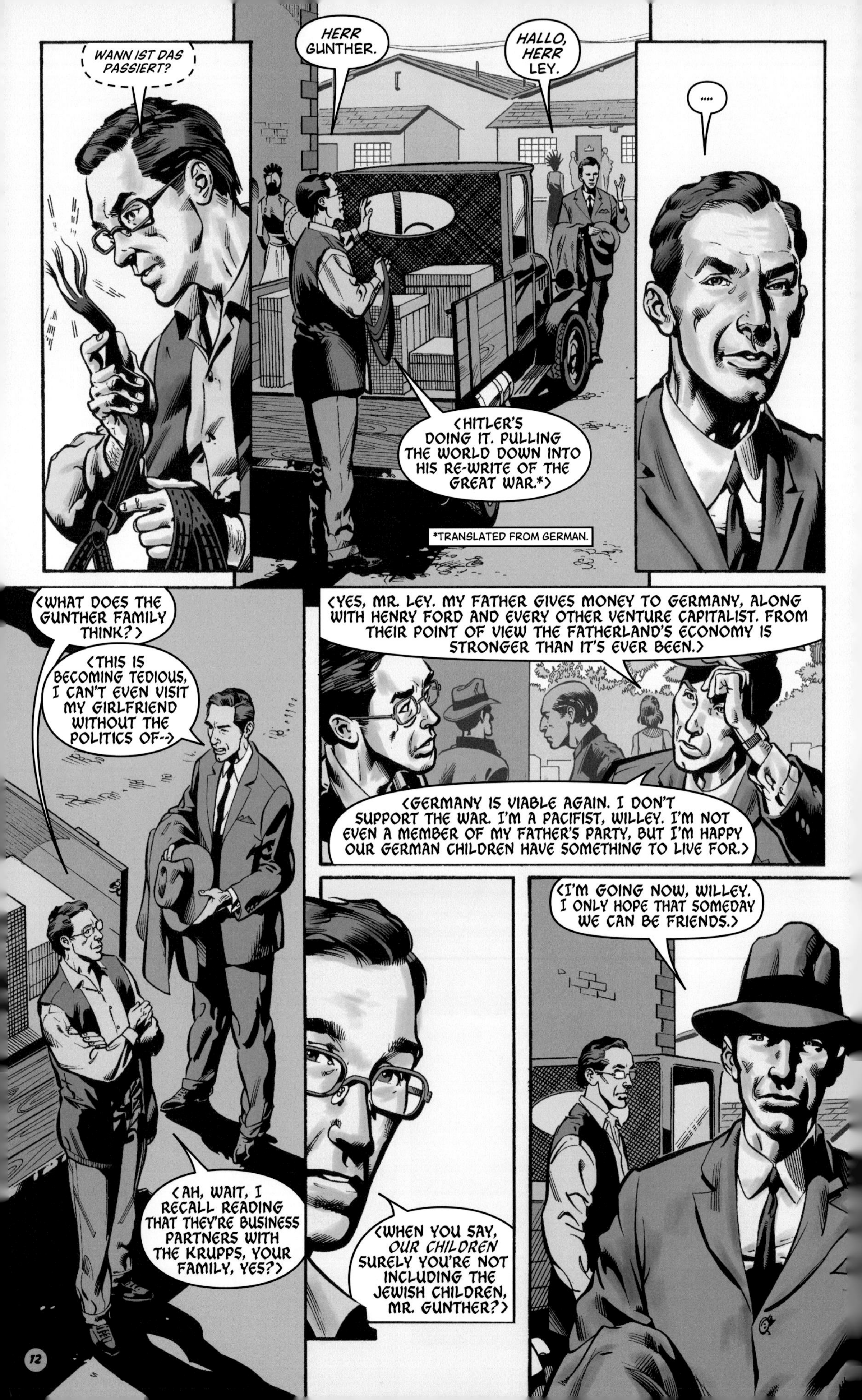
WANN IST DAS PASSIERT?
HERR GUNTHER.
HALLO, HERR LEY.
<HITLER'S DOING IT. PULLING THE WORLD DOWN INTO HIS RE-WRITE OF THE GREAT WAR.*>
*TRANSLATED FROM GERMAN.
....
<WHAT DOES THE GUNTHER FAMILY THINK?>
<THIS IS BECOMING TEDIOUS, I CAN'T EVEN VISIT MY GIRLFRIEND WITHOUT THE POLITICS OF-->
<AH, WAIT, I RECALL READING THAT THEY'RE BUSINESS PARTNERS WITH THE KRUPPS, YOUR FAMILY, YES?>
<YES, MR. LEY. MY FATHER GIVES MONEY TO GERMANY, ALONG WITH HENRY FORD AND EVERY OTHER VENTURE CAPITALIST. FROM THEIR POINT OF VIEW THE FATHERLAND'S ECONOMY IS STRONGER THAN IT'S EVER BEEN.>
<GERMANY IS VIABLE AGAIN. I DON'T SUPPORT THE WAR. I'M A PACIFIST, WILLEY. I'M NOT EVEN A MEMBER OF MY FATHER'S PARTY, BUT I'M HAPPY OUR GERMAN CHILDREN HAVE SOMETHING TO LIVE FOR.>
<WHEN YOU SAY, *OUR CHILDREN* SURELY YOU'RE NOT INCLUDING THE JEWISH CHILDREN, MR. GUNTHER?>
<I'M GOING NOW, WILLEY. I ONLY HOPE THAT SOMEDAY WE CAN BE FRIENDS.>

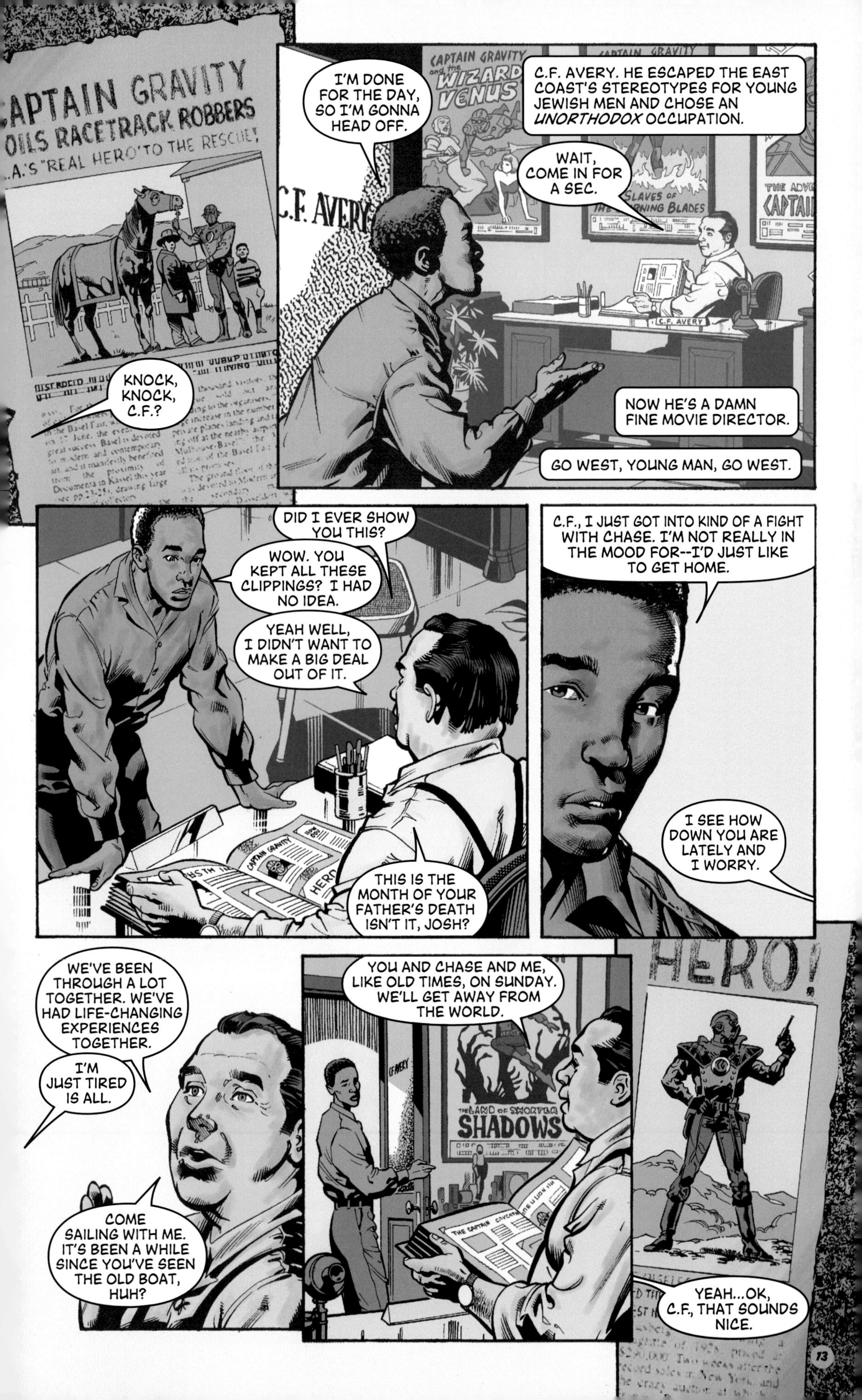

CAPTAIN GRAVITY
OILS RACETRACK ROBBERS
KNOCK, KNOCK, C.F.?
I'M DONE FOR THE DAY, SO I'M GONNA HEAD OFF.
C.F. AVERY
C.F. AVERY. HE ESCAPED THE EAST COAST'S STEREOTYPES FOR YOUNG JEWISH MEN AND CHOSE AN *UNORTHODOX* OCCUPATION.
WAIT, COME IN FOR A SEC.
NOW HE'S A DAMN FINE MOVIE DIRECTOR.
GO WEST, YOUNG MAN, GO WEST.
DID I EVER SHOW YOU THIS?
WOW. YOU KEPT ALL THESE CLIPPINGS? I HAD NO IDEA.
YEAH WELL, I DIDN'T WANT TO MAKE A BIG DEAL OUT OF IT.
THIS IS THE MONTH OF YOUR FATHER'S DEATH ISN'T IT, JOSH?
C.F., I JUST GOT INTO KIND OF A FIGHT WITH CHASE. I'M NOT REALLY IN THE MOOD FOR--I'D JUST LIKE TO GET HOME.
I SEE HOW DOWN YOU ARE LATELY AND I WORRY.
WE'VE BEEN THROUGH A LOT TOGETHER. WE'VE HAD LIFE-CHANGING EXPERIENCES TOGETHER.
I'M JUST TIRED IS ALL.
COME SAILING WITH ME. IT'S BEEN A WHILE SINCE YOU'VE SEEN THE OLD BOAT, HUH?
YOU AND CHASE AND ME, LIKE OLD TIMES, ON SUNDAY. WE'LL GET AWAY FROM THE WORLD.
THE LAND OF SHORTER SHADOWS
HERO!
YEAH...OK, C.F., THAT SOUNDS NICE.

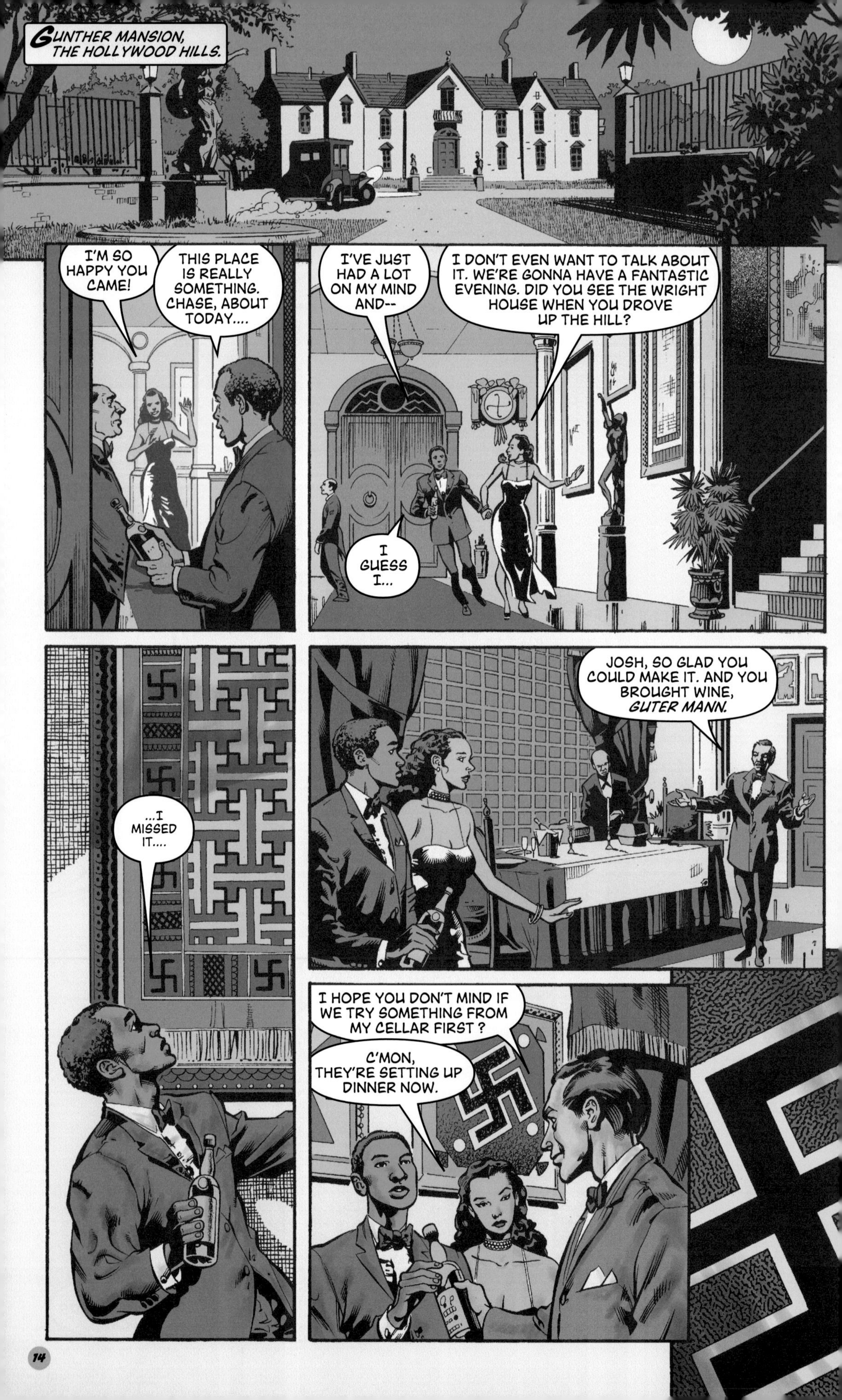
GUNTHER MANSION, THE HOLLYWOOD HILLS.
I'M SO HAPPY YOU CAME!
THIS PLACE IS REALLY SOMETHING. CHASE, ABOUT TODAY....
I'VE JUST HAD A LOT ON MY MIND AND--
I DON'T EVEN WANT TO TALK ABOUT IT. WE'RE GONNA HAVE A FANTASTIC EVENING. DID YOU SEE THE WRIGHT HOUSE WHEN YOU DROVE UP THE HILL?
I GUESS I...
...I MISSED IT....
JOSH, SO GLAD YOU COULD MAKE IT. AND YOU BROUGHT WINE, *GUTER MANN.*
I HOPE YOU DON'T MIND IF WE TRY SOMETHING FROM MY CELLAR FIRST ?
C'MON, THEY'RE SETTING UP DINNER NOW.

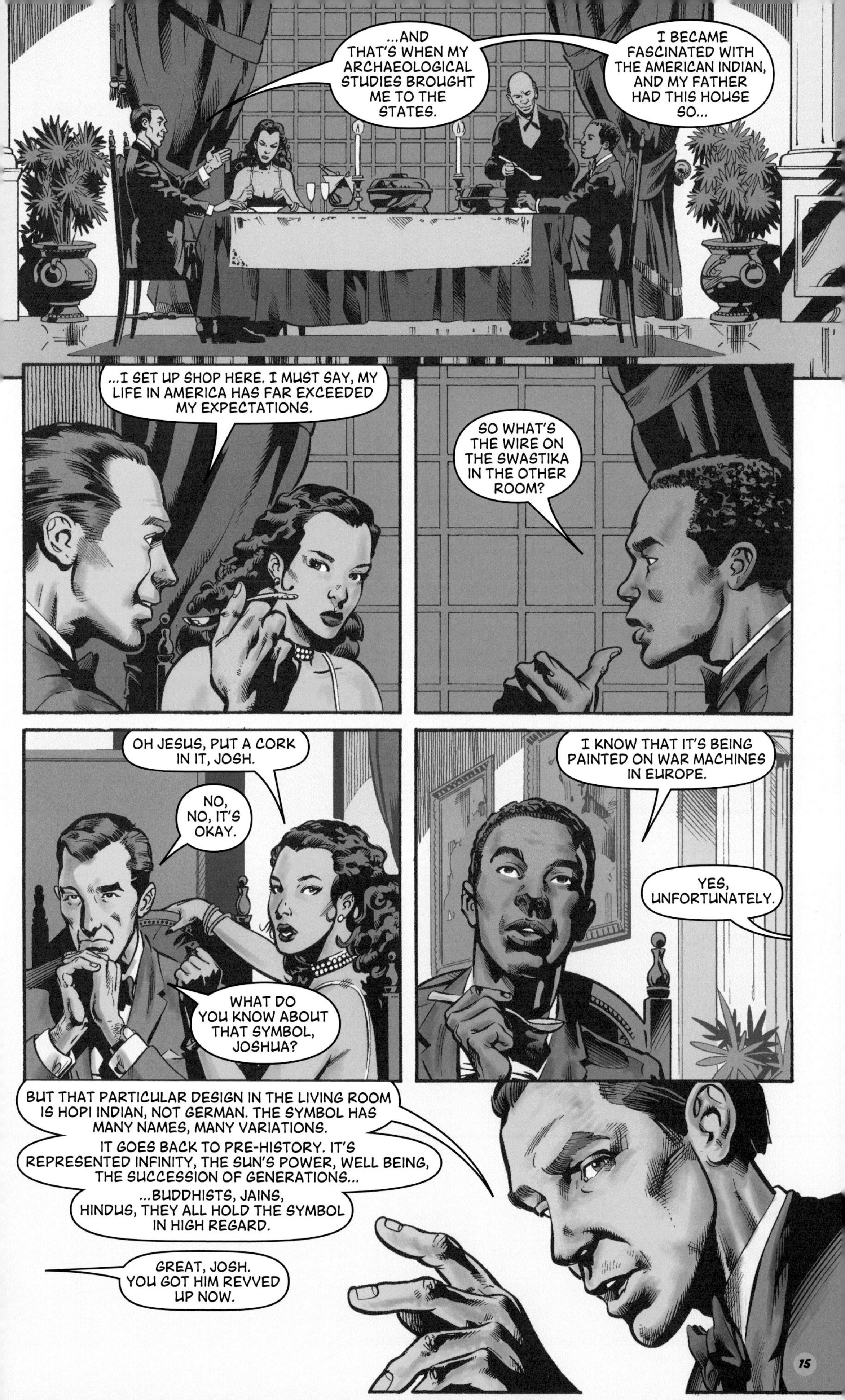
...AND THAT'S WHEN MY ARCHAEOLOGICAL STUDIES BROUGHT ME TO THE STATES.
I BECAME FASCINATED WITH THE AMERICAN INDIAN, AND MY FATHER HAD THIS HOUSE SO...
...I SET UP SHOP HERE. I MUST SAY, MY LIFE IN AMERICA HAS FAR EXCEEDED MY EXPECTATIONS.
SO WHAT'S THE WIRE ON THE SWASTIKA IN THE OTHER ROOM?
OH JESUS, PUT A CORK IN IT, JOSH.
NO, NO, IT'S OKAY.
WHAT DO YOU KNOW ABOUT THAT SYMBOL, JOSHUA?
I KNOW THAT IT'S BEING PAINTED ON WAR MACHINES IN EUROPE.
YES, UNFORTUNATELY.
BUT THAT PARTICULAR DESIGN IN THE LIVING ROOM IS HOPI INDIAN, NOT GERMAN. THE SYMBOL HAS MANY NAMES, MANY VARIATIONS.
IT GOES BACK TO PRE-HISTORY. IT'S REPRESENTED INFINITY, THE SUN'S POWER, WELL BEING, THE SUCCESSION OF GENERATIONS...
...BUDDHISTS, JAINS, HINDUS, THEY ALL HOLD THE SYMBOL IN HIGH REGARD.
GREAT, JOSH. YOU GOT HIM REVVED UP NOW.

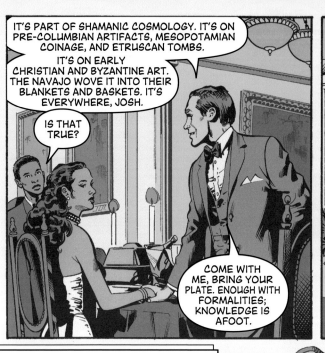

IT'S PART OF SHAMANIC COSMOLOGY. IT'S ON PRE-COLUMBIAN ARTIFACTS, MESOPOTAMIAN COINAGE, AND ETRUSCAN TOMBS.

IT'S ON EARLY CHRISTIAN AND BYZANTINE ART. THE NAVAJO WOVE IT INTO THEIR BLANKETS AND BASKETS. IT'S EVERYWHERE, JOSH.

IS THAT TRUE?

COME WITH ME, BRING YOUR PLATE. ENOUGH WITH FORMALITIES; KNOWLEDGE IS AFOOT.

I'M FASCINATED WITH HOW IT'S PERMEATED OUR SPECIES.

WAS IT CARRIED IN MIGRATION BY THE FIRST MEN WHO WERE PROBABLY SUN WORSHIPERS AND CUT THE SYMBOL FROM THE DAYSTAR'S CIRCLE?

"OR IS IT A NATURAL PATTERN, SO TRUE AND ALL INCLUSIVE, SO PART OF THE VERY FABRIC OF DESIGN, THAT IT BUBBLES UP THROUGH OUR CREATIVE SELVES?"

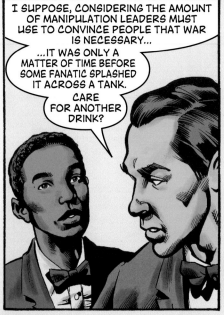

I SUPPOSE, CONSIDERING THE AMOUNT OF MANIPULATION LEADERS MUST USE TO CONVINCE PEOPLE THAT WAR IS NECESSARY...

...IT WAS ONLY A MATTER OF TIME BEFORE SOME FANATIC SPLASHED IT ACROSS A TANK.

CARE FOR ANOTHER DRINK?

LATER.

I'M SORRY.

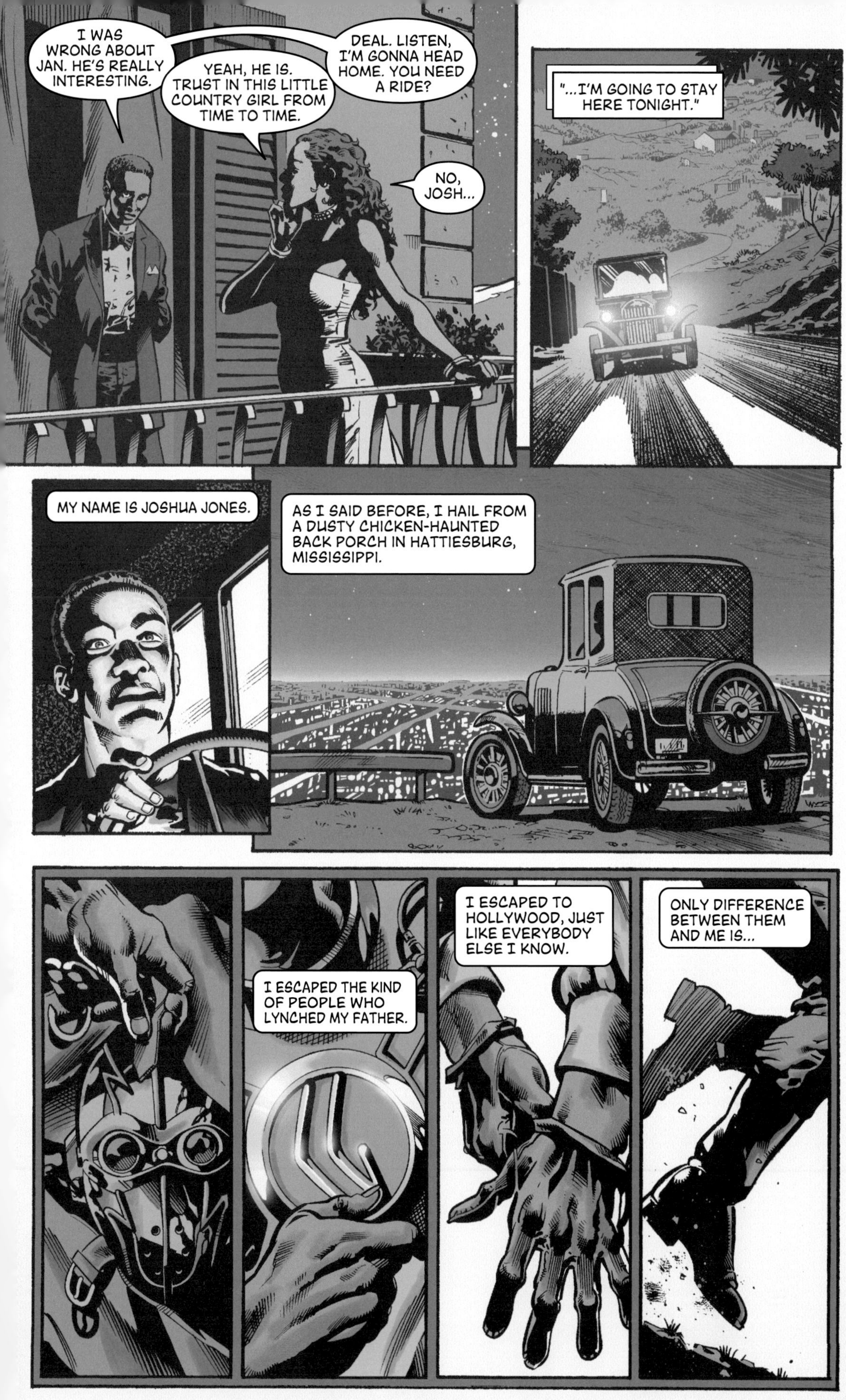
I WAS WRONG ABOUT JAN. HE'S REALLY INTERESTING.
YEAH, HE IS. TRUST IN THIS LITTLE COUNTRY GIRL FROM TIME TO TIME.
DEAL. LISTEN, I'M GONNA HEAD HOME. YOU NEED A RIDE?
NO, JOSH...
"...I'M GOING TO STAY HERE TONIGHT."
MY NAME IS JOSHUA JONES.
AS I SAID BEFORE, I HAIL FROM A DUSTY CHICKEN-HAUNTED BACK PORCH IN HATTIESBURG, MISSISSIPPI.
I ESCAPED THE KIND OF PEOPLE WHO LYNCHED MY FATHER.
I ESCAPED TO HOLLYWOOD, JUST LIKE EVERYBODY ELSE I KNOW.
ONLY DIFFERENCE BETWEEN THEM AND ME IS...

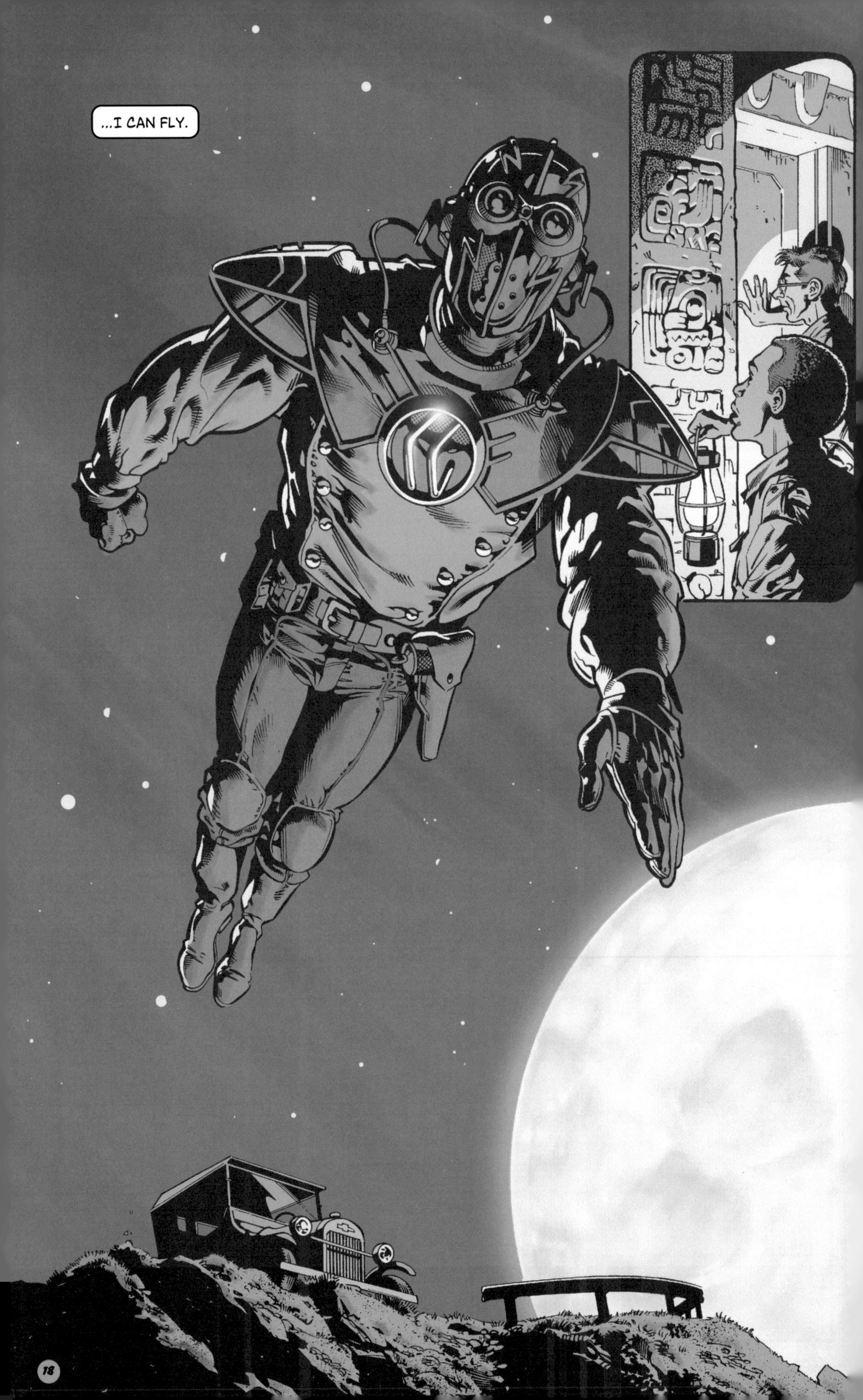
...I CAN FLY.

IT'S AN INTERESTING STORY, HOW THIS *BOY* LEARNED TO SOAR.

WHILE SHOOTING ON LOCATION AT THE MAYAN RUINS IN CHICHEN ITZA, MEXICO, WITH C.F. AND CHASE, I STUMBLED ONTO SOMETHING EXTRAORDINARY.

ELEMENT 115, A GAS ENCASED IN A CIRCULAR TRANSPARENT STONE THAT HAD LAID SEALED INSIDE THE TEMPLE KUKULCAN FOR OVER 700 YEARS.

ACCORDING TO A GERMAN PROFESSOR NAMED GOETHALS -- WHO'D SPENT THE BETTER PART OF HIS LIFE TRYING TO FIND THE ELEMENT --

-- IT HAD BEEN A GIFT FROM THE ITZA MAYA *GODS* WHO WERE ACTUALLY ALIENS STRANDED ON EARTH A THOUSAND YEARS AGO.

WHEN I TOUCHED THE CONTAINMENT STONE. I ABSORBED THE ELEMENT AND WAS GIVEN THE POWER OVER GRAVITY.

THEN THINGS GOT STICKY. THE GERMAN FINANCIERS OF OUR FILM TURNED OUT TO BE NAZIS LOOKING FOR ELEMENT 115, AS WELL AS THE ANCIENT HIDDEN SPACE SHIP WITH ITS MANY SECRETS.

ALL TO AID HITLER IN HIS PLANS FOR WORLD CONQUEST.

THAT ENDED WITH ME KILLING A MAN OUT THERE IN THE JUNGLE. HIS NAME WAS REICHSMASTER JAEGER. IT WAS THE FIRST AND ONLY TIME I'VE EVER TAKEN A LIFE.

BUT I ALSO SAVED MY FRIENDS, AND MAYBE THE WORLD...WHO KNOWS.

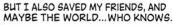

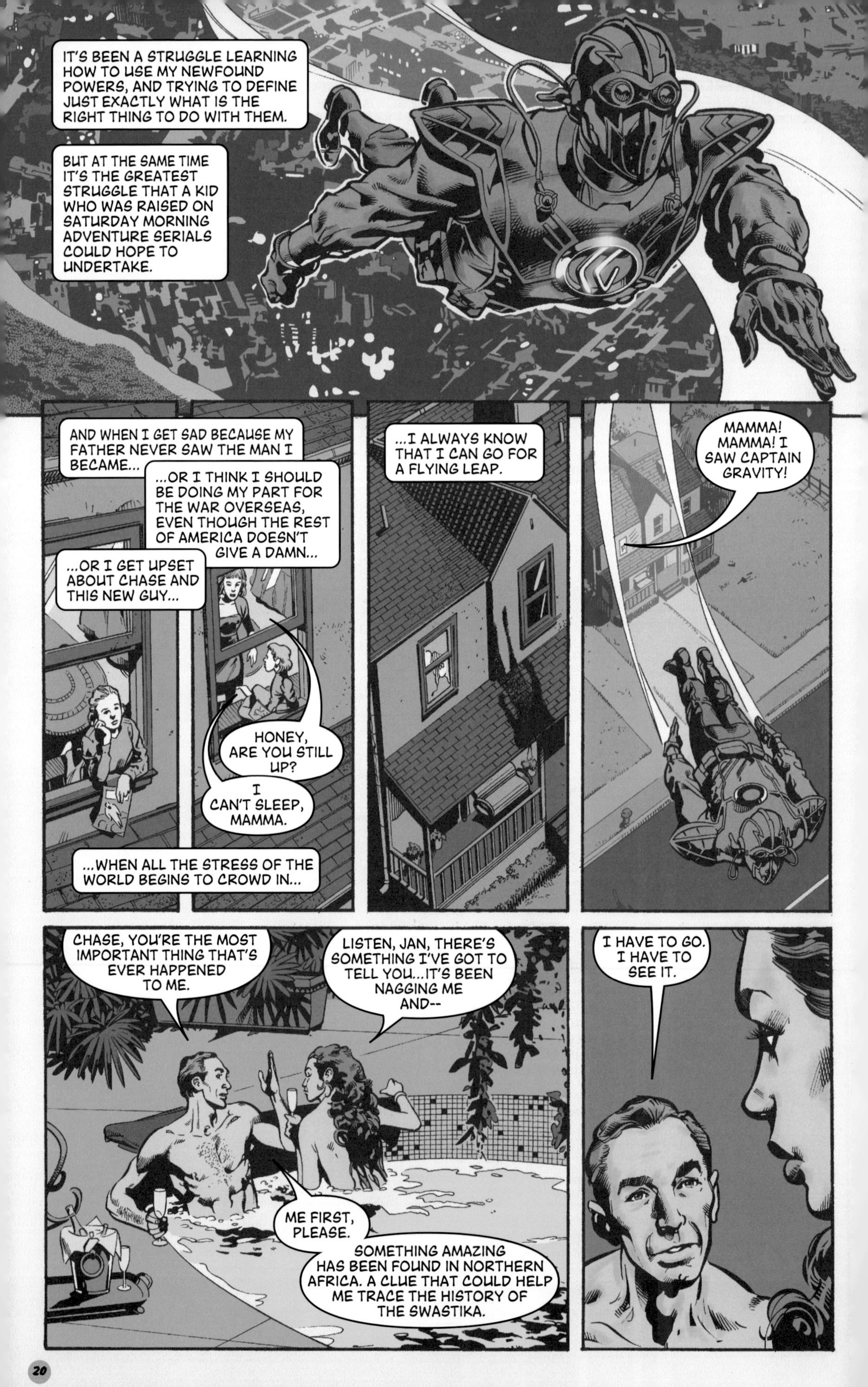
IT'S BEEN A STRUGGLE LEARNING HOW TO USE MY NEWFOUND POWERS, AND TRYING TO DEFINE JUST EXACTLY WHAT IS THE RIGHT THING TO DO WITH THEM.
BUT AT THE SAME TIME IT'S THE GREATEST STRUGGLE THAT A KID WHO WAS RAISED ON SATURDAY MORNING ADVENTURE SERIALS COULD HOPE TO UNDERTAKE.
AND WHEN I GET SAD BECAUSE MY FATHER NEVER SAW THE MAN I BECAME...
...OR I THINK I SHOULD BE DOING MY PART FOR THE WAR OVERSEAS, EVEN THOUGH THE REST OF AMERICA DOESN'T GIVE A DAMN...
...OR I GET UPSET ABOUT CHASE AND THIS NEW GUY...
HONEY, ARE YOU STILL UP?
I CAN'T SLEEP, MAMMA.
...WHEN ALL THE STRESS OF THE WORLD BEGINS TO CROWD IN...
...I ALWAYS KNOW THAT I CAN GO FOR A FLYING LEAP.
MAMMA! MAMMA! I SAW CAPTAIN GRAVITY!
CHASE, YOU'RE THE MOST IMPORTANT THING THAT'S EVER HAPPENED TO ME.
LISTEN, JAN, THERE'S SOMETHING I'VE GOT TO TELL YOU...IT'S BEEN NAGGING ME AND--
ME FIRST, PLEASE.
SOMETHING AMAZING HAS BEEN FOUND IN NORTHERN AFRICA. A CLUE THAT COULD HELP ME TRACE THE HISTORY OF THE SWASTIKA.
I HAVE TO GO. I HAVE TO SEE IT.

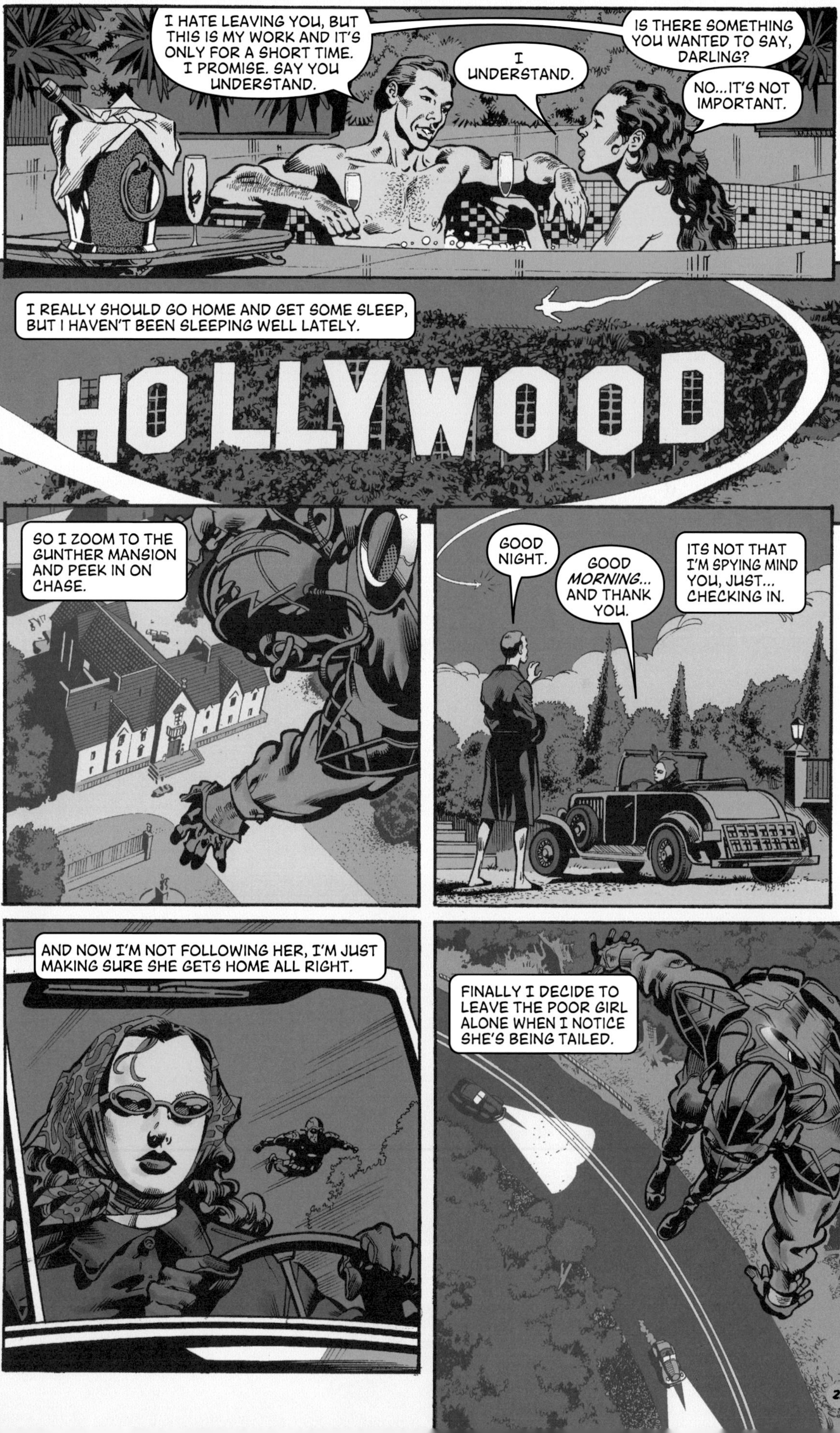
I HATE LEAVING YOU, BUT THIS IS MY WORK AND IT'S ONLY FOR A SHORT TIME. I PROMISE. SAY YOU UNDERSTAND.
I UNDERSTAND.
IS THERE SOMETHING YOU WANTED TO SAY, DARLING?
NO...IT'S NOT IMPORTANT.
I REALLY SHOULD GO HOME AND GET SOME SLEEP, BUT I HAVEN'T BEEN SLEEPING WELL LATELY.
HOLLYWOOD
SO I ZOOM TO THE GUNTHER MANSION AND PEEK IN ON CHASE.
GOOD NIGHT.
GOOD *MORNING*... AND THANK YOU.
ITS NOT THAT I'M SPYING MIND YOU, JUST... CHECKING IN.
AND NOW I'M NOT FOLLOWING HER, I'M JUST MAKING SURE SHE GETS HOME ALL RIGHT.
FINALLY I DECIDE TO LEAVE THE POOR GIRL ALONE WHEN I NOTICE SHE'S BEING TAILED.

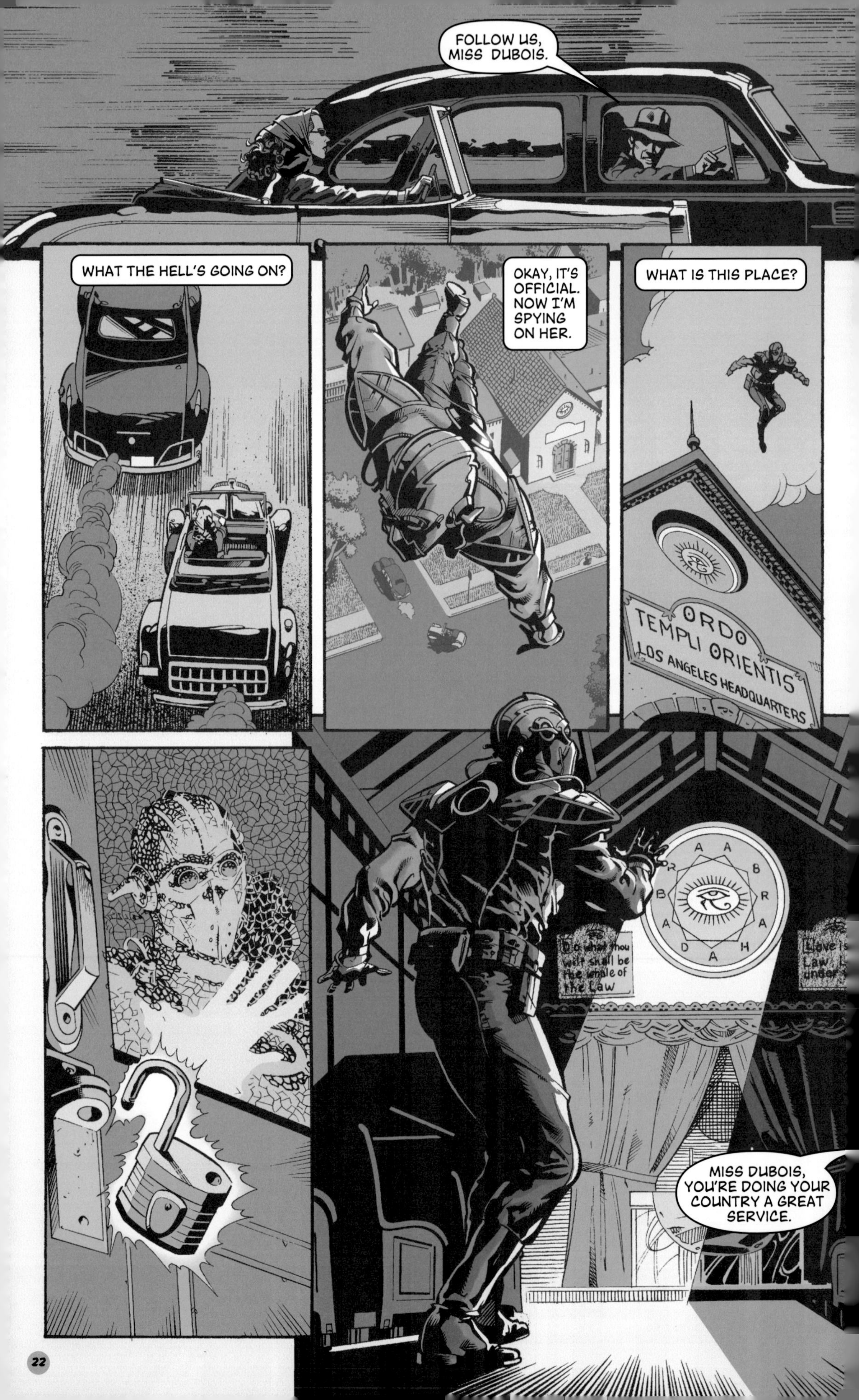
FOLLOW US, MISS DUBOIS.
WHAT THE HELL'S GOING ON?
OKAY, IT'S OFFICIAL. NOW I'M SPYING ON HER.
WHAT IS THIS PLACE?
ORDO TEMPLI ORIENTIS
LOS ANGELES HEADQUARTERS
Do what thou wilt shall be the whole of the Law
MISS DUBOIS, YOU'RE DOING YOUR COUNTRY A GREAT SERVICE.

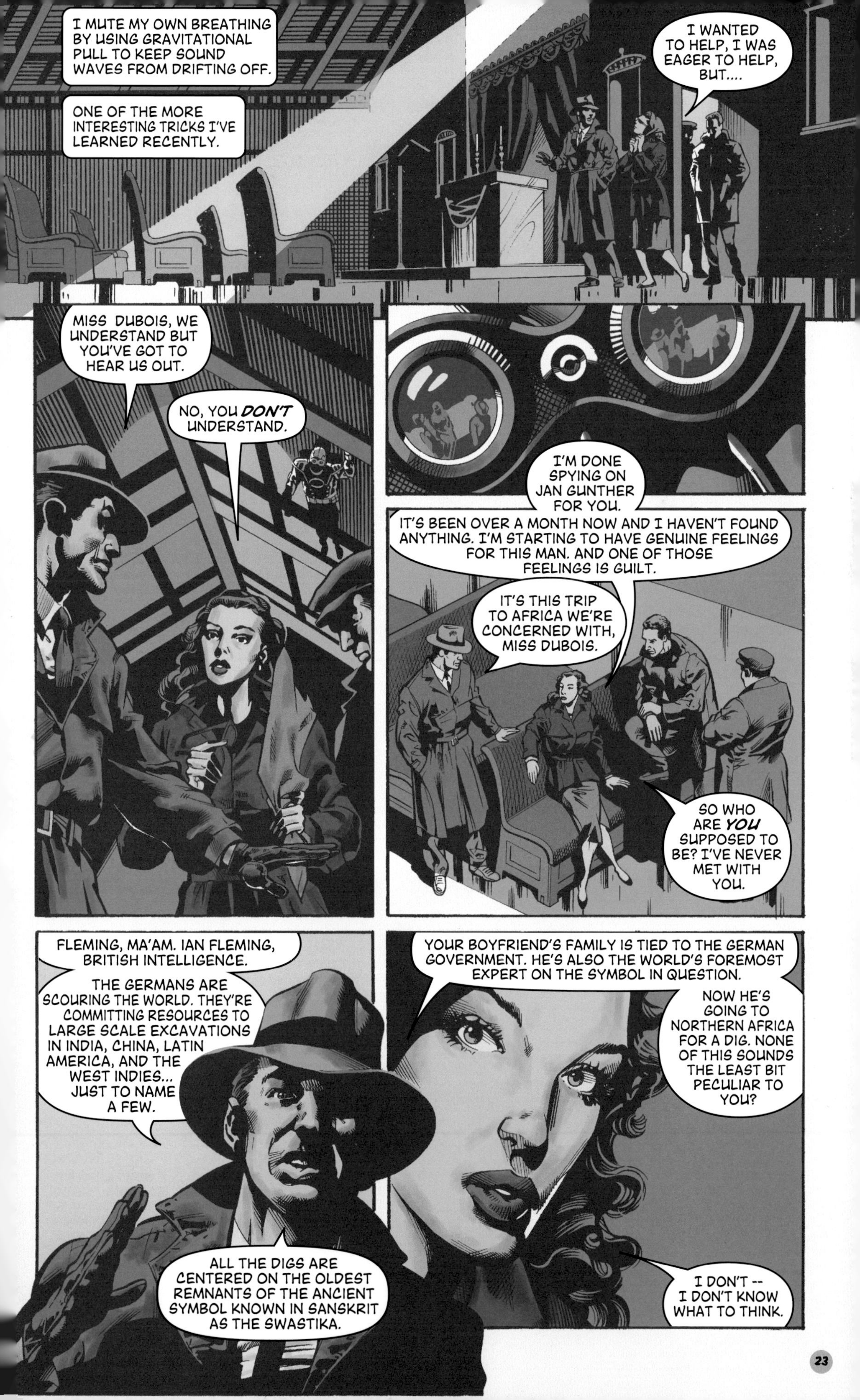
I MUTE MY OWN BREATHING BY USING GRAVITATIONAL PULL TO KEEP SOUND WAVES FROM DRIFTING OFF.
ONE OF THE MORE INTERESTING TRICKS I'VE LEARNED RECENTLY.
I WANTED TO HELP, I WAS EAGER TO HELP, BUT....
MISS DUBOIS, WE UNDERSTAND BUT YOU'VE GOT TO HEAR US OUT.
NO, YOU *DON'T* UNDERSTAND.
I'M DONE SPYING ON JAN GUNTHER FOR YOU.
IT'S BEEN OVER A MONTH NOW AND I HAVEN'T FOUND ANYTHING. I'M STARTING TO HAVE GENUINE FEELINGS FOR THIS MAN. AND ONE OF THOSE FEELINGS IS GUILT.
IT'S THIS TRIP TO AFRICA WE'RE CONCERNED WITH, MISS DUBOIS.
SO WHO ARE *YOU* SUPPOSED TO BE? I'VE NEVER MET WITH YOU.
FLEMING, MA'AM. IAN FLEMING, BRITISH INTELLIGENCE.
THE GERMANS ARE SCOURING THE WORLD. THEY'RE COMMITTING RESOURCES TO LARGE SCALE EXCAVATIONS IN INDIA, CHINA, LATIN AMERICA, AND THE WEST INDIES... JUST TO NAME A FEW.
ALL THE DIGS ARE CENTERED ON THE OLDEST REMNANTS OF THE ANCIENT SYMBOL KNOWN IN SANSKRIT AS THE SWASTIKA.
YOUR BOYFRIEND'S FAMILY IS TIED TO THE GERMAN GOVERNMENT. HE'S ALSO THE WORLD'S FOREMOST EXPERT ON THE SYMBOL IN QUESTION.
NOW HE'S GOING TO NORTHERN AFRICA FOR A DIG. NONE OF THIS SOUNDS THE LEAST BIT PECULIAR TO YOU?
I DON'T -- I DON'T KNOW WHAT TO THINK.

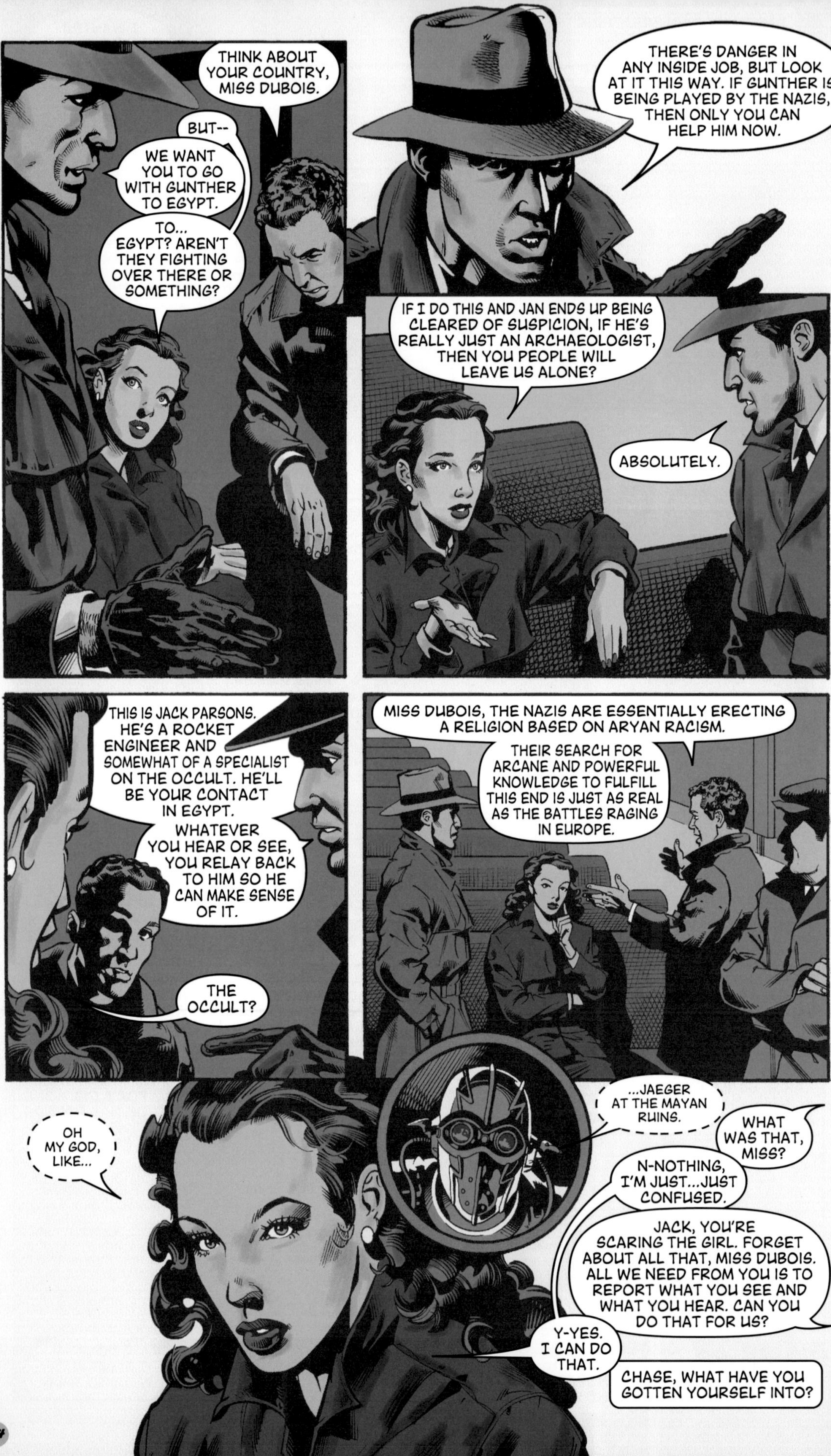
THINK ABOUT YOUR COUNTRY, MISS DUBOIS.
BUT--
WE WANT YOU TO GO WITH GUNTHER TO EGYPT.
TO... EGYPT? AREN'T THEY FIGHTING OVER THERE OR SOMETHING?
THERE'S DANGER IN ANY INSIDE JOB, BUT LOOK AT IT THIS WAY. IF GUNTHER IS BEING PLAYED BY THE NAZIS, THEN ONLY YOU CAN HELP HIM NOW.
IF I DO THIS AND JAN ENDS UP BEING CLEARED OF SUSPICION, IF HE'S REALLY JUST AN ARCHAEOLOGIST, THEN YOU PEOPLE WILL LEAVE US ALONE?
ABSOLUTELY.
THIS IS JACK PARSONS. HE'S A ROCKET ENGINEER AND SOMEWHAT OF A SPECIALIST ON THE OCCULT. HE'LL BE YOUR CONTACT IN EGYPT.
WHATEVER YOU HEAR OR SEE, YOU RELAY BACK TO HIM SO HE CAN MAKE SENSE OF IT.
THE OCCULT?
MISS DUBOIS, THE NAZIS ARE ESSENTIALLY ERECTING A RELIGION BASED ON ARYAN RACISM.
THEIR SEARCH FOR ARCANE AND POWERFUL KNOWLEDGE TO FULFILL THIS END IS JUST AS REAL AS THE BATTLES RAGING IN EUROPE.
OH MY GOD, LIKE...
...JAEGER AT THE MAYAN RUINS.
WHAT WAS THAT, MISS?
N-NOTHING, I'M JUST...JUST CONFUSED.
JACK, YOU'RE SCARING THE GIRL. FORGET ABOUT ALL THAT, MISS DUBOIS. ALL WE NEED FROM YOU IS TO REPORT WHAT YOU SEE AND WHAT YOU HEAR. CAN YOU DO THAT FOR US?
Y-YES. I CAN DO THAT.
CHASE, WHAT HAVE YOU GOTTEN YOURSELF INTO?

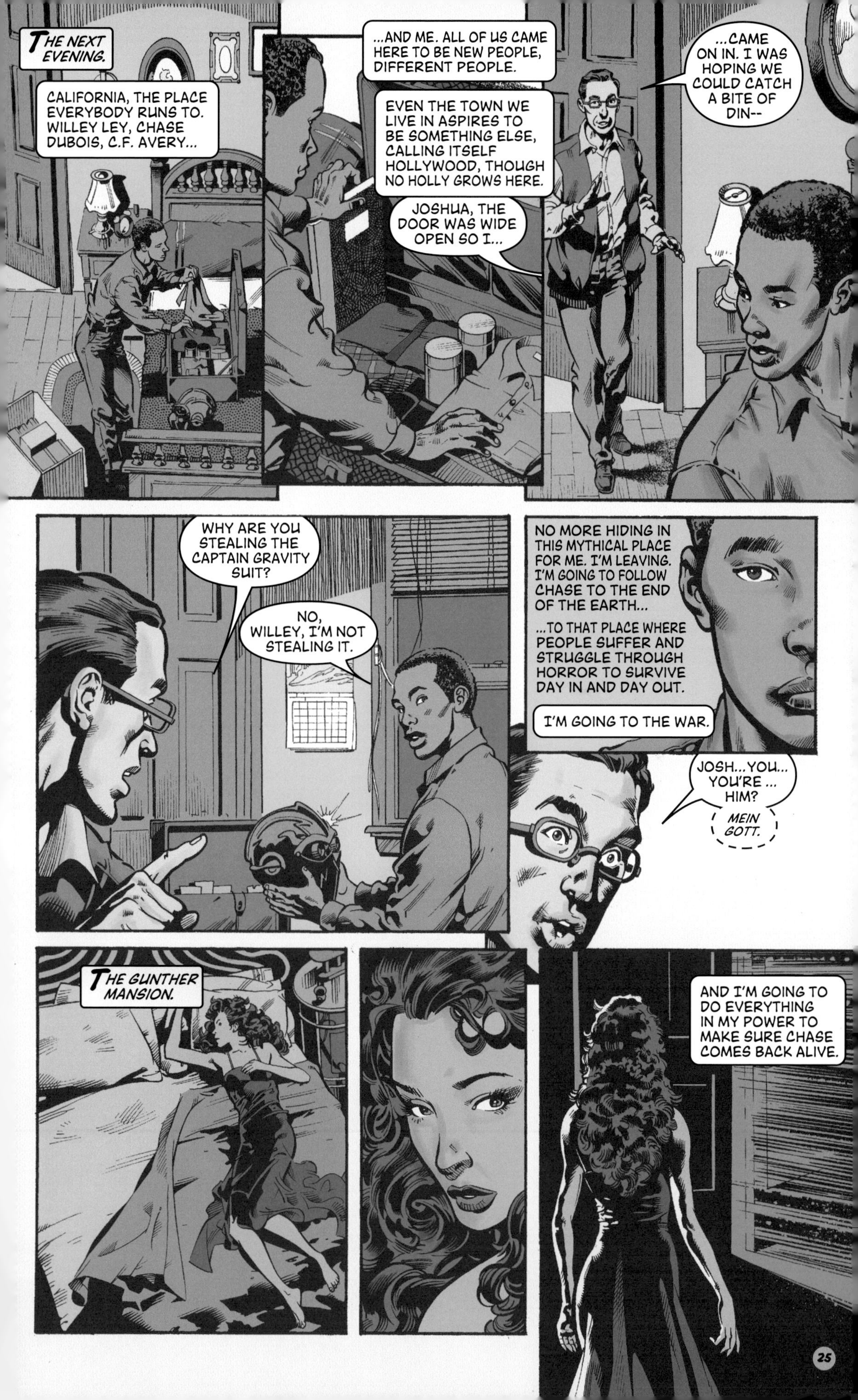
THE NEXT EVENING.
CALIFORNIA, THE PLACE EVERYBODY RUNS TO. WILLEY LEY, CHASE DUBOIS, C.F. AVERY...
...AND ME. ALL OF US CAME HERE TO BE NEW PEOPLE, DIFFERENT PEOPLE.
EVEN THE TOWN WE LIVE IN ASPIRES TO BE SOMETHING ELSE, CALLING ITSELF HOLLYWOOD, THOUGH NO HOLLY GROWS HERE.
JOSHUA, THE DOOR WAS WIDE OPEN SO I...
...CAME ON IN. I WAS HOPING WE COULD CATCH A BITE OF DIN--
WHY ARE YOU STEALING THE CAPTAIN GRAVITY SUIT?
NO, WILLEY, I'M NOT STEALING IT.
NO MORE HIDING IN THIS MYTHICAL PLACE FOR ME. I'M LEAVING. I'M GOING TO FOLLOW CHASE TO THE END OF THE EARTH...
...TO THAT PLACE WHERE PEOPLE SUFFER AND STRUGGLE THROUGH HORROR TO SURVIVE DAY IN AND DAY OUT.
I'M GOING TO THE WAR.
JOSH...YOU... YOU'RE ... HIM?
MEIN GOTT.
THE GUNTHER MANSION.
AND I'M GOING TO DO EVERYTHING IN MY POWER TO MAKE SURE CHASE COMES BACK ALIVE.

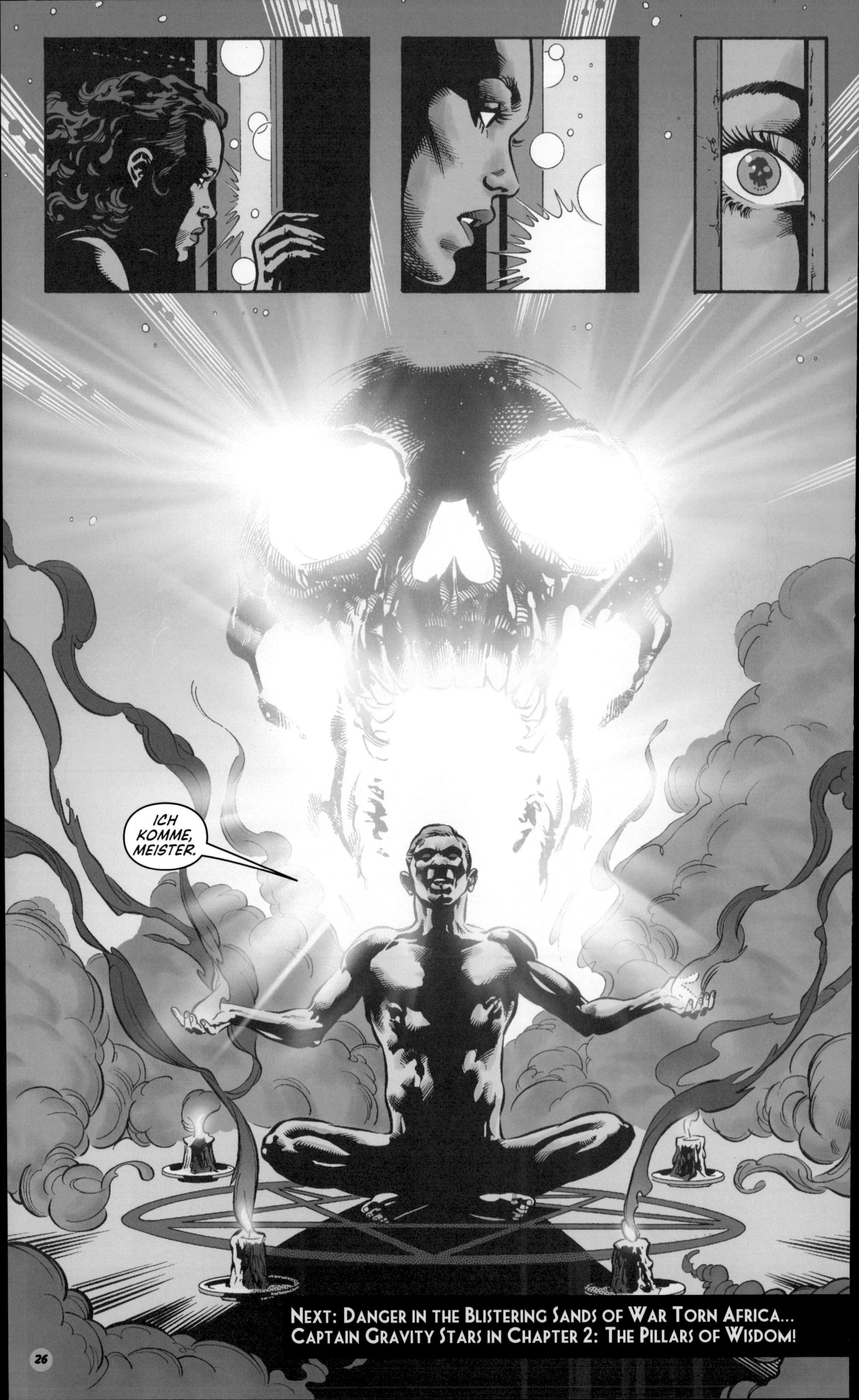
ICH KOMME, MEISTER.
Next: Danger in the Blistering Sands of War Torn Africa...
Captain Gravity Stars in Chapter 2: The Pillars of Wisdom!

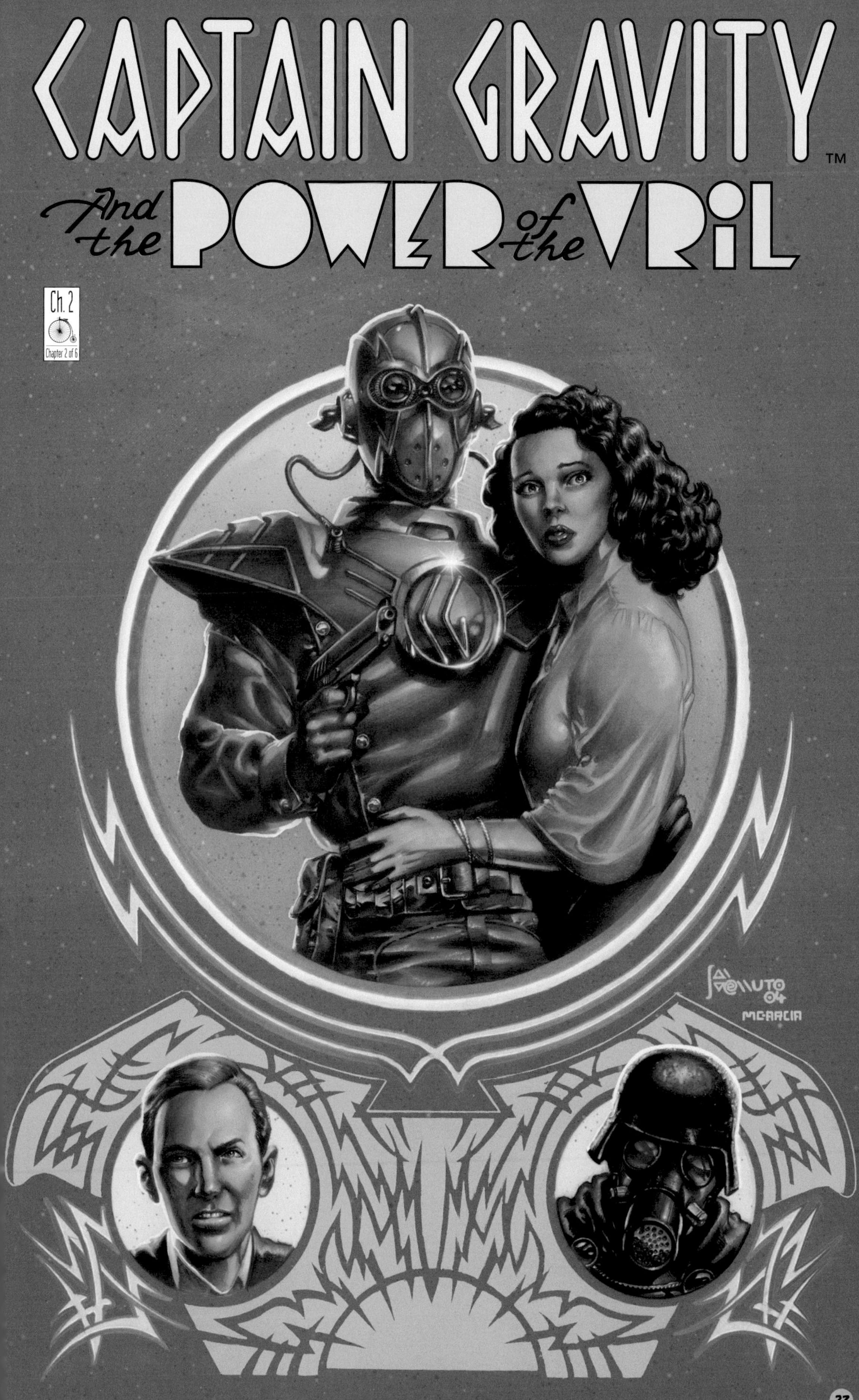
CAPTAIN GRAVITY™
And the POWER of the VRIL
Ch. 2
Chapter 2 of 6

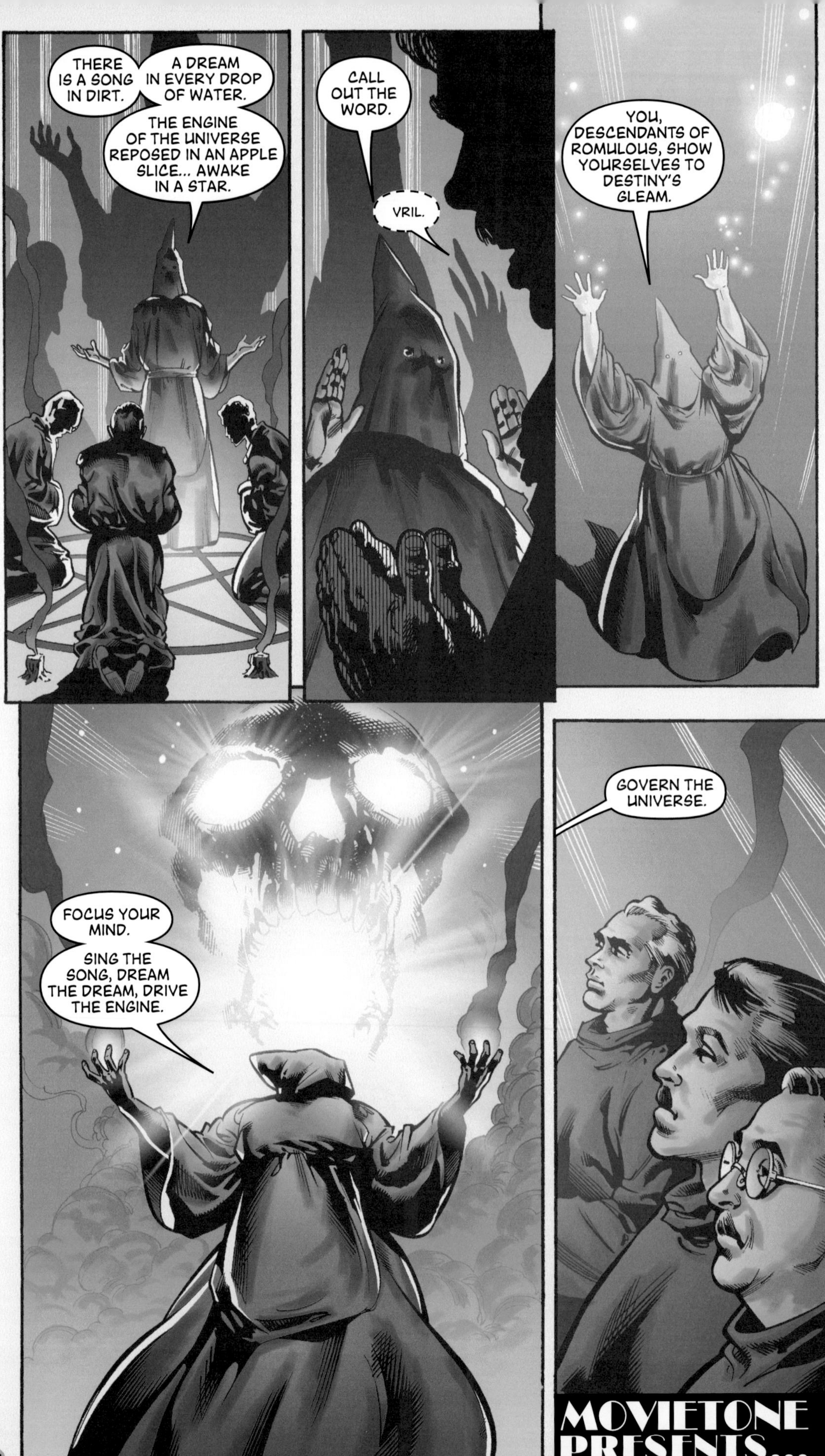
THERE IS A SONG IN DIRT.
A DREAM IN EVERY DROP OF WATER.
THE ENGINE OF THE UNIVERSE REPOSED IN AN APPLE SLICE... AWAKE IN A STAR.
CALL OUT THE WORD.
VRIL.
YOU, DESCENDANTS OF ROMULOUS, SHOW YOURSELVES TO DESTINY'S GLEAM.
FOCUS YOUR MIND.
SING THE SONG, DREAM THE DREAM, DRIVE THE ENGINE.
GOVERN THE UNIVERSE.
MOVIETONE PRESENTS...

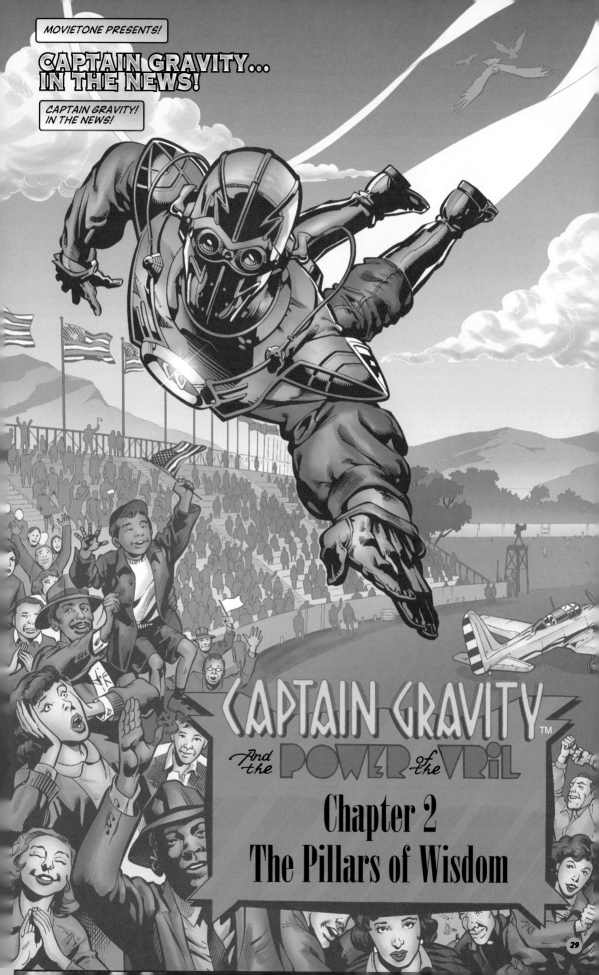

CAPTAIN GRAVITY...
IN THE NEWS!

CAPTAIN GRAVITY!
IN THE NEWS!

CAPTAIN GRAVITY
And the POWER of the VRIL

Chapter 2
The Pillars of Wisdom

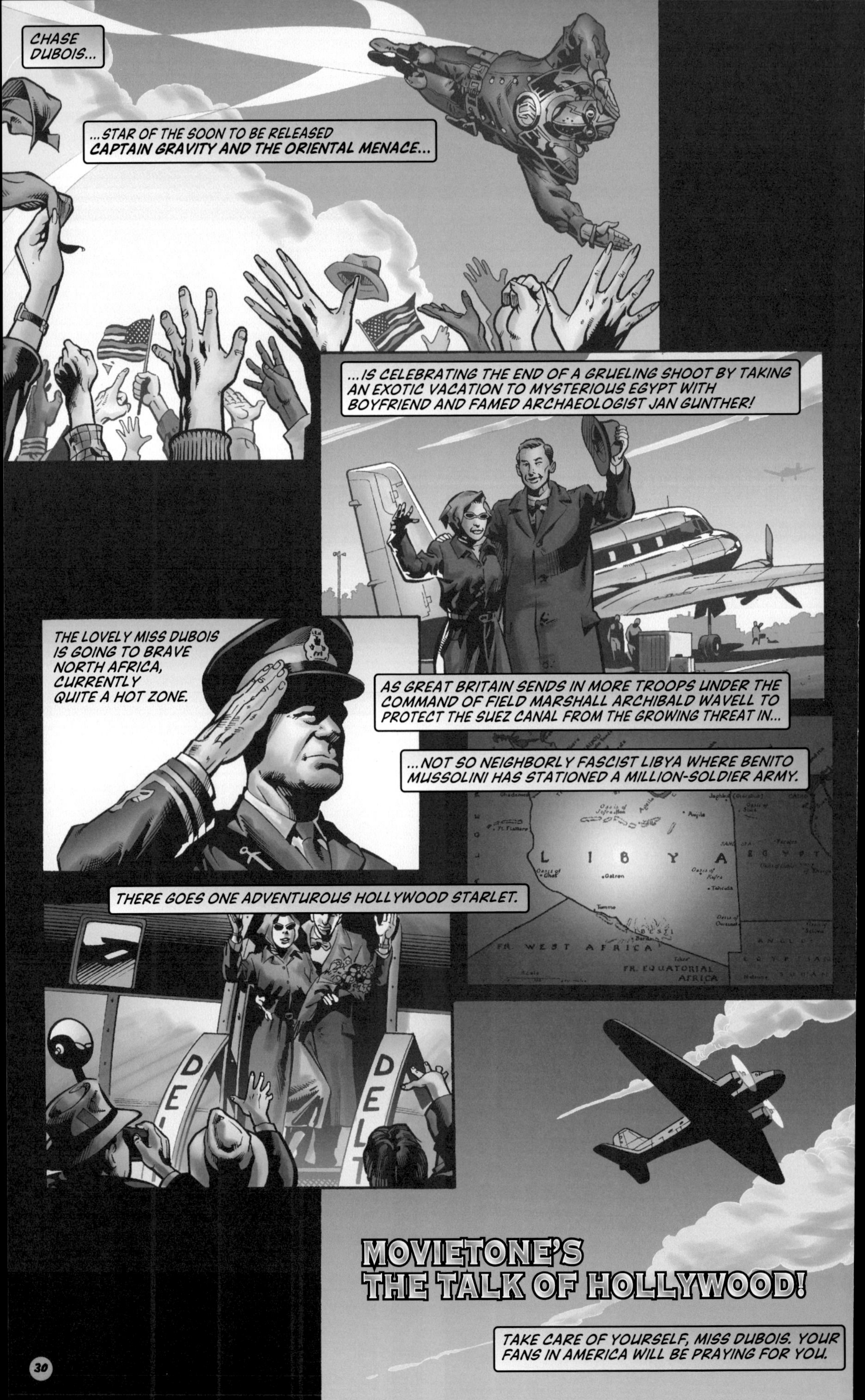
CHASE DUBOIS...
...STAR OF THE SOON TO BE RELEASED CAPTAIN GRAVITY AND THE ORIENTAL MENACE...
...IS CELEBRATING THE END OF A GRUELING SHOOT BY TAKING AN EXOTIC VACATION TO MYSTERIOUS EGYPT WITH BOYFRIEND AND FAMED ARCHAEOLOGIST JAN GUNTHER!
THE LOVELY MISS DUBOIS IS GOING TO BRAVE NORTH AFRICA, CURRENTLY QUITE A HOT ZONE.
AS GREAT BRITAIN SENDS IN MORE TROOPS UNDER THE COMMAND OF FIELD MARSHALL ARCHIBALD WAVELL TO PROTECT THE SUEZ CANAL FROM THE GROWING THREAT IN...
...NOT SO NEIGHBORLY FASCIST LIBYA WHERE BENITO MUSSOLINI HAS STATIONED A MILLION-SOLDIER ARMY.
L I B Y A
FR. WEST AFRICA
FR. EQUATORIAL AFRICA
THERE GOES ONE ADVENTUROUS HOLLYWOOD STARLET.
DEL
DELT
MOVIETONE'S THE TALK OF HOLLYWOOD!
TAKE CARE OF YOURSELF, MISS DUBOIS. YOUR FANS IN AMERICA WILL BE PRAYING FOR YOU.

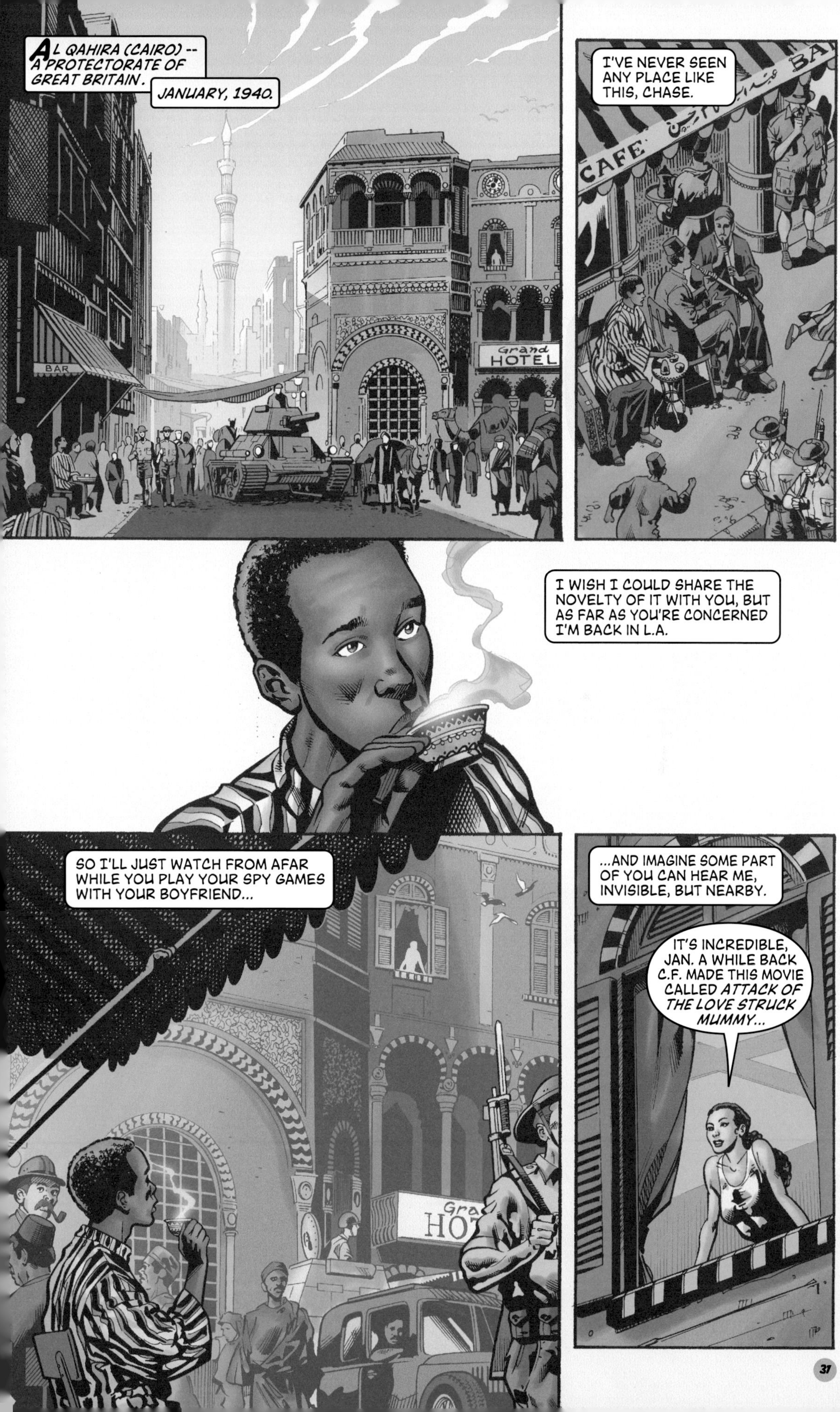
AL QAHIRA (CAIRO) -- A PROTECTORATE OF GREAT BRITAIN.
JANUARY, 1940.
BAR
Grand HOTEL
CAFE
I'VE NEVER SEEN ANY PLACE LIKE THIS, CHASE.
I WISH I COULD SHARE THE NOVELTY OF IT WITH YOU, BUT AS FAR AS YOU'RE CONCERNED I'M BACK IN L.A.
SO I'LL JUST WATCH FROM AFAR WHILE YOU PLAY YOUR SPY GAMES WITH YOUR BOYFRIEND...
...AND IMAGINE SOME PART OF YOU CAN HEAR ME, INVISIBLE, BUT NEARBY.
IT'S INCREDIBLE, JAN. A WHILE BACK C.F. MADE THIS MOVIE CALLED *ATTACK OF THE LOVE STRUCK MUMMY*...

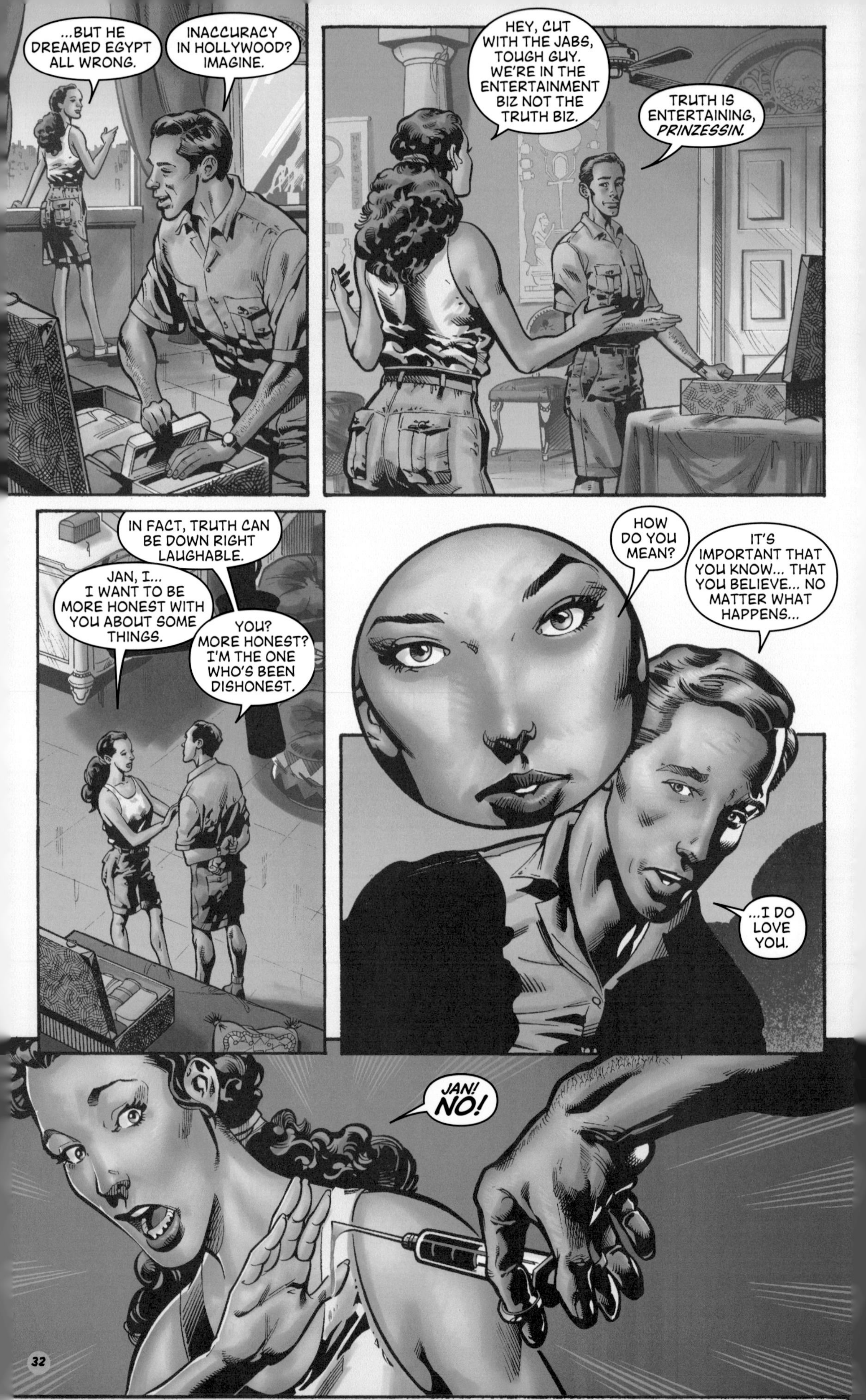

...BUT HE DREAMED EGYPT ALL WRONG.
INACCURACY IN HOLLYWOOD? IMAGINE.
HEY, CUT WITH THE JABS, TOUGH GUY. WE'RE IN THE ENTERTAINMENT BIZ NOT THE TRUTH BIZ.
TRUTH IS ENTERTAINING, *PRINZESSIN.*
IN FACT, TRUTH CAN BE DOWN RIGHT LAUGHABLE.
JAN, I... I WANT TO BE MORE HONEST WITH YOU ABOUT SOME THINGS.
YOU? MORE HONEST? I'M THE ONE WHO'S BEEN DISHONEST.
HOW DO YOU MEAN?
IT'S IMPORTANT THAT YOU KNOW... THAT YOU BELIEVE... NO MATTER WHAT HAPPENS...
...I DO LOVE YOU.
JAN! **NO!**

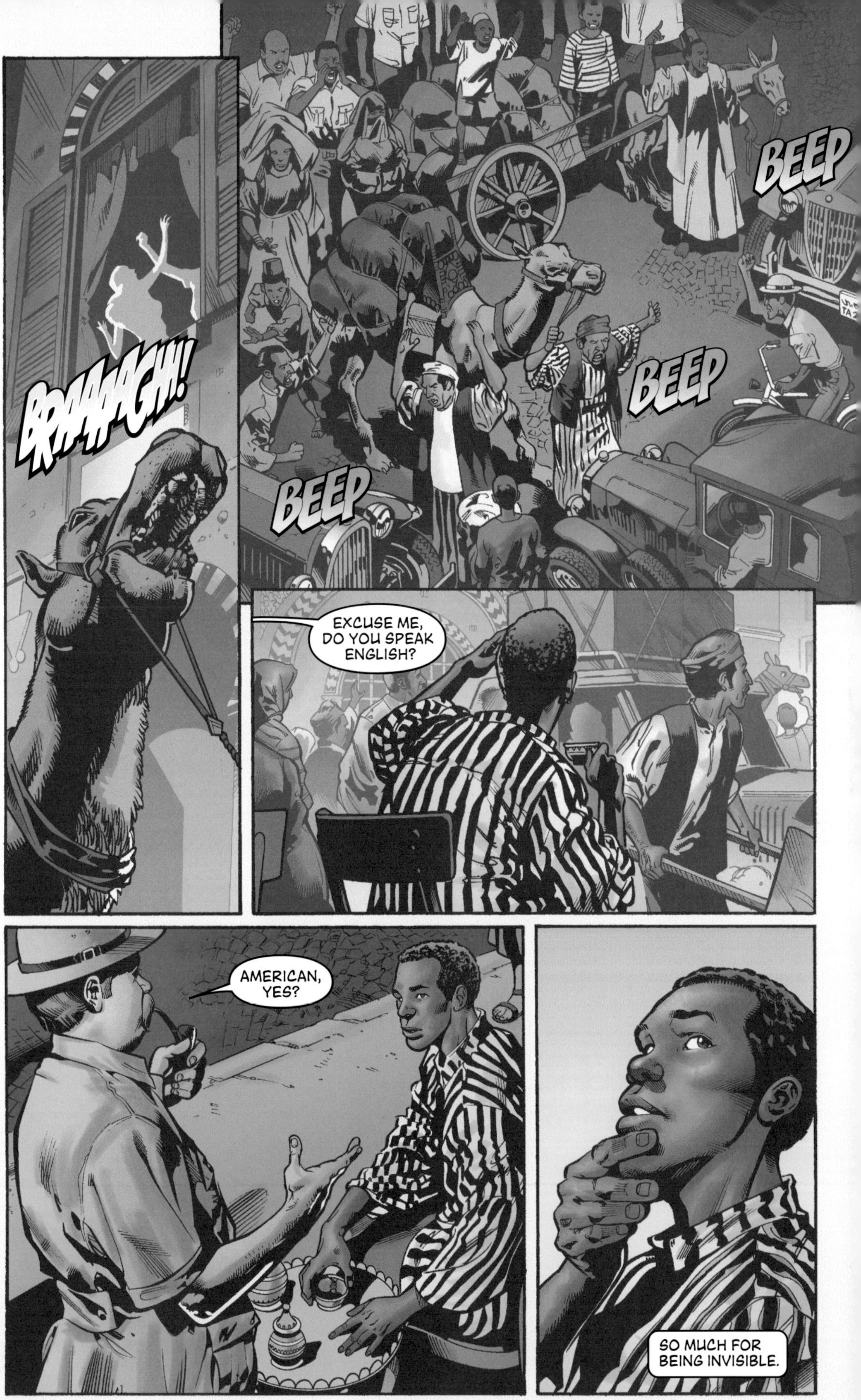
BRAAAAGH!
BEEP
BEEP
BEEP
EXCUSE ME, DO YOU SPEAK ENGLISH?
AMERICAN, YES?
SO MUCH FOR BEING INVISIBLE.

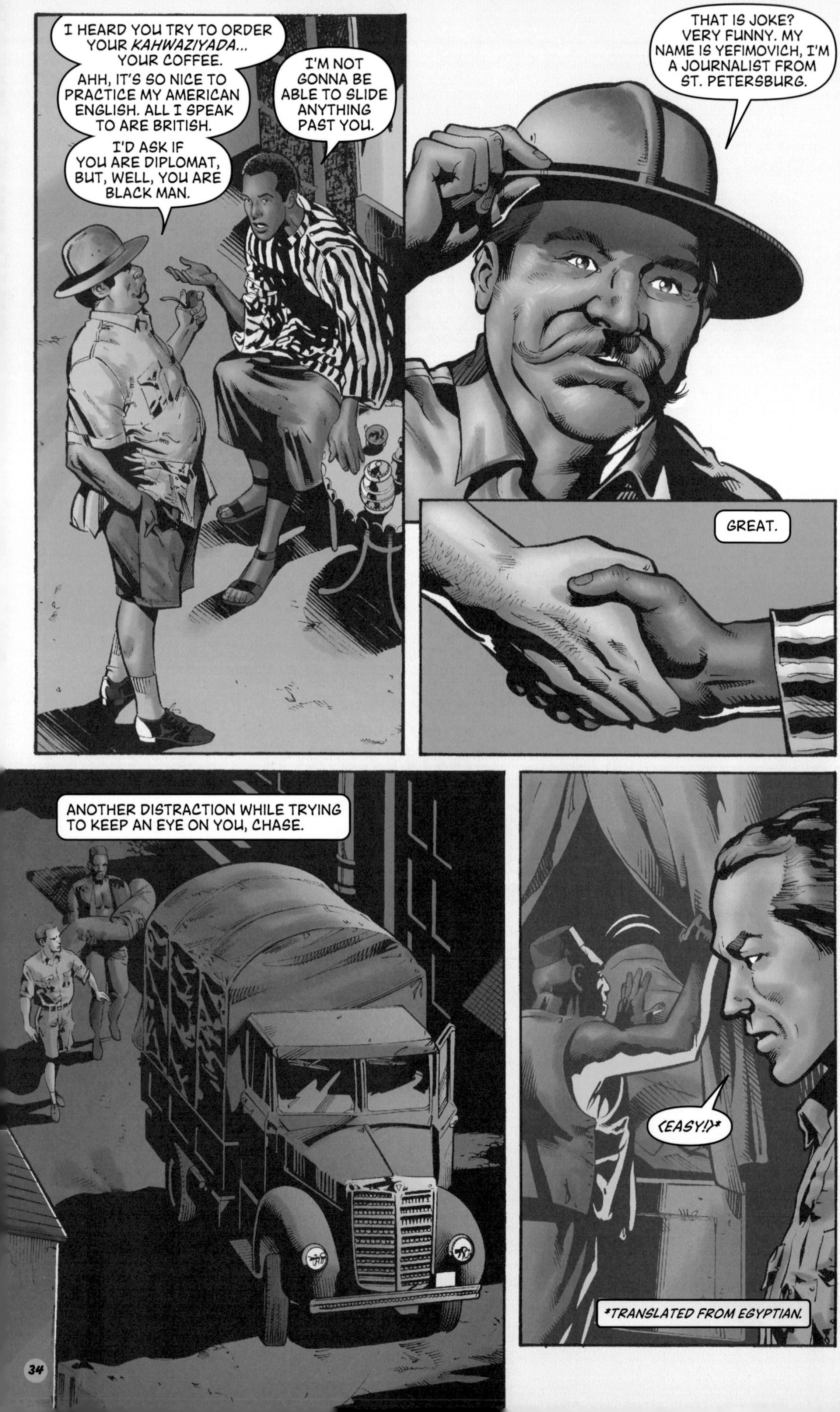

I HEARD YOU TRY TO ORDER YOUR *KAHWAZIYADA*... YOUR COFFEE.
AHH, IT'S SO NICE TO PRACTICE MY AMERICAN ENGLISH. ALL I SPEAK TO ARE BRITISH.
I'D ASK IF YOU ARE DIPLOMAT, BUT, WELL, YOU ARE BLACK MAN.
I'M NOT GONNA BE ABLE TO SLIDE ANYTHING PAST YOU.
THAT IS JOKE? VERY FUNNY. MY NAME IS YEFIMOVICH, I'M A JOURNALIST FROM ST. PETERSBURG.
GREAT.
ANOTHER DISTRACTION WHILE TRYING TO KEEP AN EYE ON YOU, CHASE.
<EASY!>*
*TRANSLATED FROM EGYPTIAN.

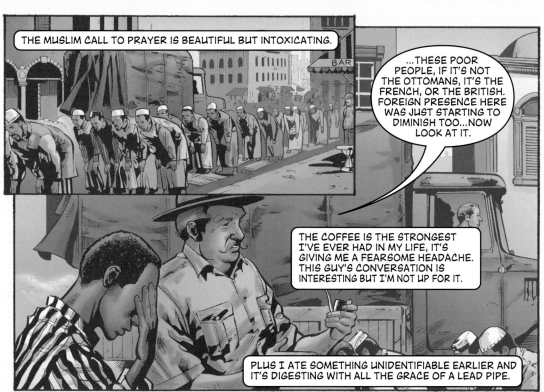

THE MUSLIM CALL TO PRAYER IS BEAUTIFUL BUT INTOXICATING.

...THESE POOR PEOPLE, IF IT'S NOT THE OTTOMANS, IT'S THE FRENCH, OR THE BRITISH. FOREIGN PRESENCE HERE WAS JUST STARTING TO DIMINISH TOO...NOW LOOK AT IT.

THE COFFEE IS THE STRONGEST I'VE EVER HAD IN MY LIFE, IT'S GIVING ME A FEARSOME HEADACHE. THIS GUY'S CONVERSATION IS INTERESTING BUT I'M NOT UP FOR IT.

PLUS I ATE SOMETHING UNIDENTIFIABLE EARLIER AND IT'S DIGESTING WITH ALL THE GRACE OF A LEAD PIPE.

IN THE MIDDLE OF MY WHINEY INTERNAL DIALOG I SEE HIM.

IT'S JACK PARSONS, CHASE. YOUR AMERICAN CONTACT.

I'M SORRY, MR. YEFA-- YEFAMIV-- I'M SORRY.

I'VE GOT TO GO.

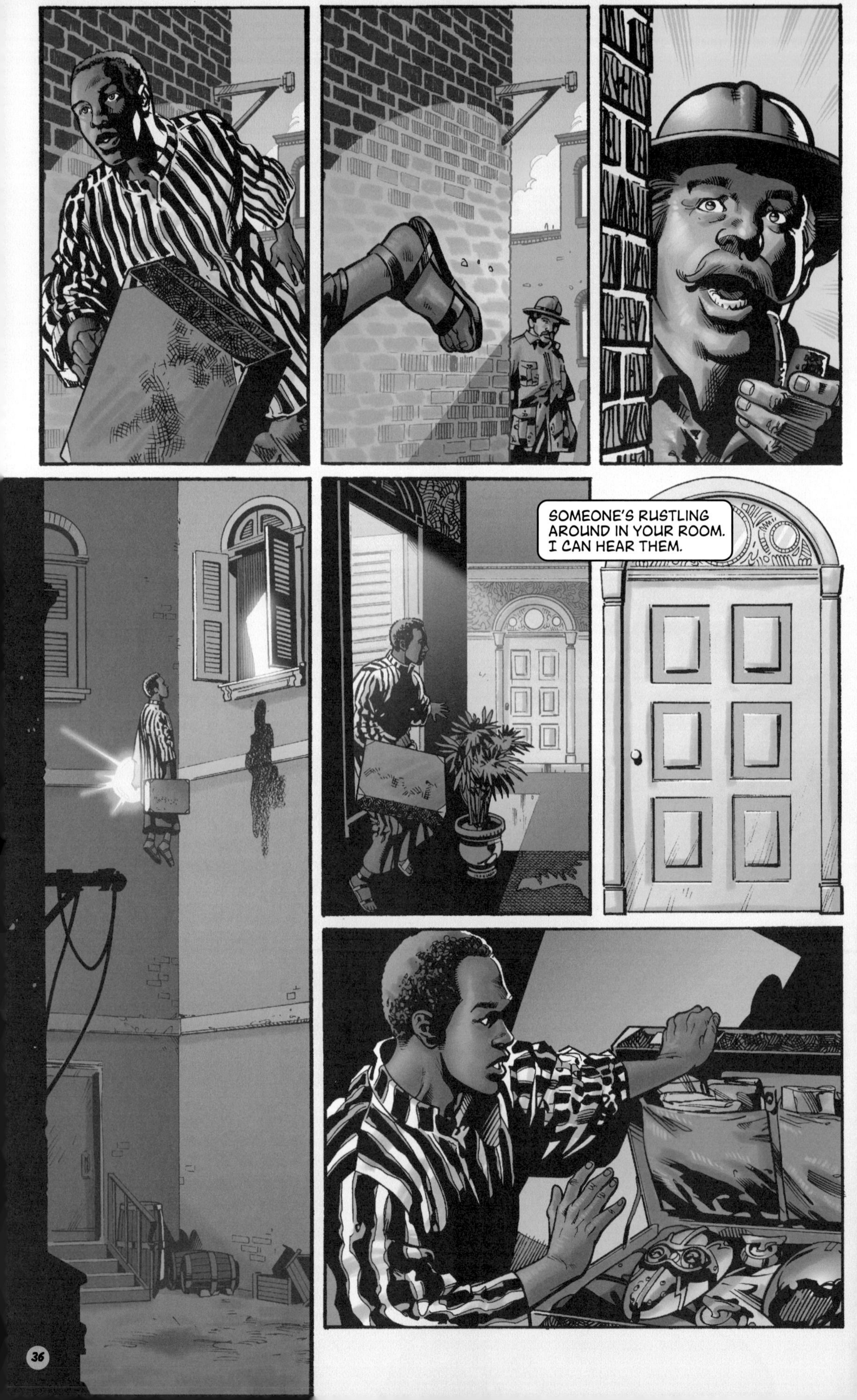
SOMEONE'S RUSTLING
AROUND IN YOUR ROOM.
I CAN HEAR THEM.

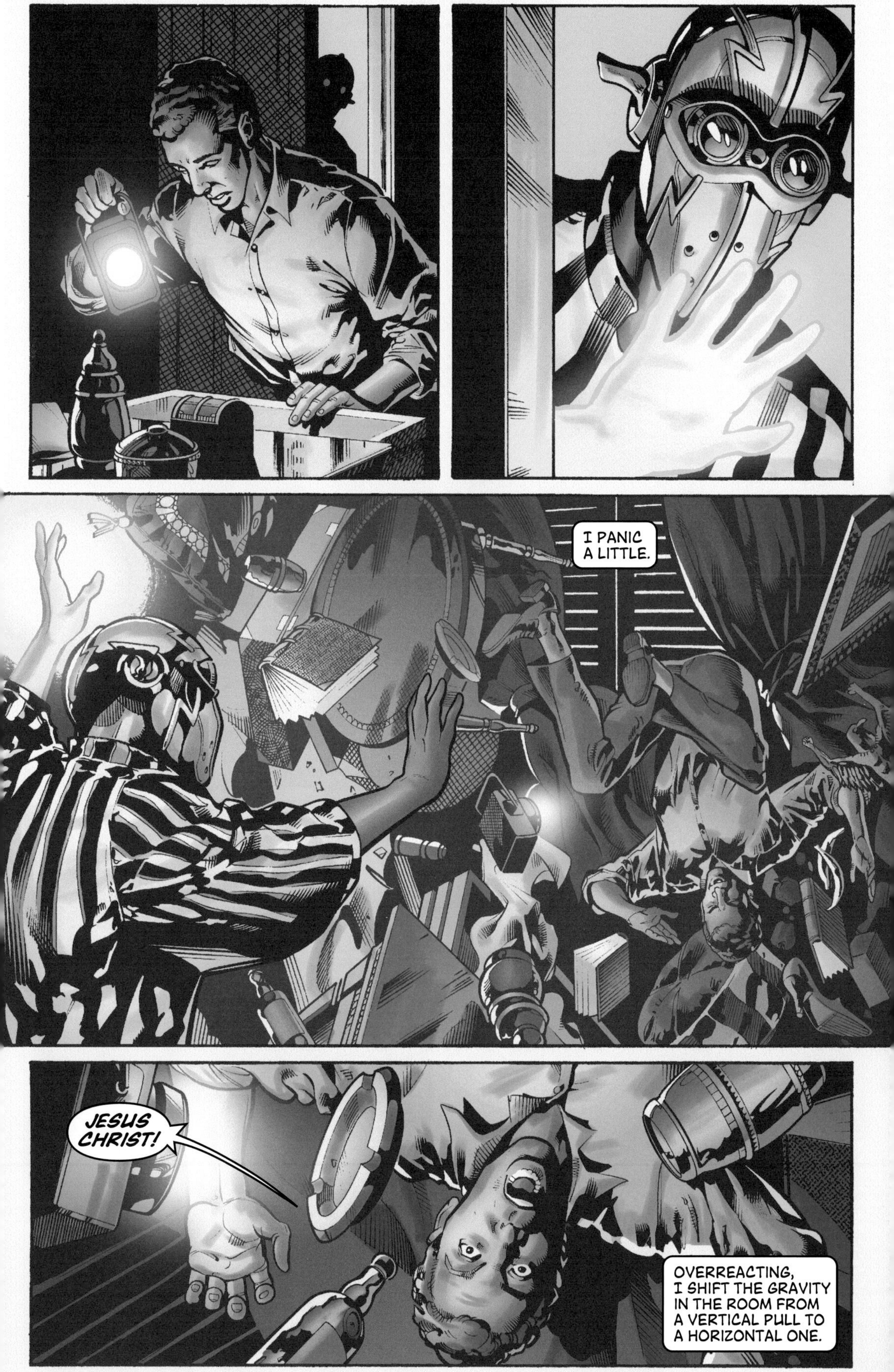
I PANIC
A LITTLE.
JESUS
CHRIST!
OVERREACTING,
I SHIFT THE GRAVITY
IN THE ROOM FROM
A VERTICAL PULL TO
A HORIZONTAL ONE.

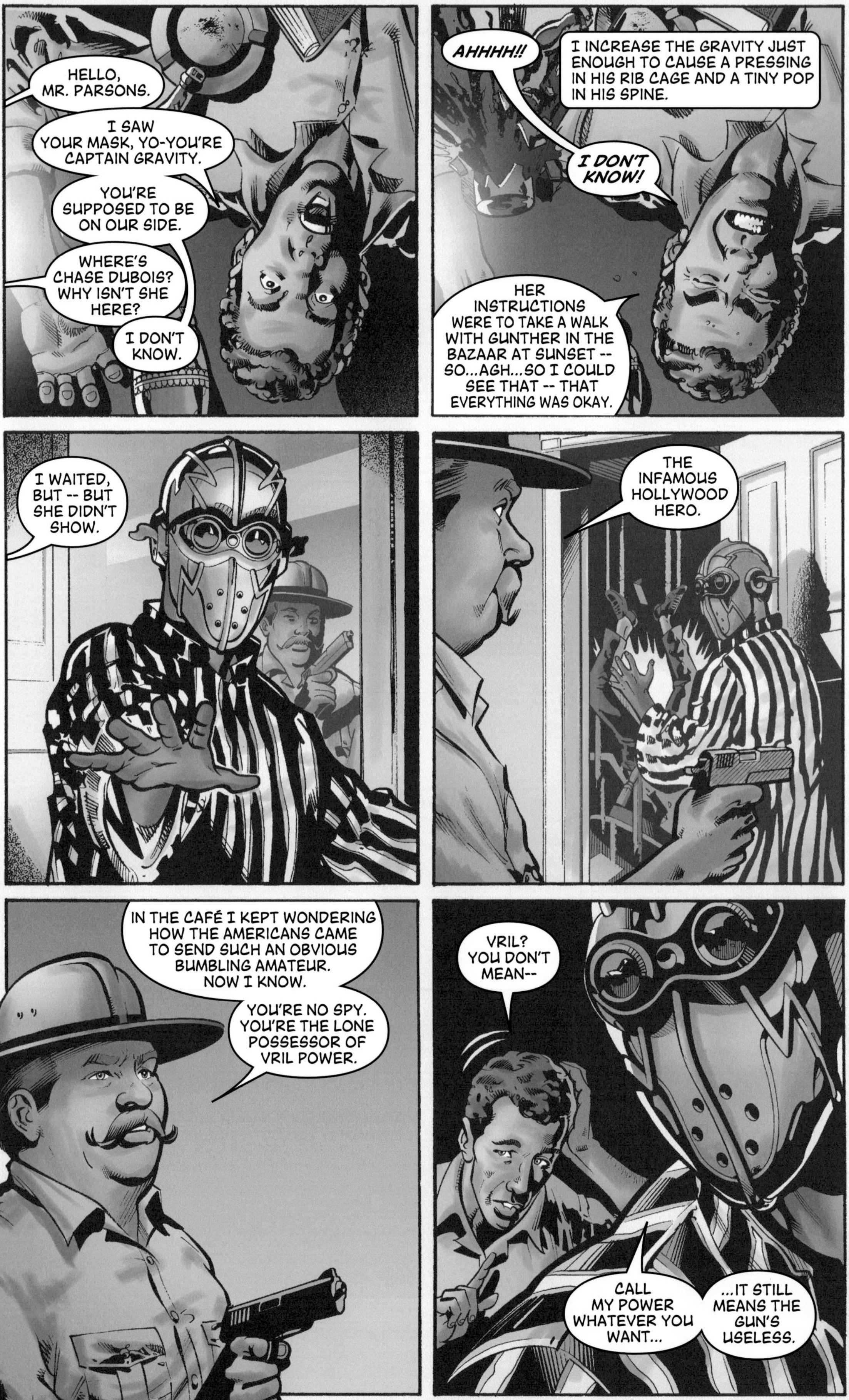
HELLO, MR. PARSONS.
I SAW YOUR MASK, YO-YOU'RE CAPTAIN GRAVITY.
YOU'RE SUPPOSED TO BE ON OUR SIDE.
WHERE'S CHASE DUBOIS? WHY ISN'T SHE HERE?
I DON'T KNOW.
AHHHH!!
I INCREASE THE GRAVITY JUST ENOUGH TO CAUSE A PRESSING IN HIS RIB CAGE AND A TINY POP IN HIS SPINE.
I DON'T KNOW!
HER INSTRUCTIONS WERE TO TAKE A WALK WITH GUNTHER IN THE BAZAAR AT SUNSET -- SO...AGH...SO I COULD SEE THAT -- THAT EVERYTHING WAS OKAY.
I WAITED, BUT -- BUT SHE DIDN'T SHOW.
THE INFAMOUS HOLLYWOOD HERO.
IN THE CAFÉ I KEPT WONDERING HOW THE AMERICANS CAME TO SEND SUCH AN OBVIOUS BUMBLING AMATEUR. NOW I KNOW.
YOU'RE NO SPY. YOU'RE THE LONE POSSESSOR OF VRIL POWER.
VRIL? YOU DON'T MEAN--
CALL MY POWER WHATEVER YOU WANT...
...IT STILL MEANS THE GUN'S USELESS.

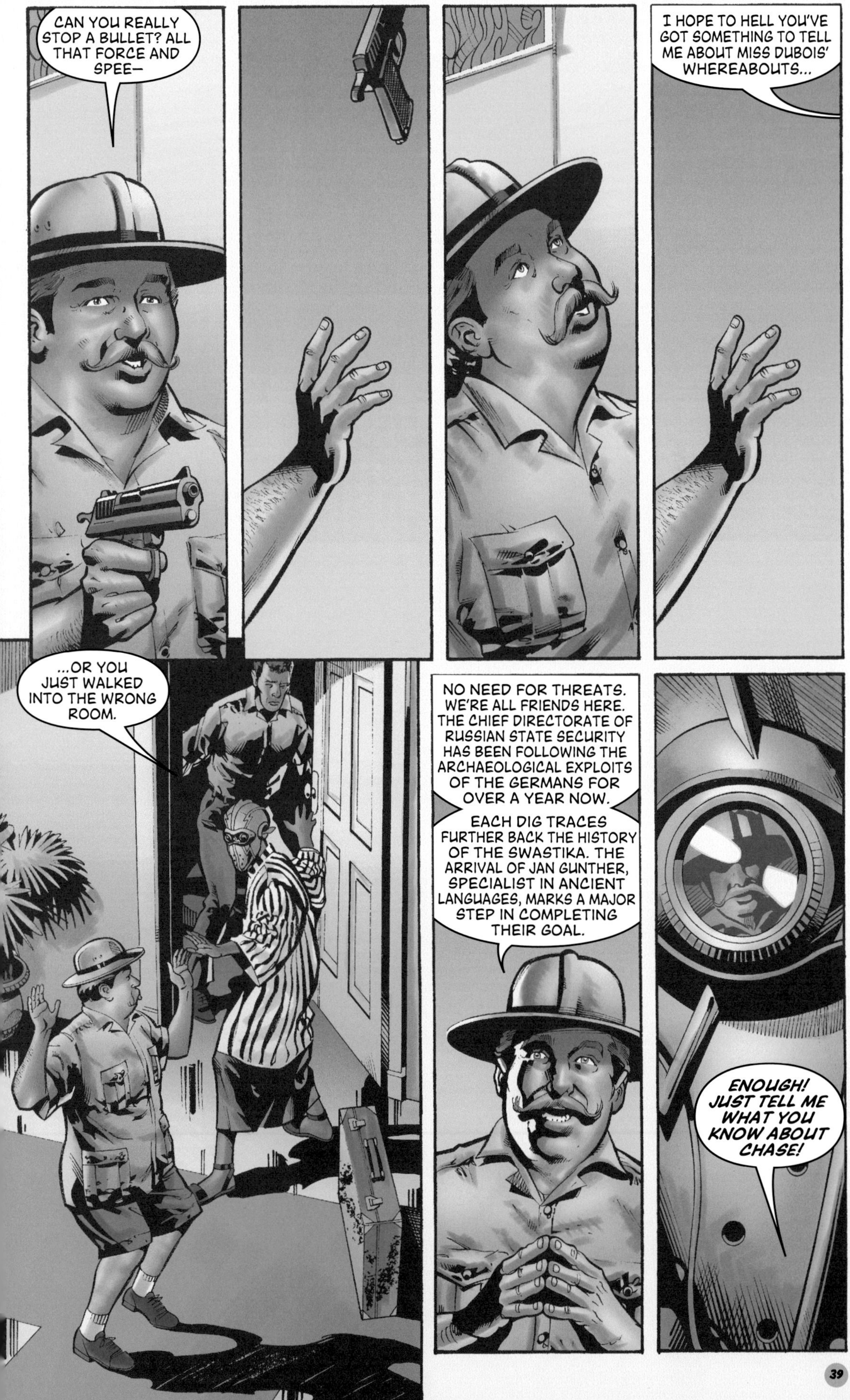
CAN YOU REALLY STOP A BULLET? ALL THAT FORCE AND SPEE—
I HOPE TO HELL YOU'VE GOT SOMETHING TO TELL ME ABOUT MISS DUBOIS' WHEREABOUTS...
...OR YOU JUST WALKED INTO THE WRONG ROOM.
NO NEED FOR THREATS. WE'RE ALL FRIENDS HERE. THE CHIEF DIRECTORATE OF RUSSIAN STATE SECURITY HAS BEEN FOLLOWING THE ARCHAEOLOGICAL EXPLOITS OF THE GERMANS FOR OVER A YEAR NOW.
EACH DIG TRACES FURTHER BACK THE HISTORY OF THE SWASTIKA. THE ARRIVAL OF JAN GUNTHER, SPECIALIST IN ANCIENT LANGUAGES, MARKS A MAJOR STEP IN COMPLETING THEIR GOAL.
ENOUGH! JUST TELL ME WHAT YOU KNOW ABOUT CHASE!

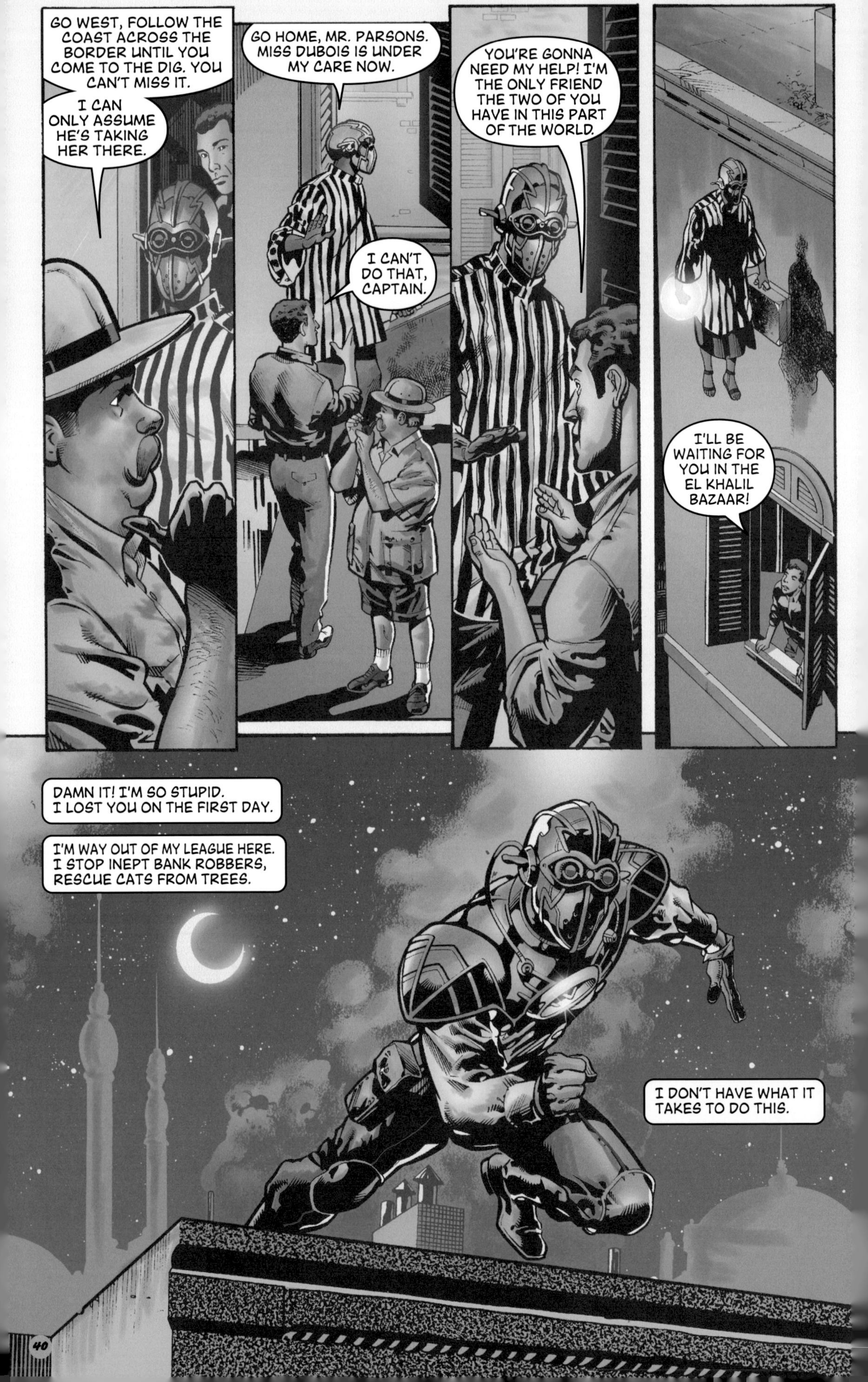
GO WEST, FOLLOW THE COAST ACROSS THE BORDER UNTIL YOU COME TO THE DIG. YOU CAN'T MISS IT.
I CAN ONLY ASSUME HE'S TAKING HER THERE.
GO HOME, MR. PARSONS. MISS DUBOIS IS UNDER MY CARE NOW.
I CAN'T DO THAT, CAPTAIN.
YOU'RE GONNA NEED MY HELP! I'M THE ONLY FRIEND THE TWO OF YOU HAVE IN THIS PART OF THE WORLD.
I'LL BE WAITING FOR YOU IN THE EL KHALIL BAZAAR!
DAMN IT! I'M SO STUPID. I LOST YOU ON THE FIRST DAY.
I'M WAY OUT OF MY LEAGUE HERE. I STOP INEPT BANK ROBBERS, RESCUE CATS FROM TREES.
I DON'T HAVE WHAT IT TAKES TO DO THIS.
40

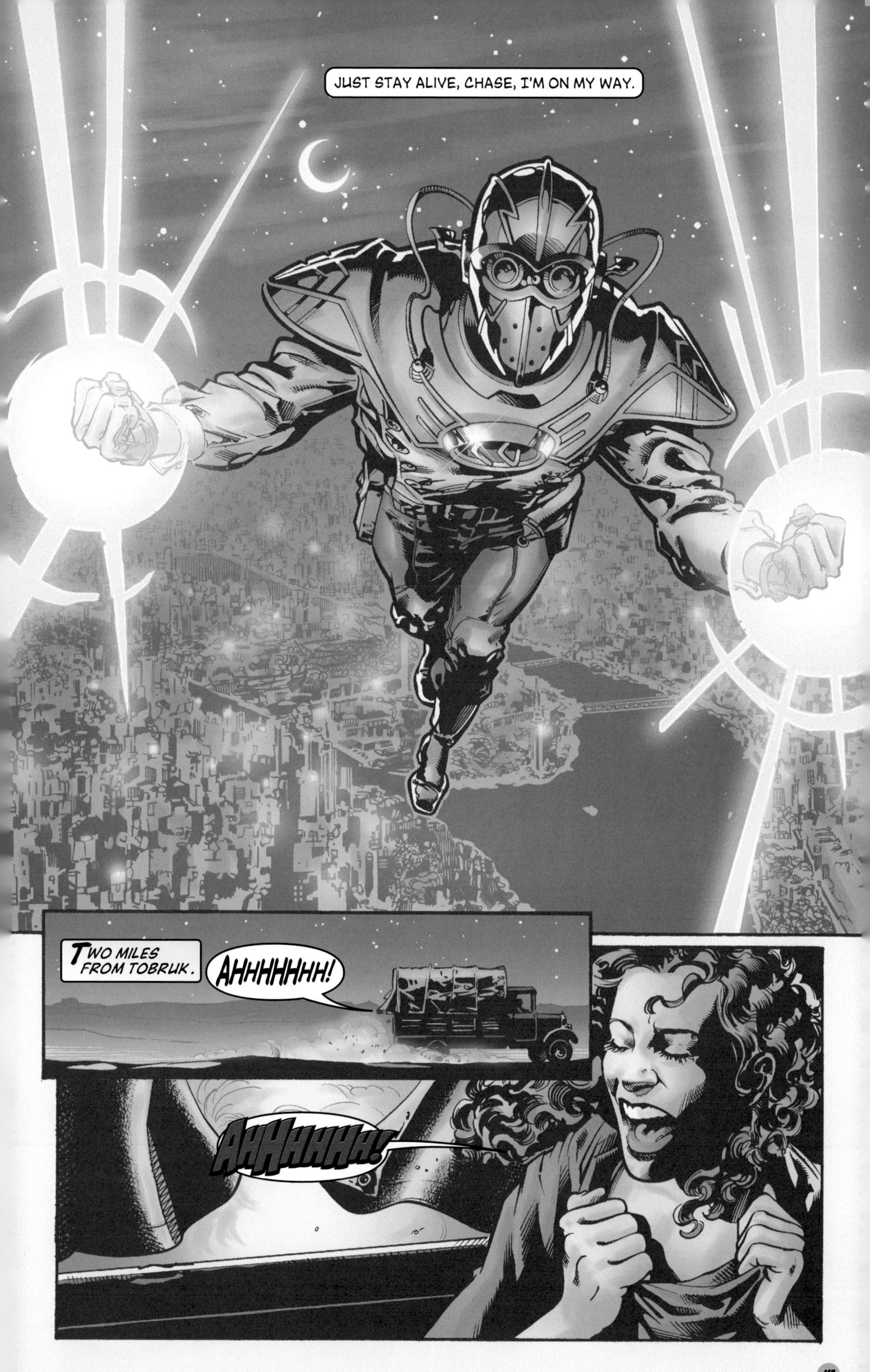
JUST STAY ALIVE, CHASE, I'M ON MY WAY.
TWO MILES FROM TOBRUK.
AHHHHHHH!
AHHHHHH!

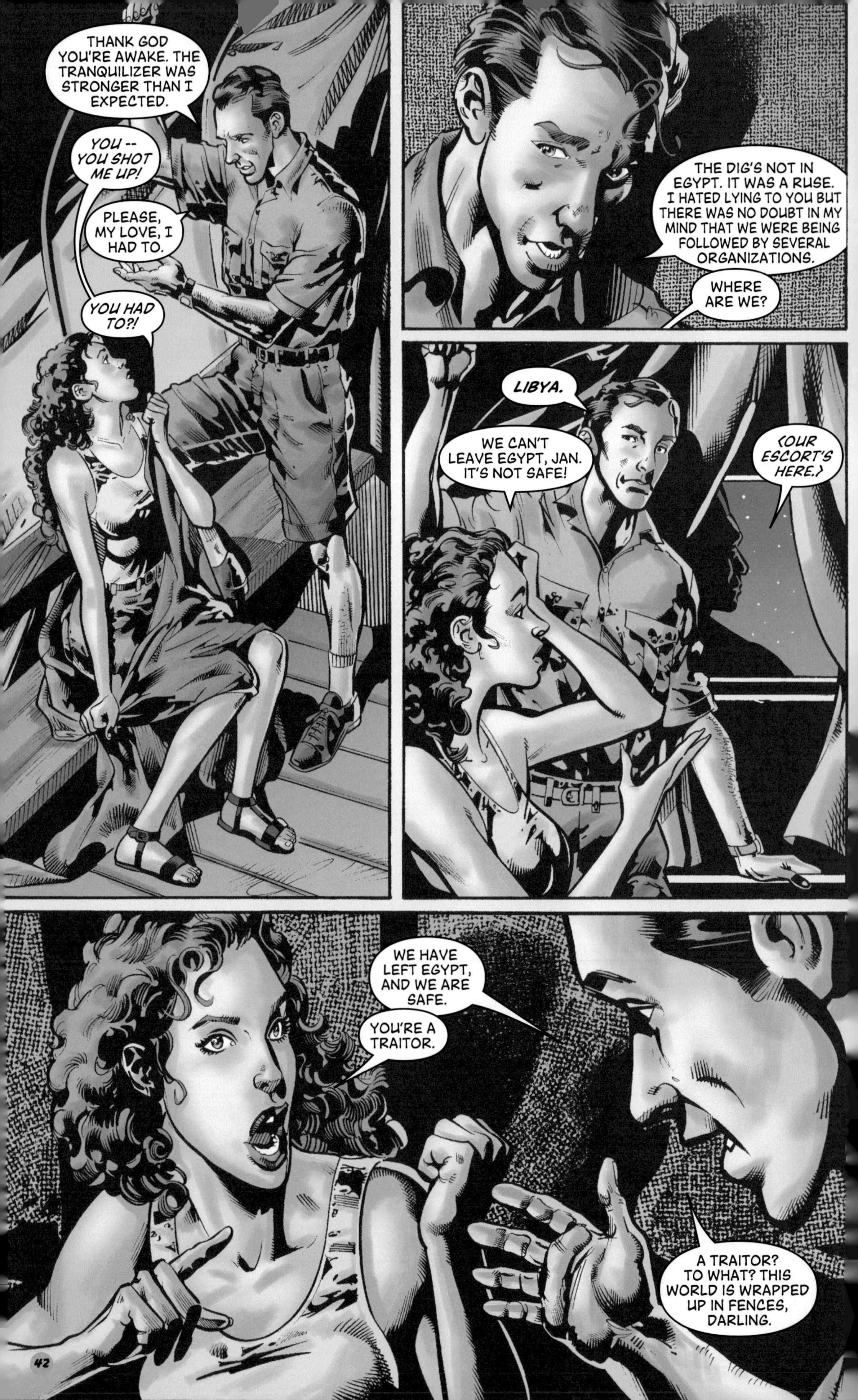
THANK GOD YOU'RE AWAKE. THE TRANQUILIZER WAS STRONGER THAN I EXPECTED.
YOU -- YOU SHOT ME UP!
PLEASE, MY LOVE, I HAD TO.
YOU HAD TO?!
THE DIG'S NOT IN EGYPT. IT WAS A RUSE. I HATED LYING TO YOU BUT THERE WAS NO DOUBT IN MY MIND THAT WE WERE BEING FOLLOWED BY SEVERAL ORGANIZATIONS.
WHERE ARE WE?
LIBYA.
WE CAN'T LEAVE EGYPT, JAN. IT'S NOT SAFE!
<OUR ESCORT'S HERE.>
WE HAVE LEFT EGYPT, AND WE ARE SAFE.
YOU'RE A TRAITOR.
A TRAITOR? TO WHAT? THIS WORLD IS WRAPPED UP IN FENCES, DARLING.

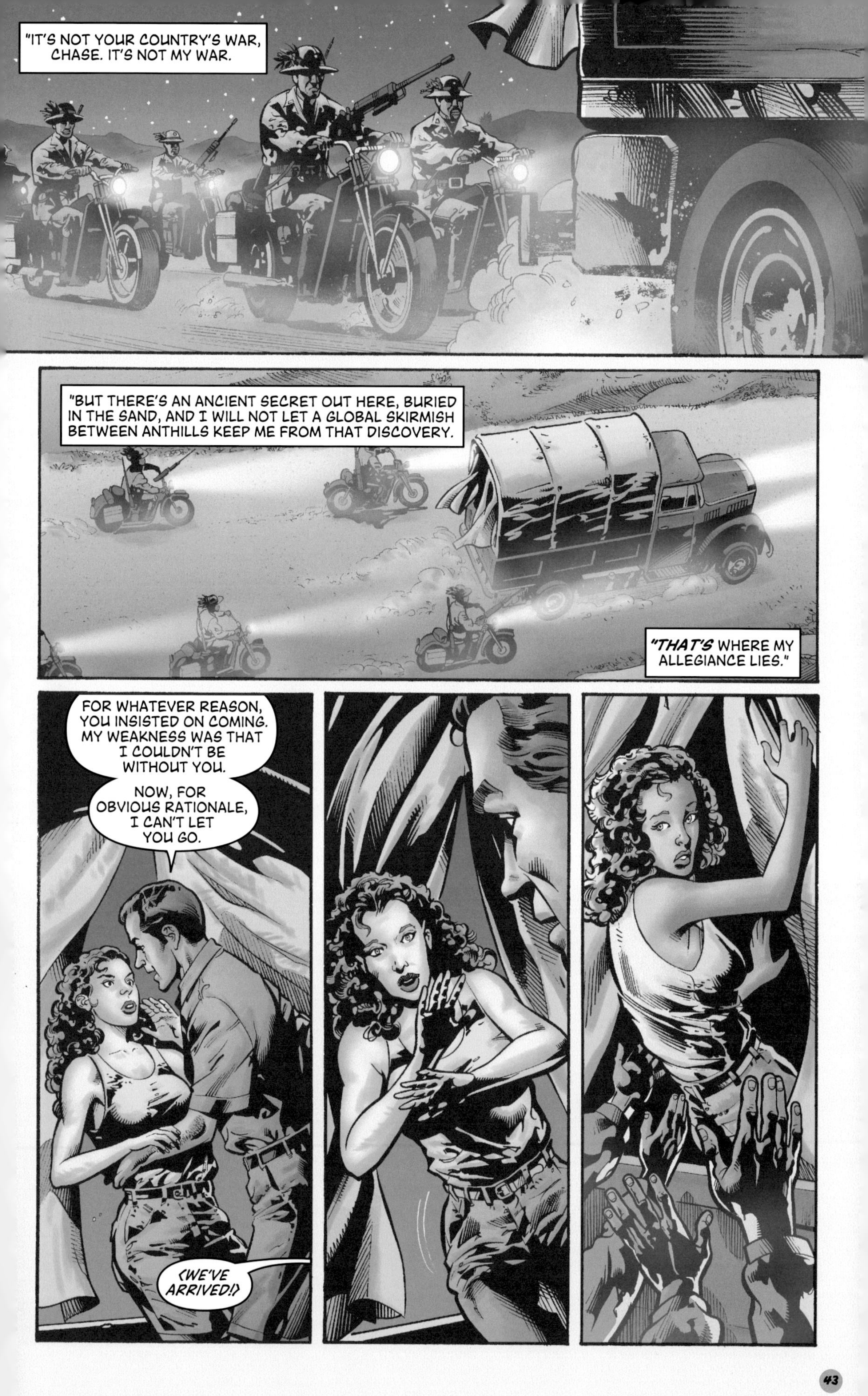
"IT'S NOT YOUR COUNTRY'S WAR, CHASE. IT'S NOT MY WAR.
"BUT THERE'S AN ANCIENT SECRET OUT HERE, BURIED IN THE SAND, AND I WILL NOT LET A GLOBAL SKIRMISH BETWEEN ANTHILLS KEEP ME FROM THAT DISCOVERY.
"*THAT'S* WHERE MY ALLEGIANCE LIES."
FOR WHATEVER REASON, YOU INSISTED ON COMING. MY WEAKNESS WAS THAT I COULDN'T BE WITHOUT YOU.
NOW, FOR OBVIOUS RATIONALE, I CAN'T LET YOU GO.
<WE'VE ARRIVED!>

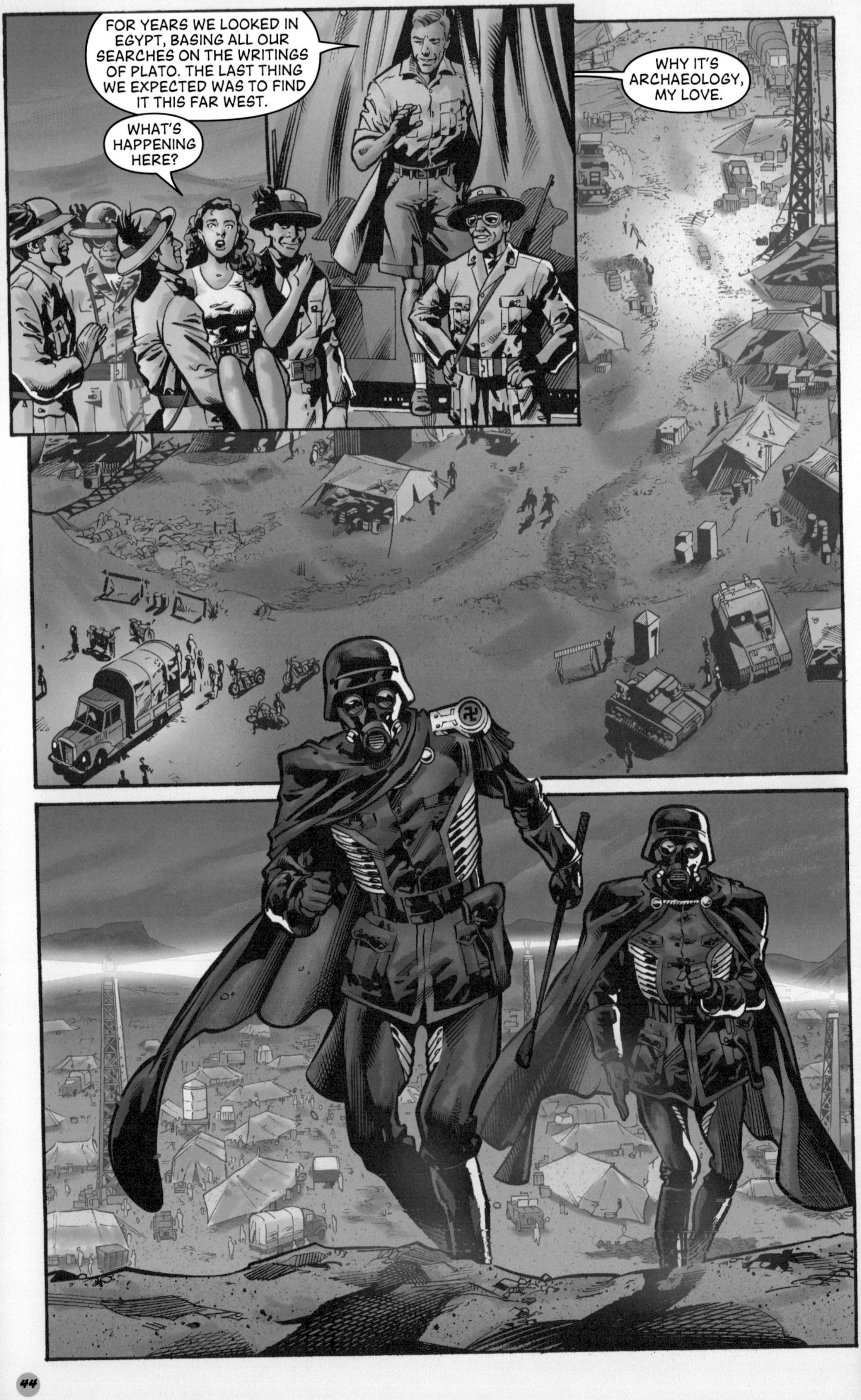
FOR YEARS WE LOOKED IN EGYPT, BASING ALL OUR SEARCHES ON THE WRITINGS OF PLATO. THE LAST THING WE EXPECTED WAS TO FIND IT THIS FAR WEST.
WHAT'S HAPPENING HERE?
WHY IT'S ARCHAEOLOGY, MY LOVE.

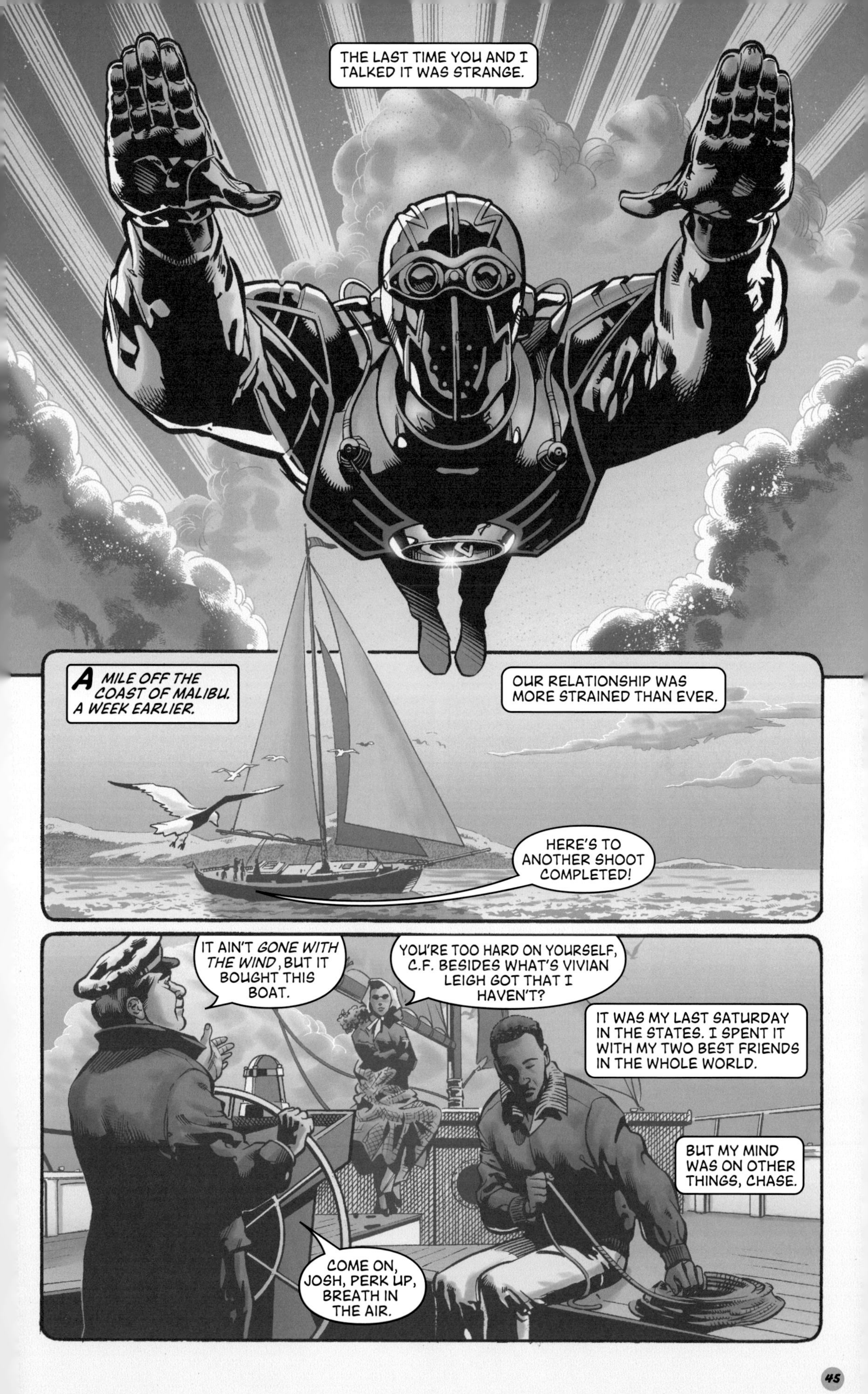
THE LAST TIME YOU AND I TALKED IT WAS STRANGE.
A MILE OFF THE COAST OF MALIBU. A WEEK EARLIER.
OUR RELATIONSHIP WAS MORE STRAINED THAN EVER.
HERE'S TO ANOTHER SHOOT COMPLETED!
IT AIN'T *GONE WITH THE WIND*, BUT IT BOUGHT THIS BOAT.
YOU'RE TOO HARD ON YOURSELF, C.F. BESIDES WHAT'S VIVIAN LEIGH GOT THAT I HAVEN'T?
IT WAS MY LAST SATURDAY IN THE STATES. I SPENT IT WITH MY TWO BEST FRIENDS IN THE WHOLE WORLD.
BUT MY MIND WAS ON OTHER THINGS, CHASE.
COME ON, JOSH, PERK UP, BREATH IN THE AIR.

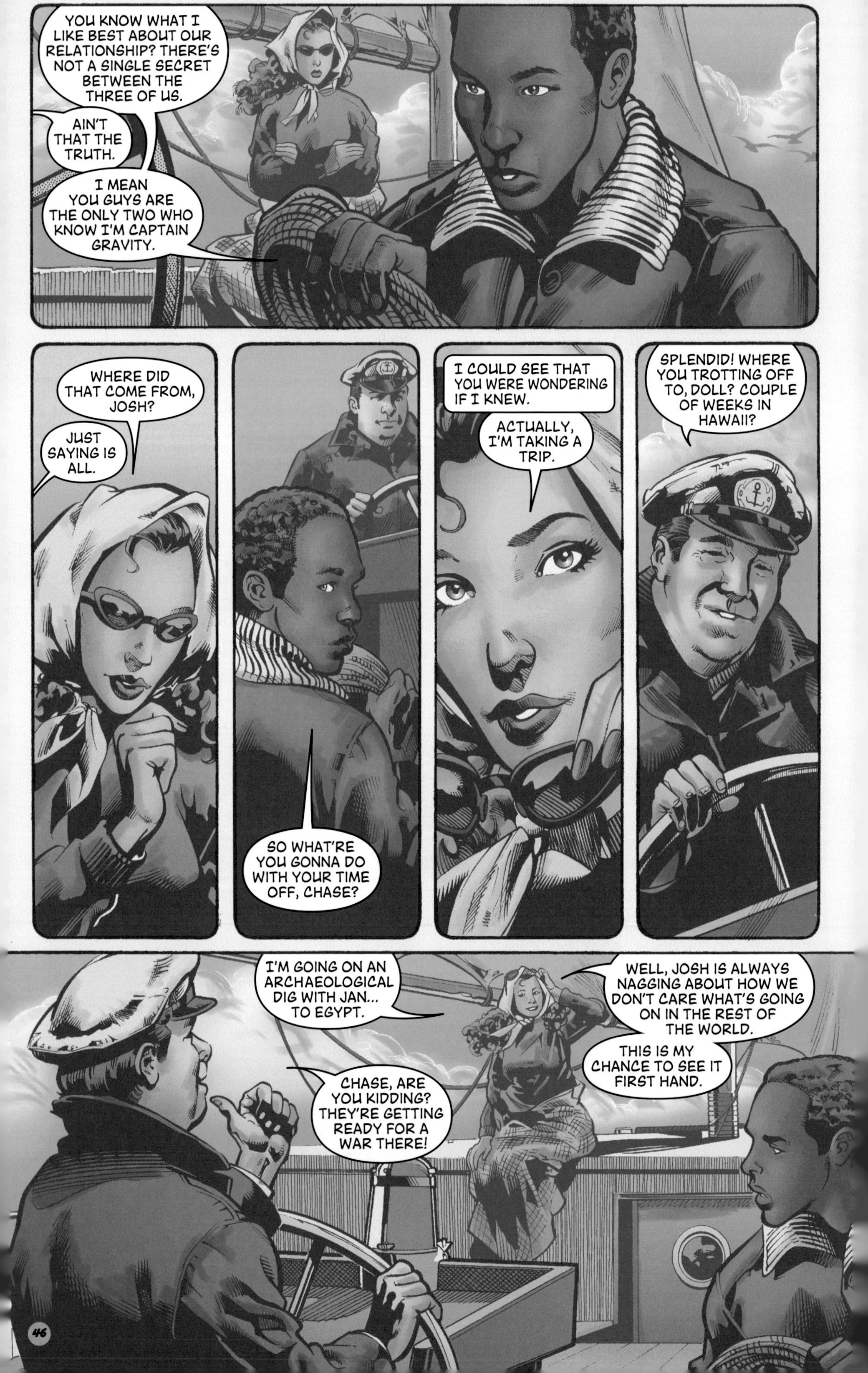

YOU KNOW WHAT I LIKE BEST ABOUT OUR RELATIONSHIP? THERE'S NOT A SINGLE SECRET BETWEEN THE THREE OF US.
AIN'T THAT THE TRUTH.
I MEAN YOU GUYS ARE THE ONLY TWO WHO KNOW I'M CAPTAIN GRAVITY.
WHERE DID THAT COME FROM, JOSH?
JUST SAYING IS ALL.
SO WHAT'RE YOU GONNA DO WITH YOUR TIME OFF, CHASE?
I COULD SEE THAT YOU WERE WONDERING IF I KNEW.
ACTUALLY, I'M TAKING A TRIP.
SPLENDID! WHERE YOU TROTTING OFF TO, DOLL? COUPLE OF WEEKS IN HAWAII?
I'M GOING ON AN ARCHAEOLOGICAL DIG WITH JAN... TO EGYPT.
CHASE, ARE YOU KIDDING? THEY'RE GETTING READY FOR A WAR THERE!
WELL, JOSH IS ALWAYS NAGGING ABOUT HOW WE DON'T CARE WHAT'S GOING ON IN THE REST OF THE WORLD.
THIS IS MY CHANCE TO SEE IT FIRST HAND.

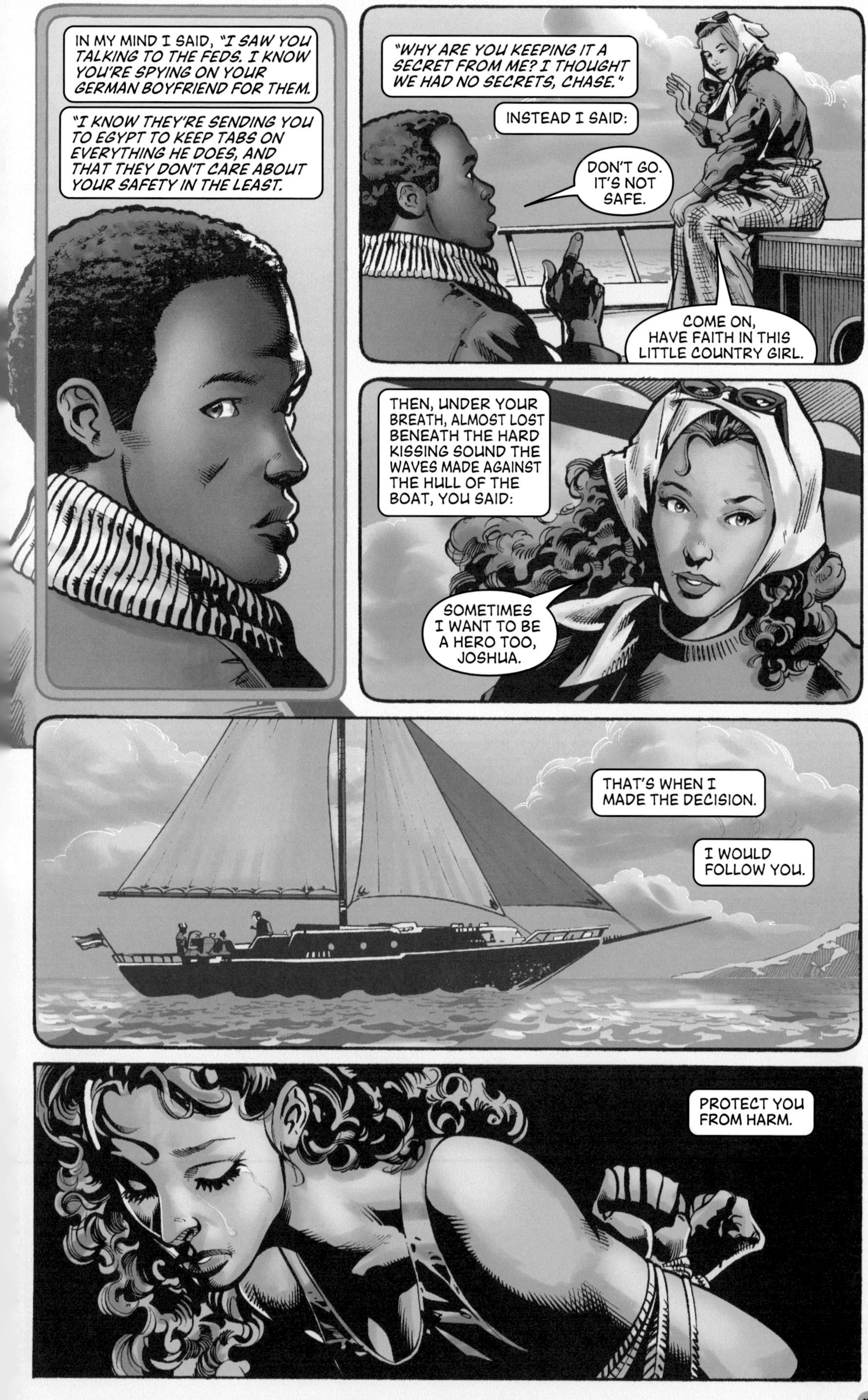
IN MY MIND I SAID, "I SAW YOU TALKING TO THE FEDS. I KNOW YOU'RE SPYING ON YOUR GERMAN BOYFRIEND FOR THEM.
"I KNOW THEY'RE SENDING YOU TO EGYPT TO KEEP TABS ON EVERYTHING HE DOES, AND THAT THEY DON'T CARE ABOUT YOUR SAFETY IN THE LEAST.
"WHY ARE YOU KEEPING IT A SECRET FROM ME? I THOUGHT WE HAD NO SECRETS, CHASE."
INSTEAD I SAID:
DON'T GO. IT'S NOT SAFE.
COME ON, HAVE FAITH IN THIS LITTLE COUNTRY GIRL.
THEN, UNDER YOUR BREATH, ALMOST LOST BENEATH THE HARD KISSING SOUND THE WAVES MADE AGAINST THE HULL OF THE BOAT, YOU SAID:
SOMETIMES I WANT TO BE A HERO TOO, JOSHUA.
THAT'S WHEN I MADE THE DECISION.
I WOULD FOLLOW YOU.
PROTECT YOU FROM HARM.

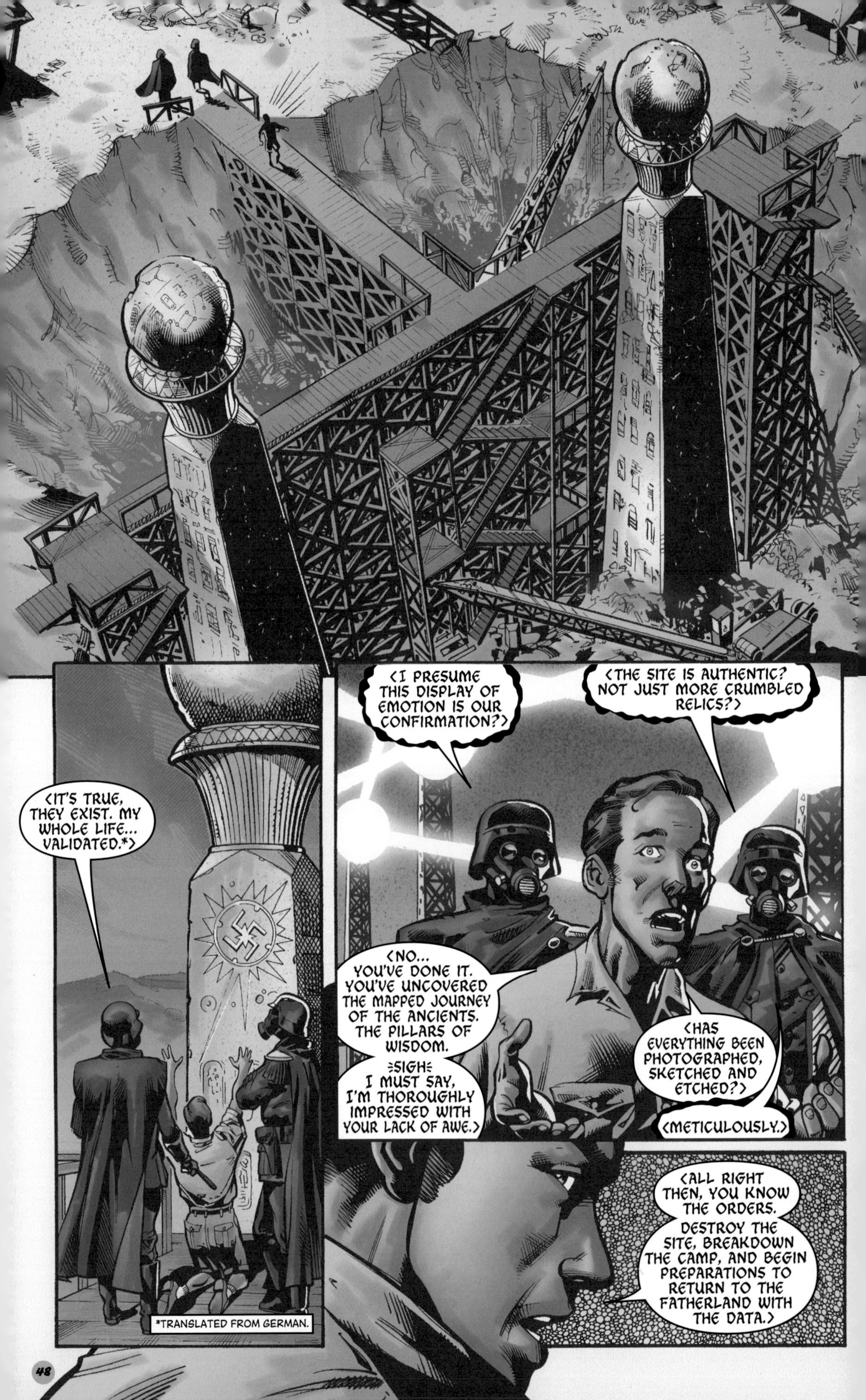

<IT'S TRUE, THEY EXIST. MY WHOLE LIFE... VALIDATED.*>
*TRANSLATED FROM GERMAN.
<I PRESUME THIS DISPLAY OF EMOTION IS OUR CONFIRMATION?>
<THE SITE IS AUTHENTIC? NOT JUST MORE CRUMBLED RELICS?>
<NO... YOU'VE DONE IT. YOU'VE UNCOVERED THE MAPPED JOURNEY OF THE ANCIENTS. THE PILLARS OF WISDOM.
=SIGH= I MUST SAY, I'M THOROUGHLY IMPRESSED WITH YOUR LACK OF AWE.>
<HAS EVERYTHING BEEN PHOTOGRAPHED, SKETCHED AND ETCHED?>
<METICULOUSLY.>
<ALL RIGHT THEN, YOU KNOW THE ORDERS.
DESTROY THE SITE, BREAKDOWN THE CAMP, AND BEGIN PREPARATIONS TO RETURN TO THE FATHERLAND WITH THE DATA.>

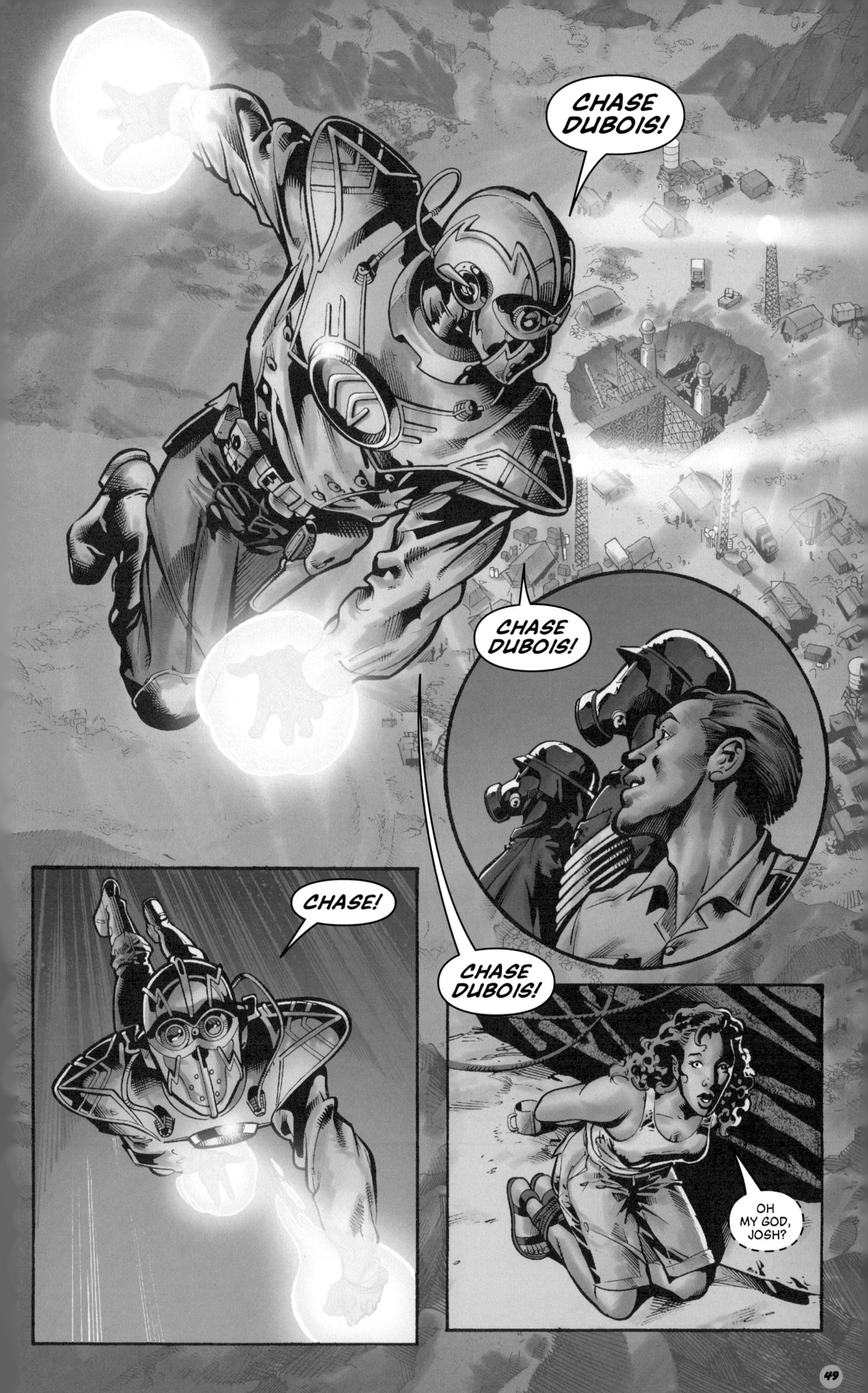
CHASE DUBOIS!
CHASE DUBOIS!
CHASE!
CHASE DUBOIS!
OH MY GOD, JOSH?

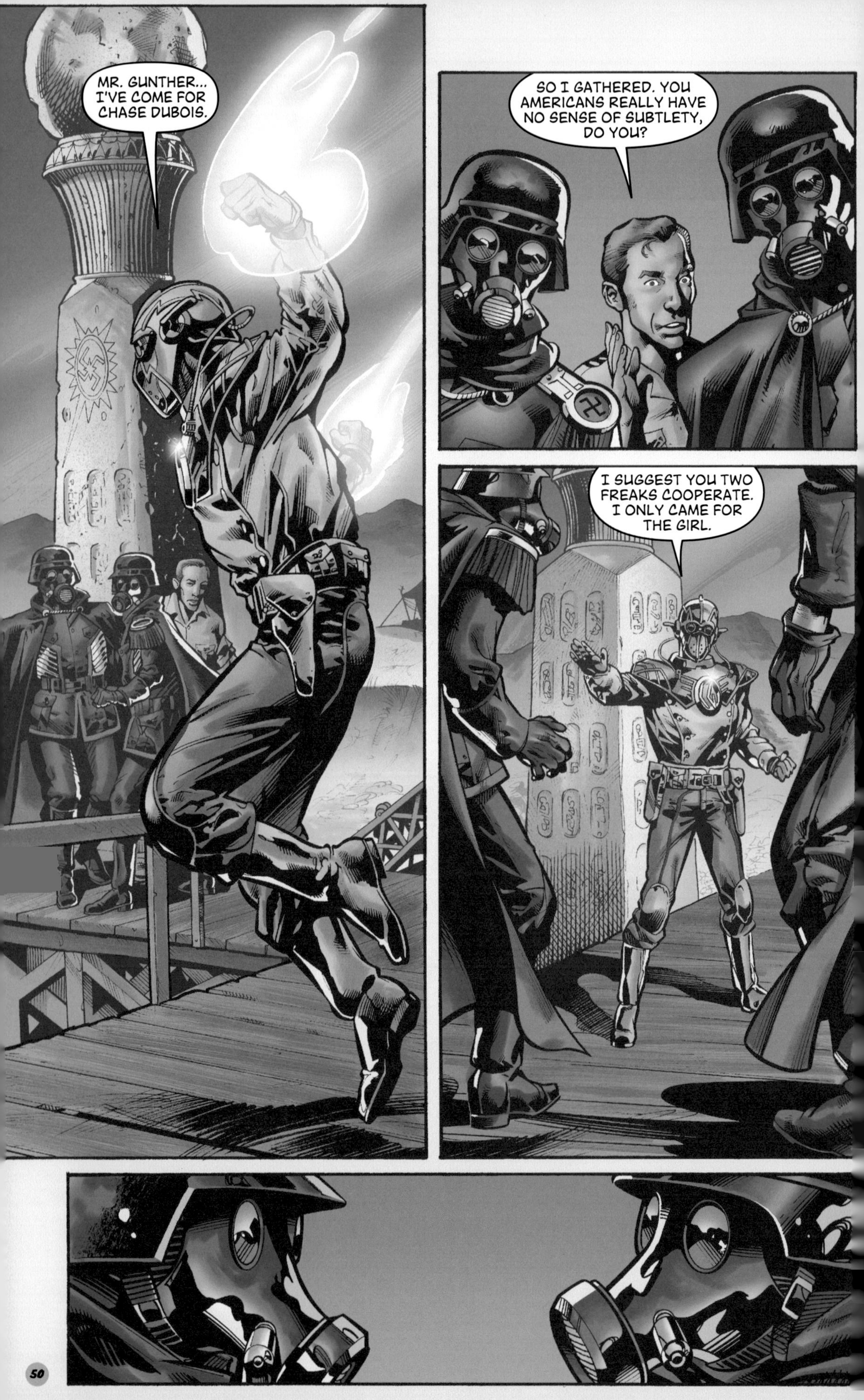
MR. GUNTHER...
I'VE COME FOR
CHASE DUBOIS.
SO I GATHERED. YOU
AMERICANS REALLY HAVE
NO SENSE OF SUBTLETY,
DO YOU?
I SUGGEST YOU TWO
FREAKS COOPERATE.
I ONLY CAME FOR
THE GIRL.

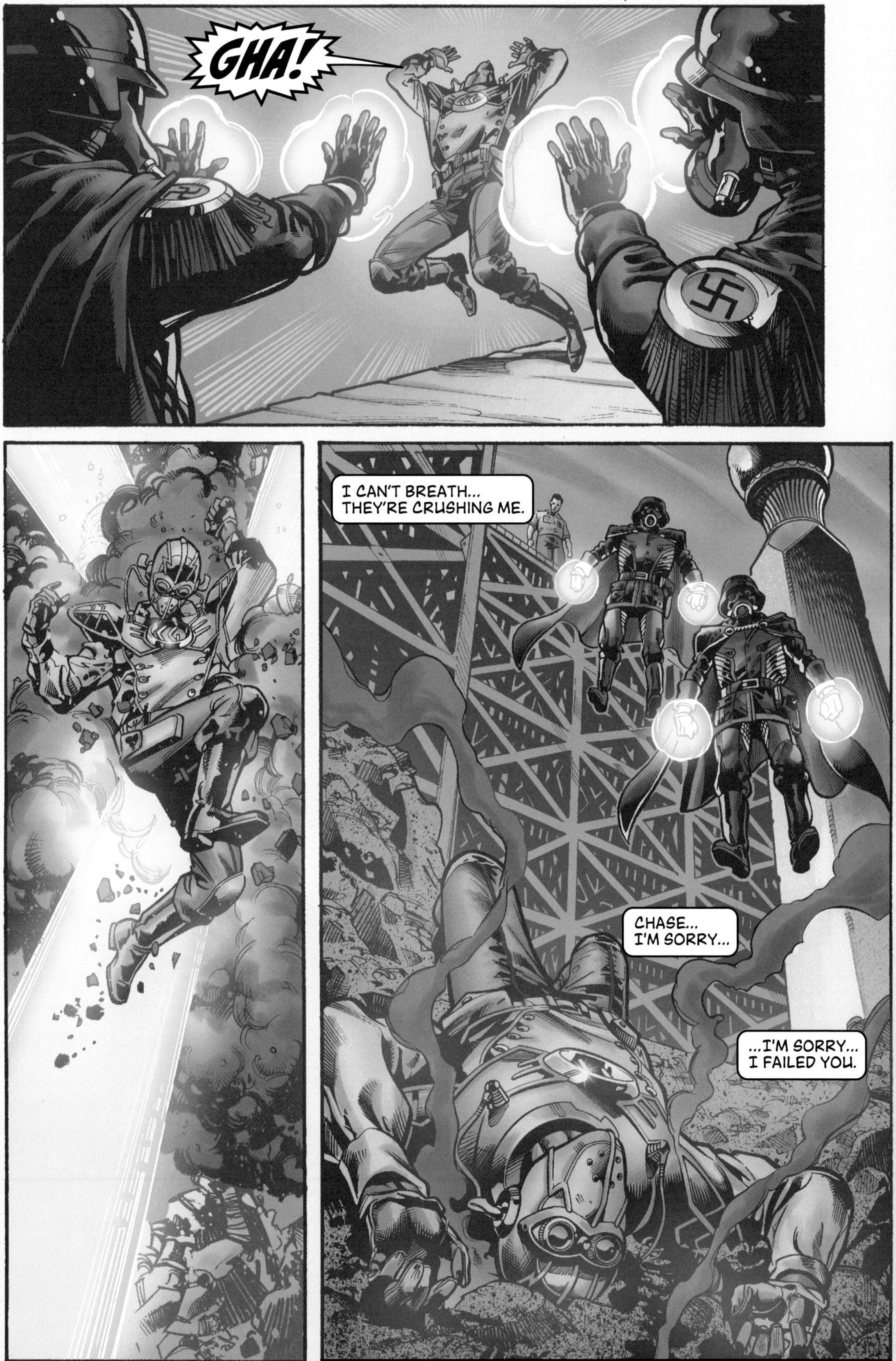
GHA!
I CAN'T BREATH... THEY'RE CRUSHING ME.
CHASE... I'M SORRY...
...I'M SORRY... I FAILED YOU.

NEXT: BATTLE IN THE SEARING SUN AND THE TRUTH ABOUT WHAT THE GERMANS SEEK...
CAPTAIN GRAVITY STARS IN CHAPTER 3: **SEARCH REVEALED!**

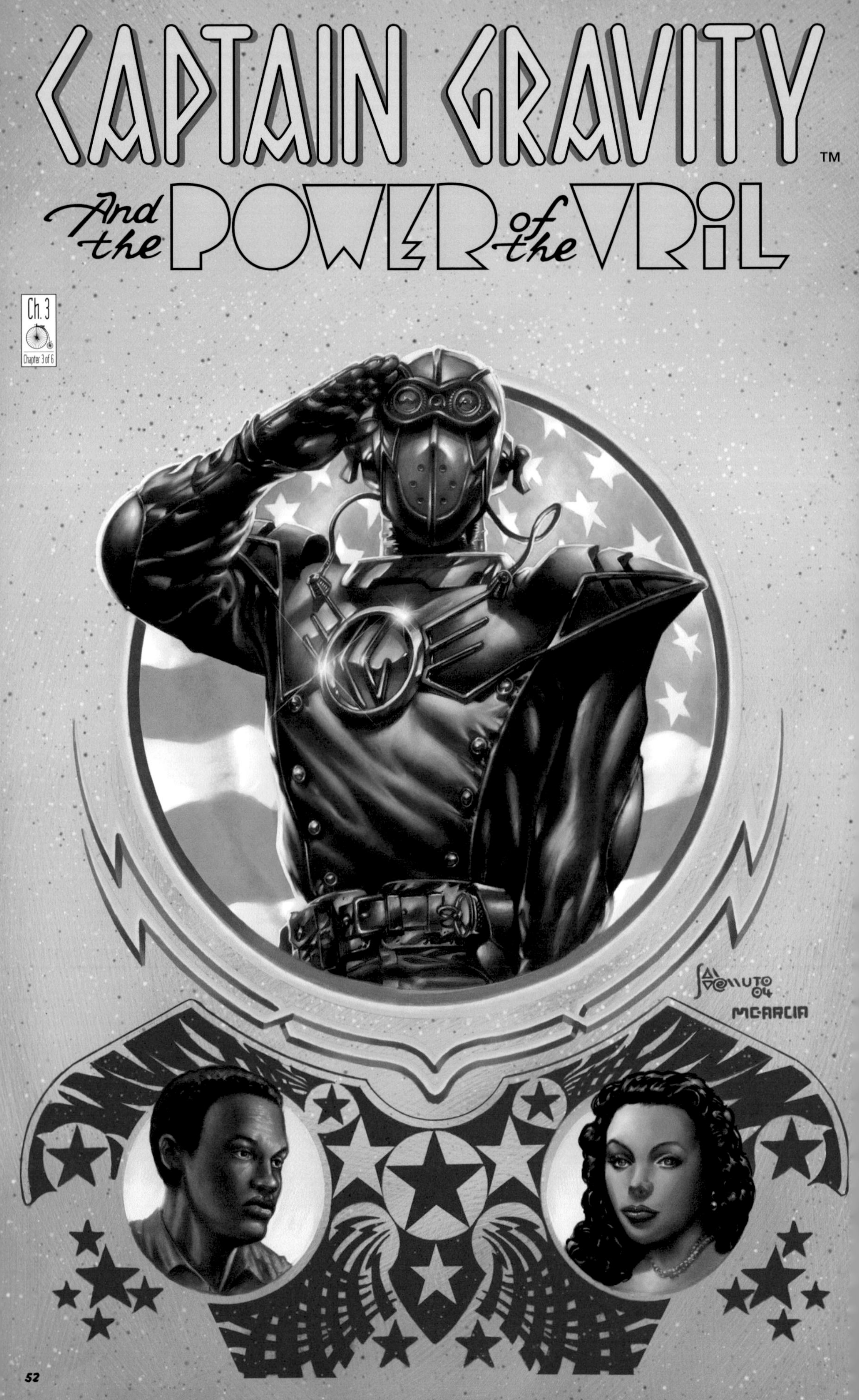
CAPTAIN GRAVITY™
And the POWER of the VRIL
Ch. 3
Chapter 3 of 6

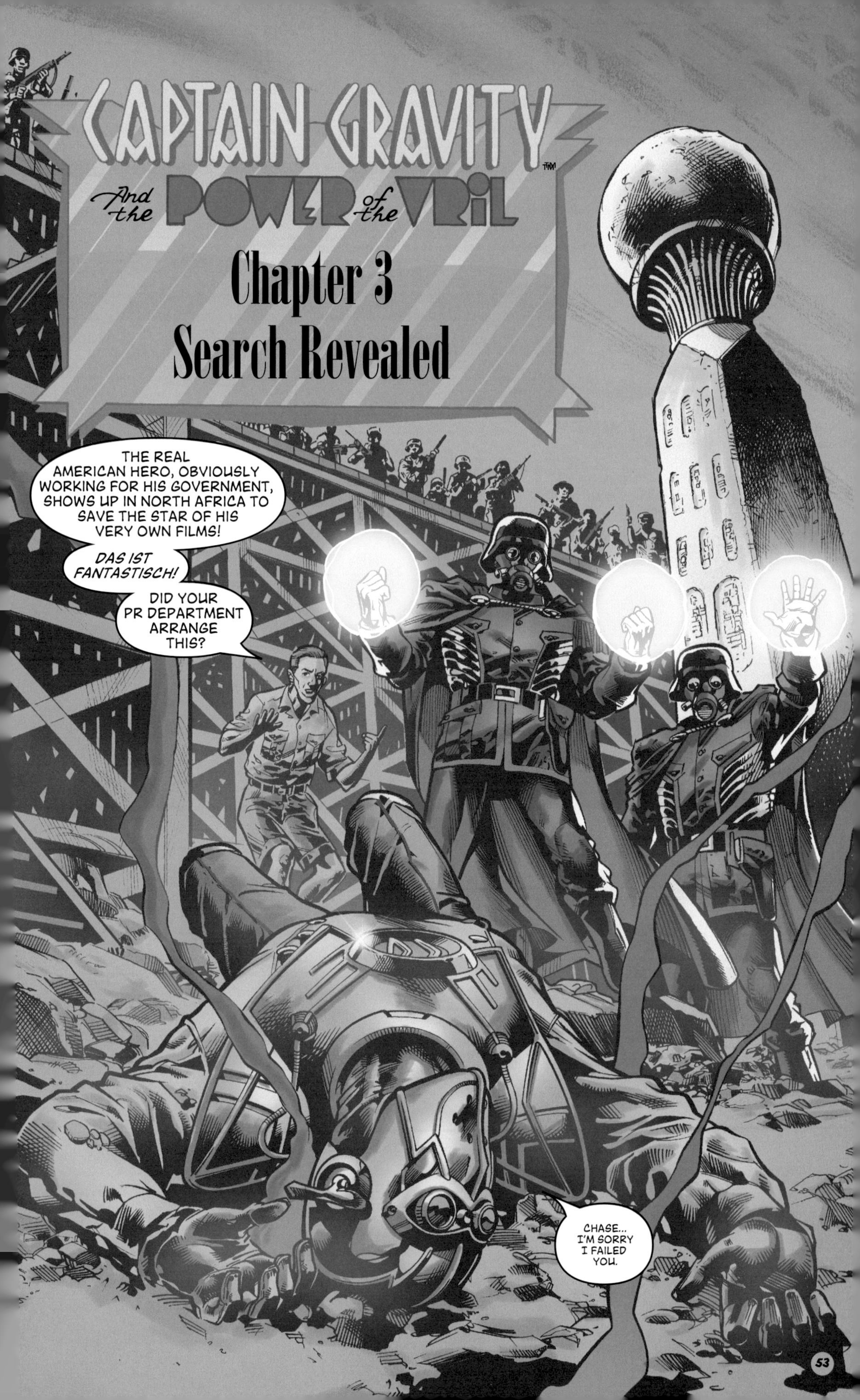
CAPTAIN GRAVITY
And the POWER of the VRIL
Chapter 3
Search Revealed
THE REAL AMERICAN HERO, OBVIOUSLY WORKING FOR HIS GOVERNMENT, SHOWS UP IN NORTH AFRICA TO SAVE THE STAR OF HIS VERY OWN FILMS!
DAS IST FANTASTISCH!
DID YOUR PR DEPARTMENT ARRANGE THIS?
CHASE... I'M SORRY I FAILED YOU.

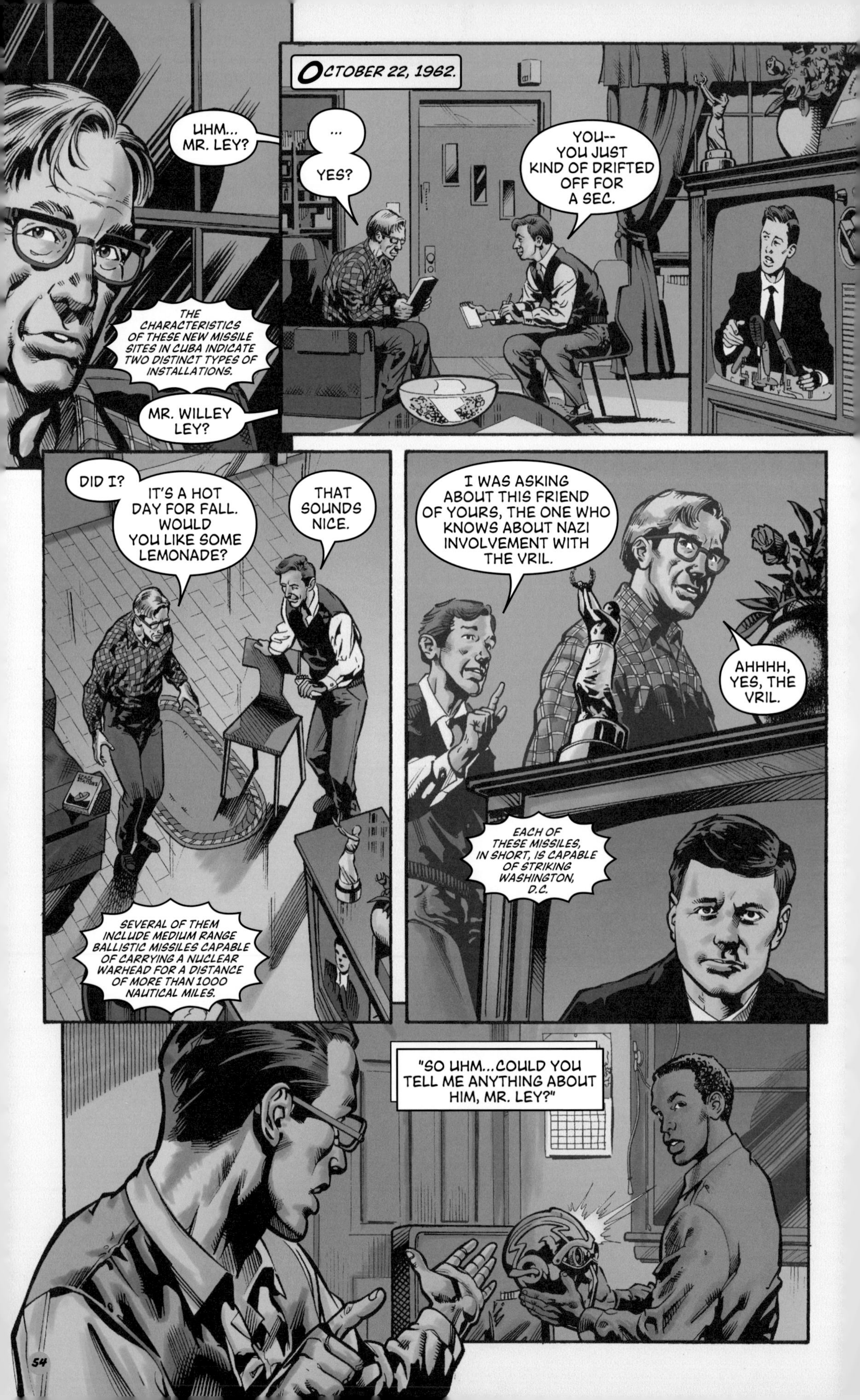
OCTOBER 22, 1962.
UHM... MR. LEY?
...
YES?
YOU-- YOU JUST KIND OF DRIFTED OFF FOR A SEC.
THE CHARACTERISTICS OF THESE NEW MISSILE SITES IN CUBA INDICATE TWO DISTINCT TYPES OF INSTALLATIONS.
MR. WILLEY LEY?
DID I?
IT'S A HOT DAY FOR FALL. WOULD YOU LIKE SOME LEMONADE?
THAT SOUNDS NICE.
SEVERAL OF THEM INCLUDE MEDIUM RANGE BALLISTIC MISSILES CAPABLE OF CARRYING A NUCLEAR WARHEAD FOR A DISTANCE OF MORE THAN 1000 NAUTICAL MILES.
I WAS ASKING ABOUT THIS FRIEND OF YOURS, THE ONE WHO KNOWS ABOUT NAZI INVOLVEMENT WITH THE VRIL.
AHHHH, YES, THE VRIL.
EACH OF THESE MISSILES, IN SHORT, IS CAPABLE OF STRIKING WASHINGTON, D.C.
"SO UHM...COULD YOU TELL ME ANYTHING ABOUT HIM, MR. LEY?"

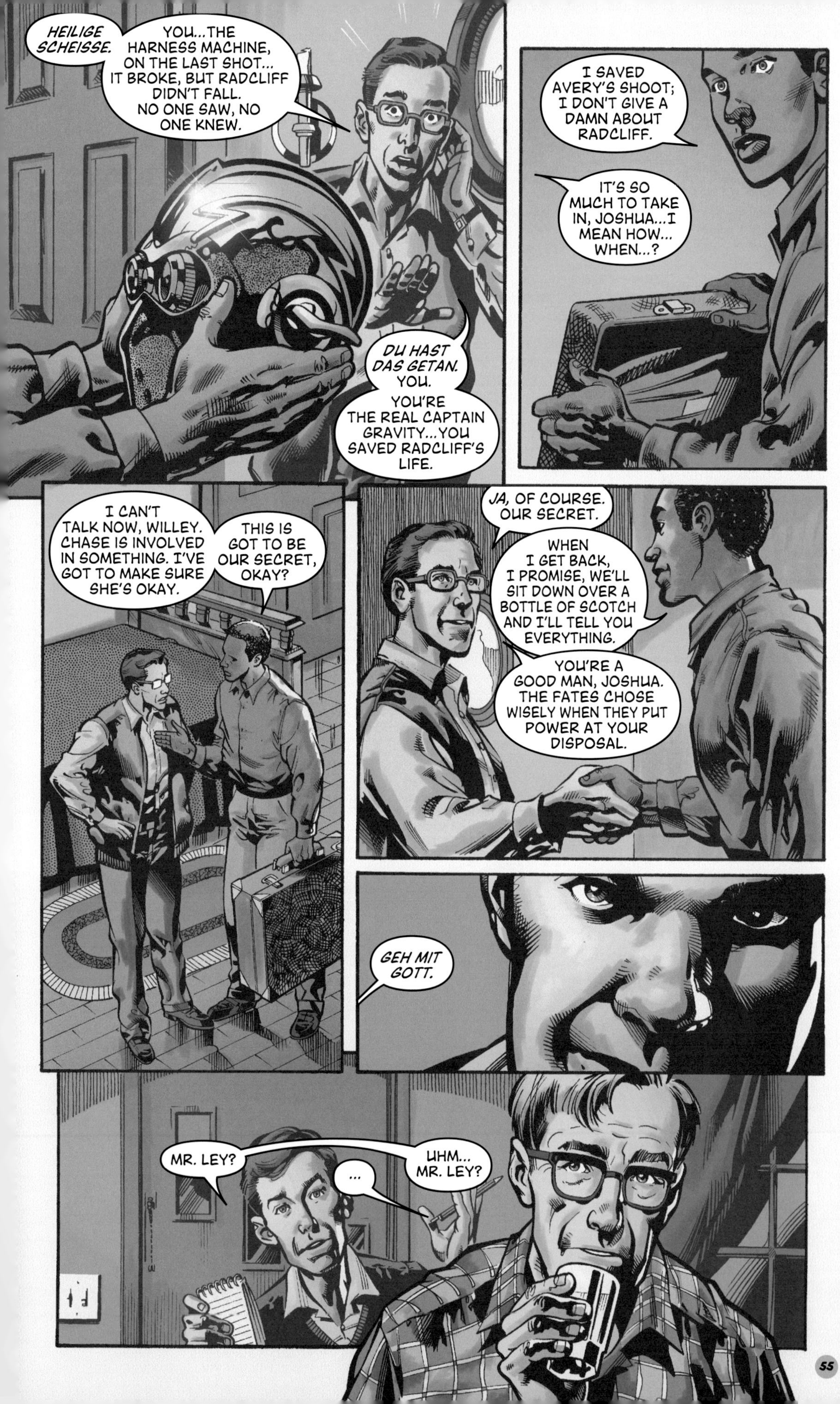
HEILIGE SCHEISSE.
YOU...THE HARNESS MACHINE, ON THE LAST SHOT... IT BROKE, BUT RADCLIFF DIDN'T FALL. NO ONE SAW, NO ONE KNEW.
DU HAST DAS GETAN. YOU.
YOU'RE THE REAL CAPTAIN GRAVITY...YOU SAVED RADCLIFF'S LIFE.
I SAVED AVERY'S SHOOT; I DON'T GIVE A DAMN ABOUT RADCLIFF.
IT'S SO MUCH TO TAKE IN, JOSHUA...I MEAN HOW... WHEN...?
I CAN'T TALK NOW, WILLEY. CHASE IS INVOLVED IN SOMETHING. I'VE GOT TO MAKE SURE SHE'S OKAY.
THIS IS GOT TO BE OUR SECRET, OKAY?
JA, OF COURSE. OUR SECRET.
WHEN I GET BACK, I PROMISE, WE'LL SIT DOWN OVER A BOTTLE OF SCOTCH AND I'LL TELL YOU EVERYTHING.
YOU'RE A GOOD MAN, JOSHUA. THE FATES CHOSE WISELY WHEN THEY PUT POWER AT YOUR DISPOSAL.
GEH MIT GOTT.
MR. LEY?
...
UHM... MR. LEY?

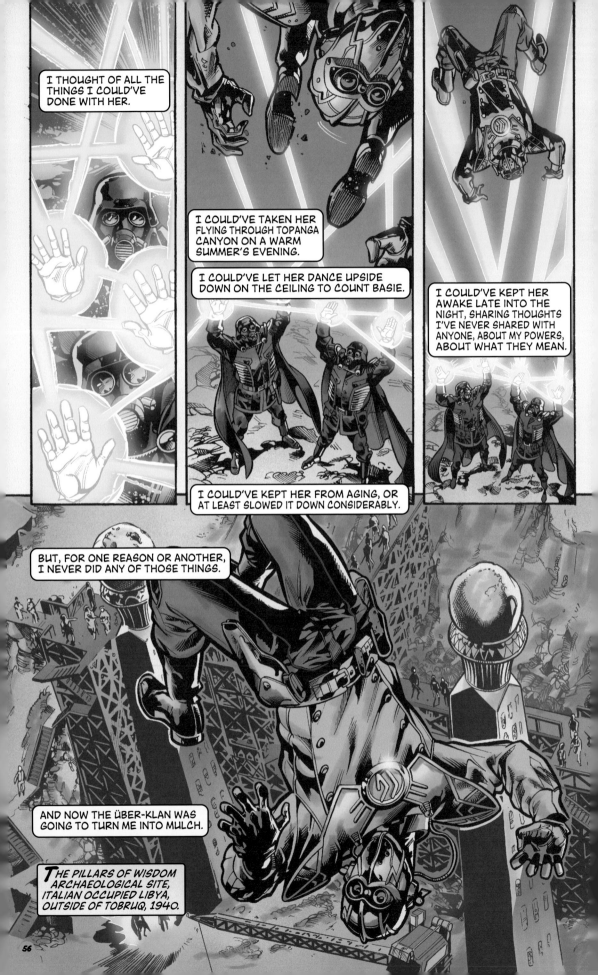

I THOUGHT OF ALL THE THINGS I COULD'VE DONE WITH HER.

I COULD'VE TAKEN HER FLYING THROUGH TOPANGA CANYON ON A WARM SUMMER'S EVENING.

I COULD'VE LET HER DANCE UPSIDE DOWN ON THE CEILING TO COUNT BASIE.

I COULD'VE KEPT HER AWAKE LATE INTO THE NIGHT, SHARING THOUGHTS I'VE NEVER SHARED WITH ANYONE, ABOUT MY POWERS, ABOUT WHAT THEY MEAN.

I COULD'VE KEPT HER FROM AGING, OR AT LEAST SLOWED IT DOWN CONSIDERABLY.

BUT, FOR ONE REASON OR ANOTHER, I NEVER DID ANY OF THOSE THINGS.

AND NOW THE ÜBER-KLAN WAS GOING TO TURN ME INTO MULCH.

THE PILLARS OF WISDOM ARCHAEOLOGICAL SITE, ITALIAN OCCUPIED LIBYA, OUTSIDE OF TOBRUQ, 1940.

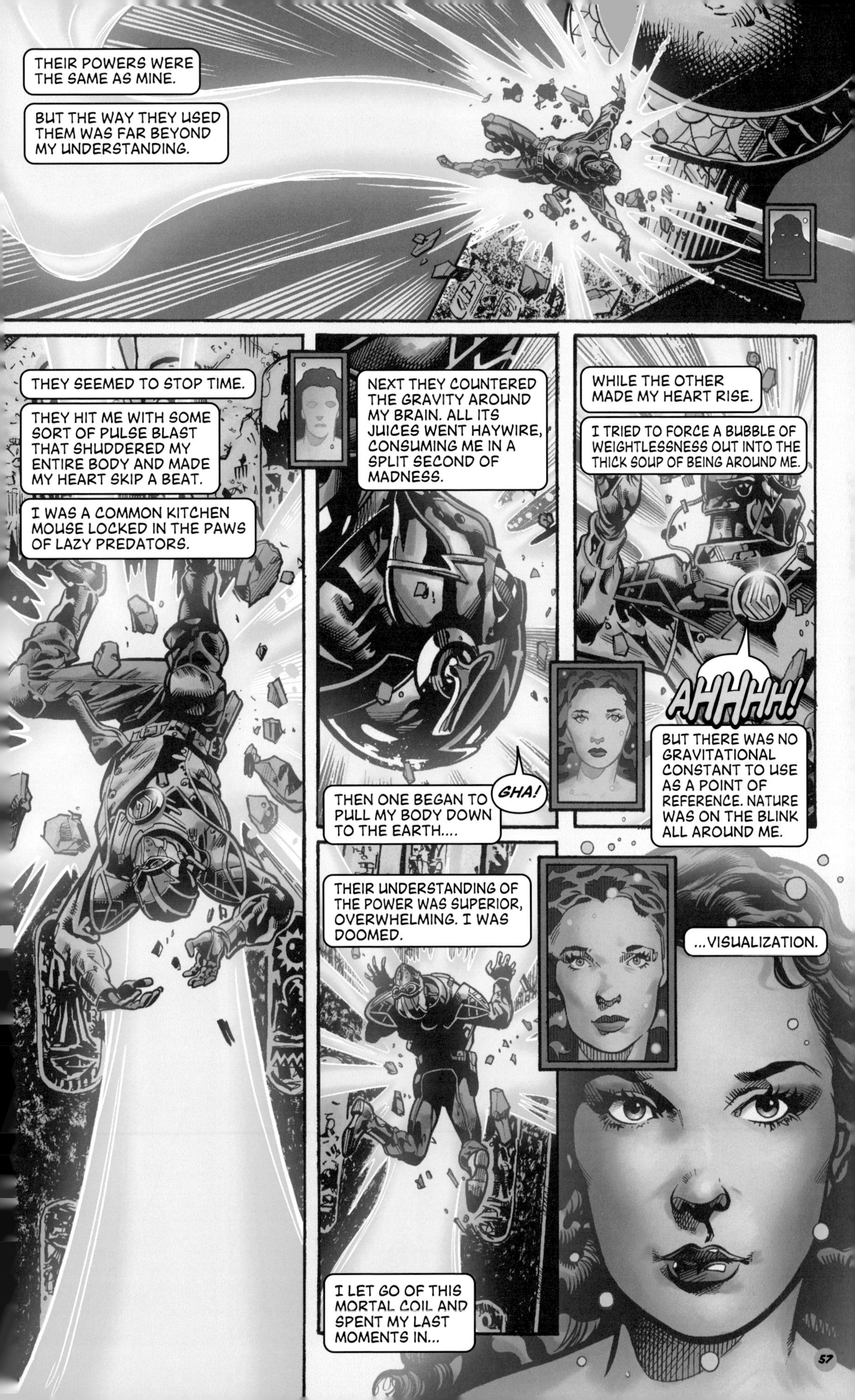
THEIR POWERS WERE THE SAME AS MINE.
BUT THE WAY THEY USED THEM WAS FAR BEYOND MY UNDERSTANDING.
THEY SEEMED TO STOP TIME.
THEY HIT ME WITH SOME SORT OF PULSE BLAST THAT SHUDDERED MY ENTIRE BODY AND MADE MY HEART SKIP A BEAT.
I WAS A COMMON KITCHEN MOUSE LOCKED IN THE PAWS OF LAZY PREDATORS.
NEXT THEY COUNTERED THE GRAVITY AROUND MY BRAIN. ALL ITS JUICES WENT HAYWIRE, CONSUMING ME IN A SPLIT SECOND OF MADNESS.
THEN ONE BEGAN TO PULL MY BODY DOWN TO THE EARTH....
GHA!
WHILE THE OTHER MADE MY HEART RISE.
I TRIED TO FORCE A BUBBLE OF WEIGHTLESSNESS OUT INTO THE THICK SOUP OF BEING AROUND ME.
AHHHH!
BUT THERE WAS NO GRAVITATIONAL CONSTANT TO USE AS A POINT OF REFERENCE. NATURE WAS ON THE BLINK ALL AROUND ME.
THEIR UNDERSTANDING OF THE POWER WAS SUPERIOR, OVERWHELMING. I WAS DOOMED.
I LET GO OF THIS MORTAL COIL AND SPENT MY LAST MOMENTS IN...
...VISUALIZATION.

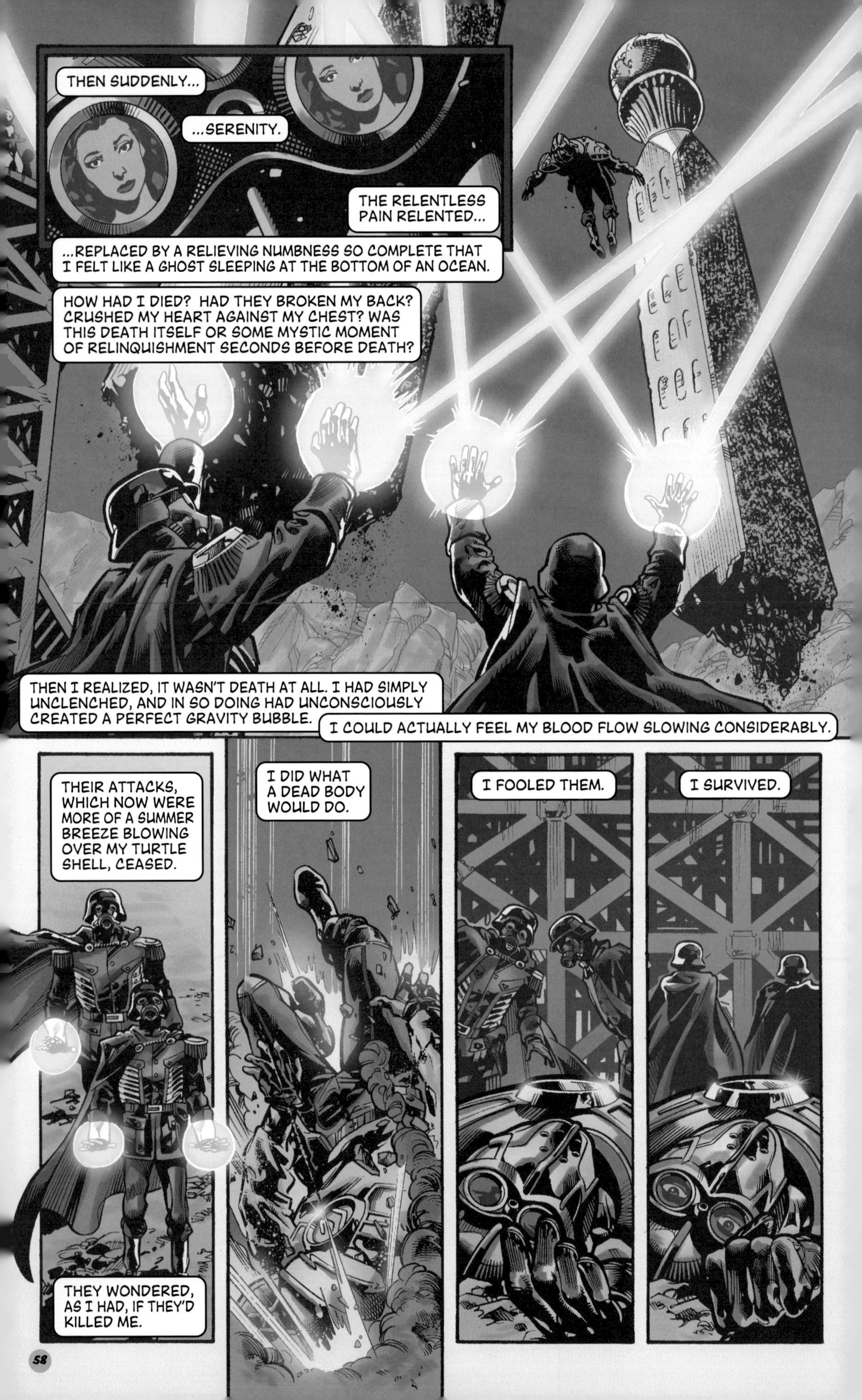

THEN SUDDENLY...
...SERENITY.
THE RELENTLESS PAIN RELENTED...
...REPLACED BY A RELIEVING NUMBNESS SO COMPLETE THAT I FELT LIKE A GHOST SLEEPING AT THE BOTTOM OF AN OCEAN.
HOW HAD I DIED? HAD THEY BROKEN MY BACK? CRUSHED MY HEART AGAINST MY CHEST? WAS THIS DEATH ITSELF OR SOME MYSTIC MOMENT OF RELINQUISHMENT SECONDS BEFORE DEATH?
THEN I REALIZED, IT WASN'T DEATH AT ALL. I HAD SIMPLY UNCLENCHED, AND IN SO DOING HAD UNCONSCIOUSLY CREATED A PERFECT GRAVITY BUBBLE.
I COULD ACTUALLY FEEL MY BLOOD FLOW SLOWING CONSIDERABLY.
THEIR ATTACKS, WHICH NOW WERE MORE OF A SUMMER BREEZE BLOWING OVER MY TURTLE SHELL, CEASED.
THEY WONDERED, AS I HAD, IF THEY'D KILLED ME.
I DID WHAT A DEAD BODY WOULD DO.
I FOOLED THEM.
I SURVIVED.

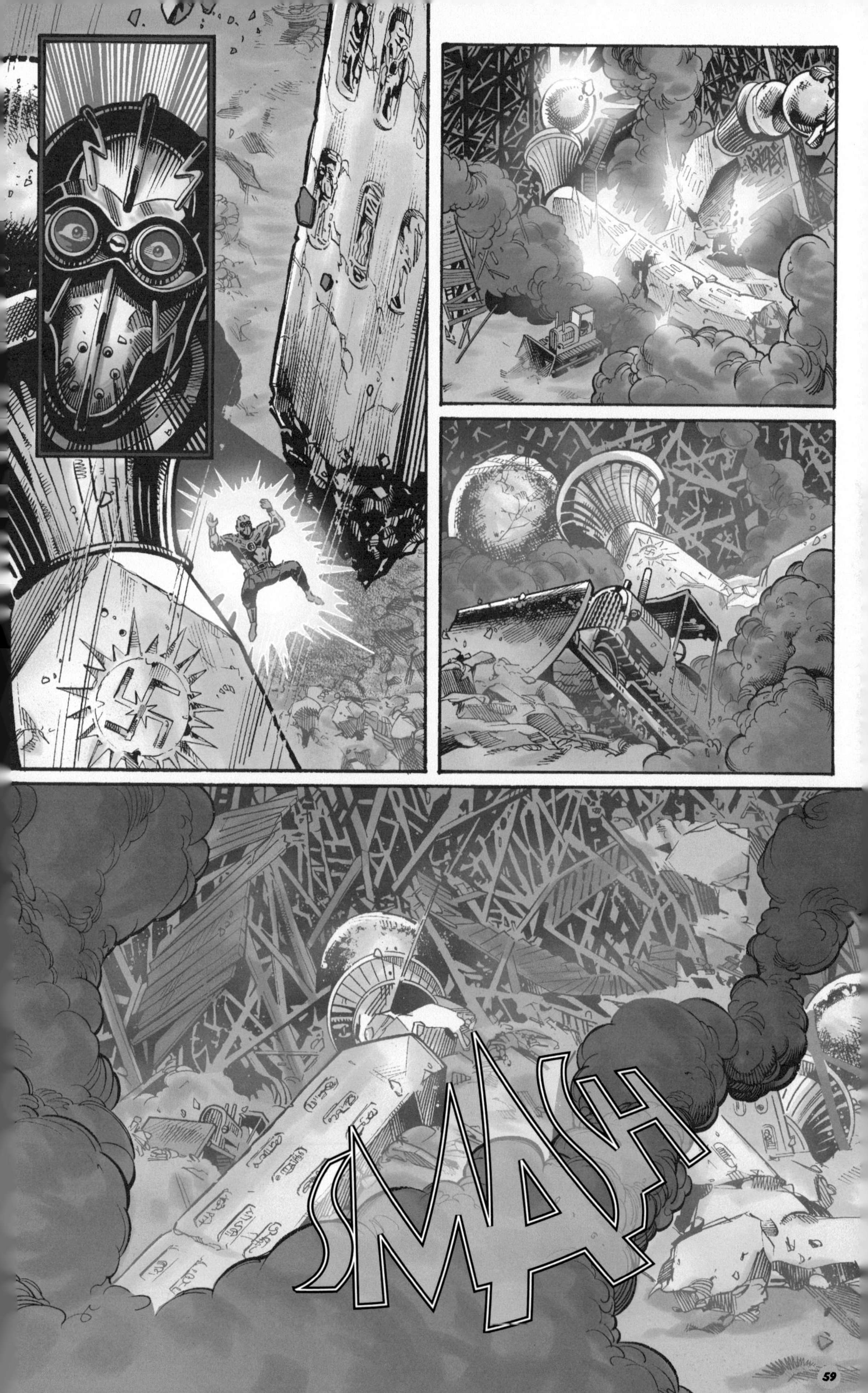
SMASH

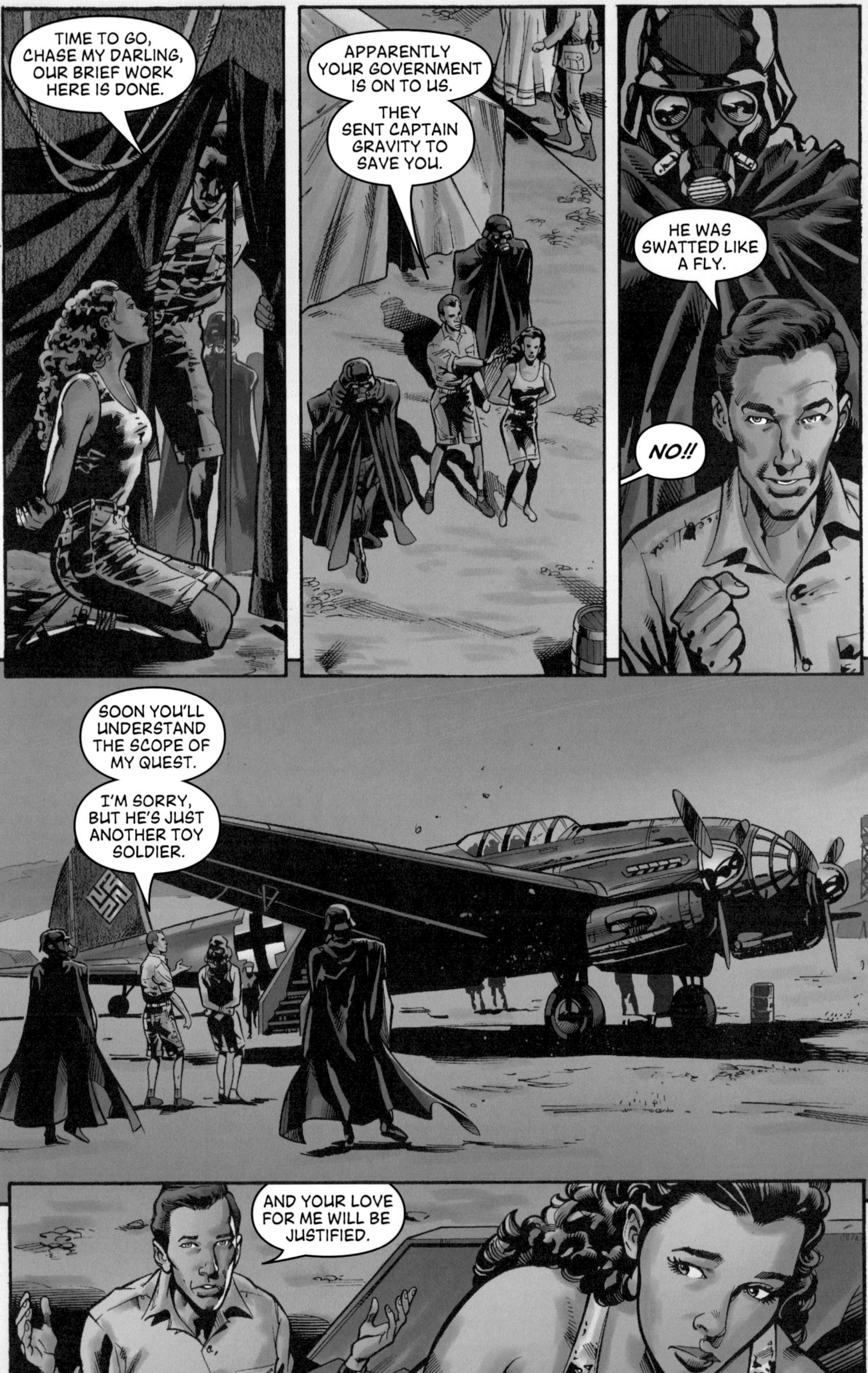
TIME TO GO, CHASE MY DARLING, OUR BRIEF WORK HERE IS DONE.
APPARENTLY YOUR GOVERNMENT IS ON TO US.
THEY SENT CAPTAIN GRAVITY TO SAVE YOU.
HE WAS SWATTED LIKE A FLY.
NO!!
SOON YOU'LL UNDERSTAND THE SCOPE OF MY QUEST.
I'M SORRY, BUT HE'S JUST ANOTHER TOY SOLDIER.
AND YOUR LOVE FOR ME WILL BE JUSTIFIED.

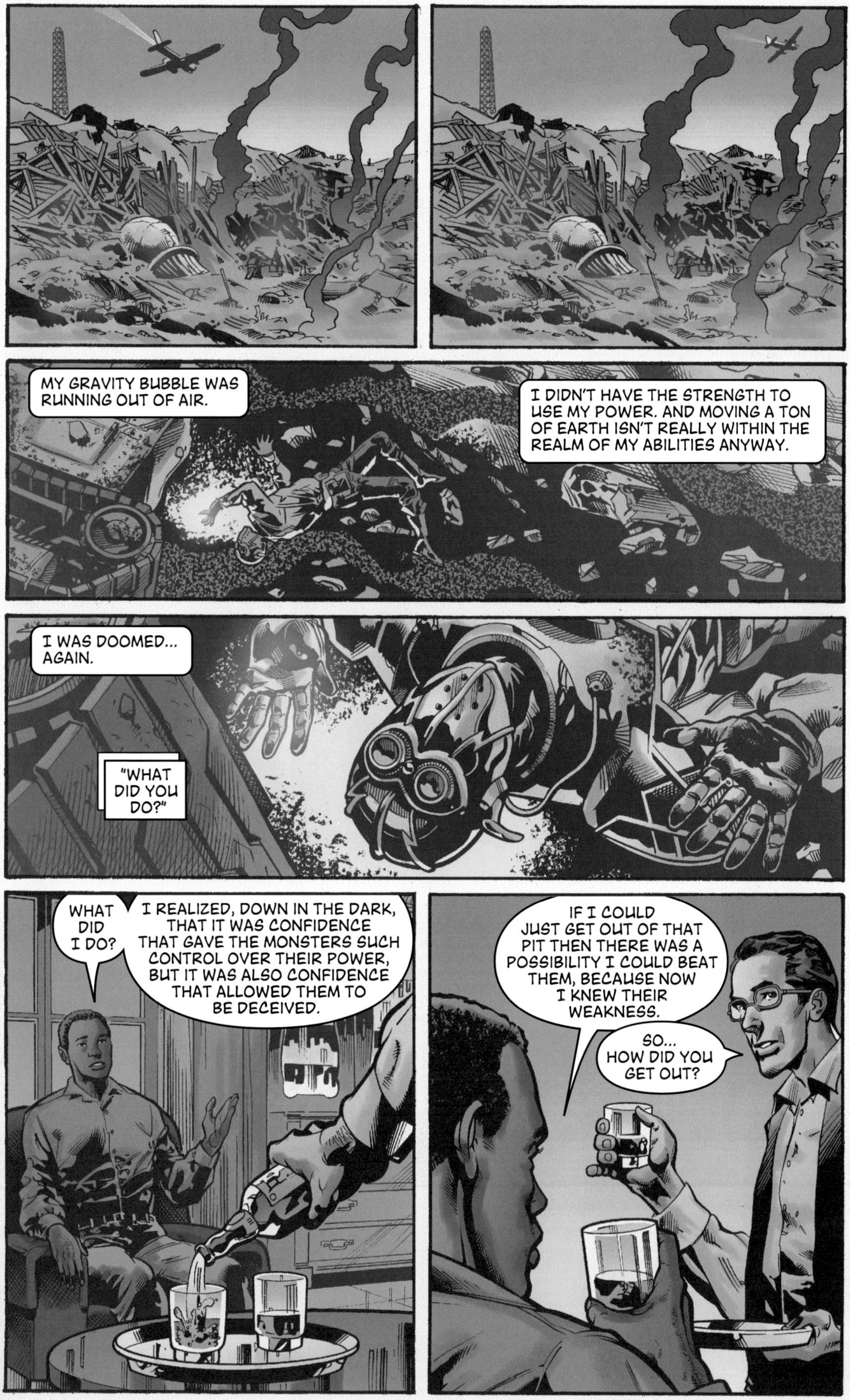
MY GRAVITY BUBBLE WAS RUNNING OUT OF AIR.
I DIDN'T HAVE THE STRENGTH TO USE MY POWER. AND MOVING A TON OF EARTH ISN'T REALLY WITHIN THE REALM OF MY ABILITIES ANYWAY.
I WAS DOOMED... AGAIN.
"WHAT DID YOU DO?"
WHAT DID I DO?
I REALIZED, DOWN IN THE DARK, THAT IT WAS CONFIDENCE THAT GAVE THE MONSTERS SUCH CONTROL OVER THEIR POWER, BUT IT WAS ALSO CONFIDENCE THAT ALLOWED THEM TO BE DECEIVED.
IF I COULD JUST GET OUT OF THAT PIT THEN THERE WAS A POSSIBILITY I COULD BEAT THEM, BECAUSE NOW I KNEW THEIR WEAKNESS.
SO... HOW DID YOU GET OUT?

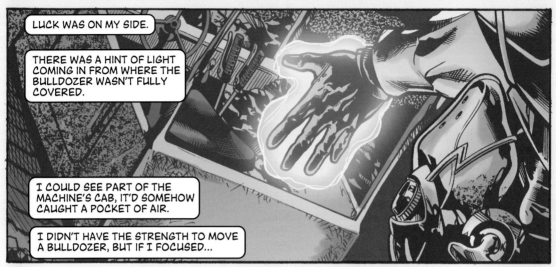

LUCK WAS ON MY SIDE.

THERE WAS A HINT OF LIGHT COMING IN FROM WHERE THE BULLDOZER WASN'T FULLY COVERED.

I COULD SEE PART OF THE MACHINE'S CAB, IT'D SOMEHOW CAUGHT A POCKET OF AIR.

I DIDN'T HAVE THE STRENGTH TO MOVE A BULLDOZER, BUT IF I FOCUSED...

...MAYBE I COULD TURN A KEY...

...PUSH A GEAR.

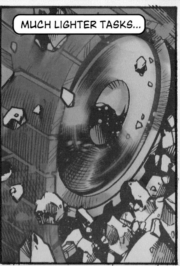

MUCH LIGHTER TASKS...

...THAT MIGHT ACHIEVE THE SAME END.

RRRRUUUUMMMBLE

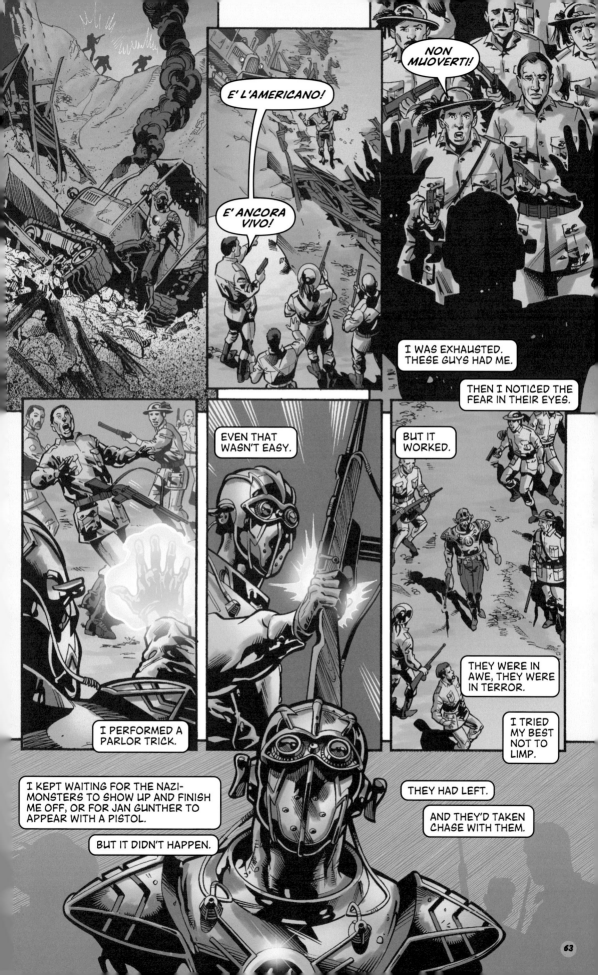

E' L'AMERICANO!

E' ANCORA VIVO!

NON MUOVERTI!!

I WAS EXHAUSTED. THESE GUYS HAD ME.

THEN I NOTICED THE FEAR IN THEIR EYES.

EVEN THAT WASN'T EASY.

BUT IT WORKED.

I PERFORMED A PARLOR TRICK.

THEY WERE IN AWE, THEY WERE IN TERROR.

I TRIED MY BEST NOT TO LIMP.

I KEPT WAITING FOR THE NAZI-MONSTERS TO SHOW UP AND FINISH ME OFF, OR FOR JAN GUNTHER TO APPEAR WITH A PISTOL.

BUT IT DIDN'T HAPPEN.

THEY HAD LEFT.

AND THEY'D TAKEN CHASE WITH THEM.

PuuuuuuuRrrrr

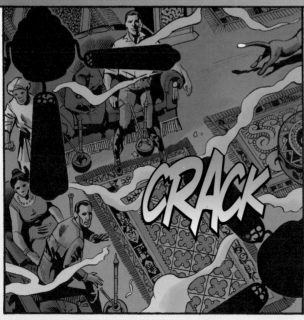

CRACK

⟨POLICE!!⟩*

⟨RAID!⟩

WHA...?

* TRANSLATED FROM EGYPTIAN

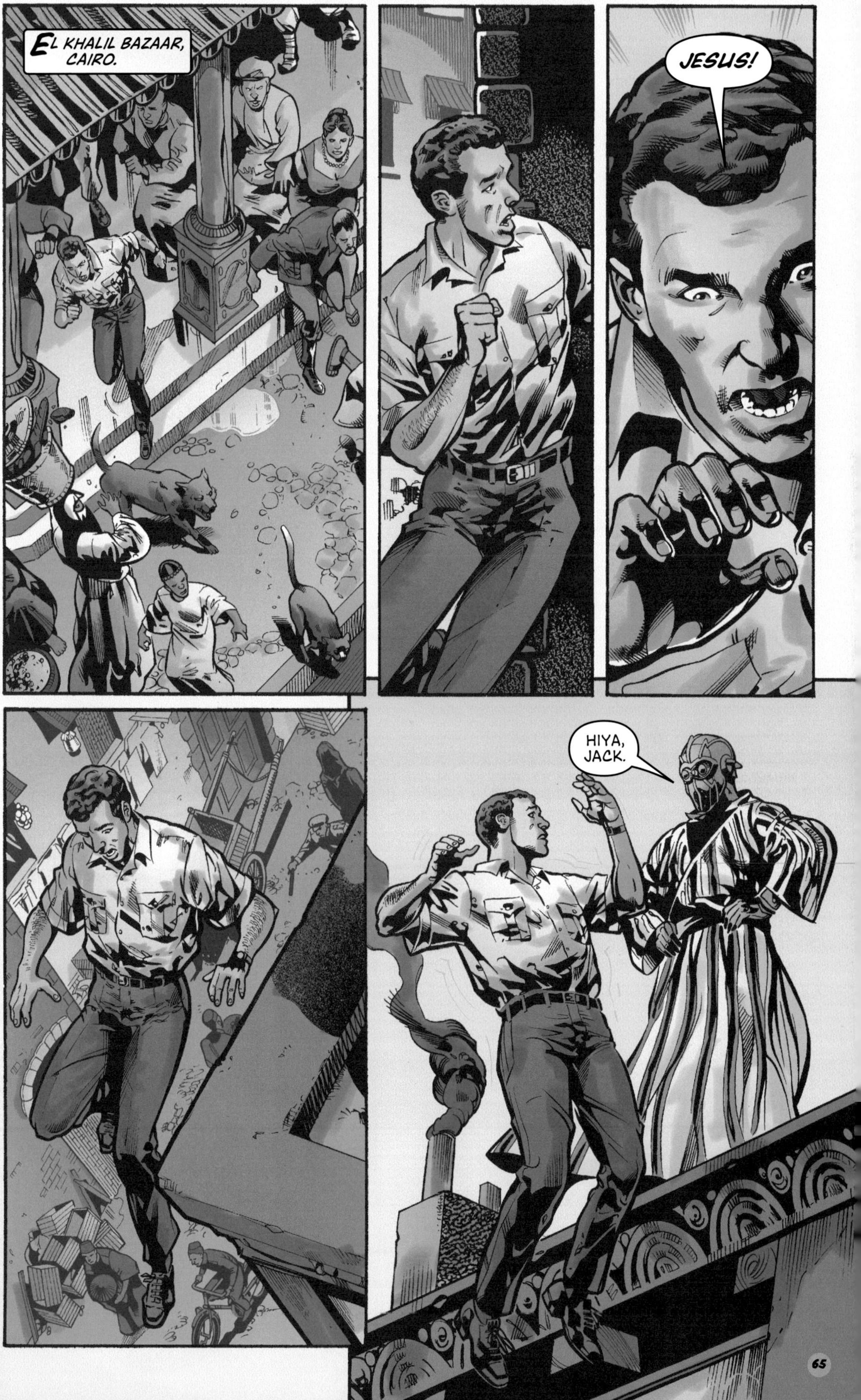
EL KHALIL BAZAAR, CAIRO.
JESUS!
HIYA, JACK.

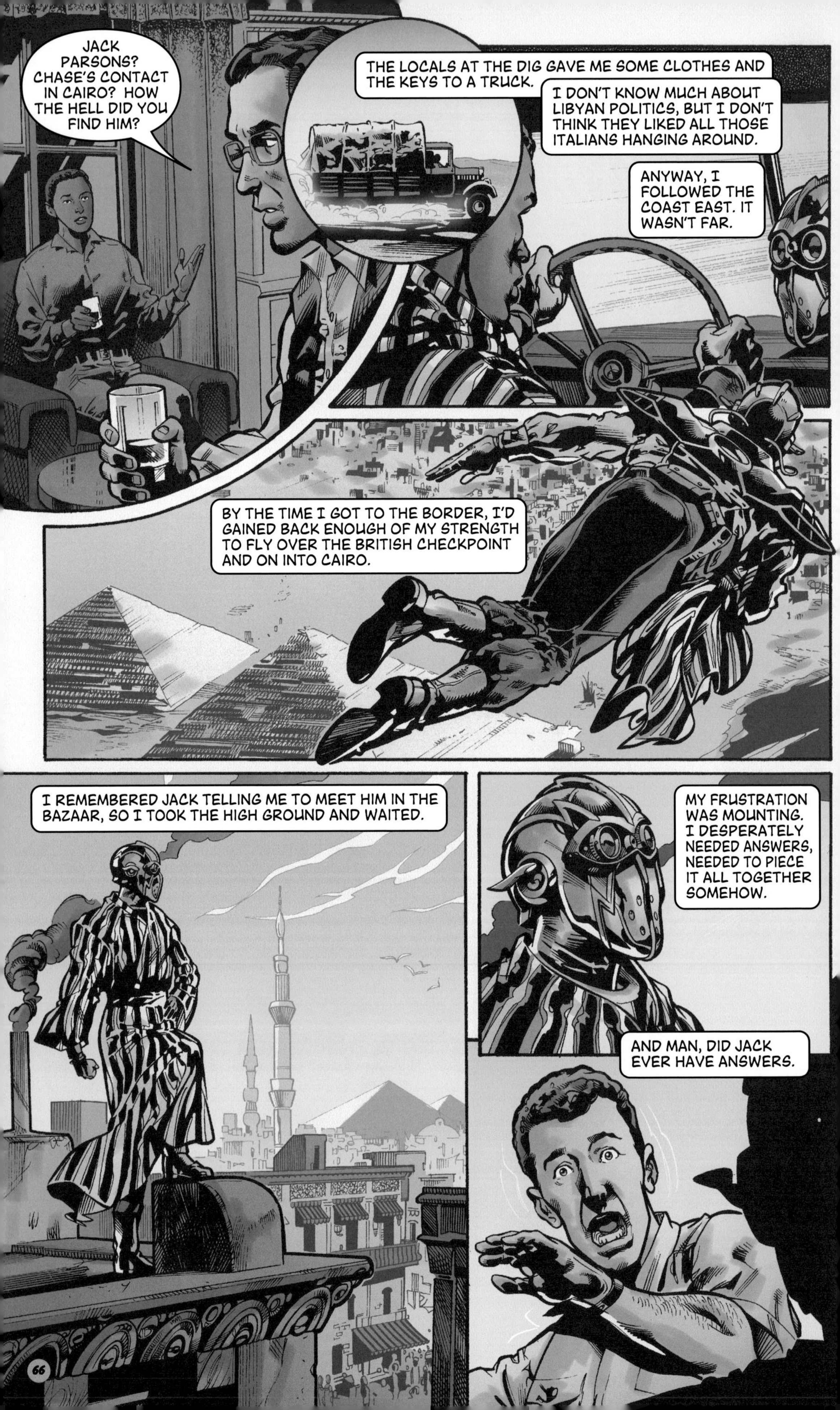
JACK PARSONS? CHASE'S CONTACT IN CAIRO? HOW THE HELL DID YOU FIND HIM?
THE LOCALS AT THE DIG GAVE ME SOME CLOTHES AND THE KEYS TO A TRUCK.
I DON'T KNOW MUCH ABOUT LIBYAN POLITICS, BUT I DON'T THINK THEY LIKED ALL THOSE ITALIANS HANGING AROUND.
ANYWAY, I FOLLOWED THE COAST EAST. IT WASN'T FAR.
BY THE TIME I GOT TO THE BORDER, I'D GAINED BACK ENOUGH OF MY STRENGTH TO FLY OVER THE BRITISH CHECKPOINT AND ON INTO CAIRO.
I REMEMBERED JACK TELLING ME TO MEET HIM IN THE BAZAAR, SO I TOOK THE HIGH GROUND AND WAITED.
MY FRUSTRATION WAS MOUNTING. I DESPERATELY NEEDED ANSWERS, NEEDED TO PIECE IT ALL TOGETHER SOMEHOW.
AND MAN, DID JACK EVER HAVE ANSWERS.

HE KNEW ABOUT THE VRIL?

HE'S MORE THAN JUST SOME SCIENTIST.

WHAT'D HE SAY?

WILLEY... THAT PART OF THE STORY HAS TO STAY A SECRET. I'VE ALREADY SAID TOO MUCH.

I KNOW I PROMISED TO TELL YOU EVERYTHING, BUT I CAN'T. I SHOULDN'T HAVE EVEN STARTED...I'M JUST -- JUST A LITTLE DRUNK AND... I WANTED TO TALK, YOU KNOW.

SO TALK.

I...IT HAS TO STAY A SECRET, WILLEY, FOREVER. BUT I'LL TELL YOU THIS...

...POWER CAN BE A SCARY THING.

"UHM... MR. LEY?"

MR. LEY?

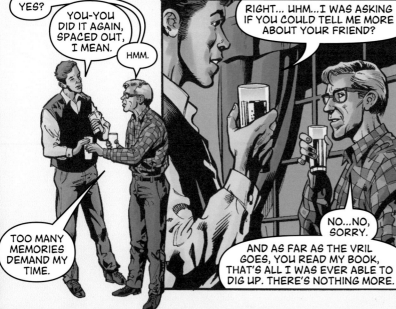

YES?

YOU-YOU DID IT AGAIN, SPACED OUT, I MEAN.

HMM.

TOO MANY MEMORIES DEMAND MY TIME.

RIGHT... UHM...I WAS ASKING IF YOU COULD TELL ME MORE ABOUT YOUR FRIEND?

NO...NO, SORRY.

AND AS FAR AS THE VRIL GOES, YOU READ MY BOOK, THAT'S ALL I WAS EVER ABLE TO DIG UP. THERE'S NOTHING MORE.

GOD BLESS THE LIMITS OF MY KNOWLEDGE, YOUNG MAN.

WHAT'S GOING ON IS A LOT BIGGER THAN JUST SAVING THE GIRL.

WHEN THAT RUSSIAN SPY MENTIONED VRIL BACK AT CHASE'S HOTEL, IT SENT A CHILL UP MY SPINE.

I'VE BEEN... SHAKY EVER SINCE.

THE WORD VRIL GETS THROWN AROUND IN CERTAIN OCCULT CIRCLES. IT'S MENTIONED IN THE OLDEST BOOKS.

IT'S AN INFINITE ENERGY SOURCE, SOMEHOW PART OF REALITY ON AN ATOMIC LEVEL. THE STUFF THAT FIRES THE UNIVERSE, FOLLOW ME?

AT DIFFERENT TIMES IN HISTORY THE HOLY, THE MAD, AND THE INNOCENT HAVE BEEN ABLE TO ACCESS VRIL IN SMALL DOSES THROUGH MEDITATION AND RITUAL.

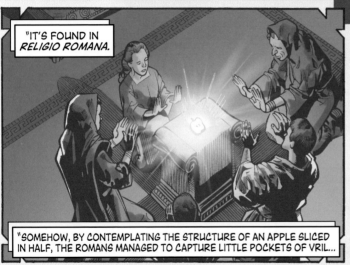

"IT'S FOUND IN *RELIGIO ROMANA*.

"SOMEHOW, BY CONTEMPLATING THE STRUCTURE OF AN APPLE SLICED IN HALF, THE ROMANS MANAGED TO CAPTURE LITTLE POCKETS OF VRIL...

"...AND ENCASE IT IN METAL BALLS THAT GUARDED THEIR HOMES FROM ILLNESS."

"CUT THE HISTORY LESSON, JACK."

PAY ATTENTION!! IT'S BELIEVED THAT THIS INFINITESIMAL PRESENCE OF VRIL ENERGY CONTRIBUTED TO THE SUCCESS OF THE ROMAN EMPIRE.

BUT ALL ACCOUNTS TRACE THE ORIGINAL DISCOVERY OF VRIL TO LONG BEFORE ROME...

...TO A CIVILIZATION THAT WAS ENTIRELY FUELED BY THE STUFF, PERMEATED WITH IT, THAT EVEN USED IT AS AN UNPARALLELED WEAPON.

THAT CIVILIZATION WAS ATLANTIS, CAPTAIN. THE NAZIS ARE LOOKING FOR ATLANTIS.

YOU STILL HIGH?

COME ON, YOU CAN FLY FOR CHRIST SAKE! I THINK YOU'VE SEEN ENOUGH TO TAKE THIS SERIOUSLY.

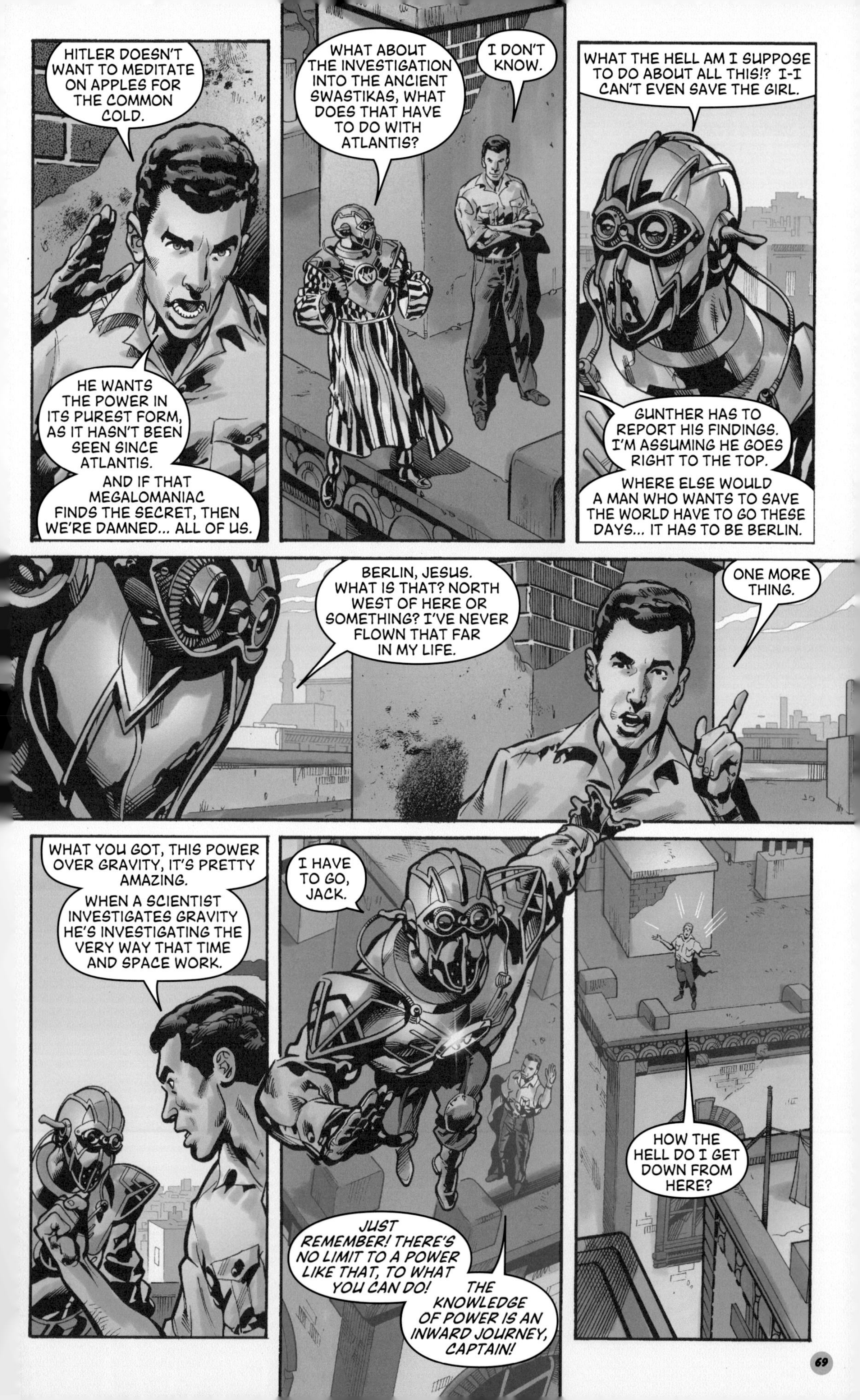
HITLER DOESN'T WANT TO MEDITATE ON APPLES FOR THE COMMON COLD.
HE WANTS THE POWER IN ITS PUREST FORM, AS IT HASN'T BEEN SEEN SINCE ATLANTIS.
AND IF THAT MEGALOMANIAC FINDS THE SECRET, THEN WE'RE DAMNED... ALL OF US.
WHAT ABOUT THE INVESTIGATION INTO THE ANCIENT SWASTIKAS, WHAT DOES THAT HAVE TO DO WITH ATLANTIS?
I DON'T KNOW.
WHAT THE HELL AM I SUPPOSE TO DO ABOUT ALL THIS!? I-I CAN'T EVEN SAVE THE GIRL.
GUNTHER HAS TO REPORT HIS FINDINGS. I'M ASSUMING HE GOES RIGHT TO THE TOP.
WHERE ELSE WOULD A MAN WHO WANTS TO SAVE THE WORLD HAVE TO GO THESE DAYS... IT HAS TO BE BERLIN.
BERLIN, JESUS. WHAT IS THAT? NORTH WEST OF HERE OR SOMETHING? I'VE NEVER FLOWN THAT FAR IN MY LIFE.
ONE MORE THING.
WHAT YOU GOT, THIS POWER OVER GRAVITY, IT'S PRETTY AMAZING.
WHEN A SCIENTIST INVESTIGATES GRAVITY HE'S INVESTIGATING THE VERY WAY THAT TIME AND SPACE WORK.
I HAVE TO GO, JACK.
JUST REMEMBER! THERE'S NO LIMIT TO A POWER LIKE THAT, TO WHAT YOU CAN DO!
THE KNOWLEDGE OF POWER IS AN INWARD JOURNEY, CAPTAIN!
HOW THE HELL DO I GET DOWN FROM HERE?

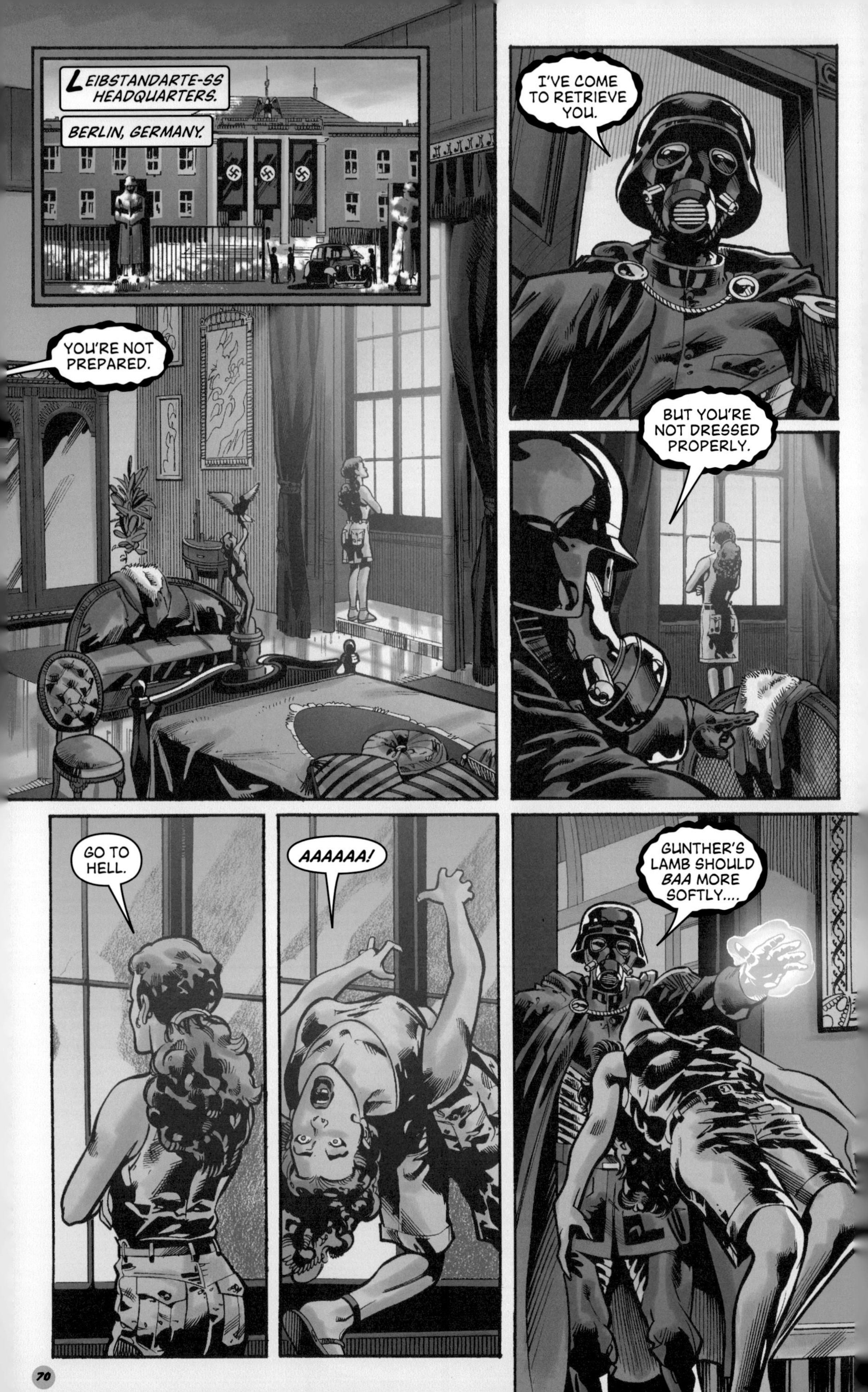
LEIBSTANDARTE-SS HEADQUARTERS.
BERLIN, GERMANY.
YOU'RE NOT PREPARED.
I'VE COME TO RETRIEVE YOU.
BUT YOU'RE NOT DRESSED PROPERLY.
GO TO HELL.
AAAAAA!
GUNTHER'S LAMB SHOULD *BAA* MORE SOFTLY....

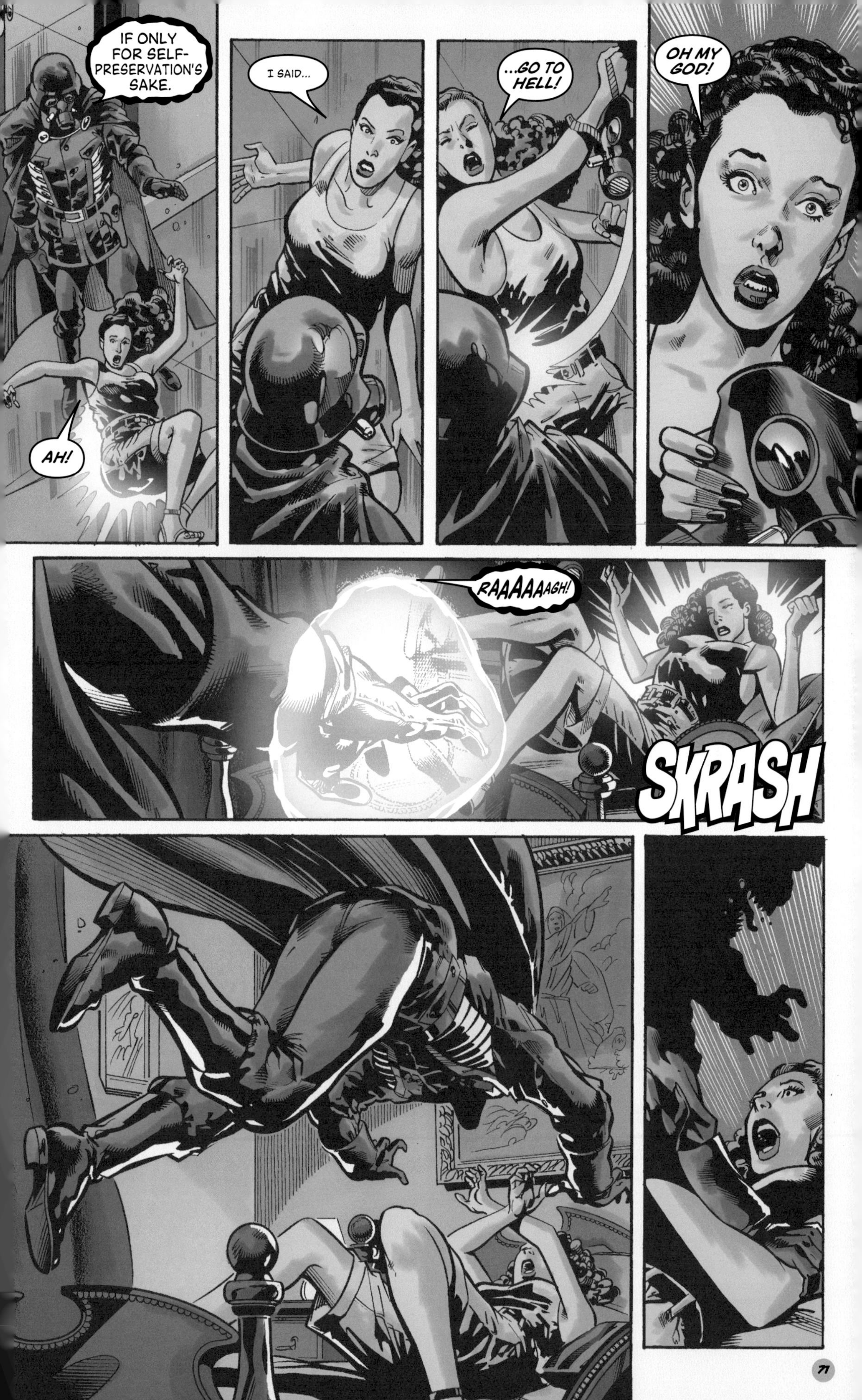
IF ONLY FOR SELF-PRESERVATION'S SAKE.
AH!
I SAID...
...GO TO HELL!
OH MY GOD!
RAAAAAAGH!
SKRASH

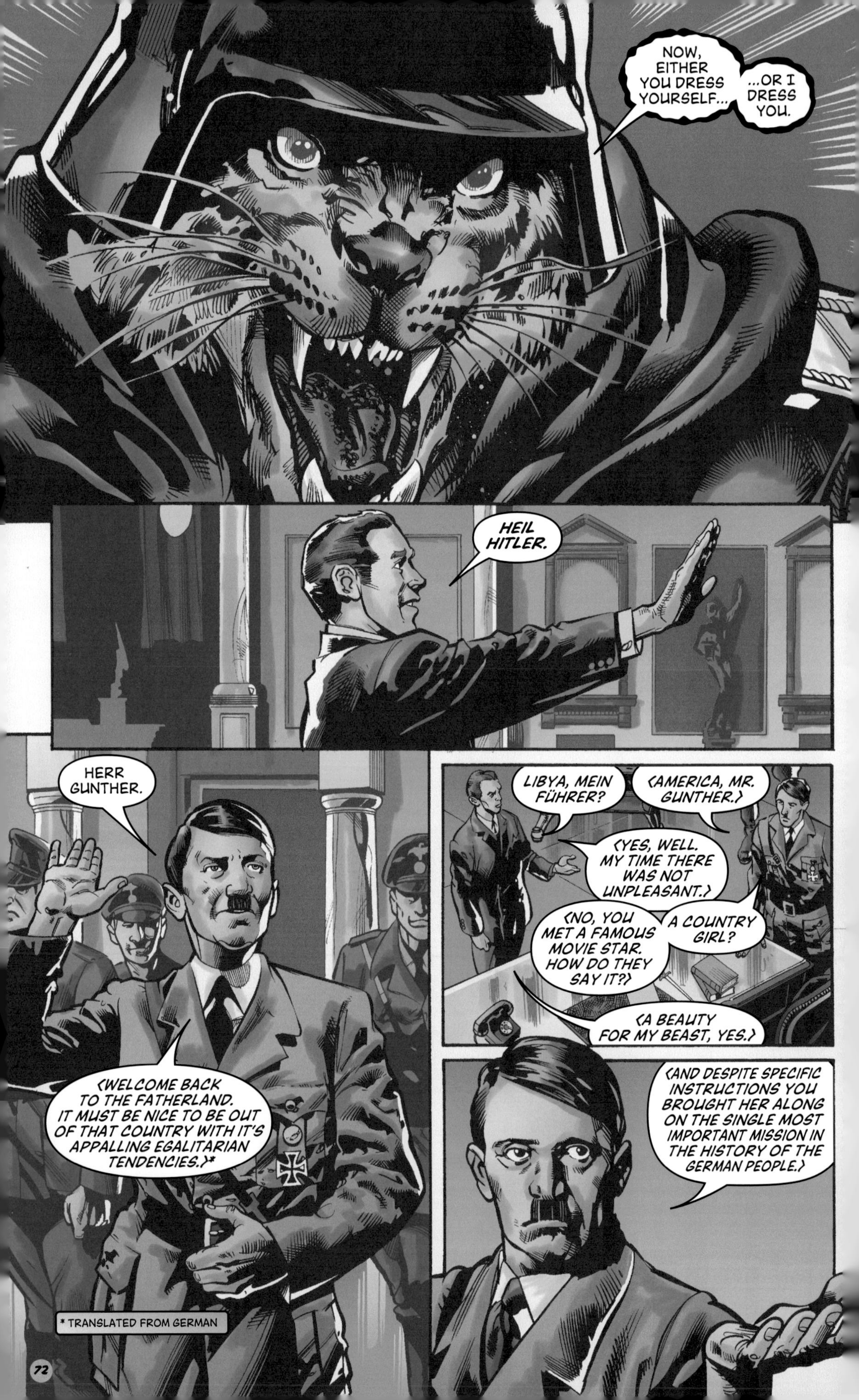
NOW, EITHER YOU DRESS YOURSELF...
...OR I DRESS YOU.
HEIL HITLER.
HERR GUNTHER.
<WELCOME BACK TO THE FATHERLAND. IT MUST BE NICE TO BE OUT OF THAT COUNTRY WITH IT'S APPALLING EGALITARIAN TENDENCIES.>*
* TRANSLATED FROM GERMAN
LIBYA, MEIN FÜHRER?
<AMERICA, MR. GUNTHER.>
<YES, WELL. MY TIME THERE WAS NOT UNPLEASANT.>
A COUNTRY GIRL?
<NO, YOU MET A FAMOUS MOVIE STAR. HOW DO THEY SAY IT?>
<A BEAUTY FOR MY BEAST, YES.>
<AND DESPITE SPECIFIC INSTRUCTIONS YOU BROUGHT HER ALONG ON THE SINGLE MOST IMPORTANT MISSION IN THE HISTORY OF THE GERMAN PEOPLE.>

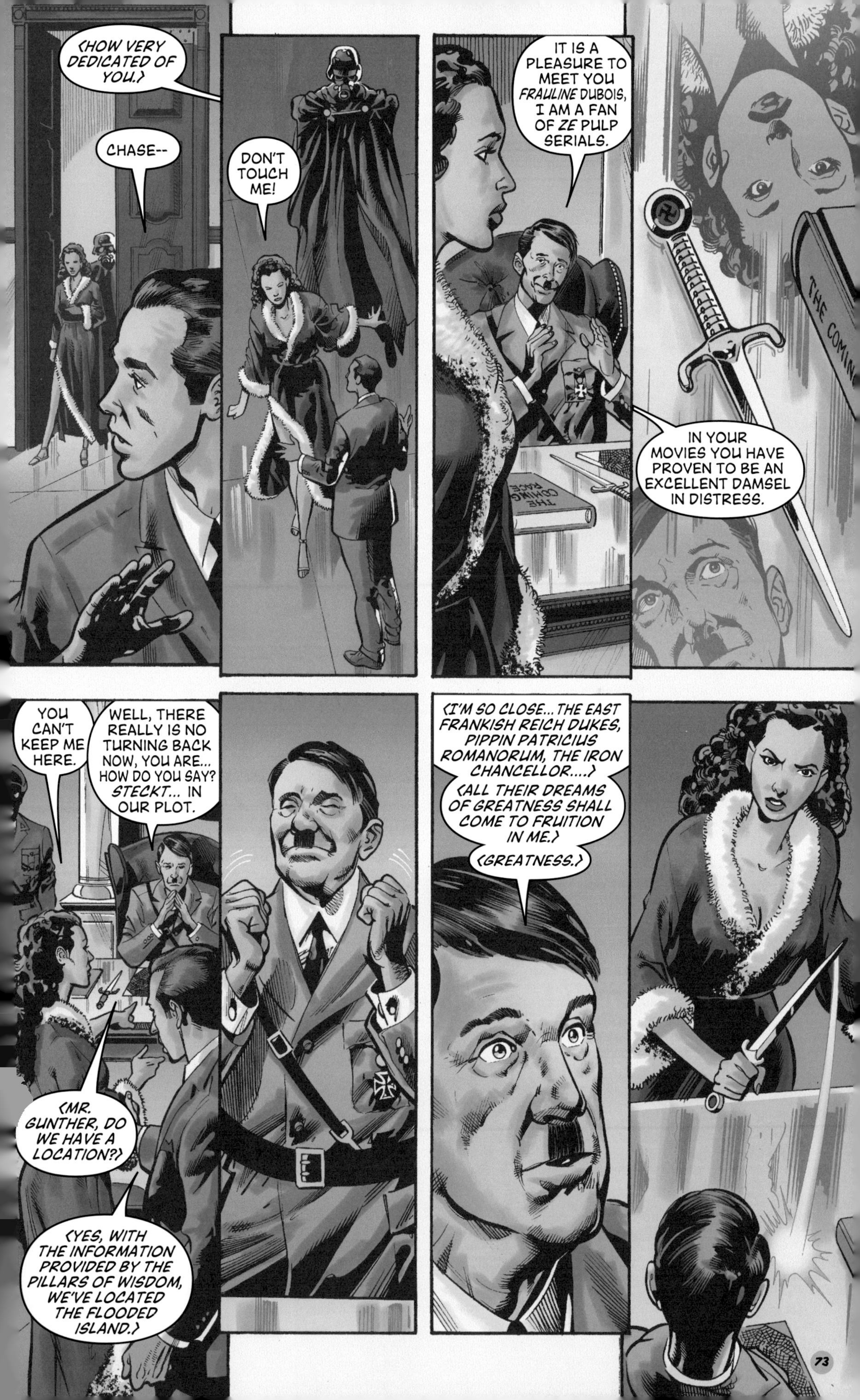

<HOW VERY DEDICATED OF YOU.>
CHASE--
DON'T TOUCH ME!
IT IS A PLEASURE TO MEET YOU FRAULINE DUBOIS, I AM A FAN OF ZE PULP SERIALS.
THE COMING RACE
IN YOUR MOVIES YOU HAVE PROVEN TO BE AN EXCELLENT DAMSEL IN DISTRESS.
YOU CAN'T KEEP ME HERE.
WELL, THERE REALLY IS NO TURNING BACK NOW, YOU ARE... HOW DO YOU SAY? STECKT... IN OUR PLOT.
<MR. GUNTHER, DO WE HAVE A LOCATION?>
<YES, WITH THE INFORMATION PROVIDED BY THE PILLARS OF WISDOM, WE'VE LOCATED THE FLOODED ISLAND.>
<I'M SO CLOSE... THE EAST FRANKISH REICH DUKES, PIPPIN PATRICIUS ROMANORUM, THE IRON CHANCELLOR....>
<ALL THEIR DREAMS OF GREATNESS SHALL COME TO FRUITION IN ME.>
<GREATNESS.>

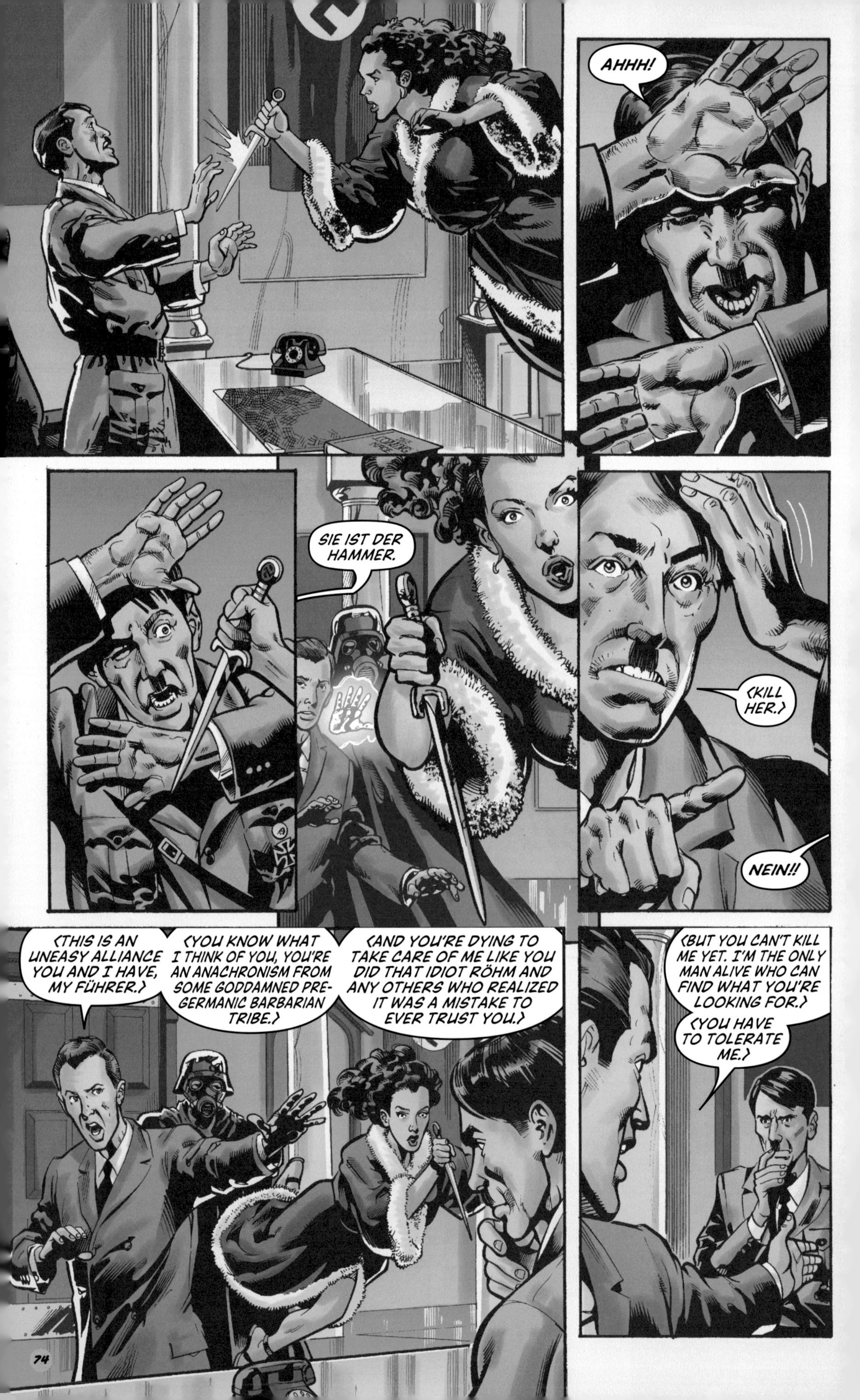
AHHH!
SIE IST DER HAMMER.
<KILL HER.>
NEIN!!
<THIS IS AN UNEASY ALLIANCE YOU AND I HAVE, MY FÜHRER.>
<YOU KNOW WHAT I THINK OF YOU, YOU'RE AN ANACHRONISM FROM SOME GODDAMNED PRE-GERMANIC BARBARIAN TRIBE.>
<AND YOU'RE DYING TO TAKE CARE OF ME LIKE YOU DID THAT IDIOT RÖHM AND ANY OTHERS WHO REALIZED IT WAS A MISTAKE TO EVER TRUST YOU.>
<BUT YOU CAN'T KILL ME YET. I'M THE ONLY MAN ALIVE WHO CAN FIND WHAT YOU'RE LOOKING FOR.>
<YOU HAVE TO TOLERATE ME.>

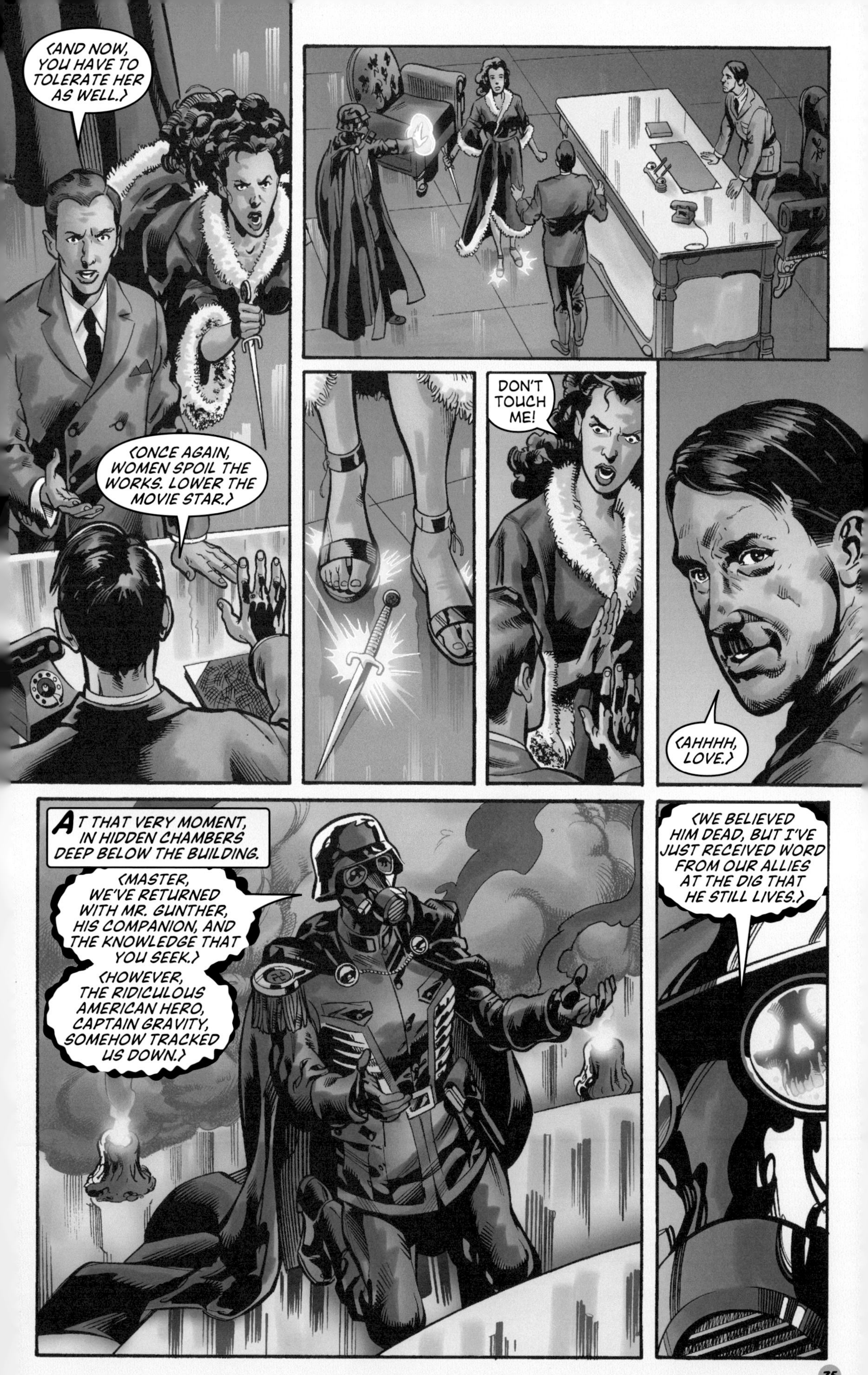

<AND NOW, YOU HAVE TO TOLERATE HER AS WELL.>
<ONCE AGAIN, WOMEN SPOIL THE WORKS. LOWER THE MOVIE STAR.>
DON'T TOUCH ME!
<AHHHH, LOVE.>
AT THAT VERY MOMENT, IN HIDDEN CHAMBERS DEEP BELOW THE BUILDING.
<MASTER, WE'VE RETURNED WITH MR. GUNTHER, HIS COMPANION, AND THE KNOWLEDGE THAT YOU SEEK.>
<HOWEVER, THE RIDICULOUS AMERICAN HERO, CAPTAIN GRAVITY, SOMEHOW TRACKED US DOWN.>
<WE BELIEVED HIM DEAD, BUT I'VE JUST RECEIVED WORD FROM OUR ALLIES AT THE DIG THAT HE STILL LIVES.>

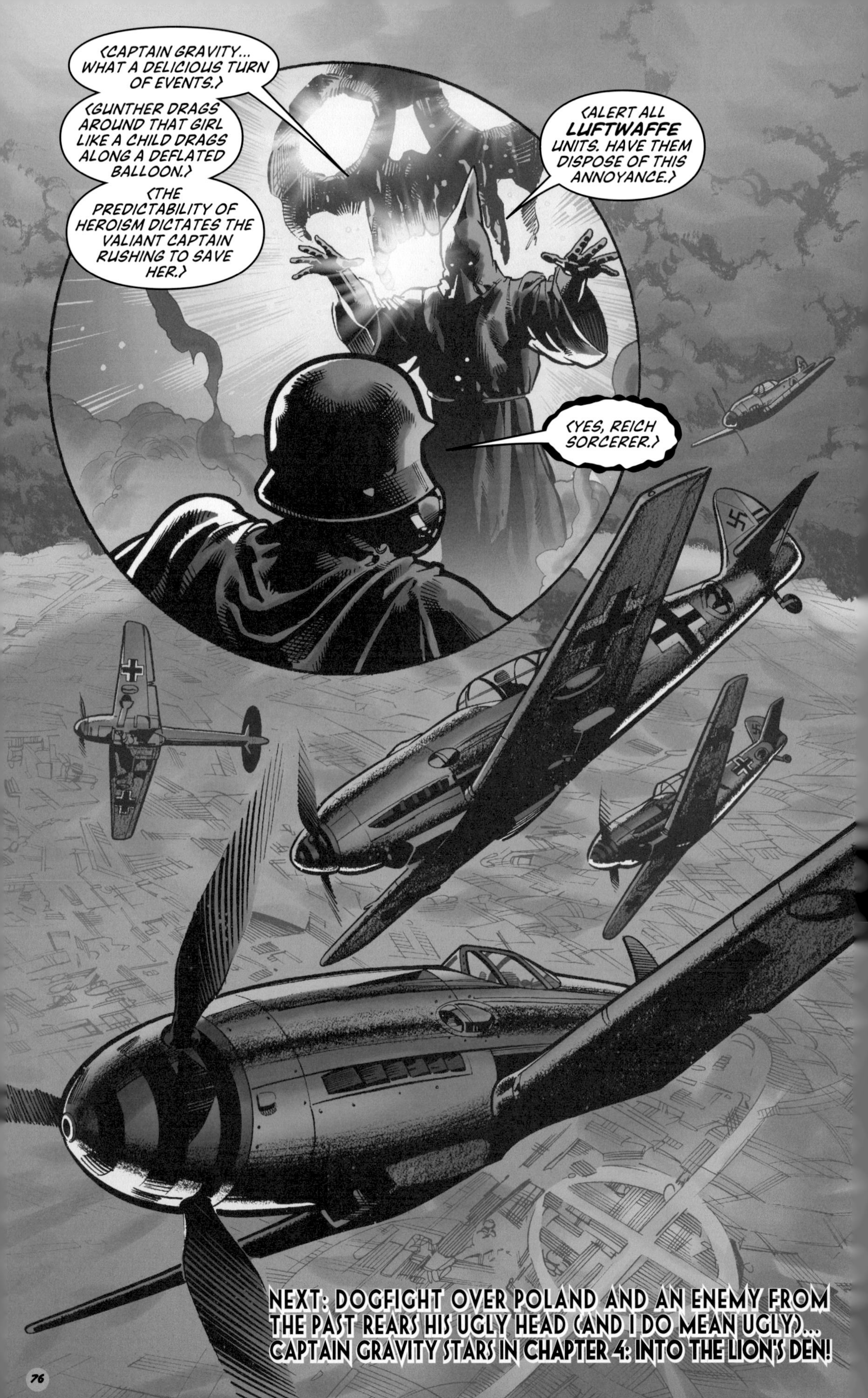
<CAPTAIN GRAVITY... WHAT A DELICIOUS TURN OF EVENTS.>
<GUNTHER DRAGS AROUND THAT GIRL LIKE A CHILD DRAGS ALONG A DEFLATED BALLOON.>
<THE PREDICTABILITY OF HEROISM DICTATES THE VALIANT CAPTAIN RUSHING TO SAVE HER.>
<ALERT ALL **LUFTWAFFE** UNITS. HAVE THEM DISPOSE OF THIS ANNOYANCE.>
<YES, REICH SORCERER.>
NEXT: DOGFIGHT OVER POLAND AND AN ENEMY FROM THE PAST REARS HIS UGLY HEAD (AND I DO MEAN UGLY)... CAPTAIN GRAVITY STARS IN CHAPTER 4: INTO THE LION'S DEN!

CAPTAIN GRAVITY™
And the POWER of the VRIL

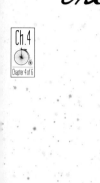

Ch.4
Chapter 4 of 6

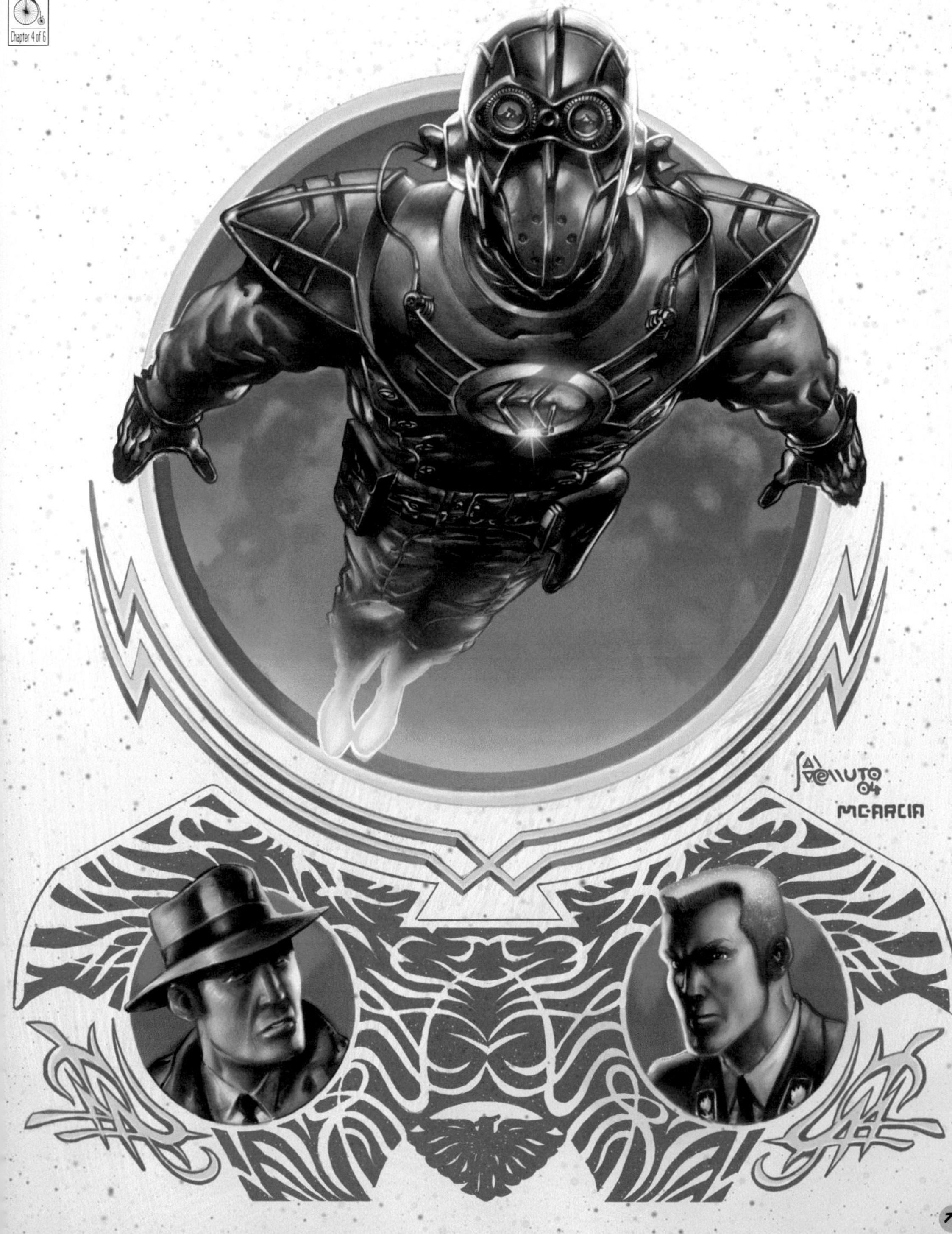

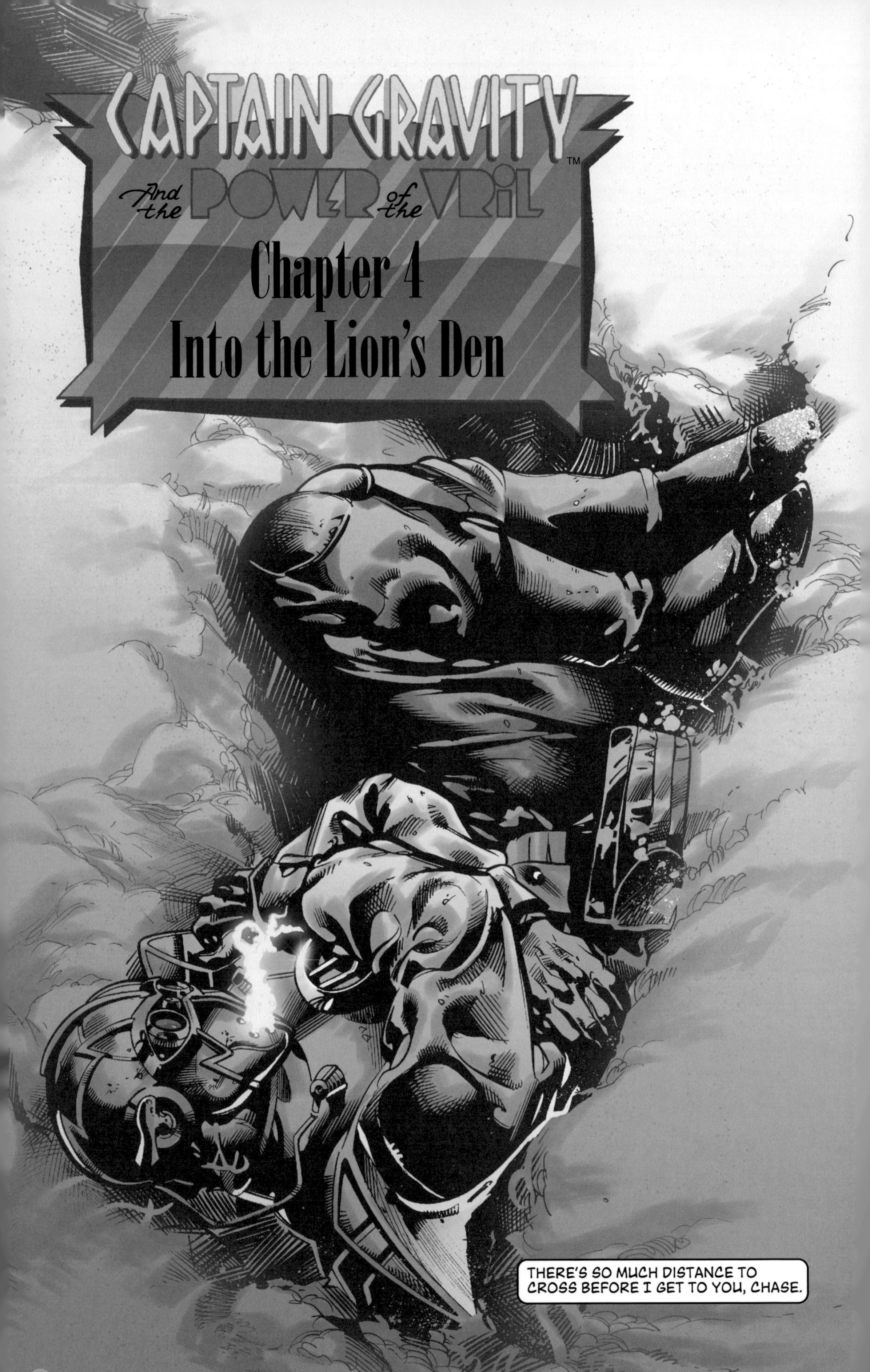
CAPTAIN GRAVITY
And the POWER of the VRIL
Chapter 4
Into the Lion's Den
THERE'S SO MUCH DISTANCE TO CROSS BEFORE I GET TO YOU, CHASE.

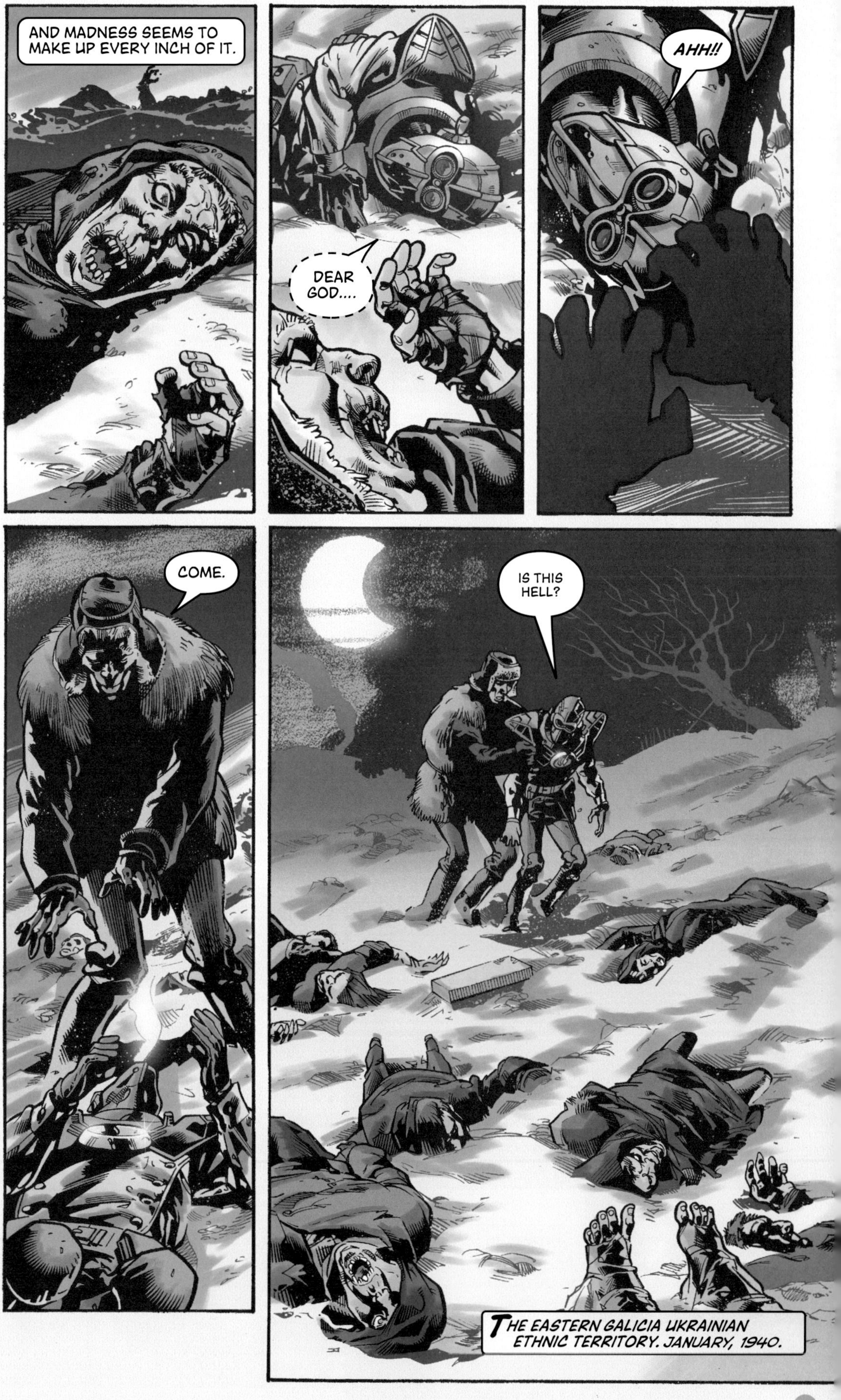

AND MADNESS SEEMS TO MAKE UP EVERY INCH OF IT.
DEAR GOD....
AHH!!
COME.
IS THIS HELL?
THE EASTERN GALICIA UKRAINIAN ETHNIC TERRITORY. JANUARY, 1940.

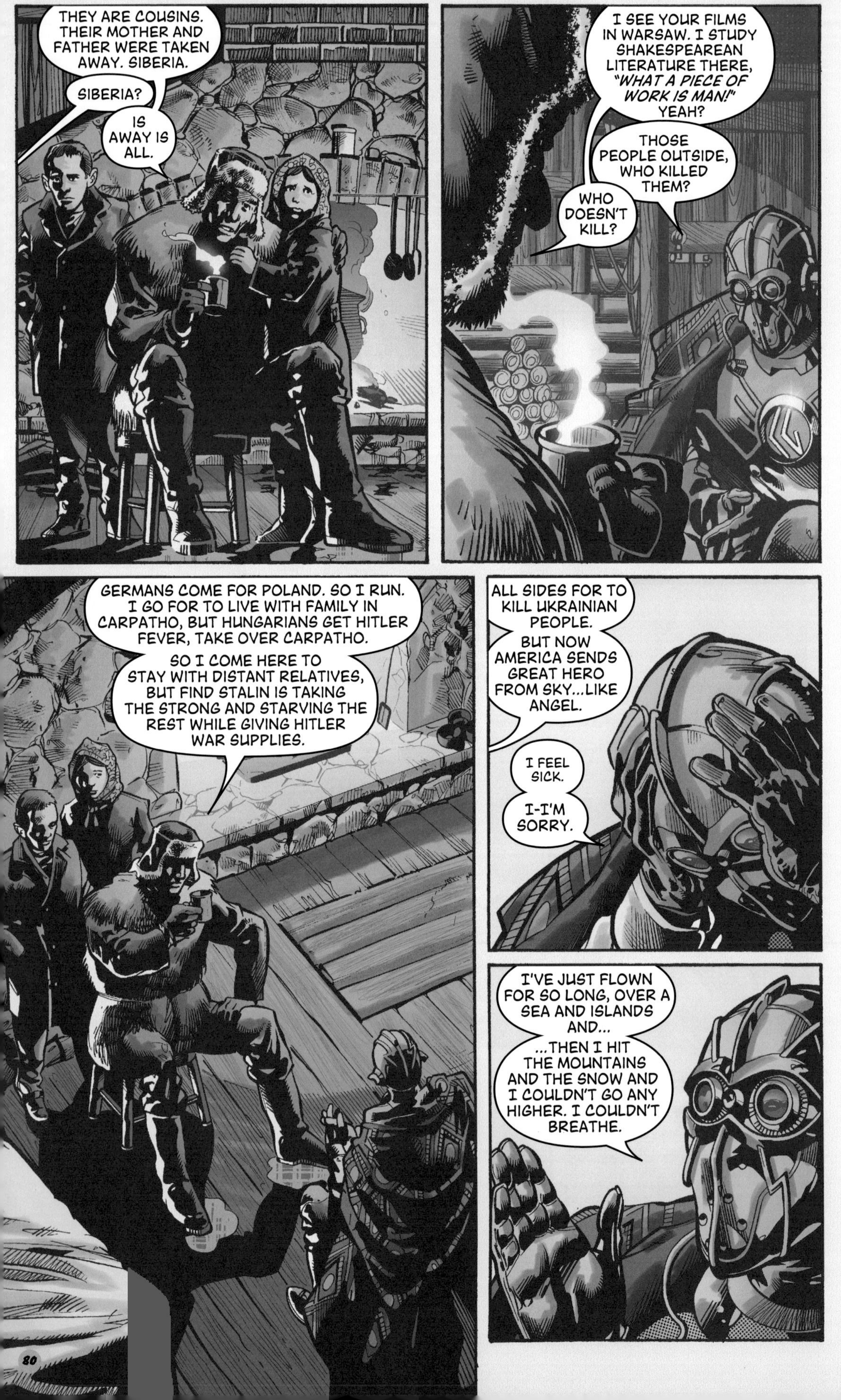

THEY ARE COUSINS. THEIR MOTHER AND FATHER WERE TAKEN AWAY. SIBERIA.
SIBERIA?
IS AWAY IS ALL.
I SEE YOUR FILMS IN WARSAW. I STUDY SHAKESPEAREAN LITERATURE THERE, "WHAT A PIECE OF WORK IS MAN!" YEAH?
THOSE PEOPLE OUTSIDE, WHO KILLED THEM?
WHO DOESN'T KILL?
GERMANS COME FOR POLAND. SO I RUN. I GO FOR TO LIVE WITH FAMILY IN CARPATHO, BUT HUNGARIANS GET HITLER FEVER, TAKE OVER CARPATHO.
SO I COME HERE TO STAY WITH DISTANT RELATIVES, BUT FIND STALIN IS TAKING THE STRONG AND STARVING THE REST WHILE GIVING HITLER WAR SUPPLIES.
ALL SIDES FOR TO KILL UKRAINIAN PEOPLE.
BUT NOW AMERICA SENDS GREAT HERO FROM SKY...LIKE ANGEL.
I FEEL SICK.
I-I'M SORRY.
I'VE JUST FLOWN FOR SO LONG, OVER A SEA AND ISLANDS AND...
...THEN I HIT THE MOUNTAINS AND THE SNOW AND I COULDN'T GO ANY HIGHER. I COULDN'T BREATHE.

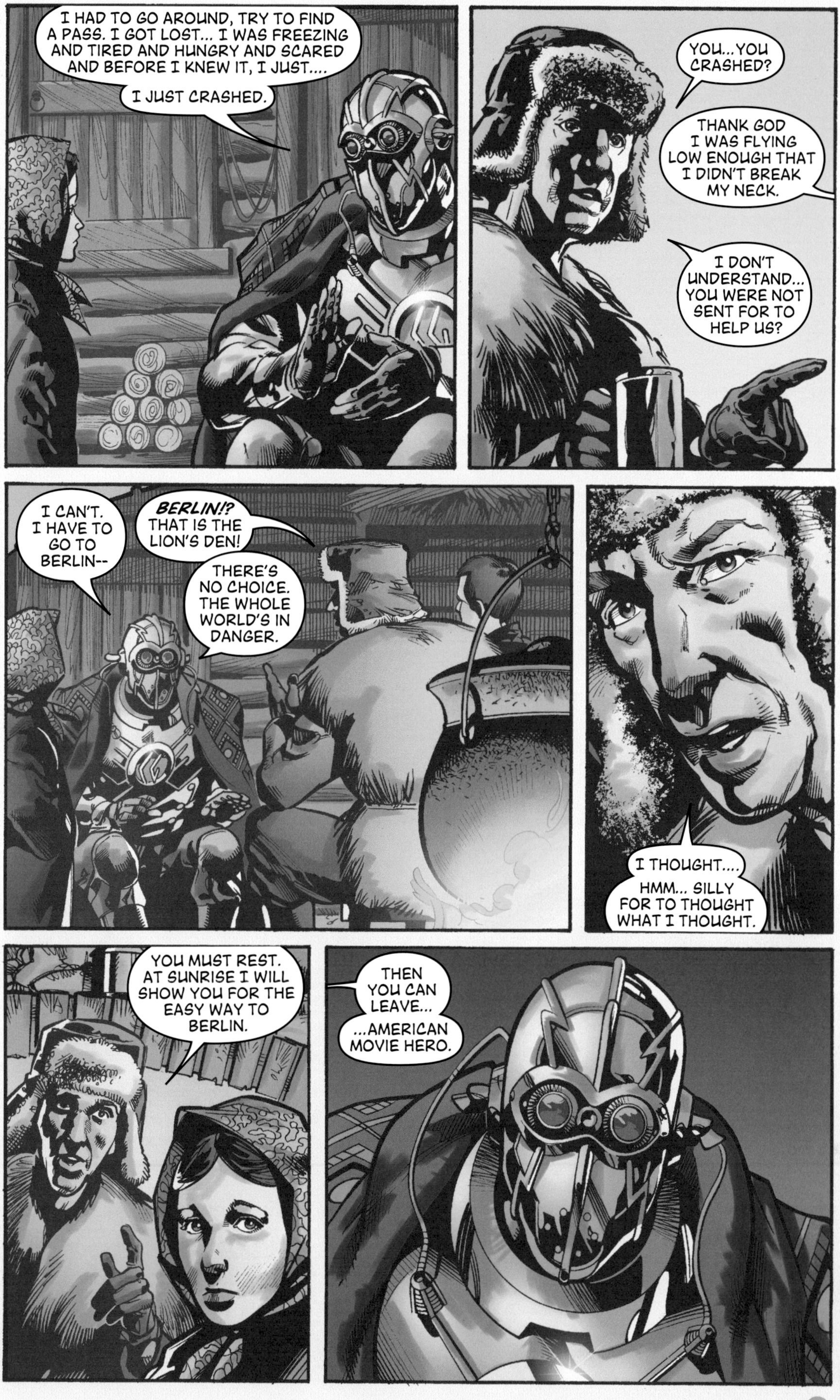
I HAD TO GO AROUND, TRY TO FIND A PASS. I GOT LOST... I WAS FREEZING AND TIRED AND HUNGRY AND SCARED AND BEFORE I KNEW IT, I JUST....
I JUST CRASHED.
YOU...YOU CRASHED?
THANK GOD I WAS FLYING LOW ENOUGH THAT I DIDN'T BREAK MY NECK.
I DON'T UNDERSTAND... YOU WERE NOT SENT FOR TO HELP US?
I CAN'T. I HAVE TO GO TO BERLIN--
BERLIN!? THAT IS THE LION'S DEN!
THERE'S NO CHOICE. THE WHOLE WORLD'S IN DANGER.
I THOUGHT....
HMM... SILLY FOR TO THOUGHT WHAT I THOUGHT.
YOU MUST REST. AT SUNRISE I WILL SHOW YOU FOR THE EASY WAY TO BERLIN.
THEN YOU CAN LEAVE...
...AMERICAN MOVIE HERO.

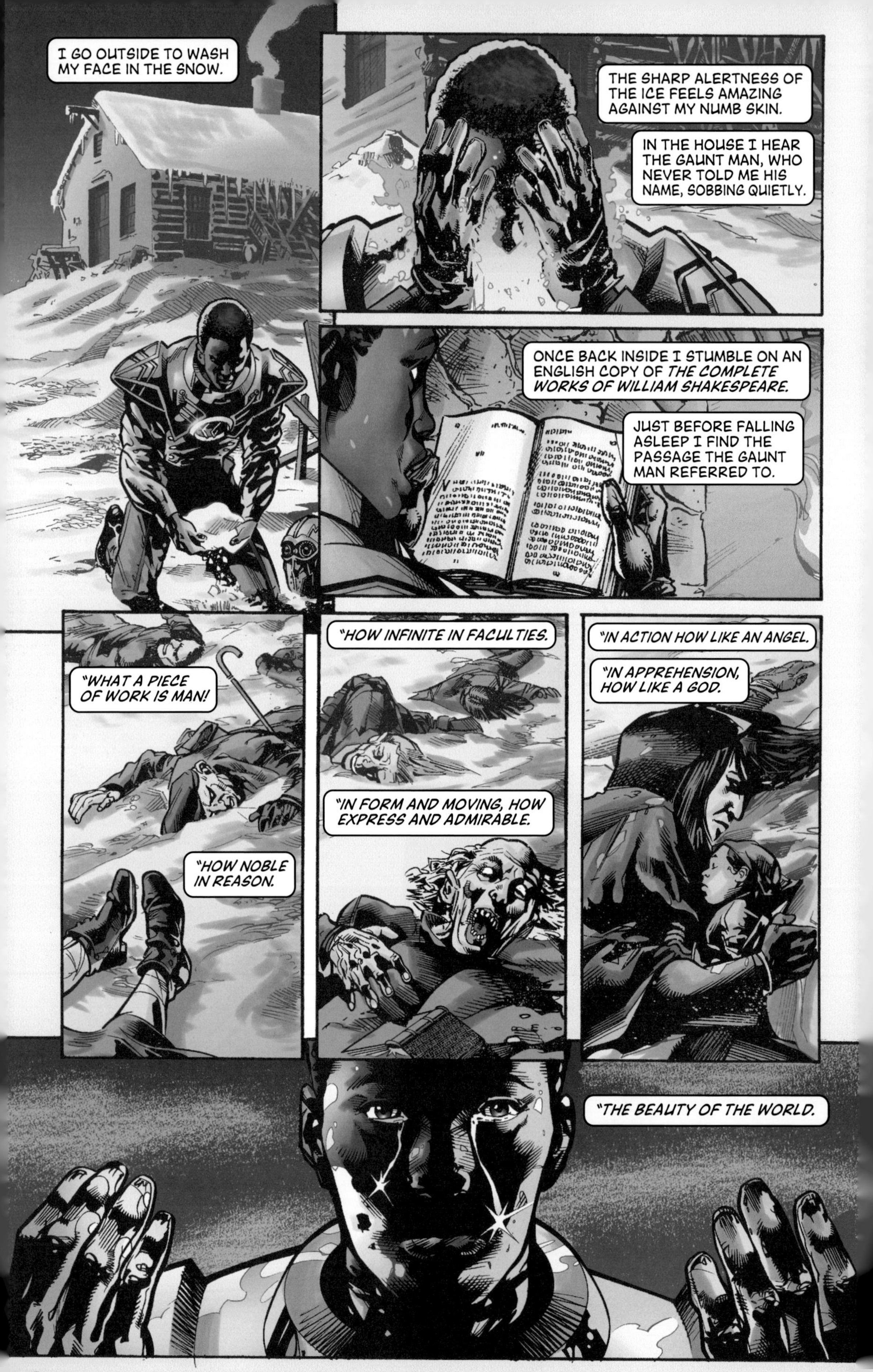
I GO OUTSIDE TO WASH MY FACE IN THE SNOW.
THE SHARP ALERTNESS OF THE ICE FEELS AMAZING AGAINST MY NUMB SKIN.
IN THE HOUSE I HEAR THE GAUNT MAN, WHO NEVER TOLD ME HIS NAME, SOBBING QUIETLY.
ONCE BACK INSIDE I STUMBLE ON AN ENGLISH COPY OF *THE COMPLETE WORKS OF WILLIAM SHAKESPEARE.*
JUST BEFORE FALLING ASLEEP I FIND THE PASSAGE THE GAUNT MAN REFERRED TO.
"WHAT A PIECE OF WORK IS MAN!
"HOW NOBLE IN REASON.
"HOW INFINITE IN FACULTIES.
"IN FORM AND MOVING, HOW EXPRESS AND ADMIRABLE.
"IN ACTION HOW LIKE AN ANGEL.
"IN APPREHENSION, HOW LIKE A GOD.
"THE BEAUTY OF THE WORLD.

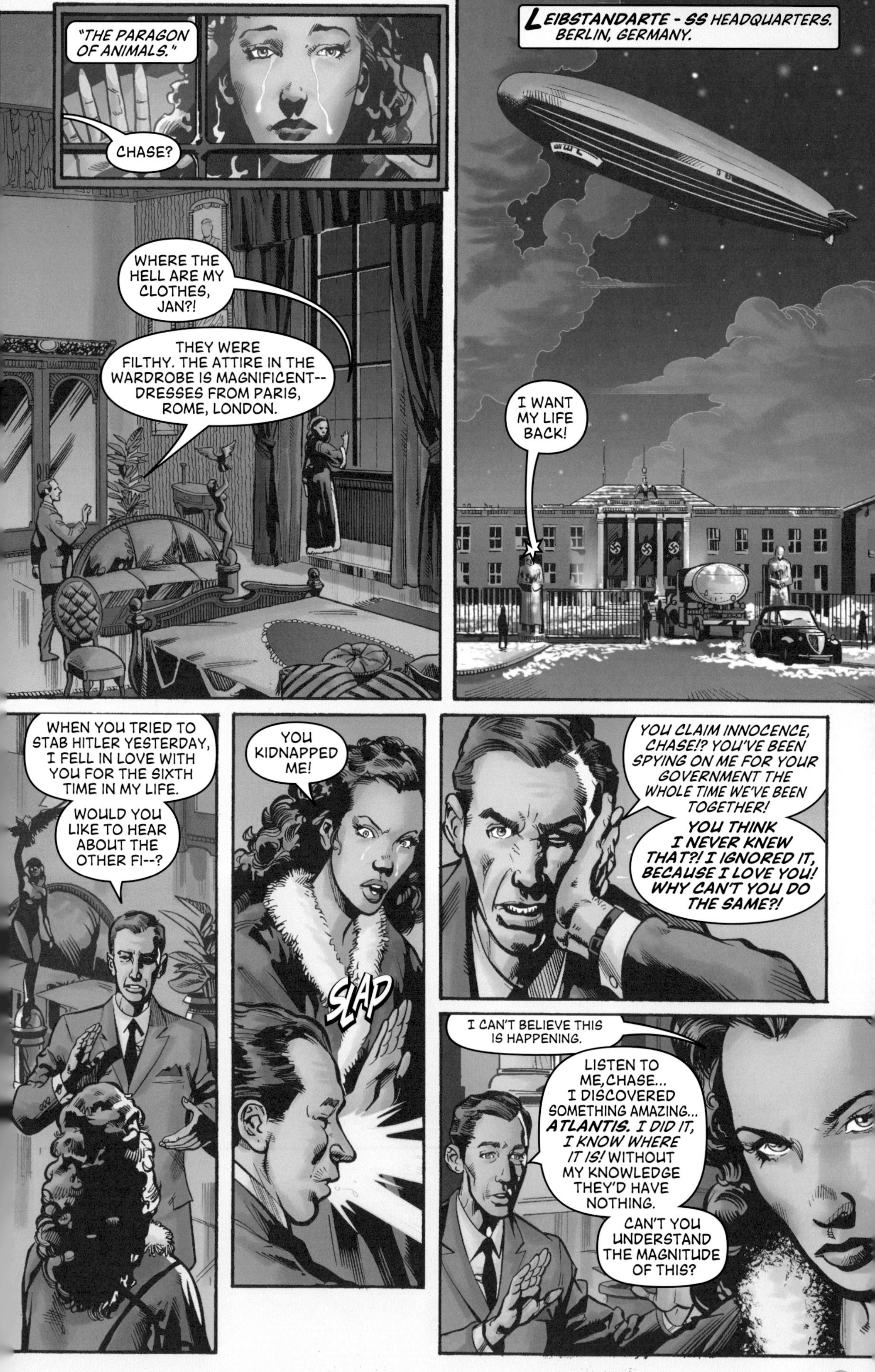
"THE PARAGON OF ANIMALS."
CHASE?
LEIBSTANDARTE - SS HEADQUARTERS. BERLIN, GERMANY.
WHERE THE HELL ARE MY CLOTHES, JAN?!
THEY WERE FILTHY. THE ATTIRE IN THE WARDROBE IS MAGNIFICENT-- DRESSES FROM PARIS, ROME, LONDON.
I WANT MY LIFE BACK!
WHEN YOU TRIED TO STAB HITLER YESTERDAY, I FELL IN LOVE WITH YOU FOR THE SIXTH TIME IN MY LIFE.
WOULD YOU LIKE TO HEAR ABOUT THE OTHER FI--?
YOU KIDNAPPED ME!
SLAP
YOU CLAIM INNOCENCE, CHASE!? YOU'VE BEEN SPYING ON ME FOR YOUR GOVERNMENT THE WHOLE TIME WE'VE BEEN TOGETHER!
YOU THINK I NEVER KNEW THAT?! I IGNORED IT, BECAUSE I LOVE YOU! WHY CAN'T YOU DO THE SAME?!
I CAN'T BELIEVE THIS IS HAPPENING.
LISTEN TO ME, CHASE... I DISCOVERED SOMETHING AMAZING... ATLANTIS. I DID IT, I KNOW WHERE IT IS! WITHOUT MY KNOWLEDGE THEY'D HAVE NOTHING.
CAN'T YOU UNDERSTAND THE MAGNITUDE OF THIS?

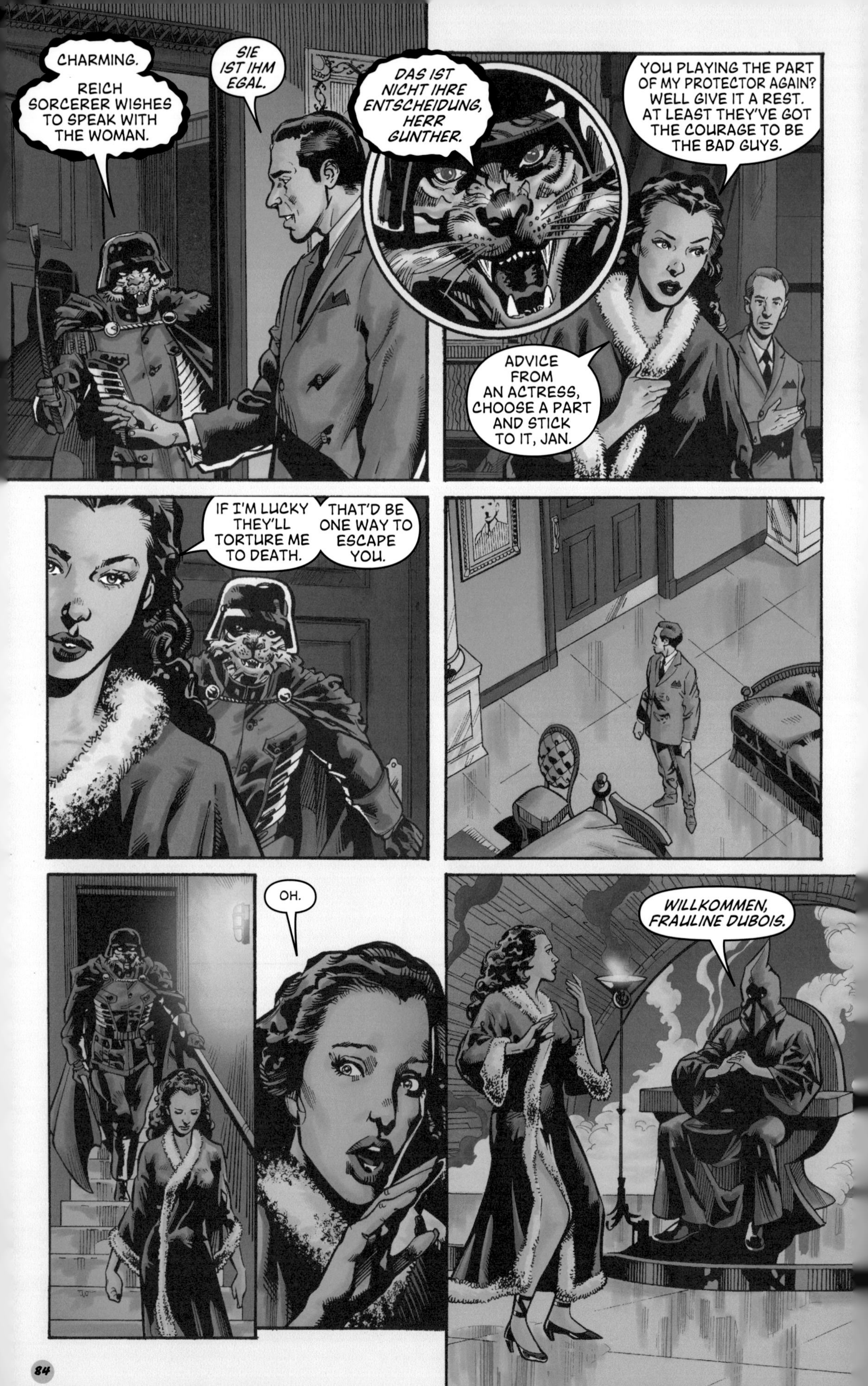
CHARMING.
REICH SORCERER WISHES TO SPEAK WITH THE WOMAN.
SIE IST IHM EGAL.
DAS IST NICHT IHRE ENTSCHEIDUNG, HERR GUNTHER.
YOU PLAYING THE PART OF MY PROTECTOR AGAIN? WELL GIVE IT A REST. AT LEAST THEY'VE GOT THE COURAGE TO BE THE BAD GUYS.
ADVICE FROM AN ACTRESS, CHOOSE A PART AND STICK TO IT, JAN.
IF I'M LUCKY THEY'LL TORTURE ME TO DEATH.
THAT'D BE ONE WAY TO ESCAPE YOU.
OH.
WILLKOMMEN, FRAULINE DUBOIS.

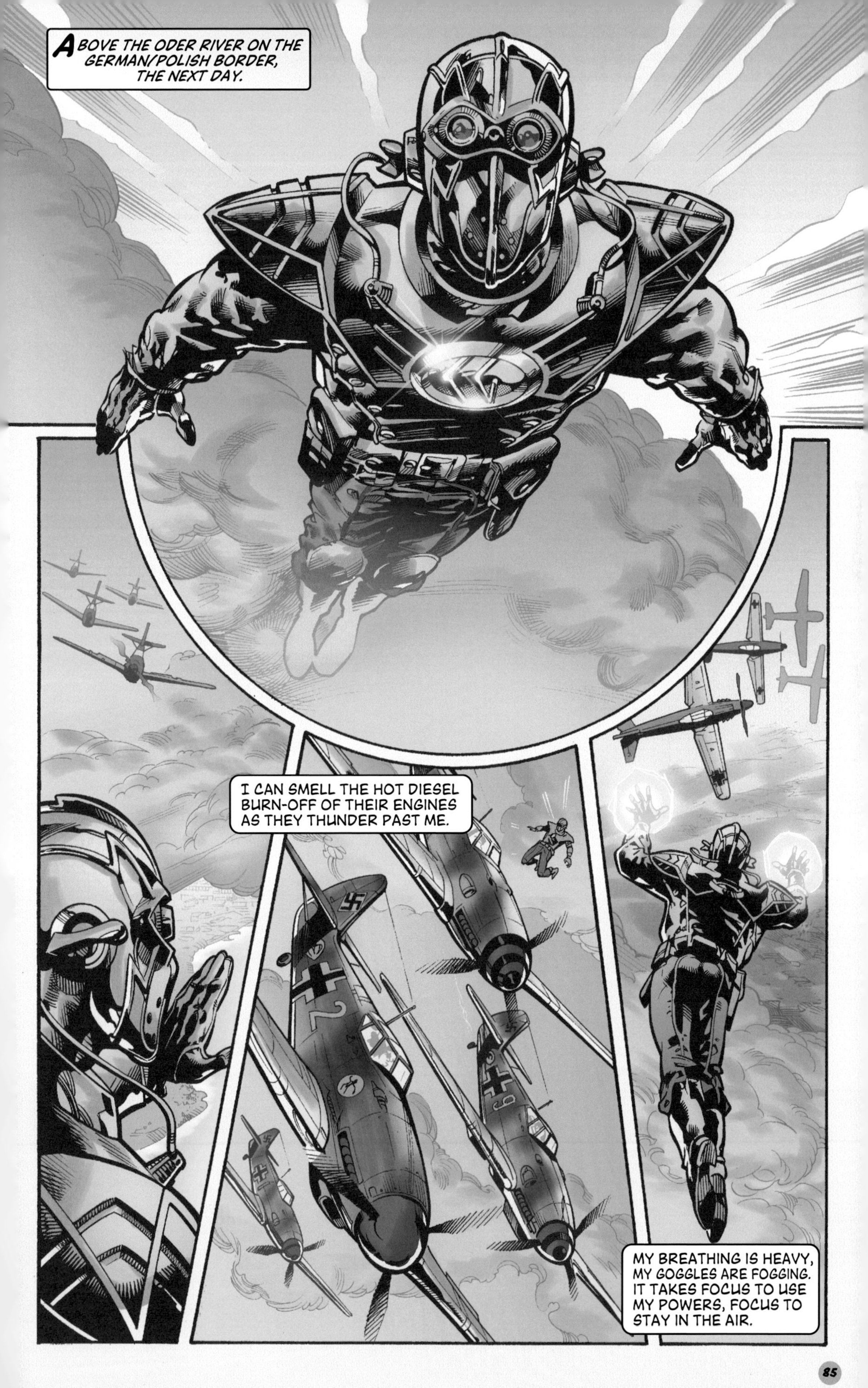
ABOVE THE ODER RIVER ON THE GERMAN/POLISH BORDER, THE NEXT DAY.
I CAN SMELL THE HOT DIESEL BURN-OFF OF THEIR ENGINES AS THEY THUNDER PAST ME.
MY BREATHING IS HEAVY, MY GOGGLES ARE FOGGING. IT TAKES FOCUS TO USE MY POWERS, FOCUS TO STAY IN THE AIR.

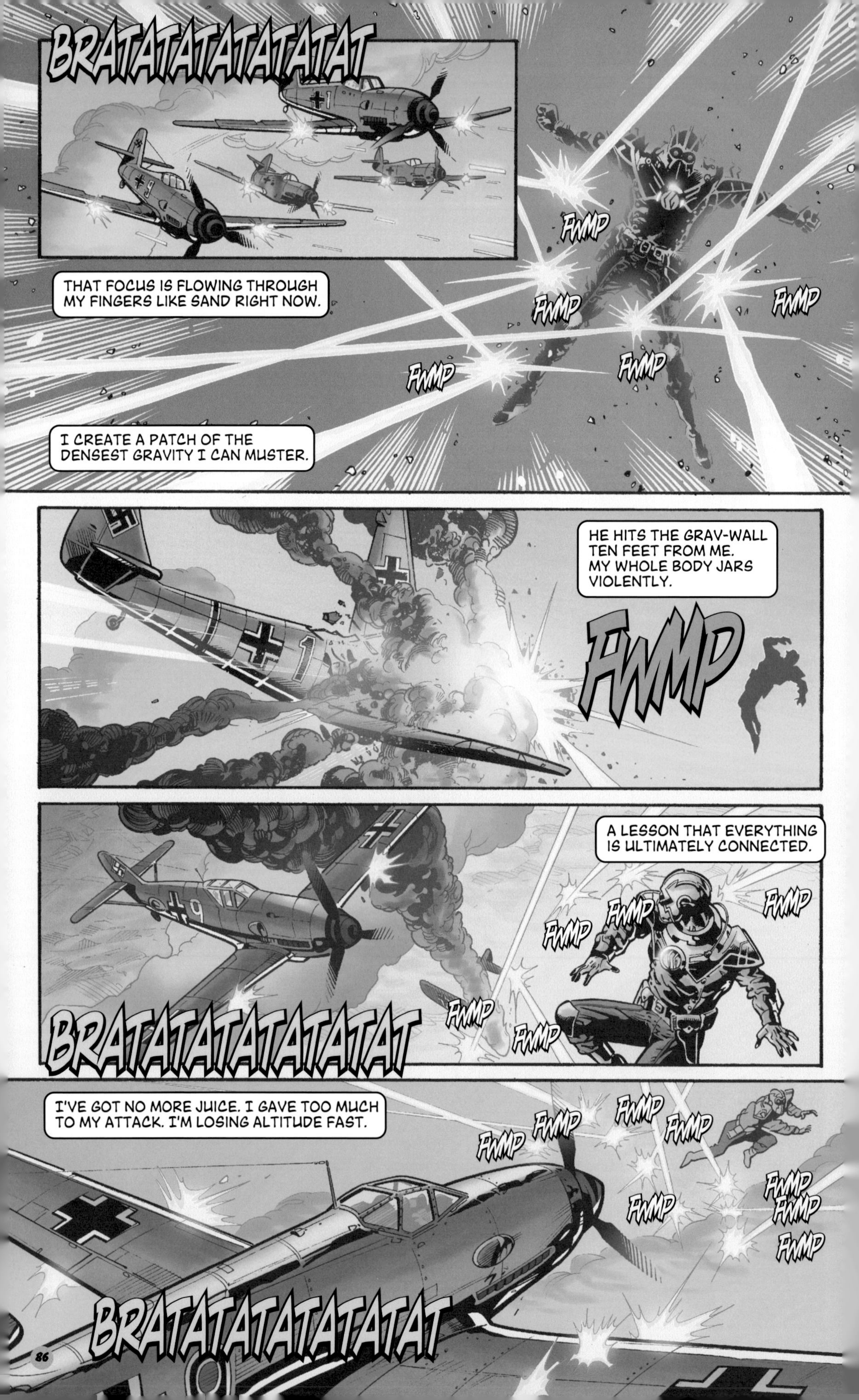
BRATATATATATATAT
THAT FOCUS IS FLOWING THROUGH MY FINGERS LIKE SAND RIGHT NOW.
FWMP
FWMP
FWMP
FWMP
FWMP
I CREATE A PATCH OF THE DENSEST GRAVITY I CAN MUSTER.
HE HITS THE GRAV-WALL TEN FEET FROM ME. MY WHOLE BODY JARS VIOLENTLY.
FWMP
A LESSON THAT EVERYTHING IS ULTIMATELY CONNECTED.
FWMP
FWMP
FWMP
FWMP
FWMP
BRATATATATATATATAT
I'VE GOT NO MORE JUICE. I GAVE TOO MUCH TO MY ATTACK. I'M LOSING ALTITUDE FAST.
FWMP
FWMP
FWMP
FWMP
FWMP
FWMP
FWMP
FWMP
BRATATATATATATATAT

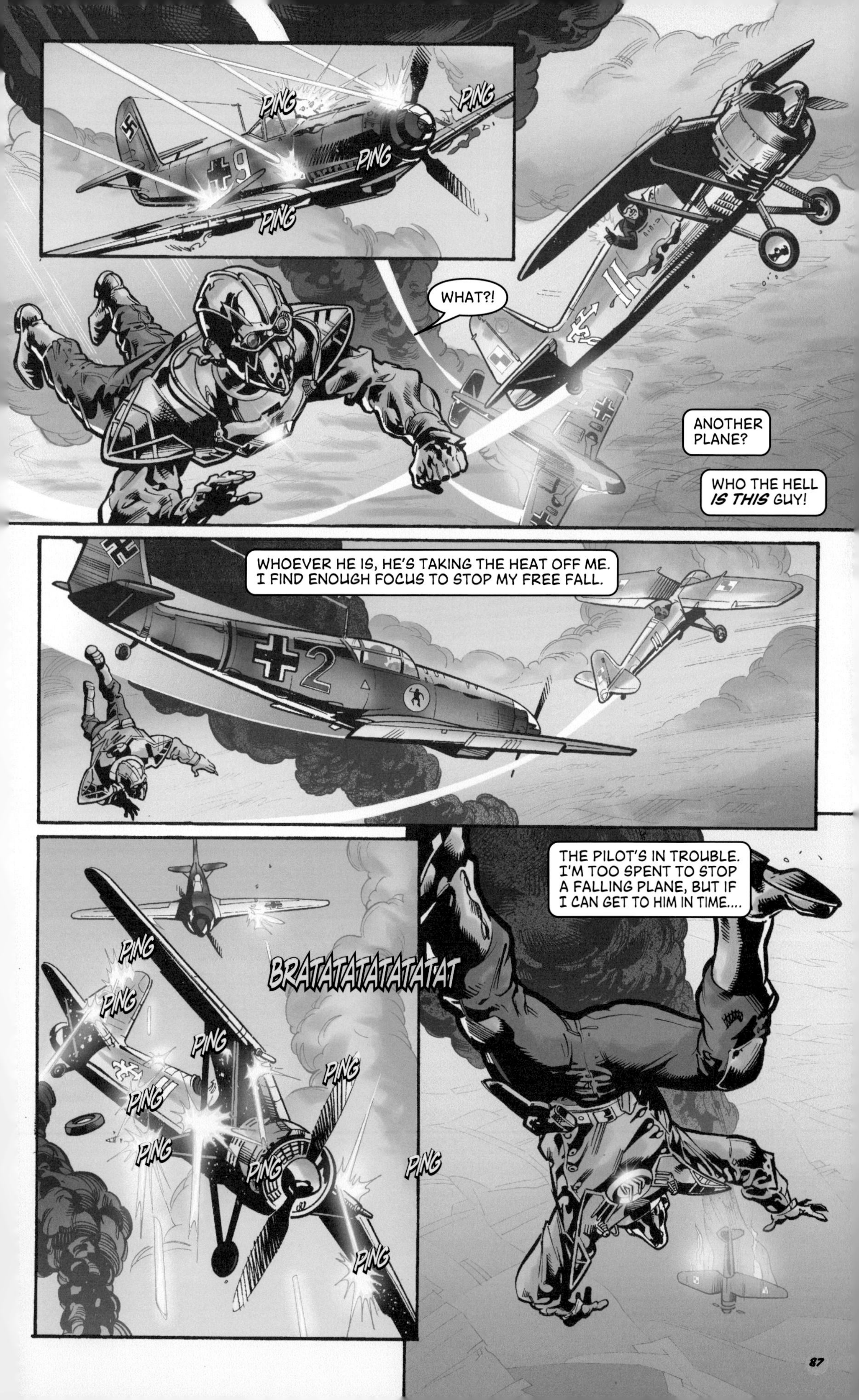
PING
PING
PING
PING
WHAT?!
ANOTHER PLANE?
WHO THE HELL IS THIS GUY!
WHOEVER HE IS, HE'S TAKING THE HEAT OFF ME. I FIND ENOUGH FOCUS TO STOP MY FREE FALL.
THE PILOT'S IN TROUBLE. I'M TOO SPENT TO STOP A FALLING PLANE, BUT IF I CAN GET TO HIM IN TIME....
BRATATATATATATAT
PING
PING
PING
PING
PING
PING
PING
PING
PING

GRAB MY HAND!

I--

--CAN'T--

--AAAAAAA!

KACHOOM

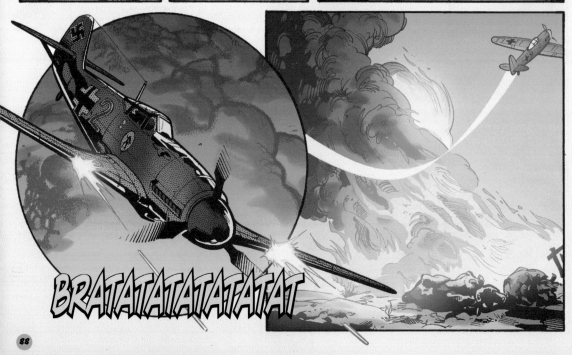

BRATATATATATAT

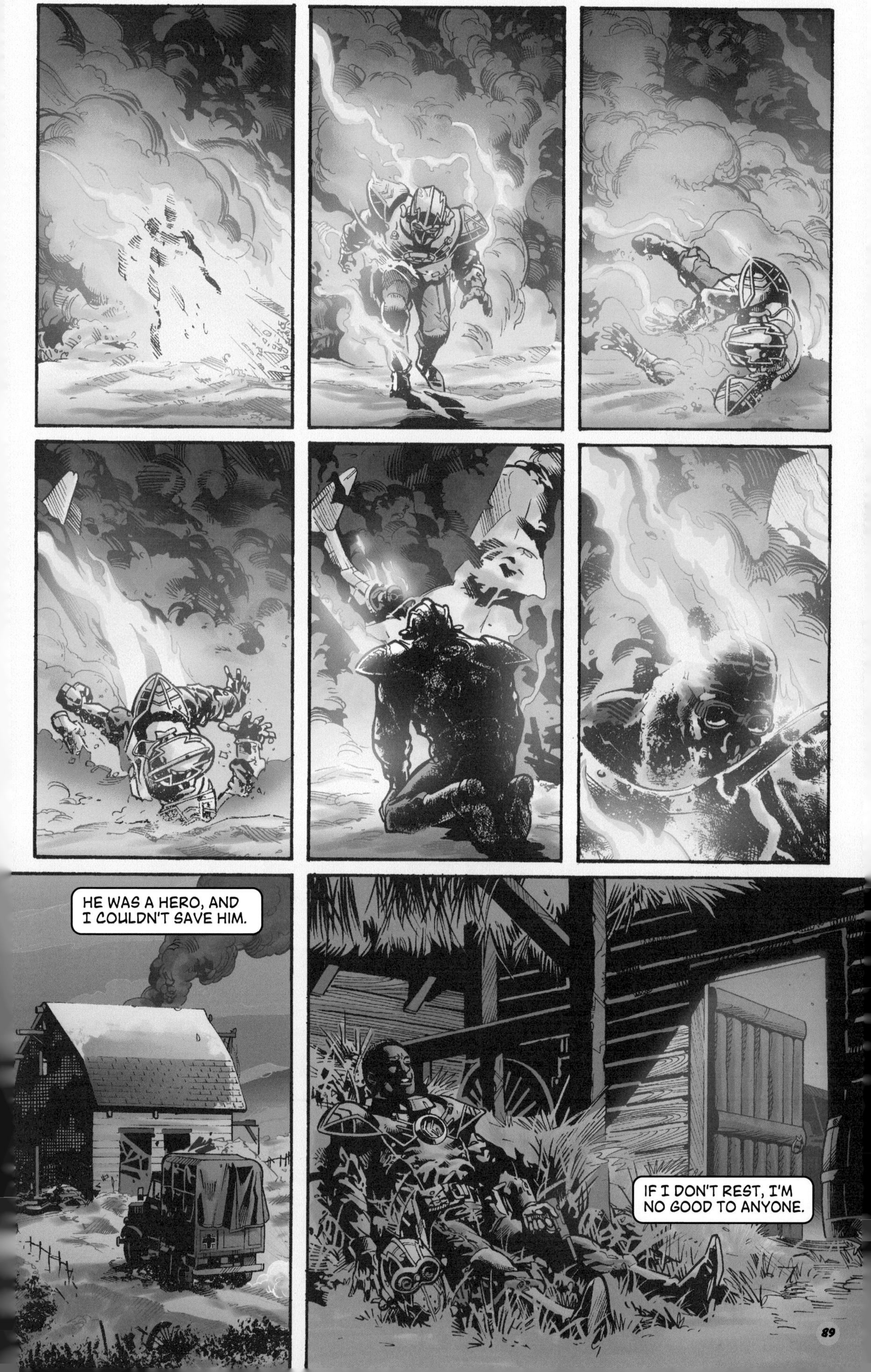
HE WAS A HERO, AND I COULDN'T SAVE HIM.
IF I DON'T REST, I'M NO GOOD TO ANYONE.

CREEEEK

WHO'S THERE?

CAPTAIN GRAVITY?

SO GLAD TO FIND YOU ALIVE, CAPTAIN.

FUNNY ACCENT FOR A KRAUT.

FLEMING, IA--

I KNOW WHO YOU ARE...BRITISH INTELLIGENCE.

YOU'RE FULL OF SURPRISES. THE GERMAN ON THE FIELD RADIO LED US TO THE WRECKAGE.

WHO WAS THE PILOT THAT SAVED MY LIFE?

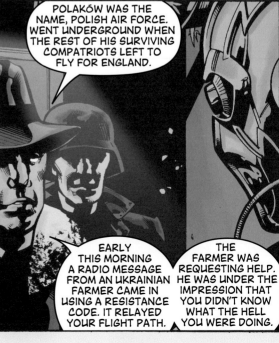

POLAKÓW WAS THE NAME, POLISH AIR FORCE. WENT UNDERGROUND WHEN THE REST OF HIS SURVIVING COMPATRIOTS LEFT TO FLY FOR ENGLAND.

EARLY THIS MORNING A RADIO MESSAGE FROM AN UKRAINIAN FARMER CAME IN USING A RESISTANCE CODE. IT RELAYED YOUR FLIGHT PATH.

THE FARMER WAS REQUESTING HELP. HE WAS UNDER THE IMPRESSION THAT YOU DIDN'T KNOW WHAT THE HELL YOU WERE DOING.

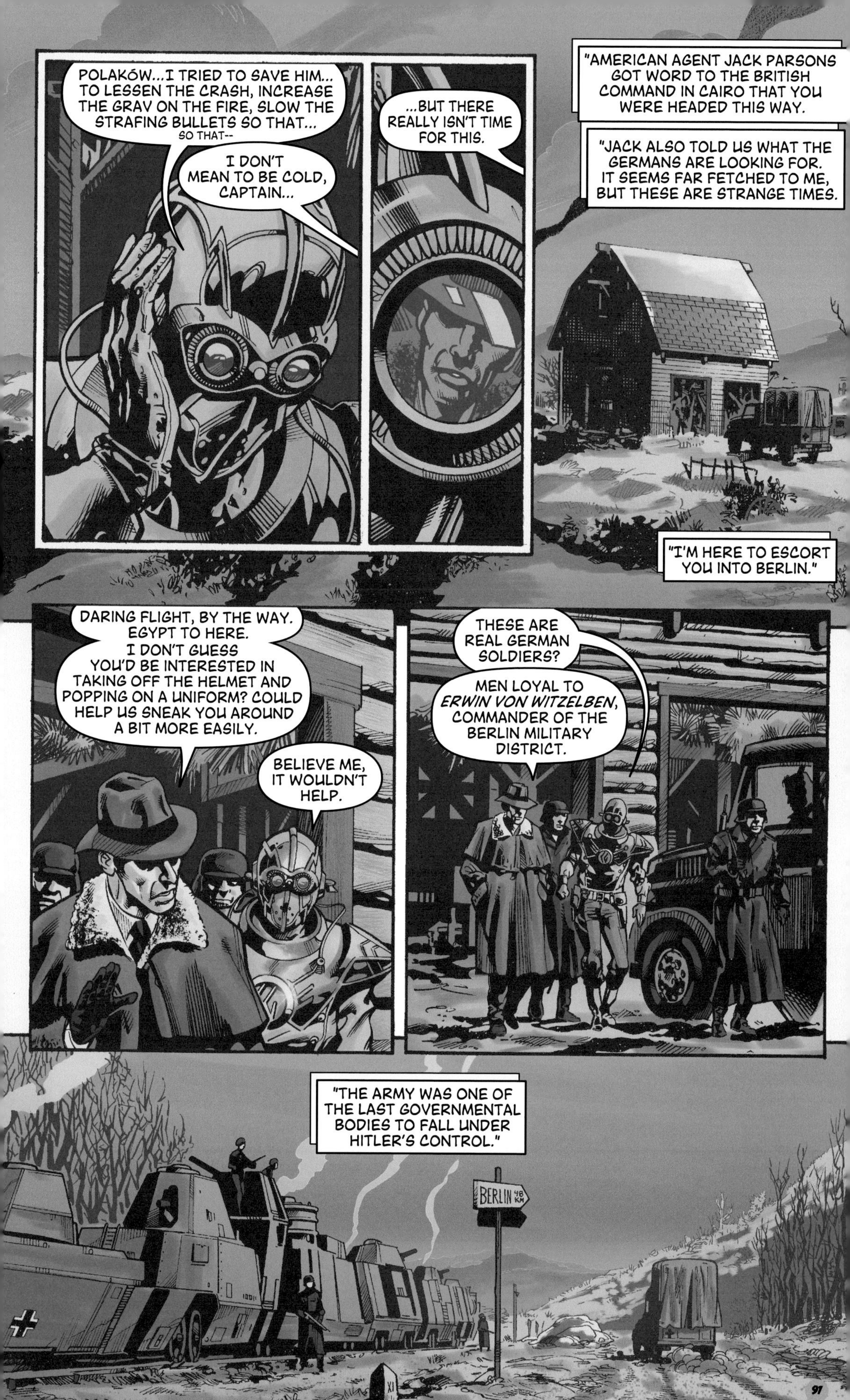

POLAKÓW...I TRIED TO SAVE HIM... TO LESSEN THE CRASH, INCREASE THE GRAV ON THE FIRE, SLOW THE STRAFING BULLETS SO THAT... SO THAT--
I DON'T MEAN TO BE COLD, CAPTAIN...
...BUT THERE REALLY ISN'T TIME FOR THIS.
"AMERICAN AGENT JACK PARSONS GOT WORD TO THE BRITISH COMMAND IN CAIRO THAT YOU WERE HEADED THIS WAY.
"JACK ALSO TOLD US WHAT THE GERMANS ARE LOOKING FOR. IT SEEMS FAR FETCHED TO ME, BUT THESE ARE STRANGE TIMES.
"I'M HERE TO ESCORT YOU INTO BERLIN."
DARING FLIGHT, BY THE WAY. EGYPT TO HERE. I DON'T GUESS YOU'D BE INTERESTED IN TAKING OFF THE HELMET AND POPPING ON A UNIFORM? COULD HELP US SNEAK YOU AROUND A BIT MORE EASILY.
BELIEVE ME, IT WOULDN'T HELP.
THESE ARE REAL GERMAN SOLDIERS?
MEN LOYAL TO *ERWIN VON WITZELBEN*, COMMANDER OF THE BERLIN MILITARY DISTRICT.
"THE ARMY WAS ONE OF THE LAST GOVERNMENTAL BODIES TO FALL UNDER HITLER'S CONTROL."
BERLIN 48 KM

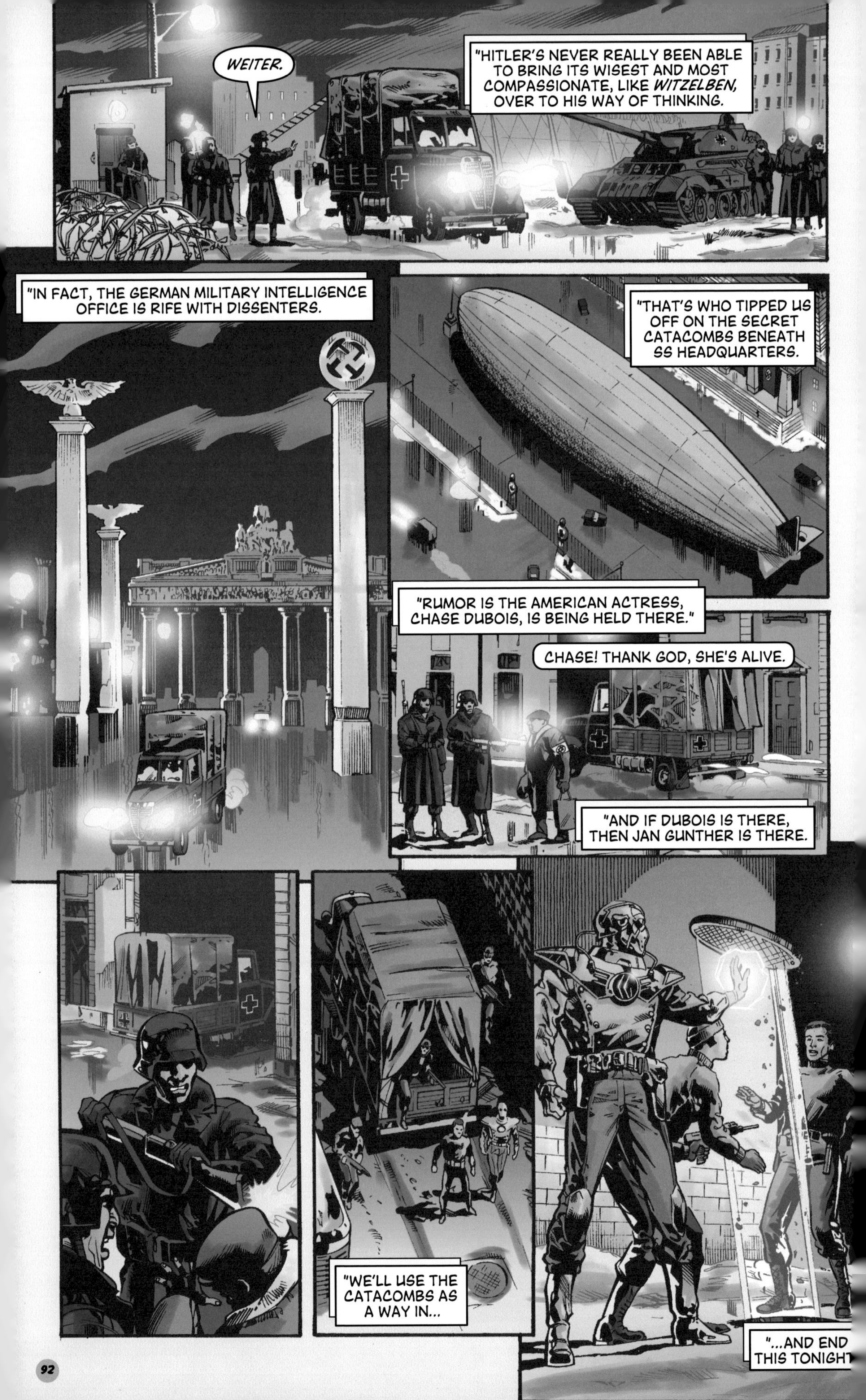
"HITLER'S NEVER REALLY BEEN ABLE TO BRING ITS WISEST AND MOST COMPASSIONATE, LIKE WITZELBEN, OVER TO HIS WAY OF THINKING.
WEITER.
"IN FACT, THE GERMAN MILITARY INTELLIGENCE OFFICE IS RIFE WITH DISSENTERS.
"THAT'S WHO TIPPED US OFF ON THE SECRET CATACOMBS BENEATH SS HEADQUARTERS.
"RUMOR IS THE AMERICAN ACTRESS, CHASE DUBOIS, IS BEING HELD THERE."
CHASE! THANK GOD, SHE'S ALIVE.
"AND IF DUBOIS IS THERE, THEN JAN GUNTHER IS THERE.
"WE'LL USE THE CATACOMBS AS A WAY IN...
"...AND END THIS TONIGHT

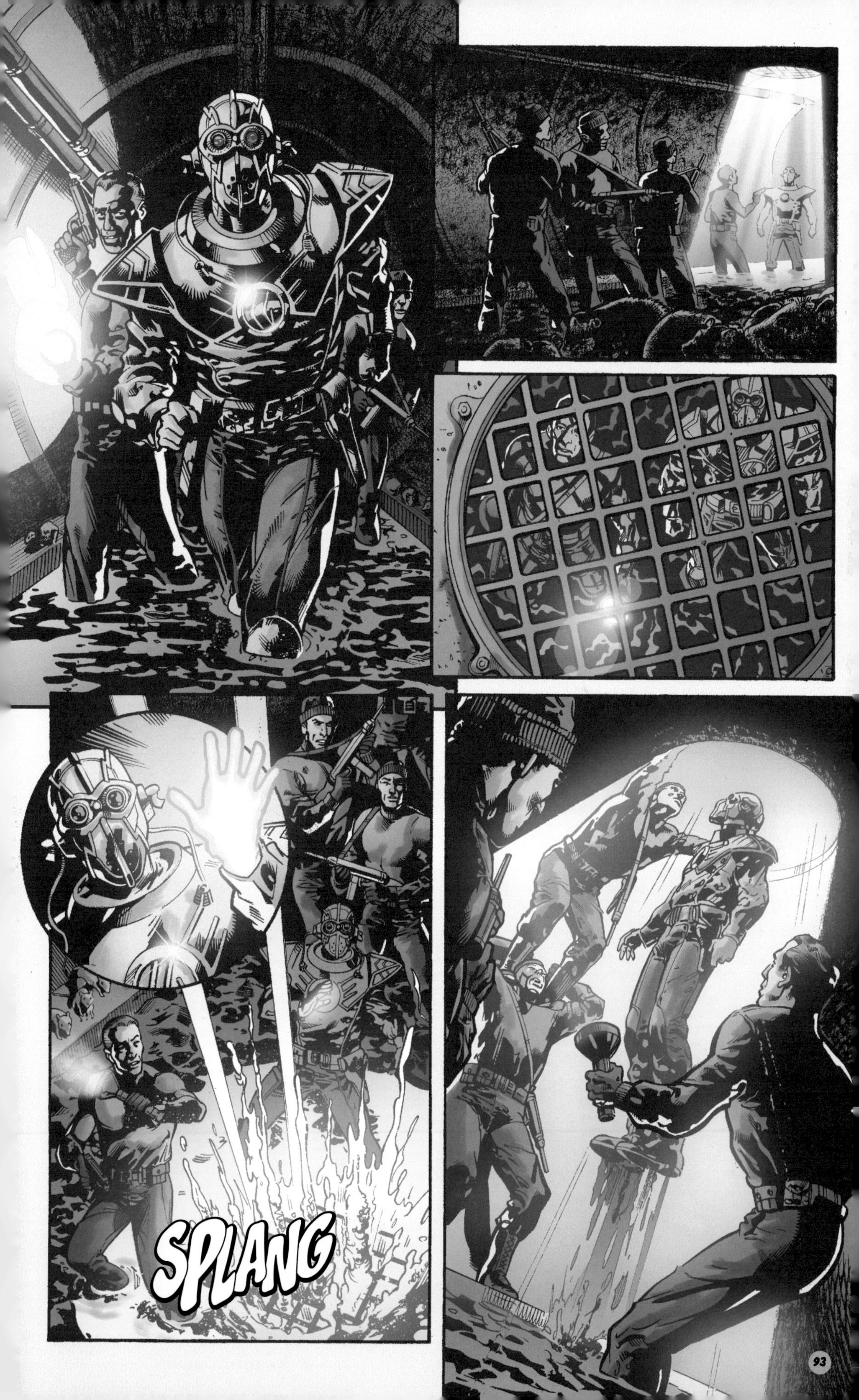
SPLANG

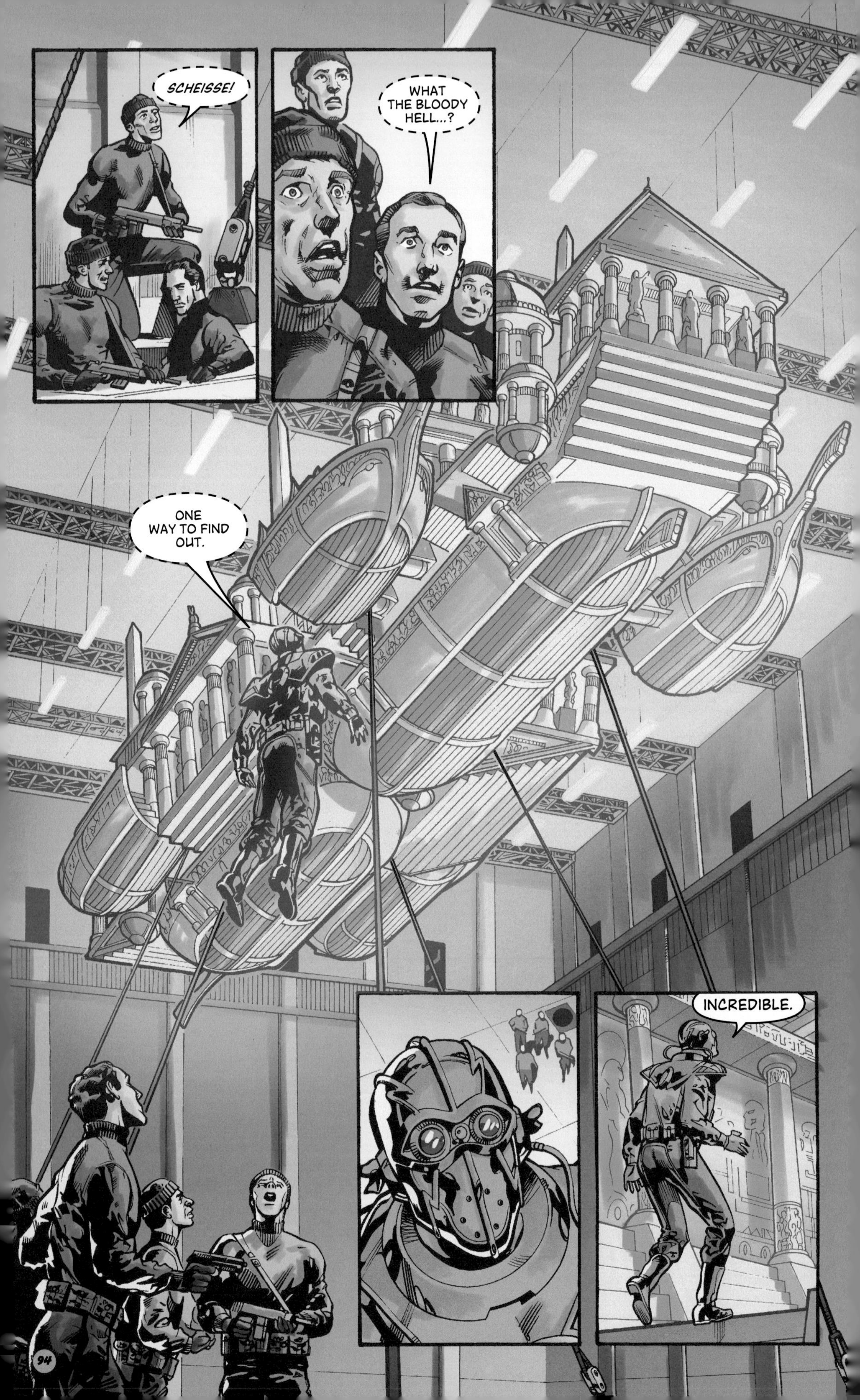
SCHEISSE!
WHAT THE BLOODY HELL...?
ONE WAY TO FIND OUT.
INCREDIBLE.

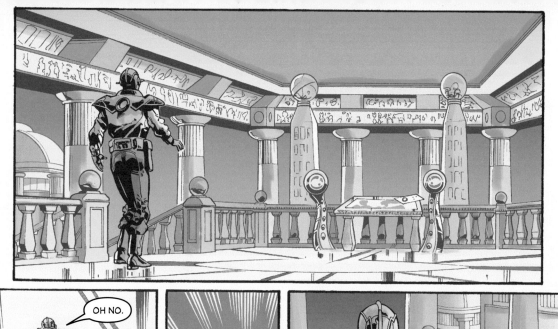

OH NO.

I MUST BE SPEAKING...

...TO THE FLYING MONGREL, JOSHUA JONES.

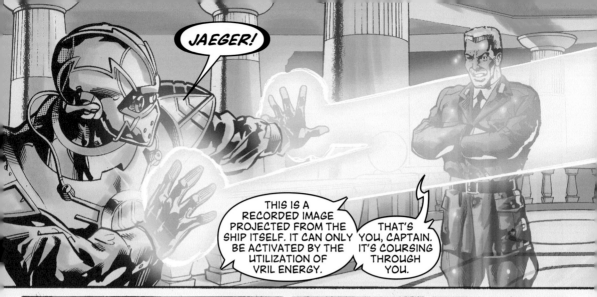

JAEGER!

THIS IS A RECORDED IMAGE PROJECTED FROM THE SHIP ITSELF. IT CAN ONLY BE ACTIVATED BY THE UTILIZATION OF VRIL ENERGY.

THAT'S YOU, CAPTAIN. IT'S COURSING THROUGH YOU.

I'VE JUST READ A REPORT FROM A *LUFTWAFFE* PILOT. IT RELAYS YET *ANOTHER* EXCITING NARRATIVE OF YOUR DEATH.

IF THIS MESSAGE IS PLAYING IT MEANS I'VE NOT UNDERESTIMATED YOUR DURABILITY.

THIS IMAGE IS A COMPOSITE OF MY FORMER SELF...

...I'M EXCITED TO SHOW YOU JUST HOW MUCH I'VE CHANGED.

EARLIER.

WILLKOMMEN, FRAU DUBOIS.

I'M DONE BEING SCARED OF YOU FREAKS.

SO IF YOU BROUGHT ME DOWN HERE TO GET YOU'RE ROCKS OFF HEARING ME SCREAM, YOU'VE PICKED THE WRONG DAME!

WHILE THAT WAS NOT MY ORIGINAL INTENTION, I MUST ADMIT...

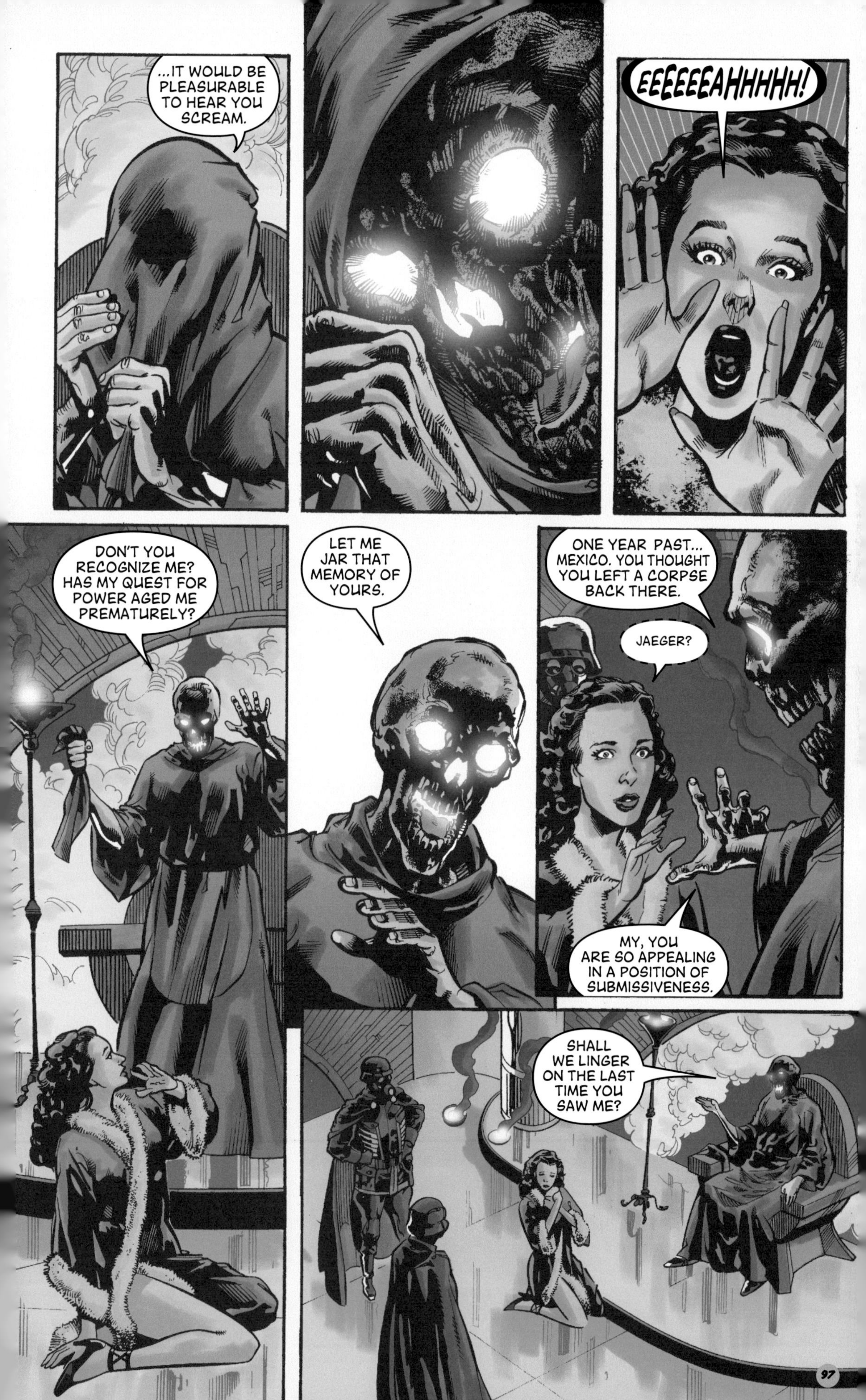
...IT WOULD BE PLEASURABLE TO HEAR YOU SCREAM.
EEEEEEAHHHHH!
DON'T YOU RECOGNIZE ME? HAS MY QUEST FOR POWER AGED ME PREMATURELY?
LET ME JAR THAT MEMORY OF YOURS.
ONE YEAR PAST... MEXICO. YOU THOUGHT YOU LEFT A CORPSE BACK THERE.
JAEGER?
MY, YOU ARE SO APPEALING IN A POSITION OF SUBMISSIVENESS.
SHALL WE LINGER ON THE LAST TIME YOU SAW ME?

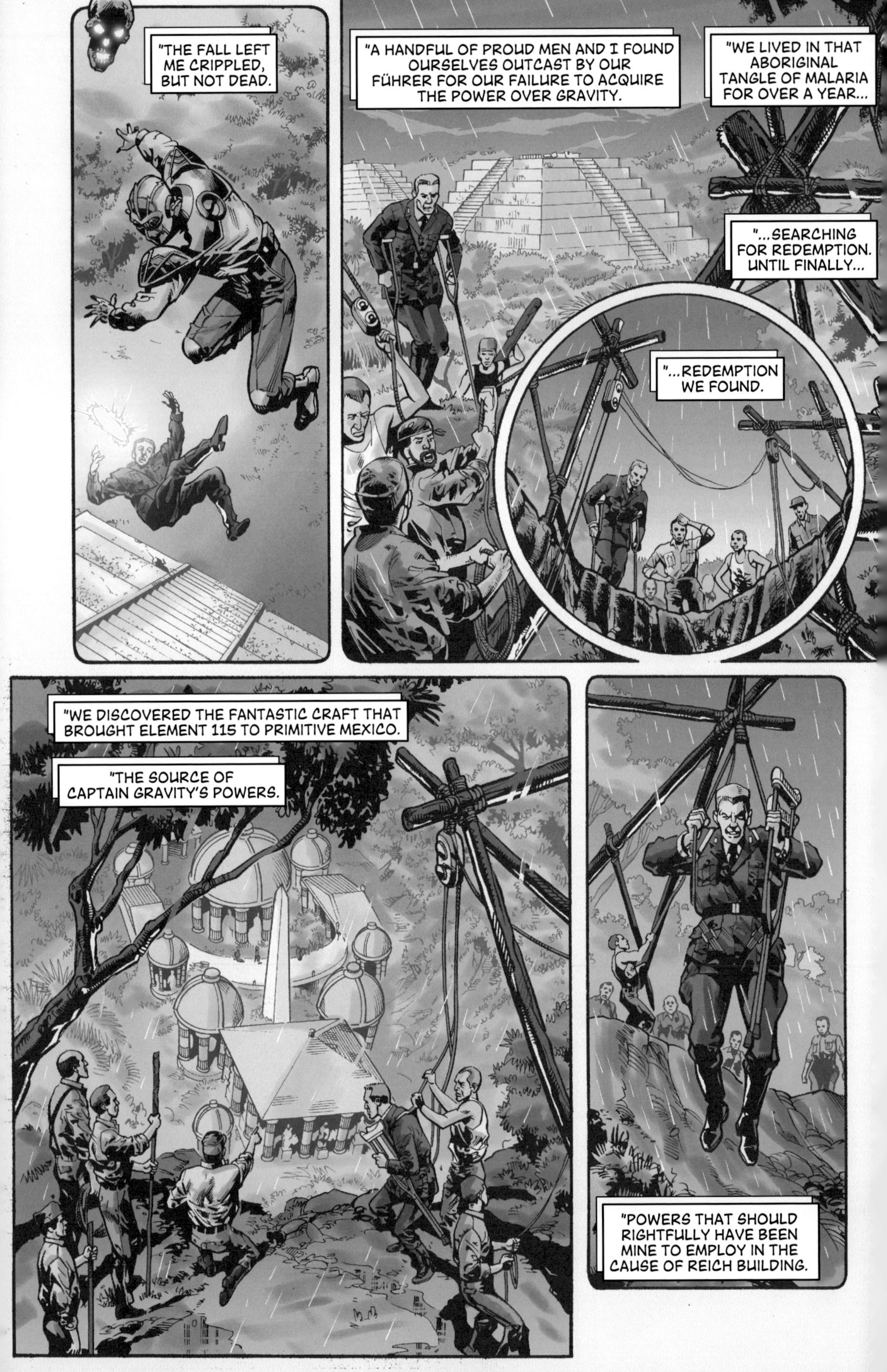
"THE FALL LEFT ME CRIPPLED, BUT NOT DEAD.
"A HANDFUL OF PROUD MEN AND I FOUND OURSELVES OUTCAST BY OUR FÜHRER FOR OUR FAILURE TO ACQUIRE THE POWER OVER GRAVITY.
"WE LIVED IN THAT ABORIGINAL TANGLE OF MALARIA FOR OVER A YEAR...
"...SEARCHING FOR REDEMPTION. UNTIL FINALLY...
"...REDEMPTION WE FOUND.
"WE DISCOVERED THE FANTASTIC CRAFT THAT BROUGHT ELEMENT 115 TO PRIMITIVE MEXICO.
"THE SOURCE OF CAPTAIN GRAVITY'S POWERS.
"POWERS THAT SHOULD RIGHTFULLY HAVE BEEN MINE TO EMPLOY IN THE CAUSE OF REICH BUILDING.

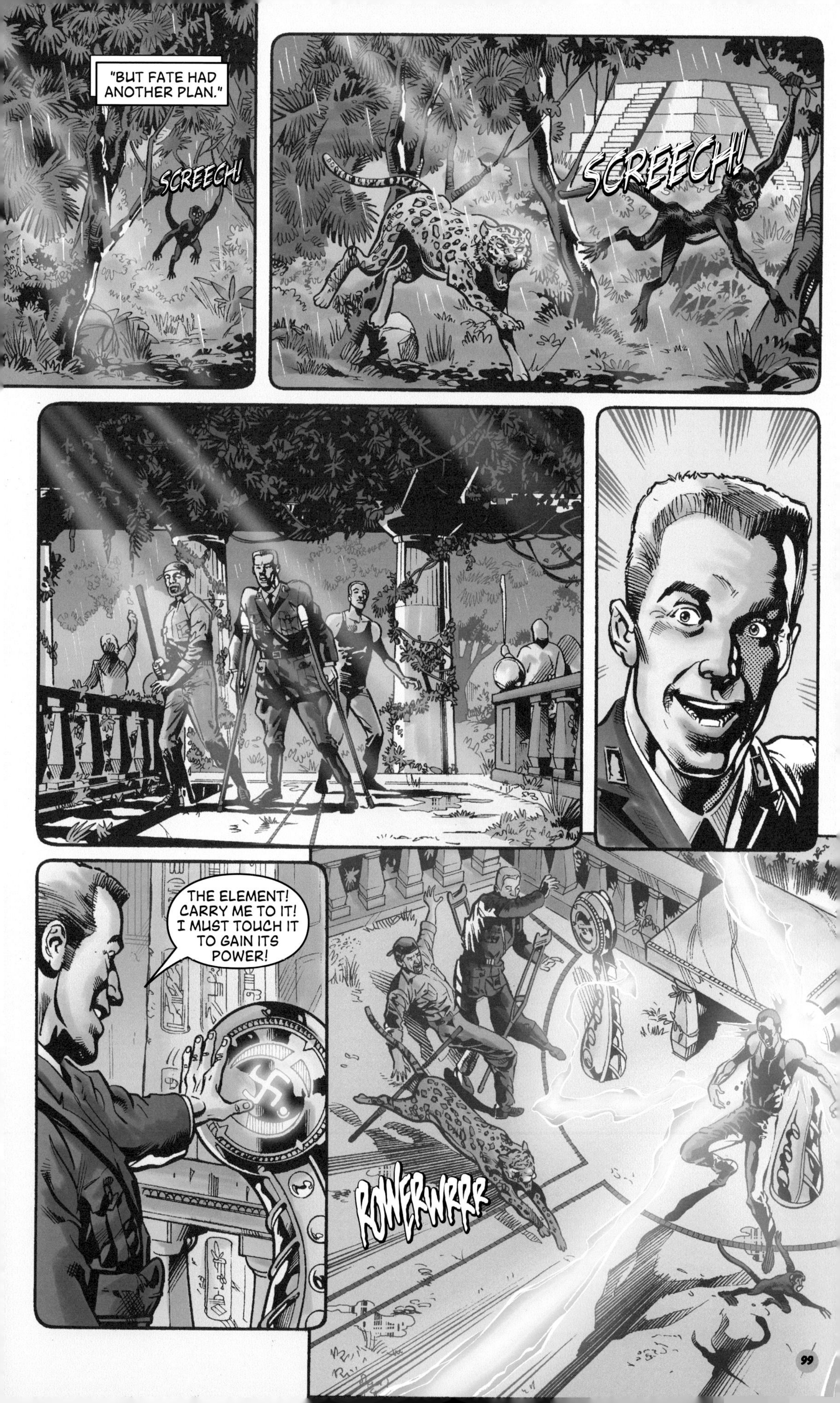
"BUT FATE HAD ANOTHER PLAN."
SCREECH!
SCREECH!
THE ELEMENT! CARRY ME TO IT! I MUST TOUCH IT TO GAIN ITS POWER!
ROWERWRRR

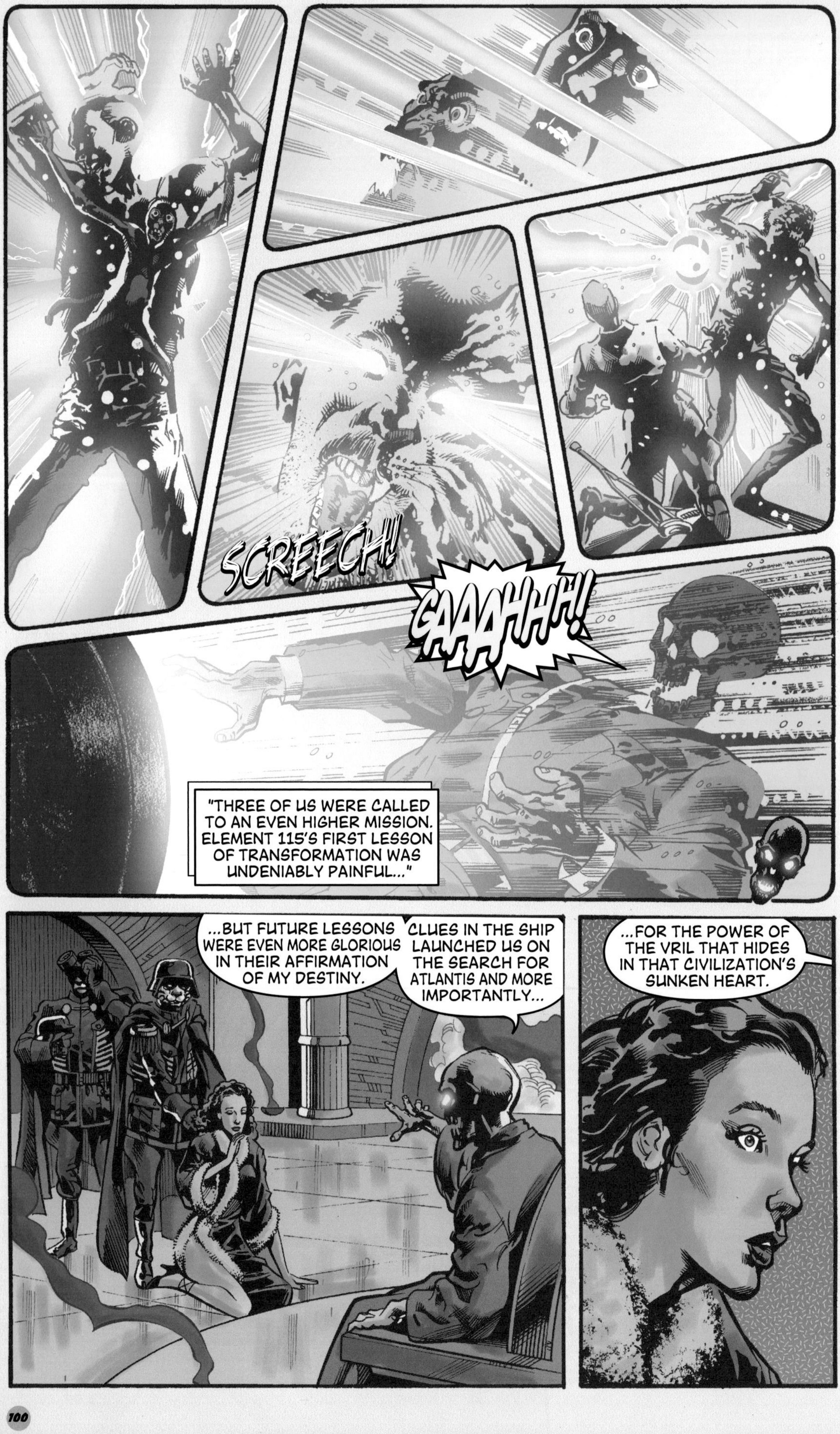
SCREECH!
GAAAHHH!
"THREE OF US WERE CALLED TO AN EVEN HIGHER MISSION. ELEMENT 115'S FIRST LESSON OF TRANSFORMATION WAS UNDENIABLY PAINFUL..."
...BUT FUTURE LESSONS WERE EVEN MORE GLORIOUS IN THEIR AFFIRMATION OF MY DESTINY.
CLUES IN THE SHIP LAUNCHED US ON THE SEARCH FOR ATLANTIS AND MORE IMPORTANTLY...
...FOR THE POWER OF THE VRIL THAT HIDES IN THAT CIVILIZATION'S SUNKEN HEART.

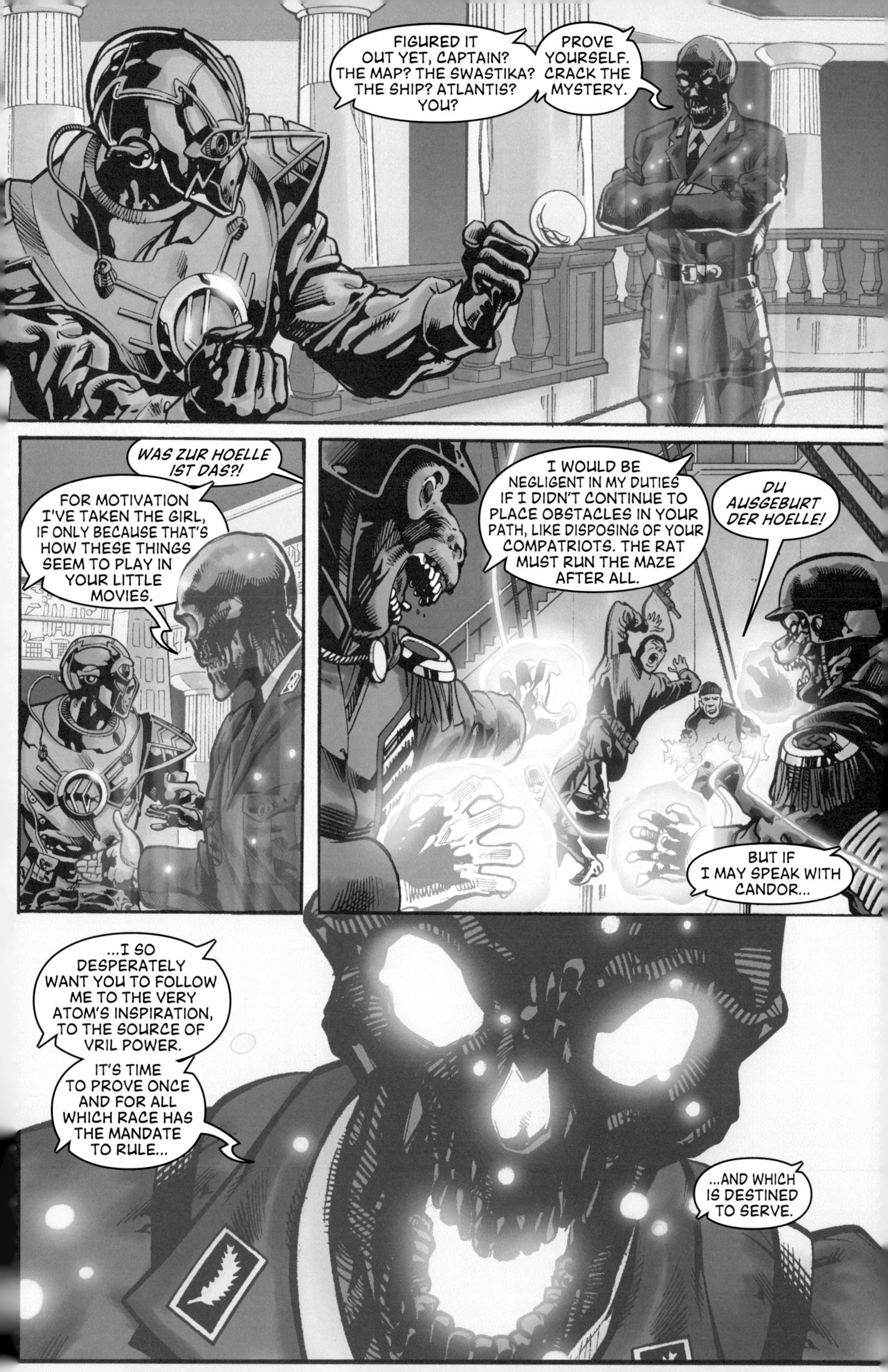
FIGURED IT OUT YET, CAPTAIN? THE MAP? THE SWASTIKA? THE SHIP? ATLANTIS? YOU?
PROVE YOURSELF. CRACK THE MYSTERY.
WAS ZUR HOELLE IST DAS?!
FOR MOTIVATION I'VE TAKEN THE GIRL, IF ONLY BECAUSE THAT'S HOW THESE THINGS SEEM TO PLAY IN YOUR LITTLE MOVIES.
I WOULD BE NEGLIGENT IN MY DUTIES IF I DIDN'T CONTINUE TO PLACE OBSTACLES IN YOUR PATH, LIKE DISPOSING OF YOUR COMPATRIOTS. THE RAT MUST RUN THE MAZE AFTER ALL.
DU AUSGEBURT DER HOELLE!
BUT IF I MAY SPEAK WITH CANDOR...
...I SO DESPERATELY WANT YOU TO FOLLOW ME TO THE VERY ATOM'S INSPIRATION, TO THE SOURCE OF VRIL POWER.
IT'S TIME TO PROVE ONCE AND FOR ALL WHICH RACE HAS THE MANDATE TO RULE...
...AND WHICH IS DESTINED TO SERVE.

NEXT: A STROLL DOWN MEMORY LANE REVEALS THE VILLAIN'S MOTIVE IN CHAPTER 4.5: IN THE SHADOW OF DIVINE LIGHT

Die fehlende Ausgabe

THE MISSING ISSUE

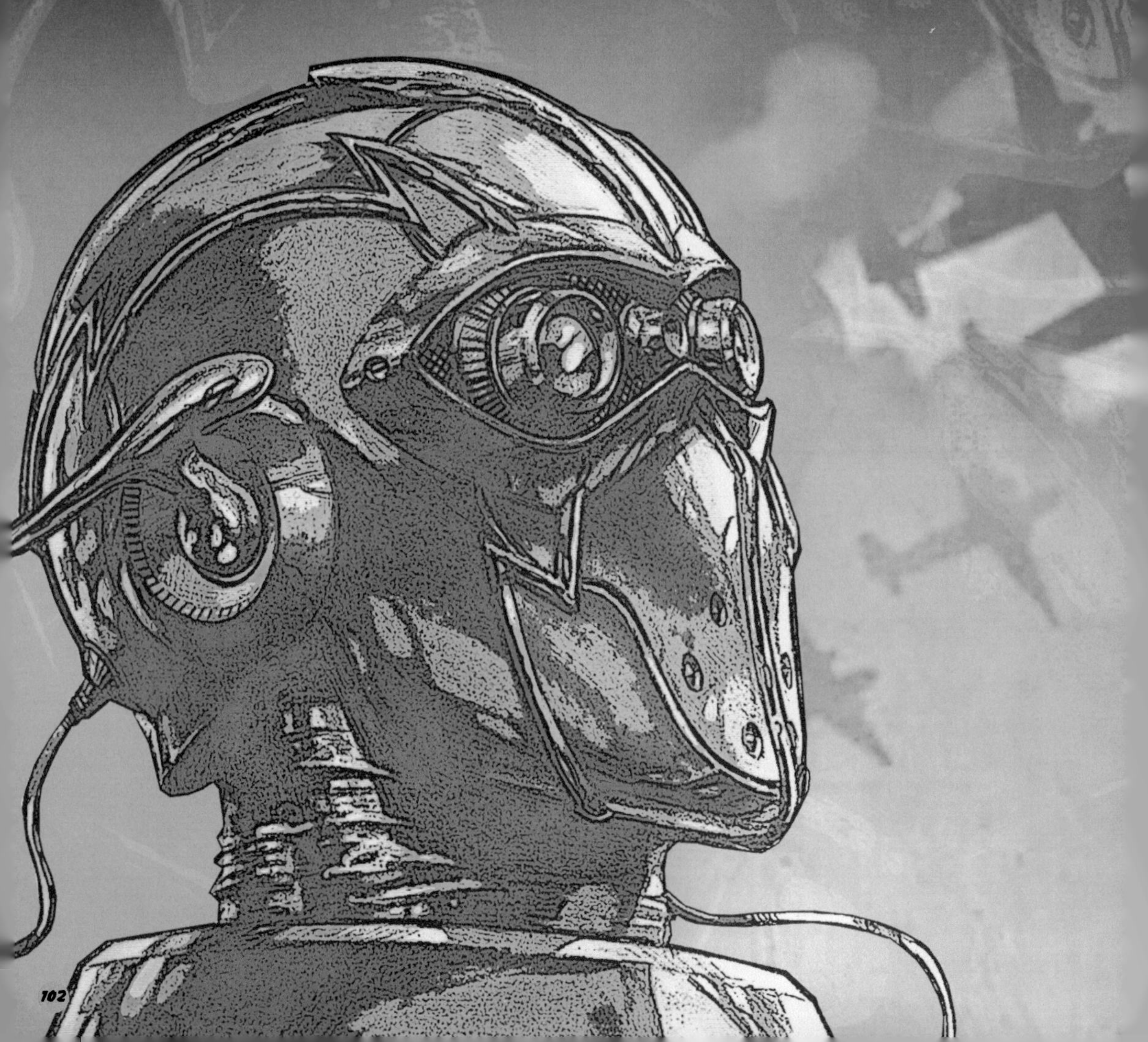

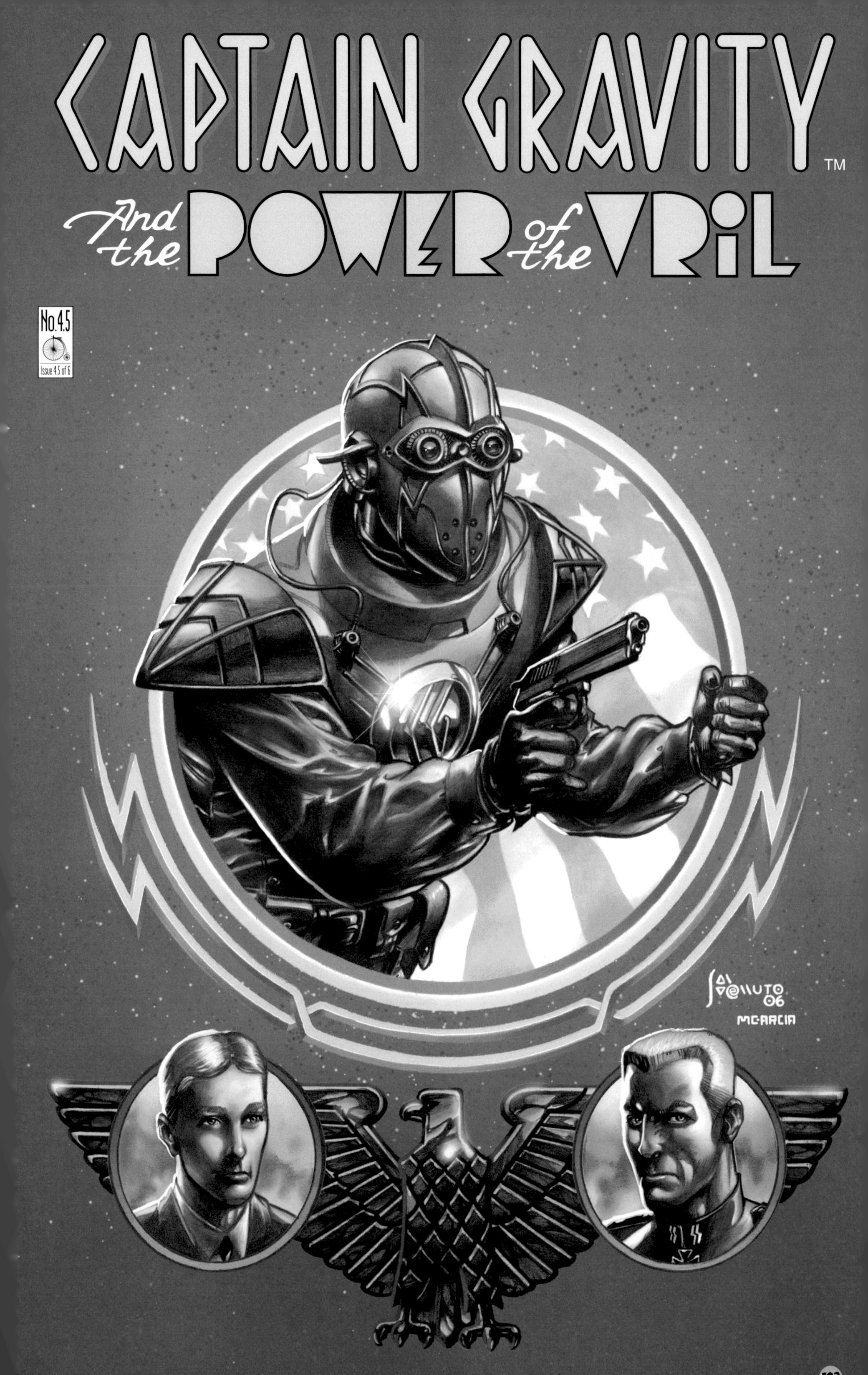
CAPTAIN GRAVITY™
And the POWER of the VRIL
No.4.5
Issue 4.5 of 6
SAL VELLUTO 06
MCGARCIA

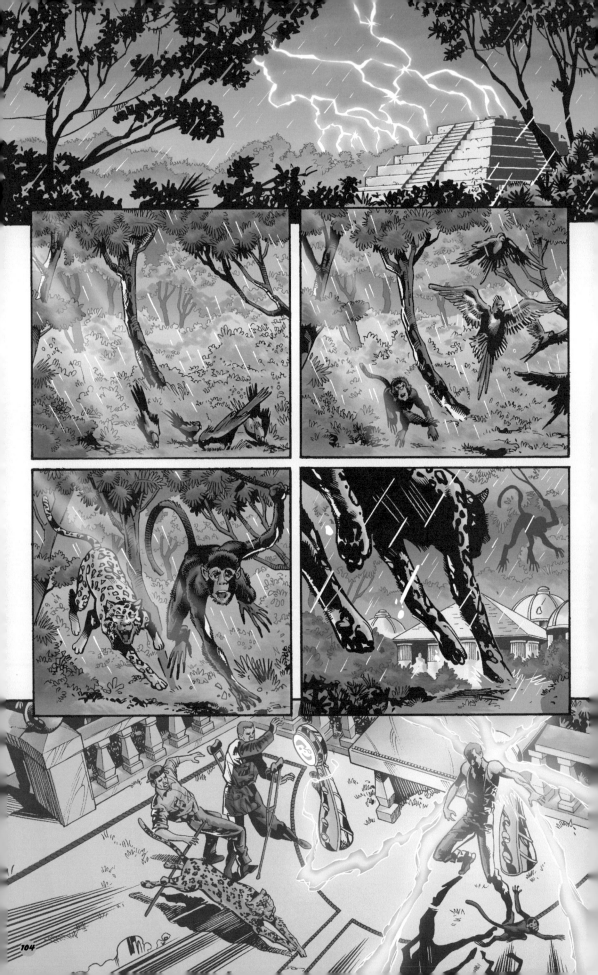

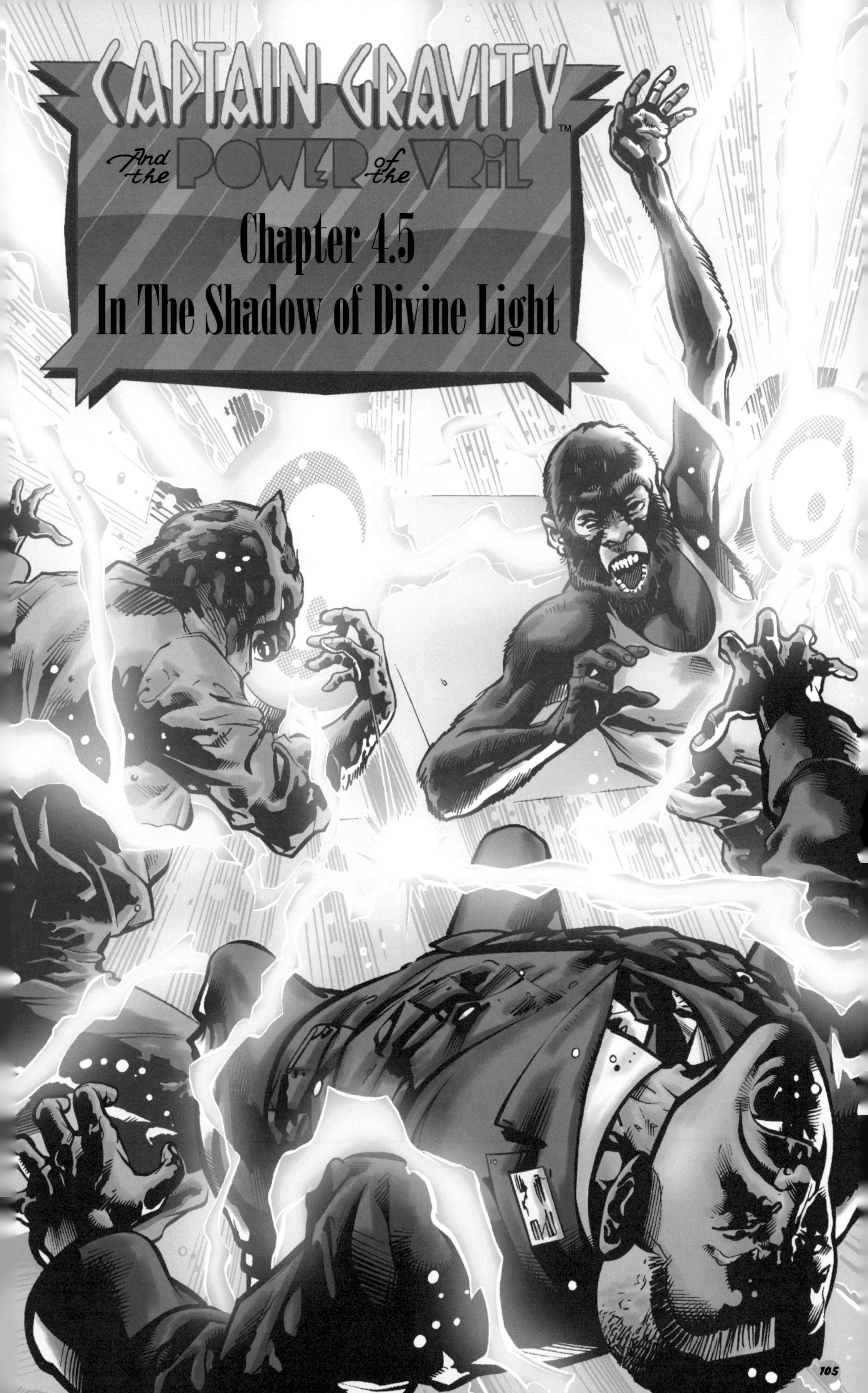

CAPTAIN GRAVITY™
And the POWER of the VRIL
Chapter 4.5
In The Shadow of Divine Light

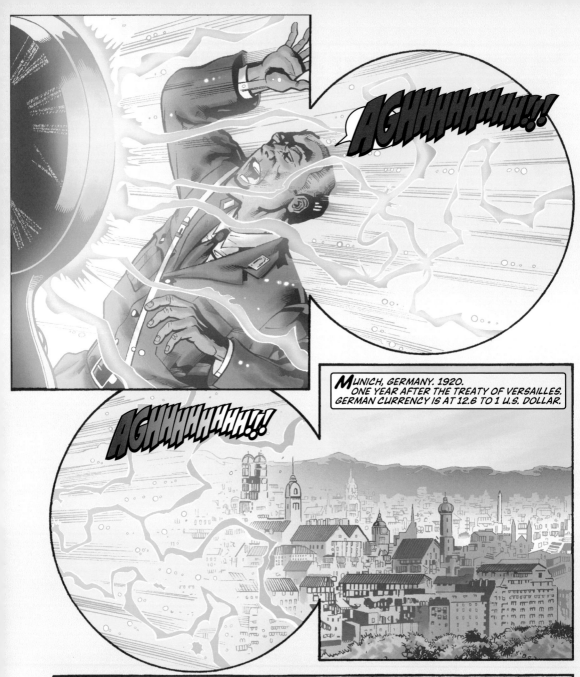

AGHHHHHHHH!!

AGHHHHHHHH!!

MUNICH, GERMANY. 1920.
ONE YEAR AFTER THE TREATY OF VERSAILLES.
GERMAN CURRENCY IS AT 12.6 TO 1 U.S. DOLLAR.

UNIVERSITY OF MUNICH.

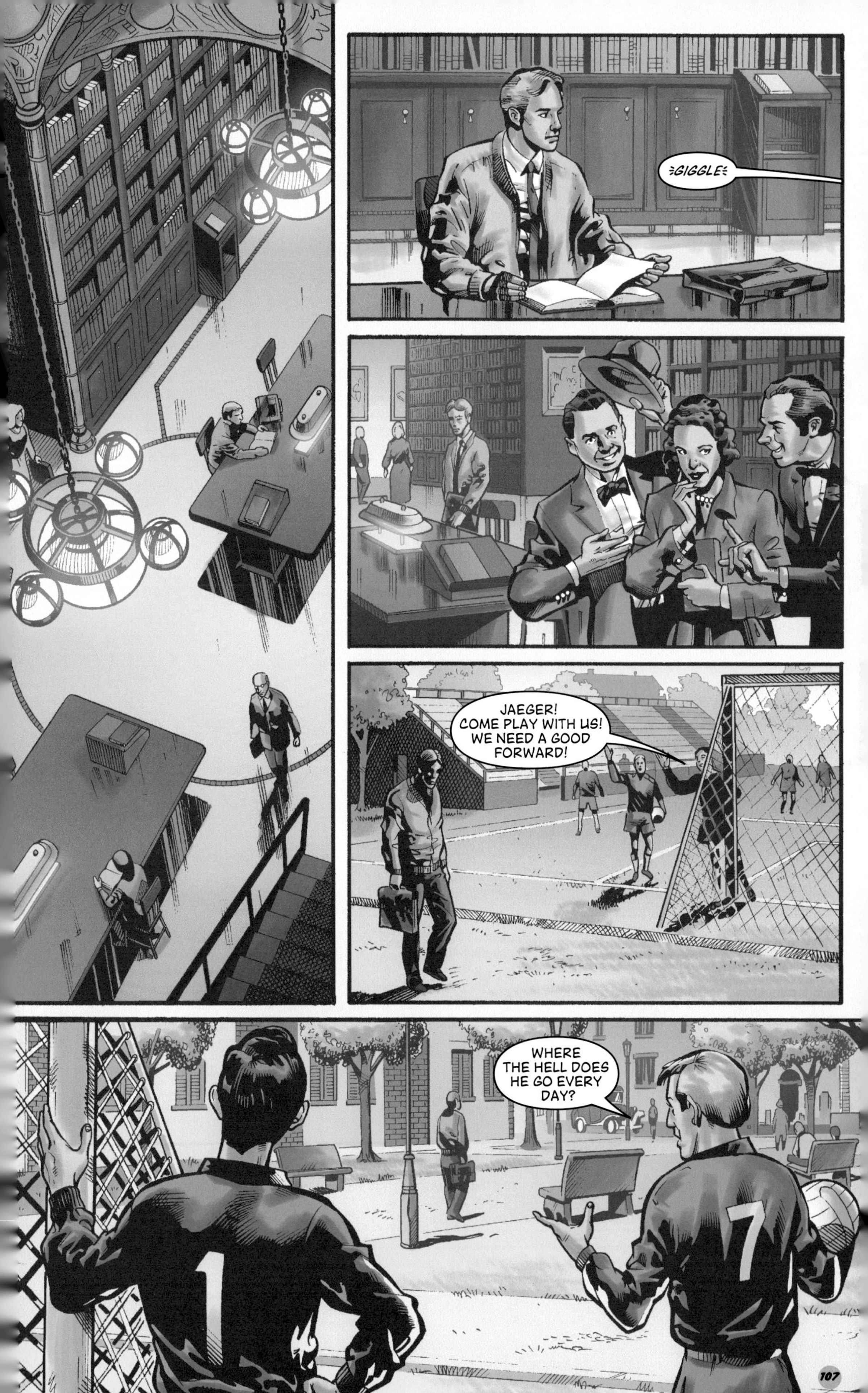
GIGGLE
JAEGER! COME PLAY WITH US! WE NEED A GOOD FORWARD!
WHERE THE HELL DOES HE GO EVERY DAY?

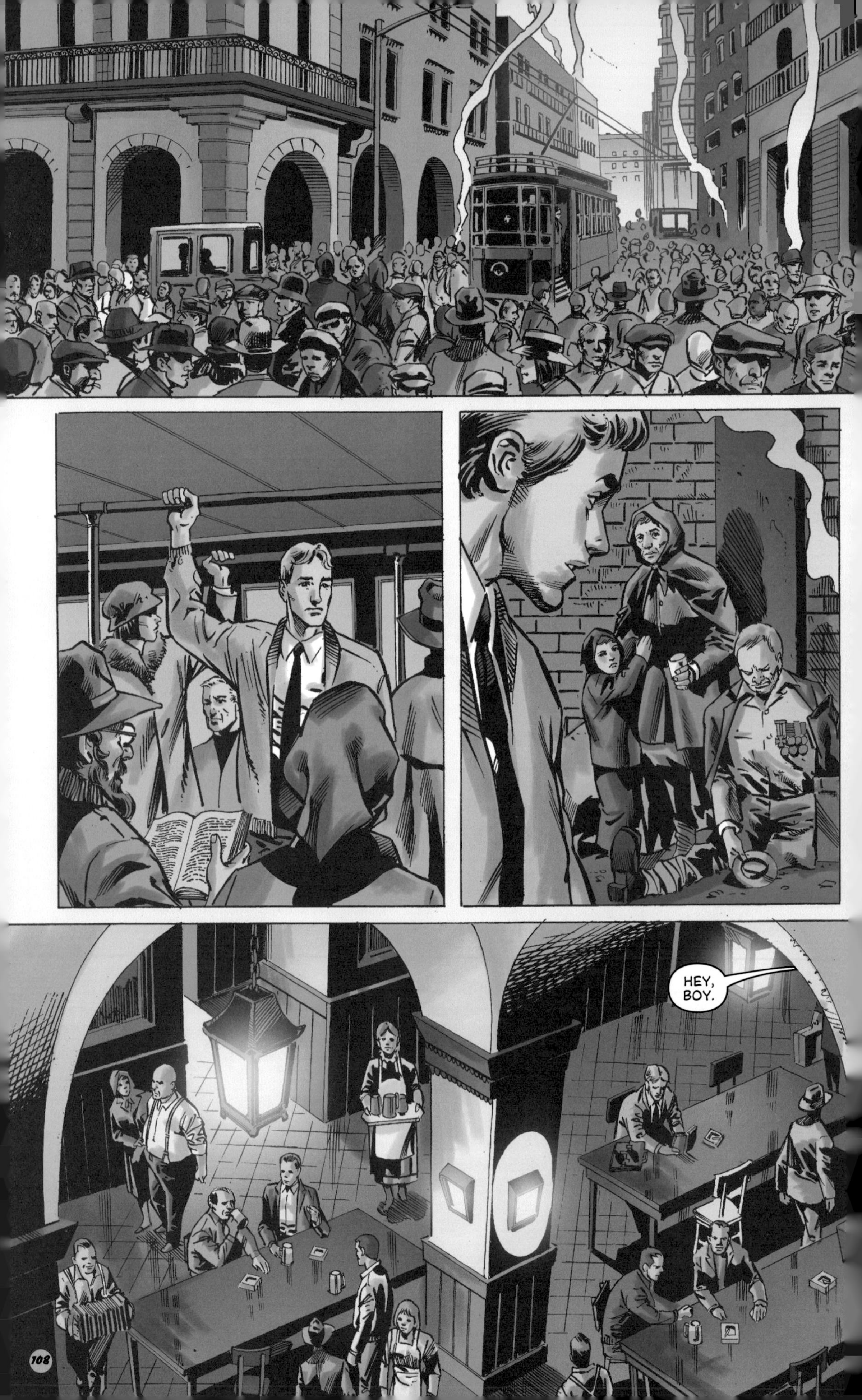
HEY, BOY.

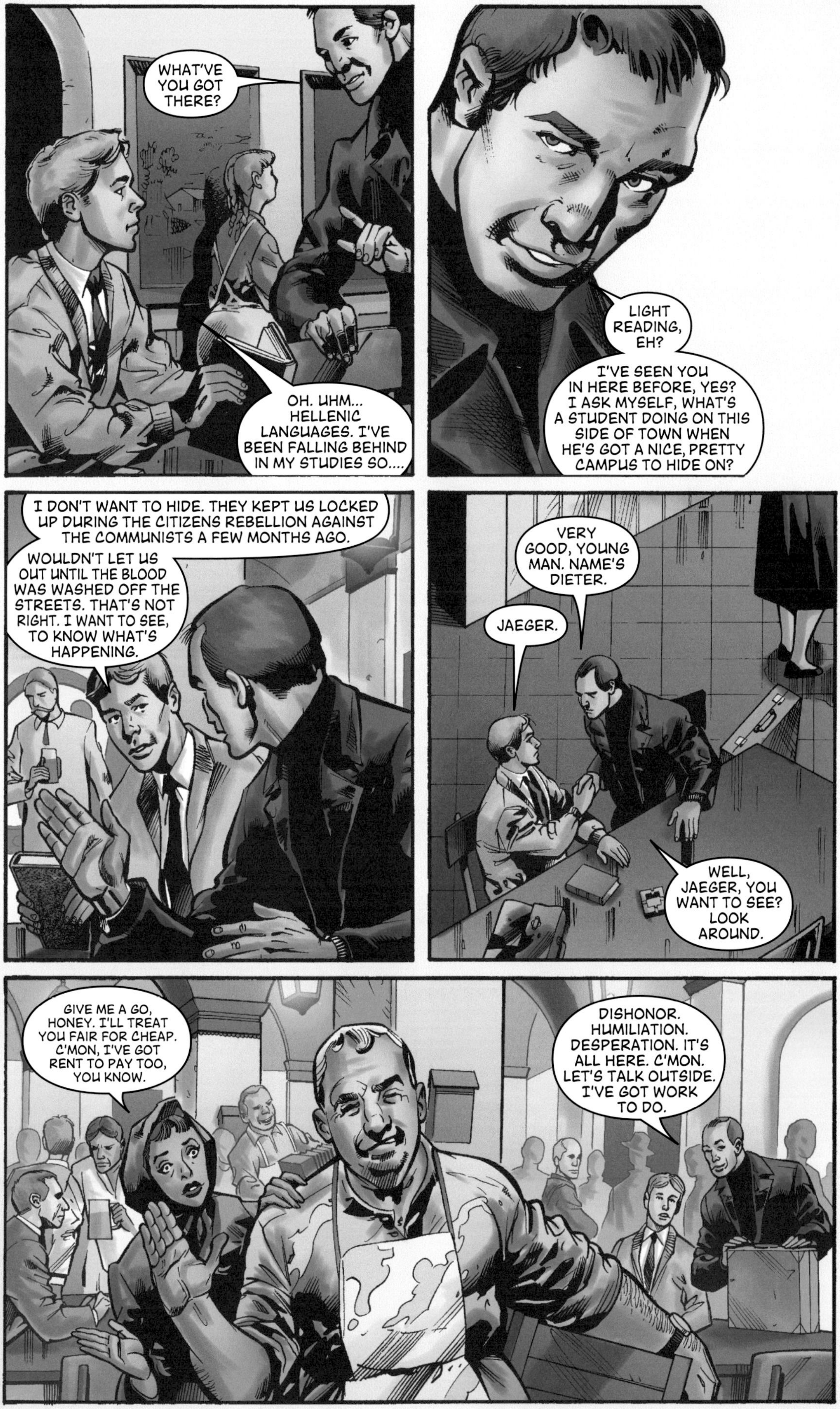
WHAT'VE YOU GOT THERE?
OH. UHM... HELLENIC LANGUAGES. I'VE BEEN FALLING BEHIND IN MY STUDIES SO....
LIGHT READING, EH?
I'VE SEEN YOU IN HERE BEFORE, YES? I ASK MYSELF, WHAT'S A STUDENT DOING ON THIS SIDE OF TOWN WHEN HE'S GOT A NICE, PRETTY CAMPUS TO HIDE ON?
I DON'T WANT TO HIDE. THEY KEPT US LOCKED UP DURING THE CITIZENS REBELLION AGAINST THE COMMUNISTS A FEW MONTHS AGO.
WOULDN'T LET US OUT UNTIL THE BLOOD WAS WASHED OFF THE STREETS. THAT'S NOT RIGHT. I WANT TO SEE, TO KNOW WHAT'S HAPPENING.
VERY GOOD, YOUNG MAN. NAME'S DIETER.
JAEGER.
WELL, JAEGER, YOU WANT TO SEE? LOOK AROUND.
GIVE ME A GO, HONEY. I'LL TREAT YOU FAIR FOR CHEAP. C'MON, I'VE GOT RENT TO PAY TOO, YOU KNOW.
DISHONOR. HUMILIATION. DESPERATION. IT'S ALL HERE. C'MON. LET'S TALK OUTSIDE. I'VE GOT WORK TO DO.

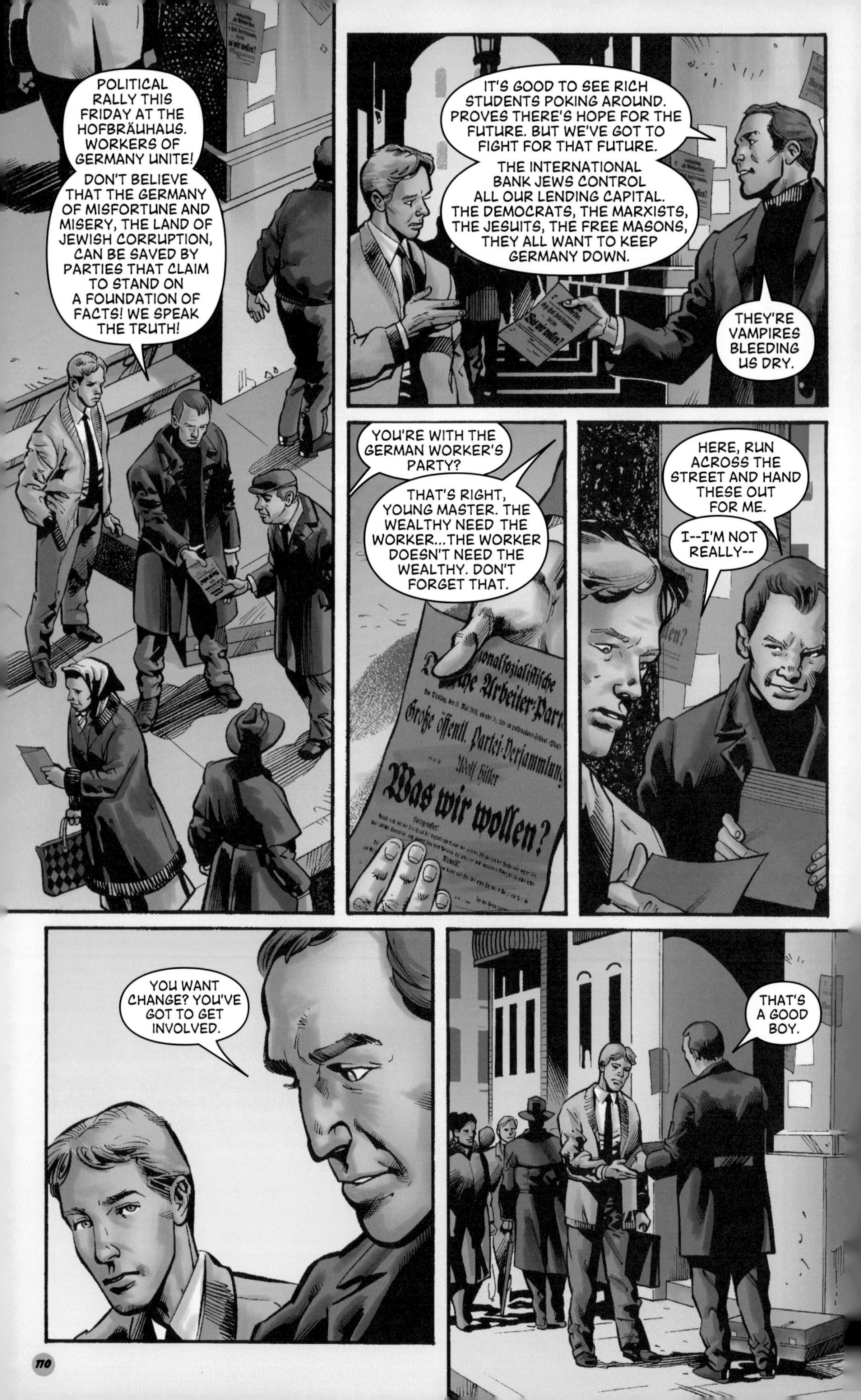
POLITICAL RALLY THIS FRIDAY AT THE HOFBRÄUHAUS. WORKERS OF GERMANY UNITE!
DON'T BELIEVE THAT THE GERMANY OF MISFORTUNE AND MISERY, THE LAND OF JEWISH CORRUPTION, CAN BE SAVED BY PARTIES THAT CLAIM TO STAND ON A FOUNDATION OF FACTS! WE SPEAK THE TRUTH!
IT'S GOOD TO SEE RICH STUDENTS POKING AROUND. PROVES THERE'S HOPE FOR THE FUTURE. BUT WE'VE GOT TO FIGHT FOR THAT FUTURE.
THE INTERNATIONAL BANK JEWS CONTROL ALL OUR LENDING CAPITAL. THE DEMOCRATS, THE MARXISTS, THE JESUITS, THE FREE MASONS, THEY ALL WANT TO KEEP GERMANY DOWN.
THEY'RE VAMPIRES BLEEDING US DRY.
YOU'RE WITH THE GERMAN WORKER'S PARTY?
THAT'S RIGHT, YOUNG MASTER. THE WEALTHY NEED THE WORKER...THE WORKER DOESN'T NEED THE WEALTHY. DON'T FORGET THAT.
Was wir wollen?
HERE, RUN ACROSS THE STREET AND HAND THESE OUT FOR ME.
I--I'M NOT REALLY--
YOU WANT CHANGE? YOU'VE GOT TO GET INVOLVED.
THAT'S A GOOD BOY.

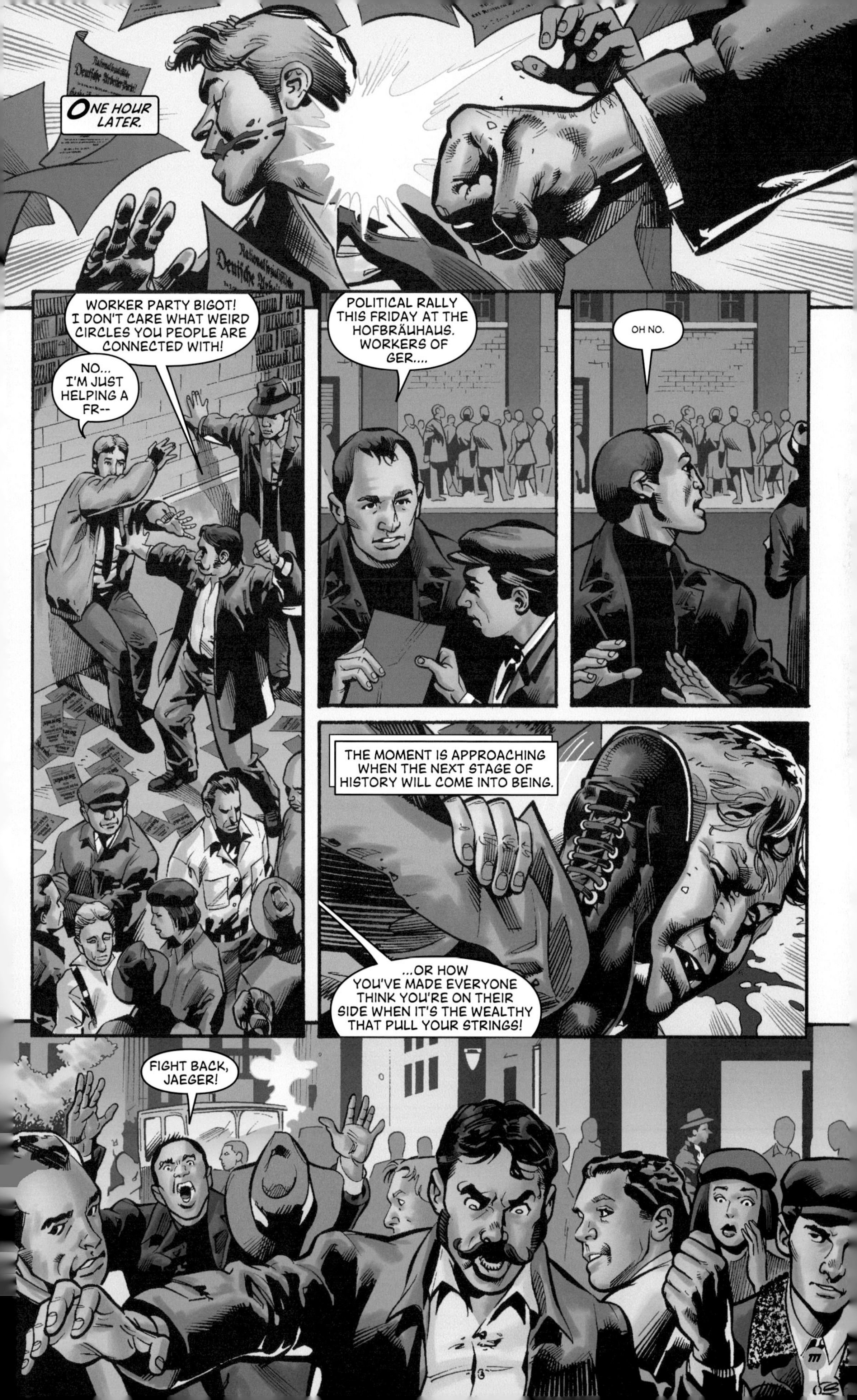
ONE HOUR LATER.
WORKER PARTY BIGOT! I DON'T CARE WHAT WEIRD CIRCLES YOU PEOPLE ARE CONNECTED WITH!
NO... I'M JUST HELPING A FR--
POLITICAL RALLY THIS FRIDAY AT THE HOFBRÄUHAUS. WORKERS OF GER....
OH NO.
THE MOMENT IS APPROACHING WHEN THE NEXT STAGE OF HISTORY WILL COME INTO BEING.
...OR HOW YOU'VE MADE EVERYONE THINK YOU'RE ON THEIR SIDE WHEN IT'S THE WEALTHY THAT PULL YOUR STRINGS!
FIGHT BACK, JAEGER!

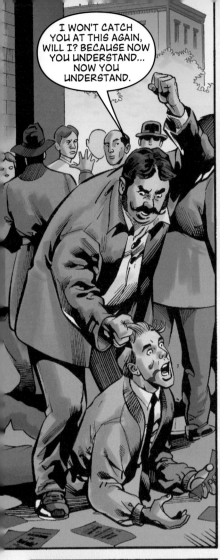

I WON'T CATCH YOU AT THIS AGAIN, WILL I? BECAUSE NOW YOU UNDERSTAND... NOW YOU UNDERSTAND.

COMMIE BASTARD!

UHH!

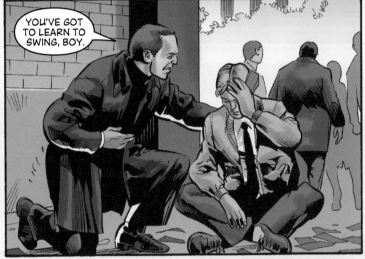

YOU'VE GOT TO LEARN TO SWING, BOY.

DON'T WORRY. IT'S JUST POLITICS. SOMETIMES THEY GET THE BETTER OF US. SOMETIMES WE GET THE BETTER OF THEM.

LET'S CALL IT A NIGHT. COME WITH ME TO THE PARTY HEADQUARTERS. YOU'LL GET A HERO'S WELCOME.

NO. I-I HAVE TO GO HOME.

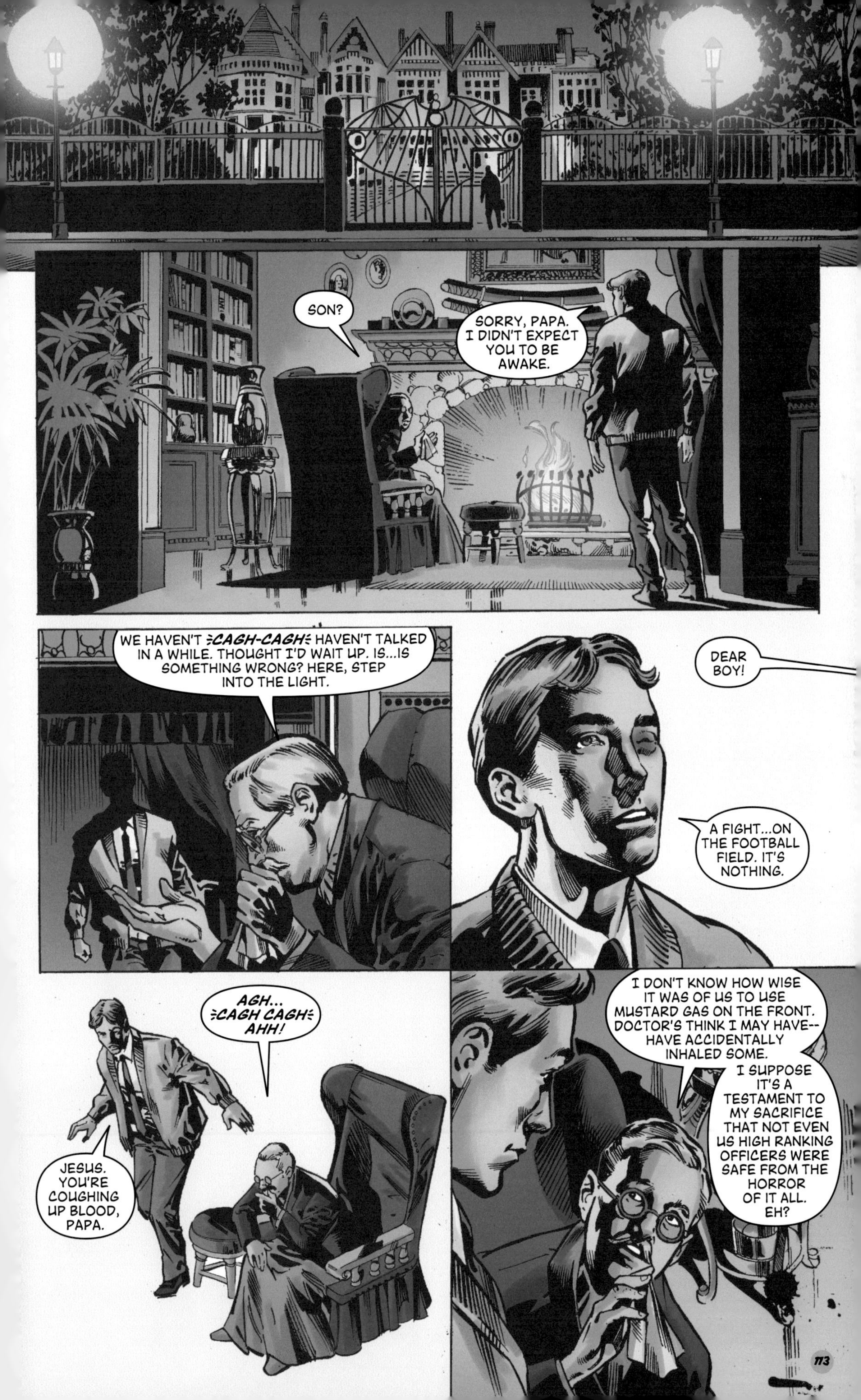
SON?
SORRY, PAPA. I DIDN'T EXPECT YOU TO BE AWAKE.
WE HAVEN'T ≈CAGH-CAGH≈ HAVEN'T TALKED IN A WHILE. THOUGHT I'D WAIT UP. IS...IS SOMETHING WRONG? HERE, STEP INTO THE LIGHT.
DEAR BOY!
A FIGHT...ON THE FOOTBALL FIELD. IT'S NOTHING.
AGH... ≈CAGH CAGH≈ AHH!
JESUS. YOU'RE COUGHING UP BLOOD, PAPA.
I DON'T KNOW HOW WISE IT WAS OF US TO USE MUSTARD GAS ON THE FRONT. DOCTOR'S THINK I MAY HAVE-- HAVE ACCIDENTALLY INHALED SOME.
I SUPPOSE IT'S A TESTAMENT TO MY SACRIFICE THAT NOT EVEN US HIGH RANKING OFFICERS WERE SAFE FROM THE HORROR OF IT ALL. EH?

I'VE BEEN THINKING. MAYBE I SHOULD DROP UNIVERSITY. GET MORE INVOLVED IN THE POLITICS OF THE HERE AND NOW. THESE JEWS AND--

FIRST OF ALL, AVOID THE TANGLE OF POLITICS. THERE ARE SNAKES IN THAT GRASS. EDUCATION IS POWER... NOT OFFICES AND STATIONS.

AND SECONDLY, I KNOW THIS RHETORIC OF HATE YOU'RE ABOUT TO INDULGE IN. I HEAR IT EVERYWHERE THESE DAYS.
BUT YOU COME FROM A NOBLE LINE OF GERMAN SOLDIERS. WE'RE TOLERANT, INTELLECTUAL. IT'S OUR HONOR ÷CA-CAGH÷ HONOR TO SERVE THE GOVERNMENT.

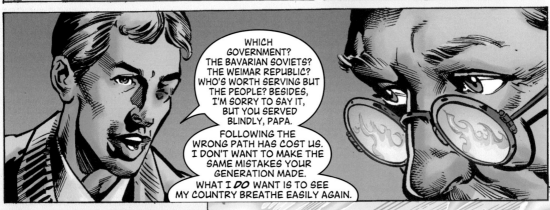

WHICH GOVERNMENT? THE BAVARIAN SOVIETS? THE WEIMAR REPUBLIC? WHO'S WORTH SERVING BUT THE PEOPLE? BESIDES, I'M SORRY TO SAY IT, BUT YOU SERVED BLINDLY, PAPA.
FOLLOWING THE WRONG PATH HAS COST US. I DON'T WANT TO MAKE THE SAME MISTAKES YOUR GENERATION MADE.
WHAT I DO WANT IS TO SEE MY COUNTRY BREATHE EASILY AGAIN.

IT'S LATE. WE'LL DISCUSS THIS MORE WHEN YOU COME HOME AT A REASONABLE HOUR TOMORROW. BUT HERE'S A SECRET, SON...

"...NO NATION EVER BREATHES EASY."

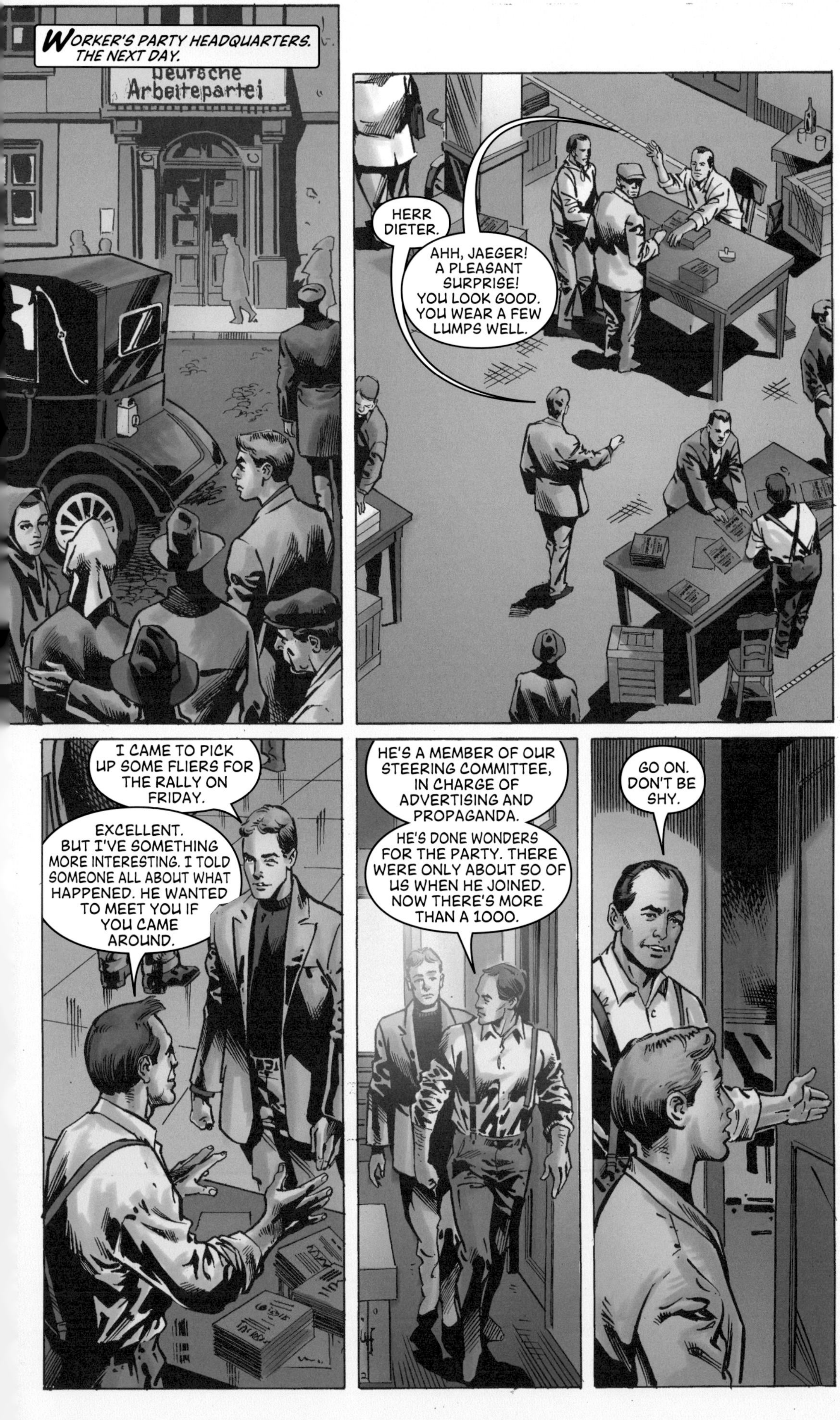
WORKER'S PARTY HEADQUARTERS. THE NEXT DAY.
Deutsche Arbeitepartei
HERR DIETER.
AHH, JAEGER! A PLEASANT SURPRISE! YOU LOOK GOOD. YOU WEAR A FEW LUMPS WELL.
I CAME TO PICK UP SOME FLIERS FOR THE RALLY ON FRIDAY.
EXCELLENT. BUT I'VE SOMETHING MORE INTERESTING. I TOLD SOMEONE ALL ABOUT WHAT HAPPENED. HE WANTED TO MEET YOU IF YOU CAME AROUND.
HE'S A MEMBER OF OUR STEERING COMMITTEE, IN CHARGE OF ADVERTISING AND PROPAGANDA.
HE'S DONE WONDERS FOR THE PARTY. THERE WERE ONLY ABOUT 50 OF US WHEN HE JOINED. NOW THERE'S MORE THAN A 1000.
GO ON. DON'T BE SHY.

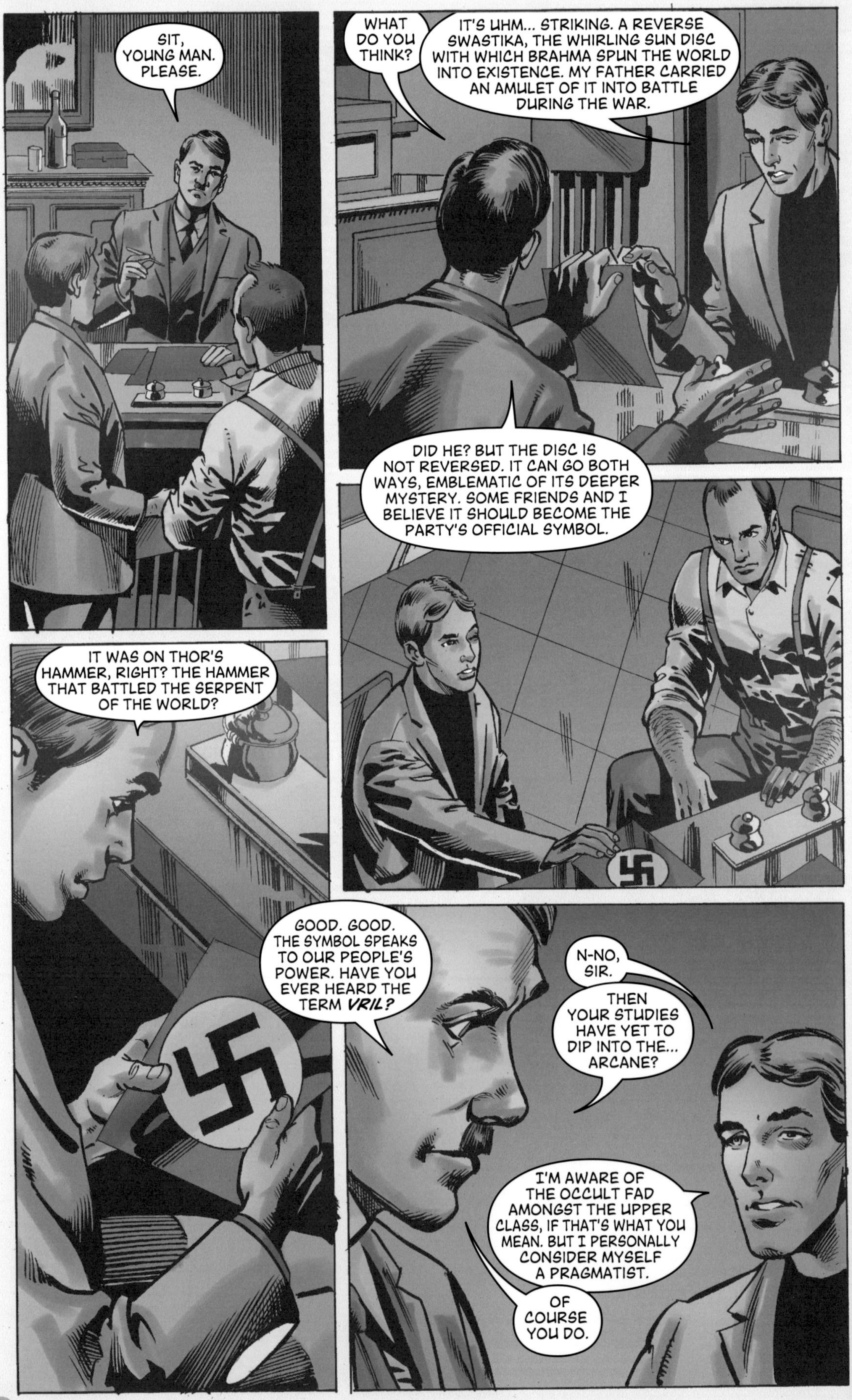
SIT, YOUNG MAN. PLEASE.
WHAT DO YOU THINK?
IT'S UHM... STRIKING. A REVERSE SWASTIKA, THE WHIRLING SUN DISC WITH WHICH BRAHMA SPUN THE WORLD INTO EXISTENCE. MY FATHER CARRIED AN AMULET OF IT INTO BATTLE DURING THE WAR.
DID HE? BUT THE DISC IS NOT REVERSED. IT CAN GO BOTH WAYS, EMBLEMATIC OF ITS DEEPER MYSTERY. SOME FRIENDS AND I BELIEVE IT SHOULD BECOME THE PARTY'S OFFICIAL SYMBOL.
IT WAS ON THOR'S HAMMER, RIGHT? THE HAMMER THAT BATTLED THE SERPENT OF THE WORLD?
GOOD. GOOD. THE SYMBOL SPEAKS TO OUR PEOPLE'S POWER. HAVE YOU EVER HEARD THE TERM *VRIL?*
N-NO, SIR.
THEN YOUR STUDIES HAVE YET TO DIP INTO THE... ARCANE?
I'M AWARE OF THE OCCULT FAD AMONGST THE UPPER CLASS, IF THAT'S WHAT YOU MEAN. BUT I PERSONALLY CONSIDER MYSELF A PRAGMATIST.
OF COURSE YOU DO.

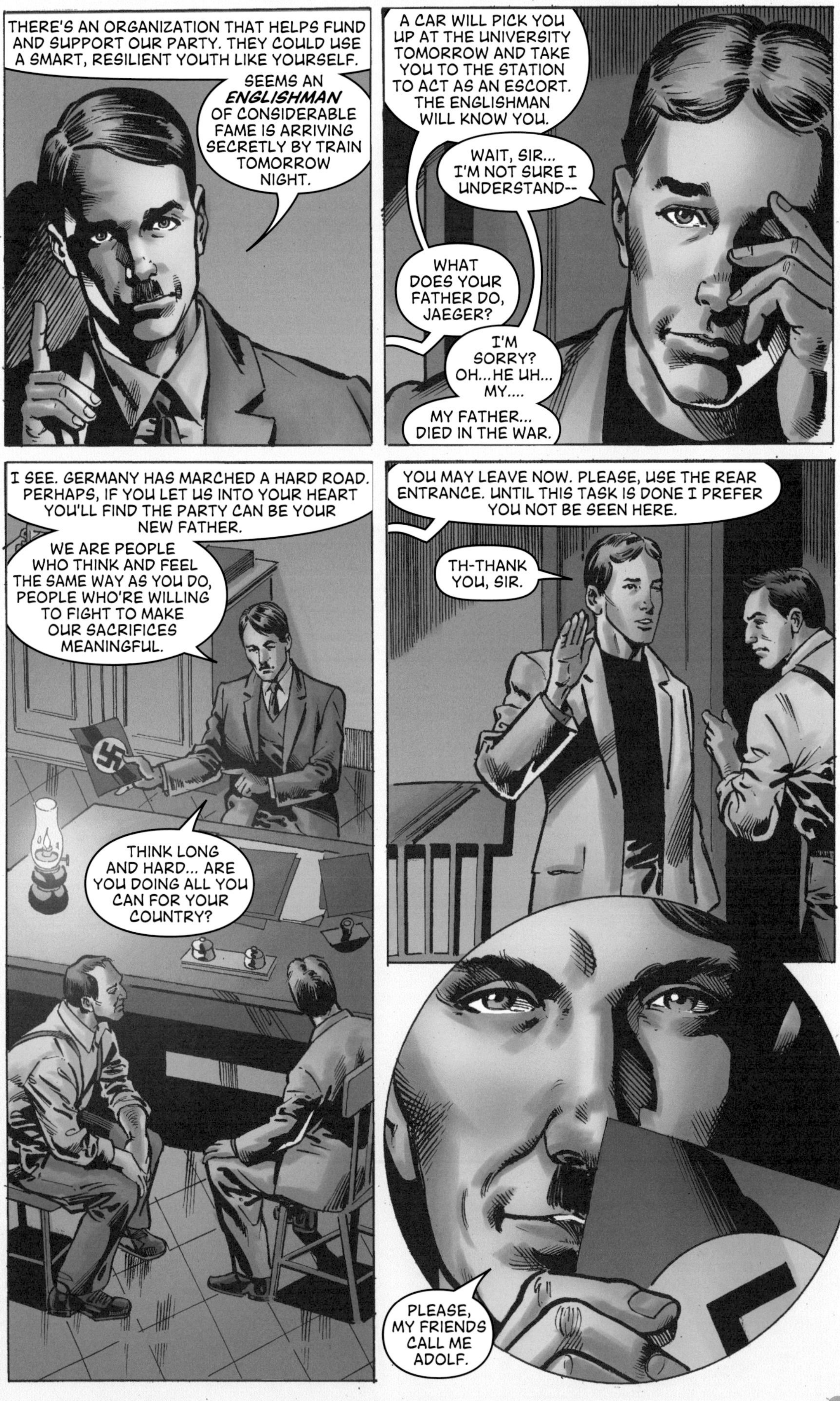

THERE'S AN ORGANIZATION THAT HELPS FUND AND SUPPORT OUR PARTY. THEY COULD USE A SMART, RESILIENT YOUTH LIKE YOURSELF.
SEEMS AN ENGLISHMAN OF CONSIDERABLE FAME IS ARRIVING SECRETLY BY TRAIN TOMORROW NIGHT.
A CAR WILL PICK YOU UP AT THE UNIVERSITY TOMORROW AND TAKE YOU TO THE STATION TO ACT AS AN ESCORT. THE ENGLISHMAN WILL KNOW YOU.
WAIT, SIR... I'M NOT SURE I UNDERSTAND--
WHAT DOES YOUR FATHER DO, JAEGER?
I'M SORRY? OH...HE UH... MY....
MY FATHER... DIED IN THE WAR.
I SEE. GERMANY HAS MARCHED A HARD ROAD. PERHAPS, IF YOU LET US INTO YOUR HEART YOU'LL FIND THE PARTY CAN BE YOUR NEW FATHER.
WE ARE PEOPLE WHO THINK AND FEEL THE SAME WAY AS YOU DO, PEOPLE WHO'RE WILLING TO FIGHT TO MAKE OUR SACRIFICES MEANINGFUL.
THINK LONG AND HARD... ARE YOU DOING ALL YOU CAN FOR YOUR COUNTRY?
YOU MAY LEAVE NOW. PLEASE, USE THE REAR ENTRANCE. UNTIL THIS TASK IS DONE I PREFER YOU NOT BE SEEN HERE.
TH-THANK YOU, SIR.
PLEASE, MY FRIENDS CALL ME ADOLF.

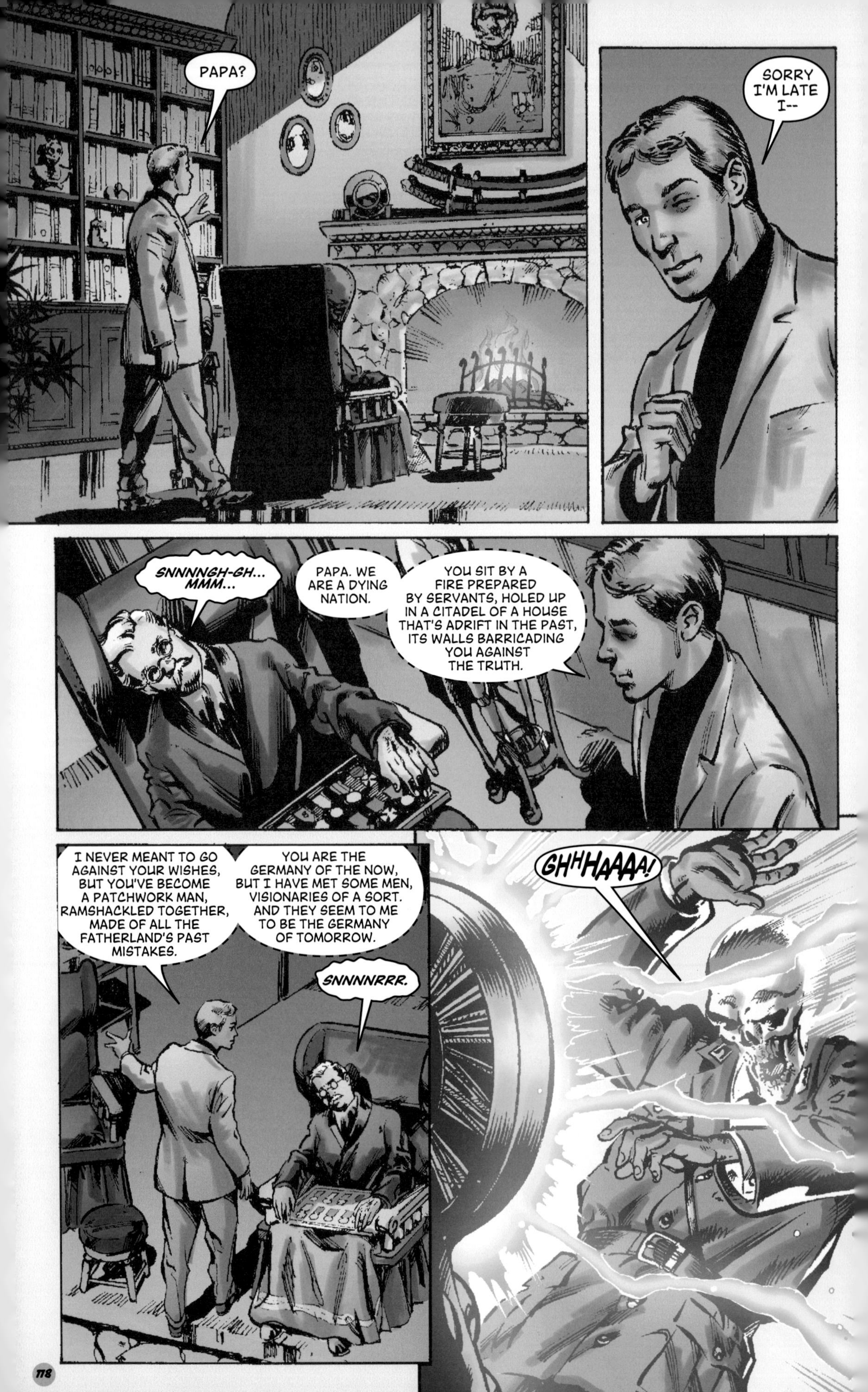
PAPA?
SORRY I'M LATE I--
SNNNNGH-GH... MMM...
PAPA. WE ARE A DYING NATION.
YOU SIT BY A FIRE PREPARED BY SERVANTS, HOLED UP IN A CITADEL OF A HOUSE THAT'S ADRIFT IN THE PAST, ITS WALLS BARRICADING YOU AGAINST THE TRUTH.
I NEVER MEANT TO GO AGAINST YOUR WISHES, BUT YOU'VE BECOME A PATCHWORK MAN, RAMSHACKLED TOGETHER, MADE OF ALL THE FATHERLAND'S PAST MISTAKES.
YOU ARE THE GERMANY OF THE NOW, BUT I HAVE MET SOME MEN, VISIONARIES OF A SORT. AND THEY SEEM TO ME TO BE THE GERMANY OF TOMORROW.
SNNNNRRR.
GHHHAAAA!

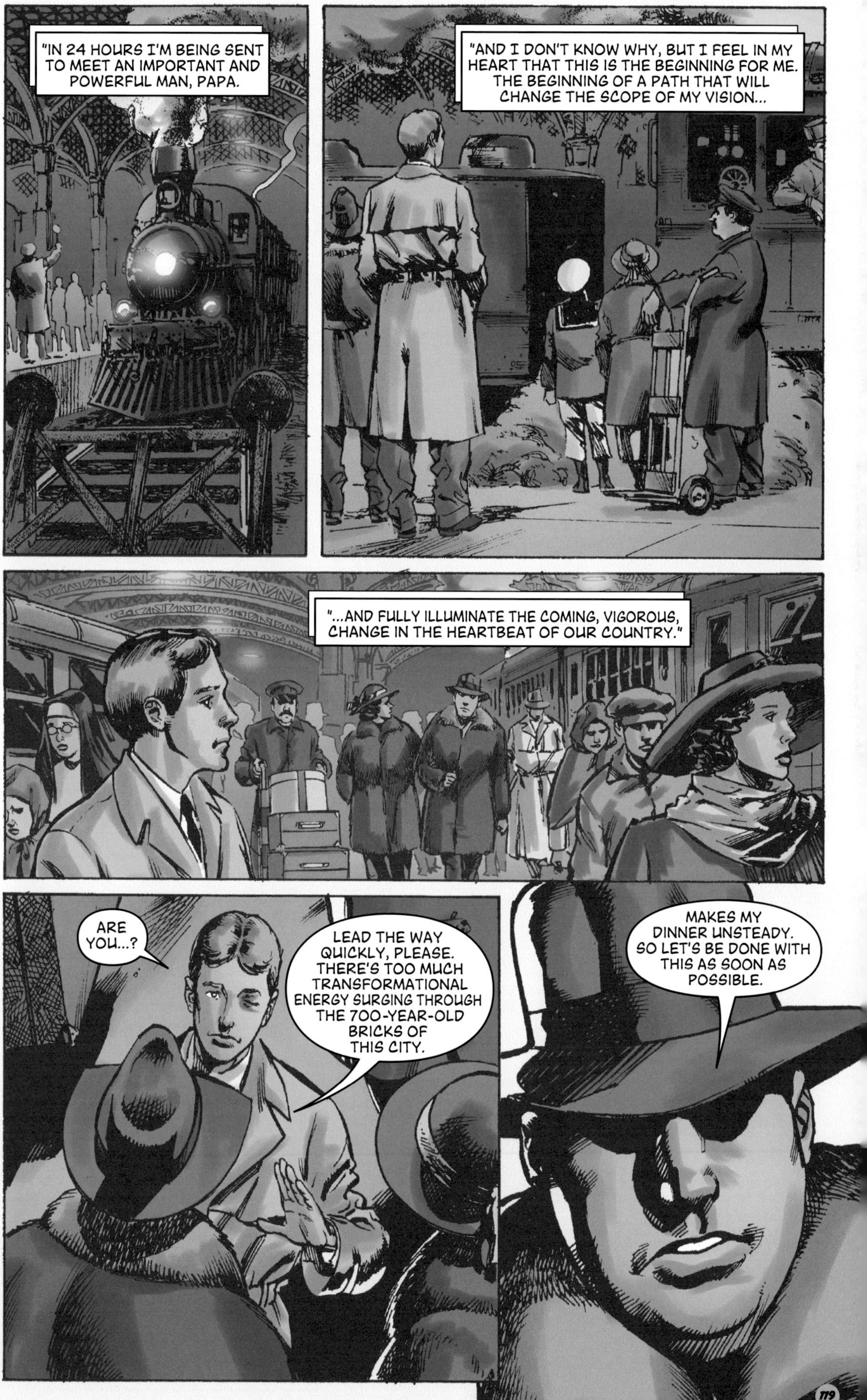
"IN 24 HOURS I'M BEING SENT TO MEET AN IMPORTANT AND POWERFUL MAN, PAPA.
"AND I DON'T KNOW WHY, BUT I FEEL IN MY HEART THAT THIS IS THE BEGINNING FOR ME. THE BEGINNING OF A PATH THAT WILL CHANGE THE SCOPE OF MY VISION...
"...AND FULLY ILLUMINATE THE COMING, VIGOROUS, CHANGE IN THE HEARTBEAT OF OUR COUNTRY."
ARE YOU...?
LEAD THE WAY QUICKLY, PLEASE. THERE'S TOO MUCH TRANSFORMATIONAL ENERGY SURGING THROUGH THE 700-YEAR-OLD BRICKS OF THIS CITY.
MAKES MY DINNER UNSTEADY. SO LET'S BE DONE WITH THIS AS SOON AS POSSIBLE.

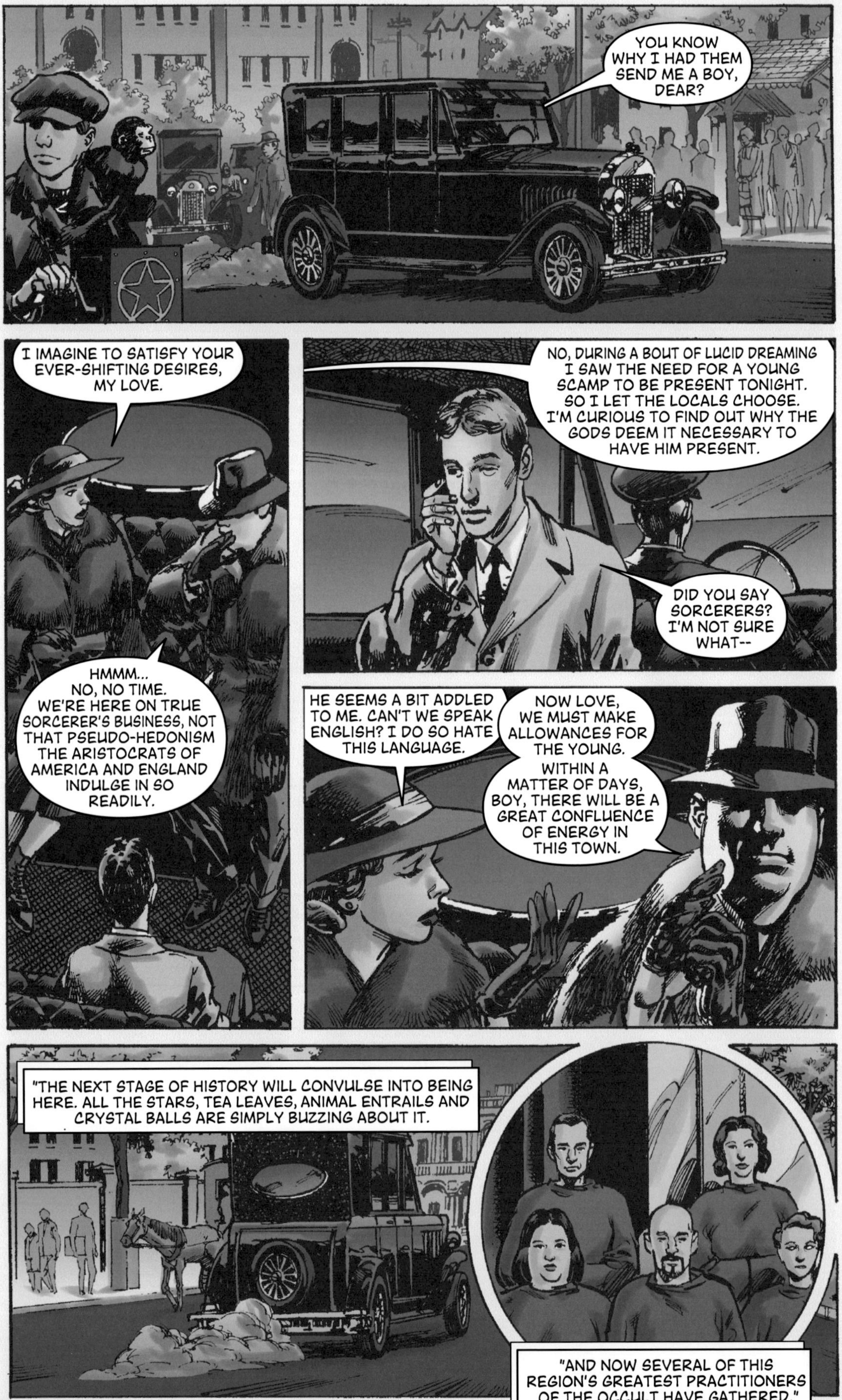
YOU KNOW WHY I HAD THEM SEND ME A BOY, DEAR?
I IMAGINE TO SATISFY YOUR EVER-SHIFTING DESIRES, MY LOVE.
NO, DURING A BOUT OF LUCID DREAMING I SAW THE NEED FOR A YOUNG SCAMP TO BE PRESENT TONIGHT. SO I LET THE LOCALS CHOOSE. I'M CURIOUS TO FIND OUT WHY THE GODS DEEM IT NECESSARY TO HAVE HIM PRESENT.
DID YOU SAY SORCERERS? I'M NOT SURE WHAT--
HMMM... NO, NO TIME. WE'RE HERE ON TRUE SORCERER'S BUSINESS, NOT THAT PSEUDO-HEDONISM THE ARISTOCRATS OF AMERICA AND ENGLAND INDULGE IN SO READILY.
HE SEEMS A BIT ADDLED TO ME. CAN'T WE SPEAK ENGLISH? I DO SO HATE THIS LANGUAGE.
NOW LOVE, WE MUST MAKE ALLOWANCES FOR THE YOUNG.
WITHIN A MATTER OF DAYS, BOY, THERE WILL BE A GREAT CONFLUENCE OF ENERGY IN THIS TOWN.
"THE NEXT STAGE OF HISTORY WILL CONVULSE INTO BEING HERE. ALL THE STARS, TEA LEAVES, ANIMAL ENTRAILS AND CRYSTAL BALLS ARE SIMPLY BUZZING ABOUT IT.
"AND NOW SEVERAL OF THIS REGION'S GREATEST PRACTITIONERS OF THE OCCULT HAVE GATHERED."

WE'RE GOING TO COMBINE OUR POWERS AND HOPEFULLY GLEAN SOMETHING OF THAT COMING EVENT, AND SO...CAPITALIZE UPON IT.

I DON'T THINK OUR YOUNG MAN BELIEVES YOUR WICKED MUMBO-JUMBO, DARLING. PERHAPS HE'S A FORTHRIGHT CHRISTIAN.

NO SUCH THING AMONG THE GERMANICS. TEUTONIC PAGANISM GLOWS AT THE HEART OF THEM.

SOMEBODY'S GIVEN YOU QUITE THE BEATING, EH? I SENSE MUCH CONFUSION HERE. YOU SEEM... DRAGGED ALONG IN THE WORLD.

PERHAPS IT'S THE DRAGGING THAT'S GIVEN HIM SUCH A BATTERING.

I BELIEVE HE'S LOOKING AT YOUR BIRTHMARK, DARLING.

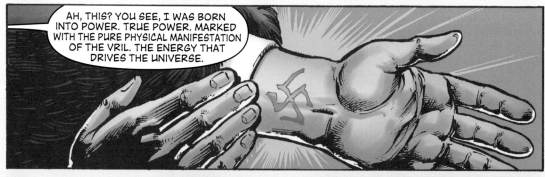

AH, THIS? YOU SEE, I WAS BORN INTO POWER. TRUE POWER. MARKED WITH THE PURE PHYSICAL MANIFESTATION OF THE VRIL. THE ENERGY THAT DRIVES THE UNIVERSE.

IF YOU LEARN ONE THING THIS EVENING, MY YOUNG MAN, LEARN THIS...YOU *CAN* IMPOSE YOUR DESIRES UPON THE UNIVERSE.

THERE'S NO NEED TO BE DRAGGED ALONG. YOUR *WILL* IS ALL THE TOOLS YOU'LL NEED.

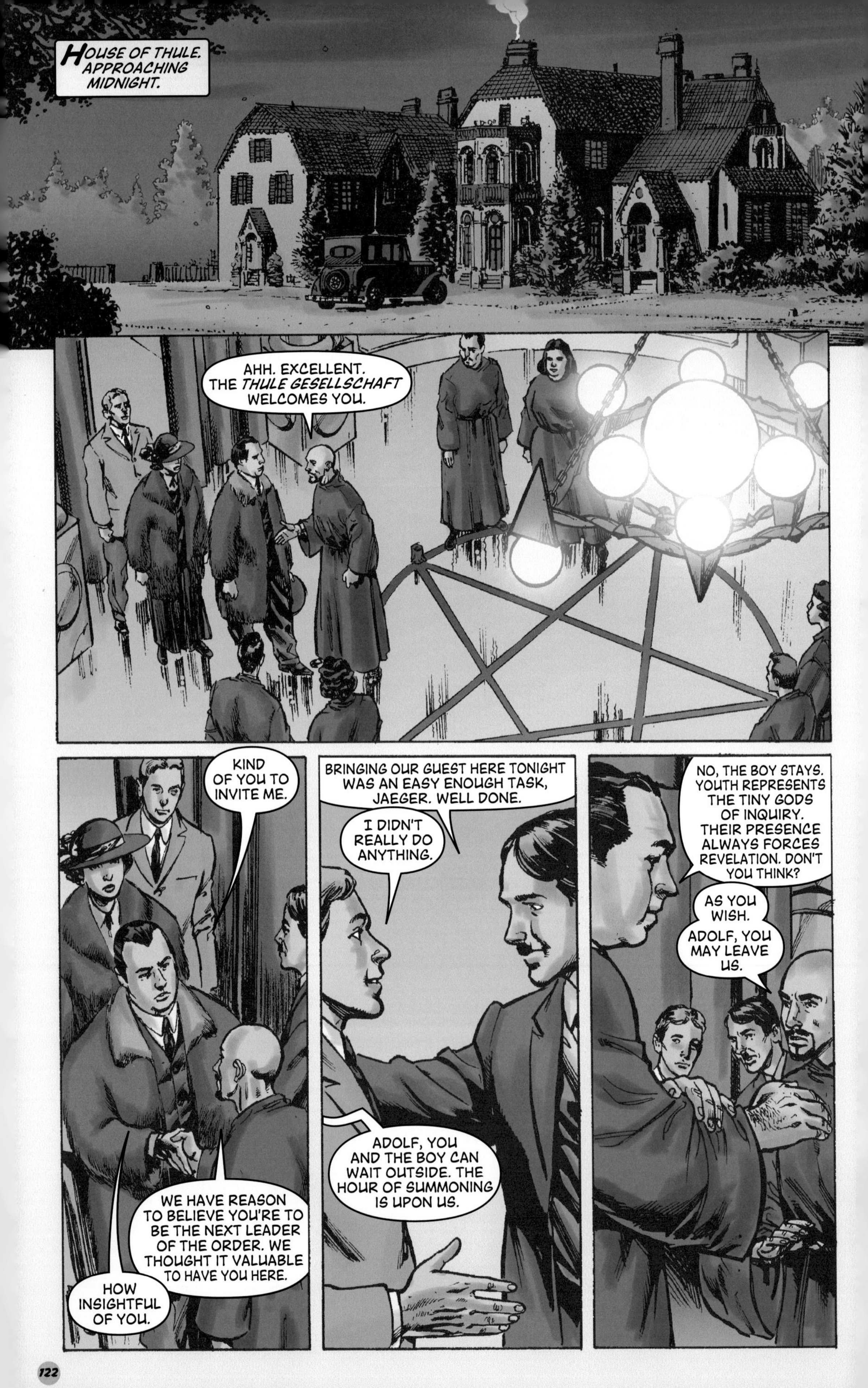
HOUSE OF THULE. APPROACHING MIDNIGHT.
AHH. EXCELLENT. THE *THULE GESELLSCHAFT* WELCOMES YOU.
KIND OF YOU TO INVITE ME.
WE HAVE REASON TO BELIEVE YOU'RE TO BE THE NEXT LEADER OF THE ORDER. WE THOUGHT IT VALUABLE TO HAVE YOU HERE.
HOW INSIGHTFUL OF YOU.
BRINGING OUR GUEST HERE TONIGHT WAS AN EASY ENOUGH TASK, JAEGER. WELL DONE.
I DIDN'T REALLY DO ANYTHING.
ADOLF, YOU AND THE BOY CAN WAIT OUTSIDE. THE HOUR OF SUMMONING IS UPON US.
NO, THE BOY STAYS. YOUTH REPRESENTS THE TINY GODS OF INQUIRY. THEIR PRESENCE ALWAYS FORCES REVELATION. DON'T YOU THINK?
AS YOU WISH.
ADOLF, YOU MAY LEAVE US.

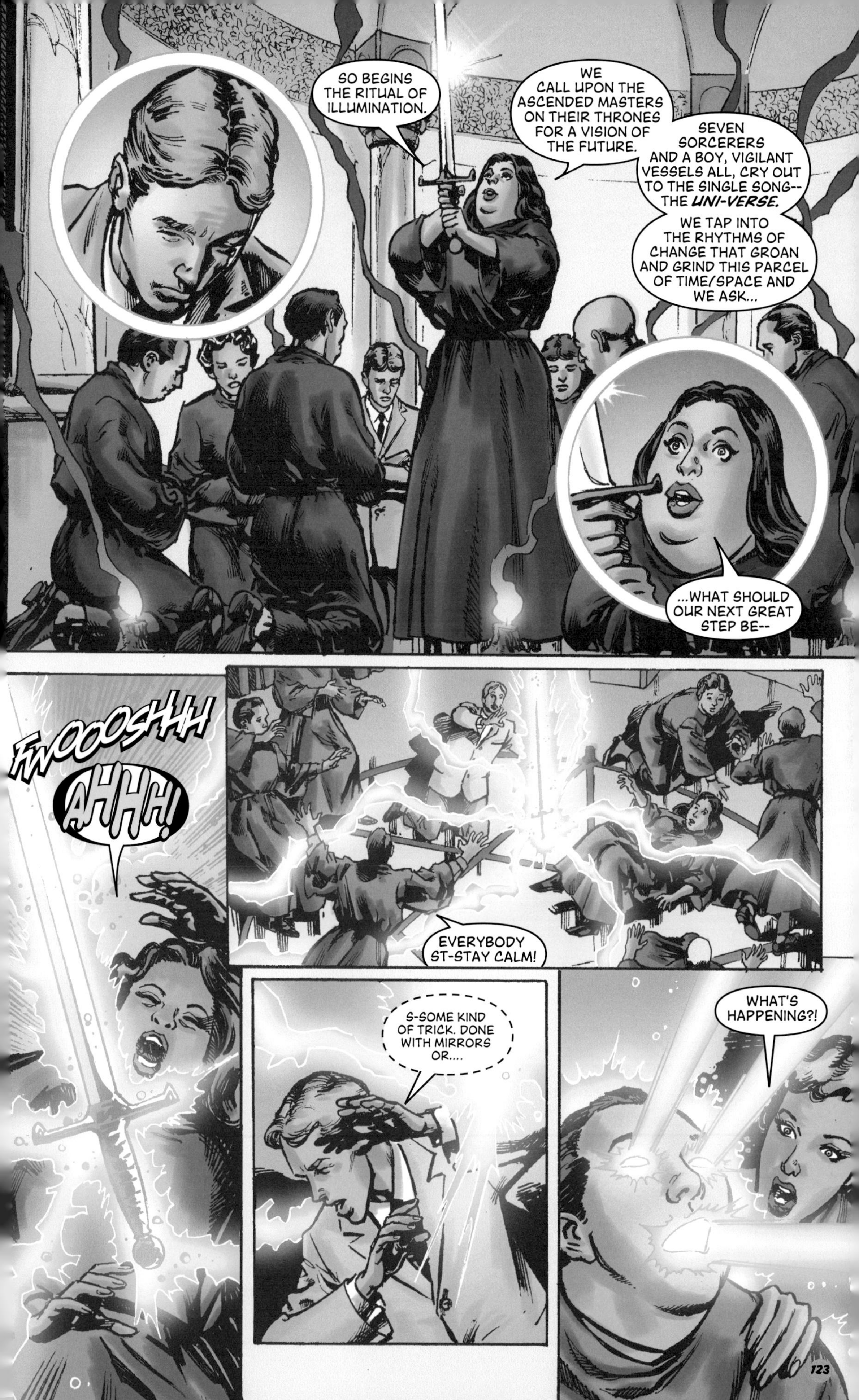

SO BEGINS THE RITUAL OF ILLUMINATION.
WE CALL UPON THE ASCENDED MASTERS ON THEIR THRONES FOR A VISION OF THE FUTURE.
SEVEN SORCERERS AND A BOY, VIGILANT VESSELS ALL, CRY OUT TO THE SINGLE SONG-- THE UNI-VERSE.
WE TAP INTO THE RHYTHMS OF CHANGE THAT GROAN AND GRIND THIS PARCEL OF TIME/SPACE AND WE ASK...
...WHAT SHOULD OUR NEXT GREAT STEP BE--
FWOOOSHHH
AHHH!
EVERYBODY ST-STAY CALM!
S-SOME KIND OF TRICK. DONE WITH MIRRORS OR....
WHAT'S HAPPENING?!

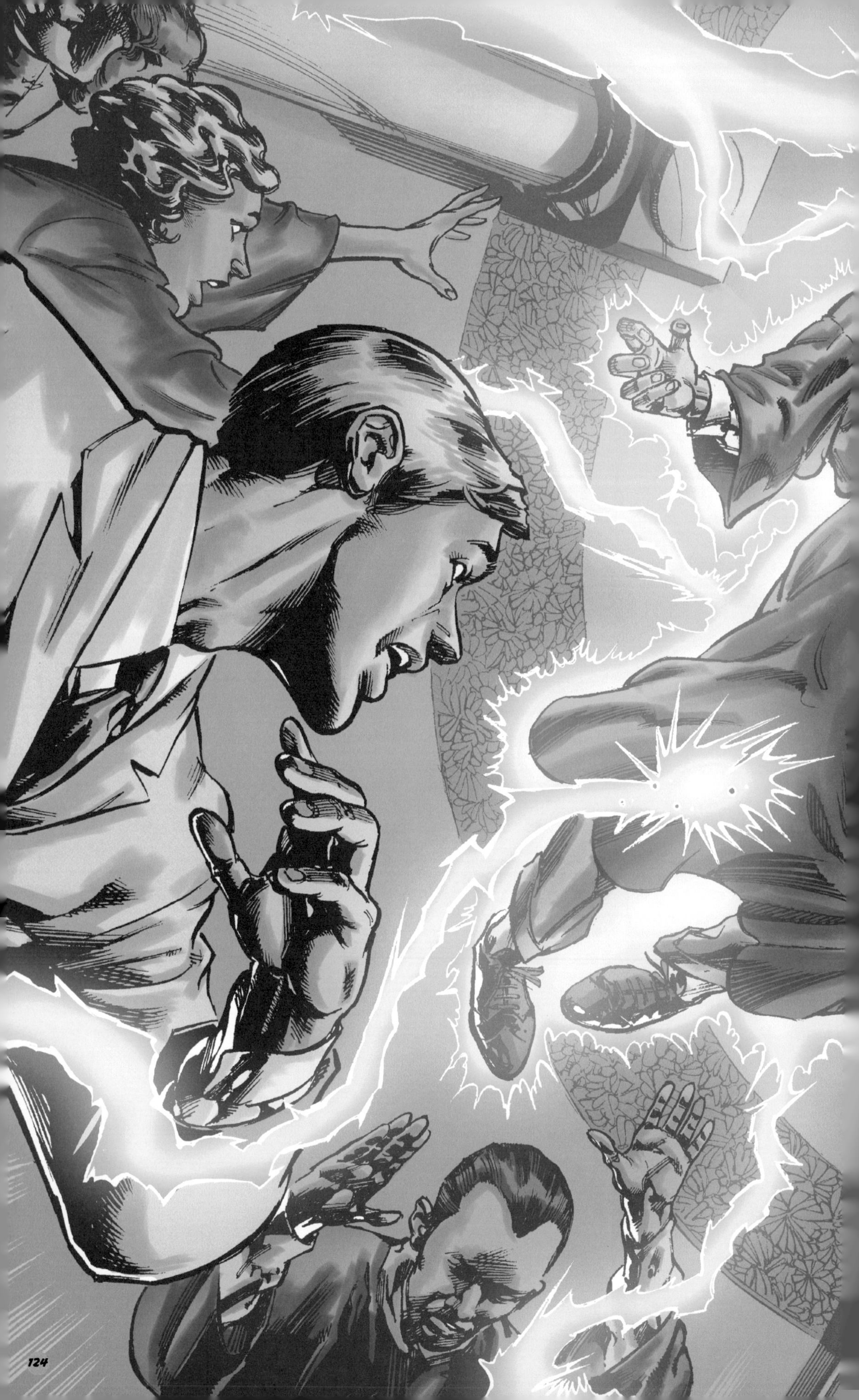

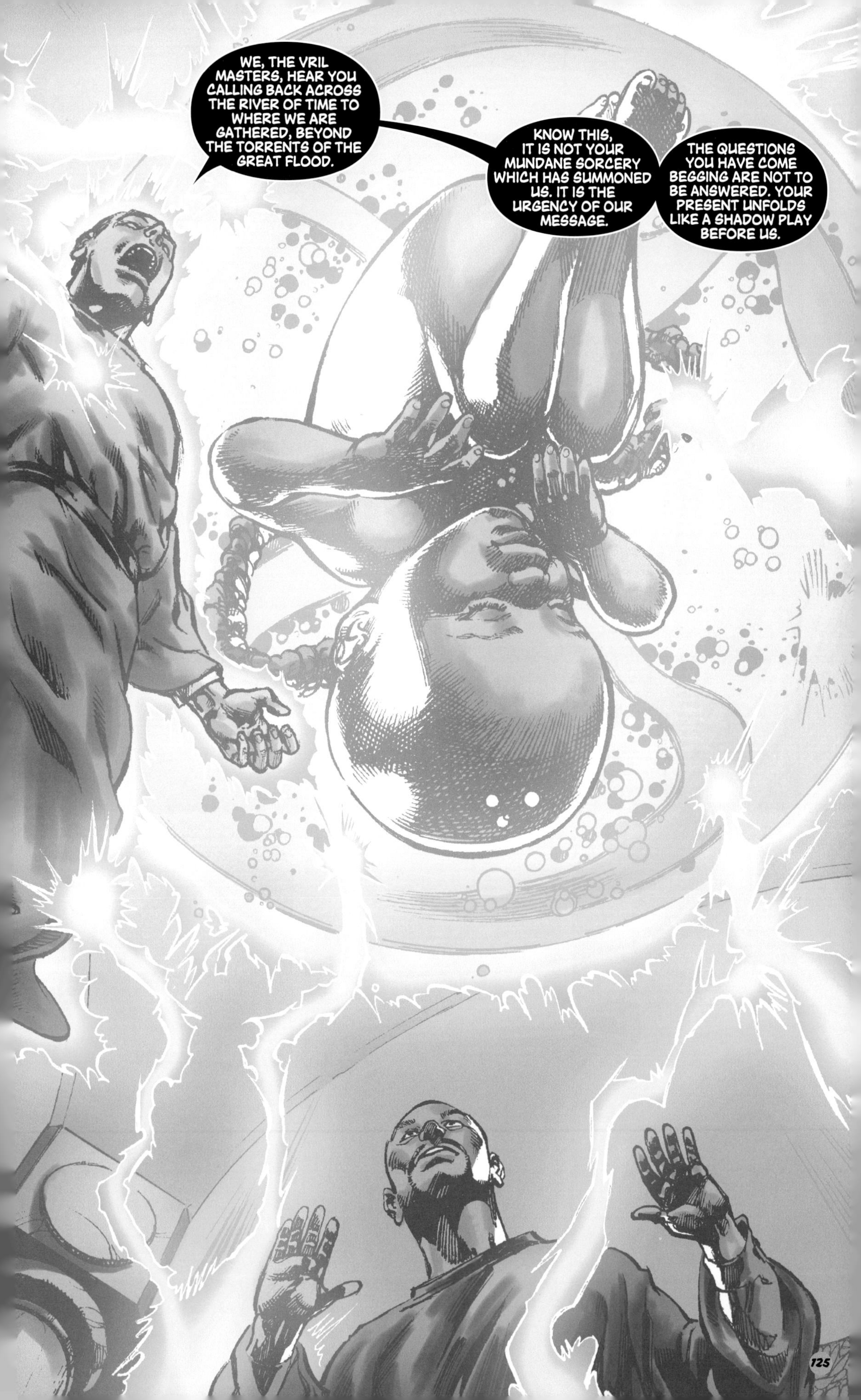
WE, THE VRIL MASTERS, HEAR YOU CALLING BACK ACROSS THE RIVER OF TIME TO WHERE WE ARE GATHERED, BEYOND THE TORRENTS OF THE GREAT FLOOD.
KNOW THIS, IT IS NOT YOUR MUNDANE SORCERY WHICH HAS SUMMONED US. IT IS THE URGENCY OF OUR MESSAGE.
THE QUESTIONS YOU HAVE COME BEGGING ARE NOT TO BE ANSWERED. YOUR PRESENT UNFOLDS LIKE A SHADOW PLAY BEFORE US.

MANY POSSIBLE PATHS ARC OUT. MOST TOO GOSSAMER AND INDISTINCT FOR US TO SEE. YET ONE THING IS CERTAIN.

THE CEASELESS TIDE OF STRUGGLE IS SOON TO REACH ANOTHER CLIMAX IN ITS CYCLE.

A VILLAIN IS UNKNOWINGLY CRAFTING HIMSELF, AND SO TOO WILL THE *SINGLE SONG* BE FORCED TO BUILD A HERO. BALANCE IS TRUTH. BOTH WILL BE TOUCHED BY THE VRIL IN THEIR WAY.

THE HERO SHALL BE AMBITIONLESS, DESIRE LITTLE. HE WILL BE FORCED INTO THE FRAY.
BUT AT THE PITH OF THE VILLAIN WILL BE HIDING AN URGE FOR GREATNESS. AND THE *VRIL* WILL RAVAGE THROUGH THAT URGE LIKE A STORM.

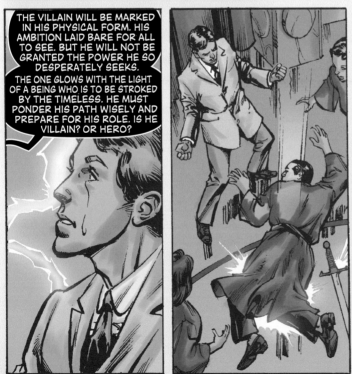

THE VILLAIN WILL BE MARKED IN HIS PHYSICAL FORM. HIS AMBITION LAID BARE FOR ALL TO SEE. BUT HE WILL NOT BE GRANTED THE POWER HE SO DESPERATELY SEEKS.
THE ONE GLOWS WITH THE LIGHT OF A BEING WHO IS TO BE STROKED BY THE TIMELESS. HE MUST PONDER HIS PATH WISELY AND PREPARE FOR HIS ROLE. IS HE VILLAIN? OR HERO?

ARE YOU OKAY?

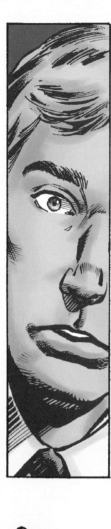

JAEGER?

WAIT!

GHHHAAAA!

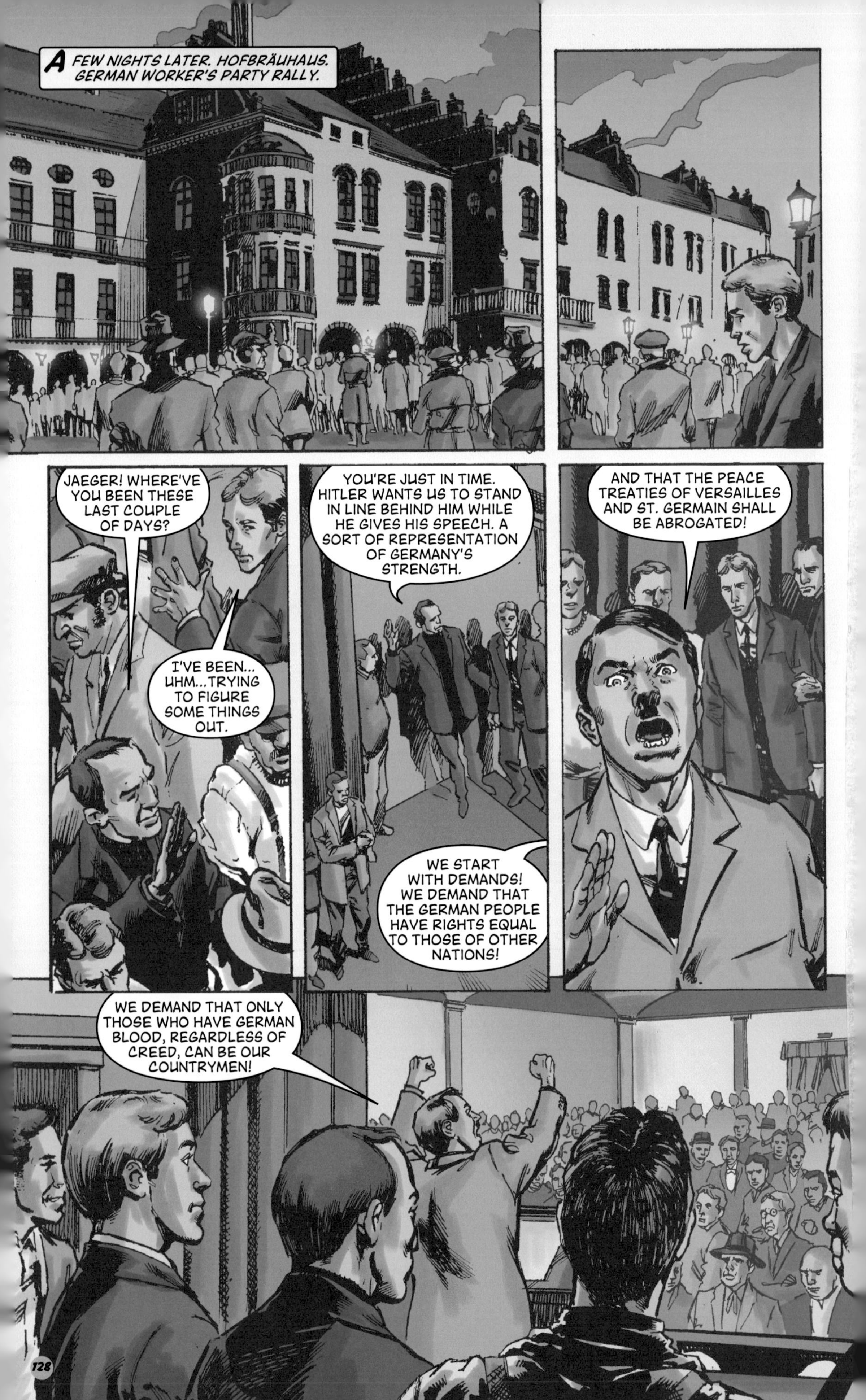
A FEW NIGHTS LATER. HOFBRÄUHAUS. GERMAN WORKER'S PARTY RALLY.
JAEGER! WHERE'VE YOU BEEN THESE LAST COUPLE OF DAYS?
I'VE BEEN... UHM...TRYING TO FIGURE SOME THINGS OUT.
YOU'RE JUST IN TIME. HITLER WANTS US TO STAND IN LINE BEHIND HIM WHILE HE GIVES HIS SPEECH. A SORT OF REPRESENTATION OF GERMANY'S STRENGTH.
WE START WITH DEMANDS! WE DEMAND THAT THE GERMAN PEOPLE HAVE RIGHTS EQUAL TO THOSE OF OTHER NATIONS!
AND THAT THE PEACE TREATIES OF VERSAILLES AND ST. GERMAIN SHALL BE ABROGATED!
WE DEMAND THAT ONLY THOSE WHO HAVE GERMAN BLOOD, REGARDLESS OF CREED, CAN BE OUR COUNTRYMEN!

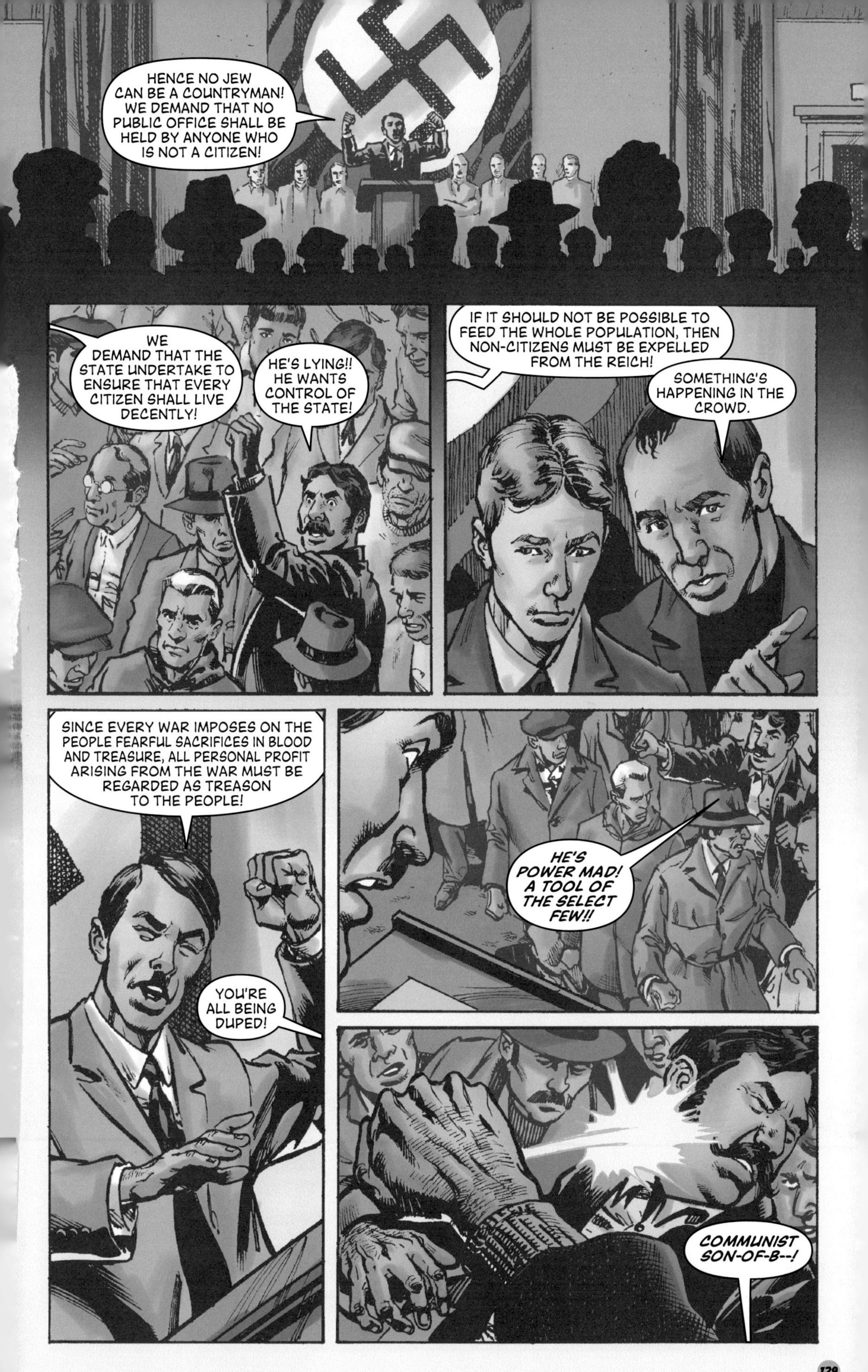
HENCE NO JEW CAN BE A COUNTRYMAN! WE DEMAND THAT NO PUBLIC OFFICE SHALL BE HELD BY ANYONE WHO IS NOT A CITIZEN!
WE DEMAND THAT THE STATE UNDERTAKE TO ENSURE THAT EVERY CITIZEN SHALL LIVE DECENTLY!
HE'S LYING!! HE WANTS CONTROL OF THE STATE!
IF IT SHOULD NOT BE POSSIBLE TO FEED THE WHOLE POPULATION, THEN NON-CITIZENS MUST BE EXPELLED FROM THE REICH!
SOMETHING'S HAPPENING IN THE CROWD.
SINCE EVERY WAR IMPOSES ON THE PEOPLE FEARFUL SACRIFICES IN BLOOD AND TREASURE, ALL PERSONAL PROFIT ARISING FROM THE WAR MUST BE REGARDED AS TREASON TO THE PEOPLE!
YOU'RE ALL BEING DUPED!
HE'S POWER MAD! A TOOL OF THE SELECT FEW!!
COMMUNIST SON-OF-B--!

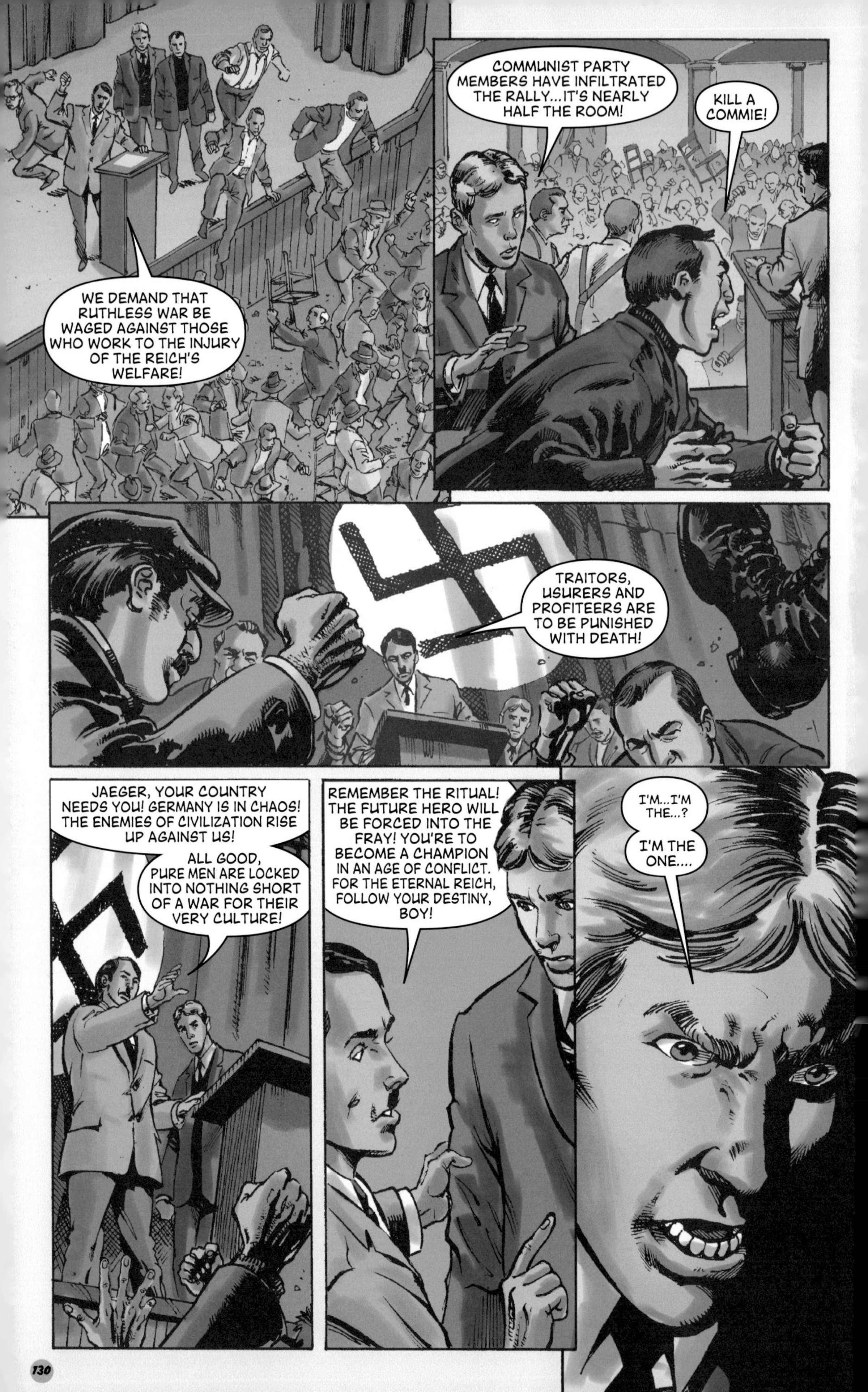
WE DEMAND THAT RUTHLESS WAR BE WAGED AGAINST THOSE WHO WORK TO THE INJURY OF THE REICH'S WELFARE!
COMMUNIST PARTY MEMBERS HAVE INFILTRATED THE RALLY...IT'S NEARLY HALF THE ROOM!
KILL A COMMIE!
TRAITORS, USURERS AND PROFITEERS ARE TO BE PUNISHED WITH DEATH!
JAEGER, YOUR COUNTRY NEEDS YOU! GERMANY IS IN CHAOS! THE ENEMIES OF CIVILIZATION RISE UP AGAINST US!
ALL GOOD, PURE MEN ARE LOCKED INTO NOTHING SHORT OF A WAR FOR THEIR VERY CULTURE!
REMEMBER THE RITUAL! THE FUTURE HERO WILL BE FORCED INTO THE FRAY! YOU'RE TO BECOME A CHAMPION IN AN AGE OF CONFLICT. FOR THE ETERNAL REICH, FOLLOW YOUR DESTINY, BOY!
I'M...I'M THE...?
I'M THE ONE....

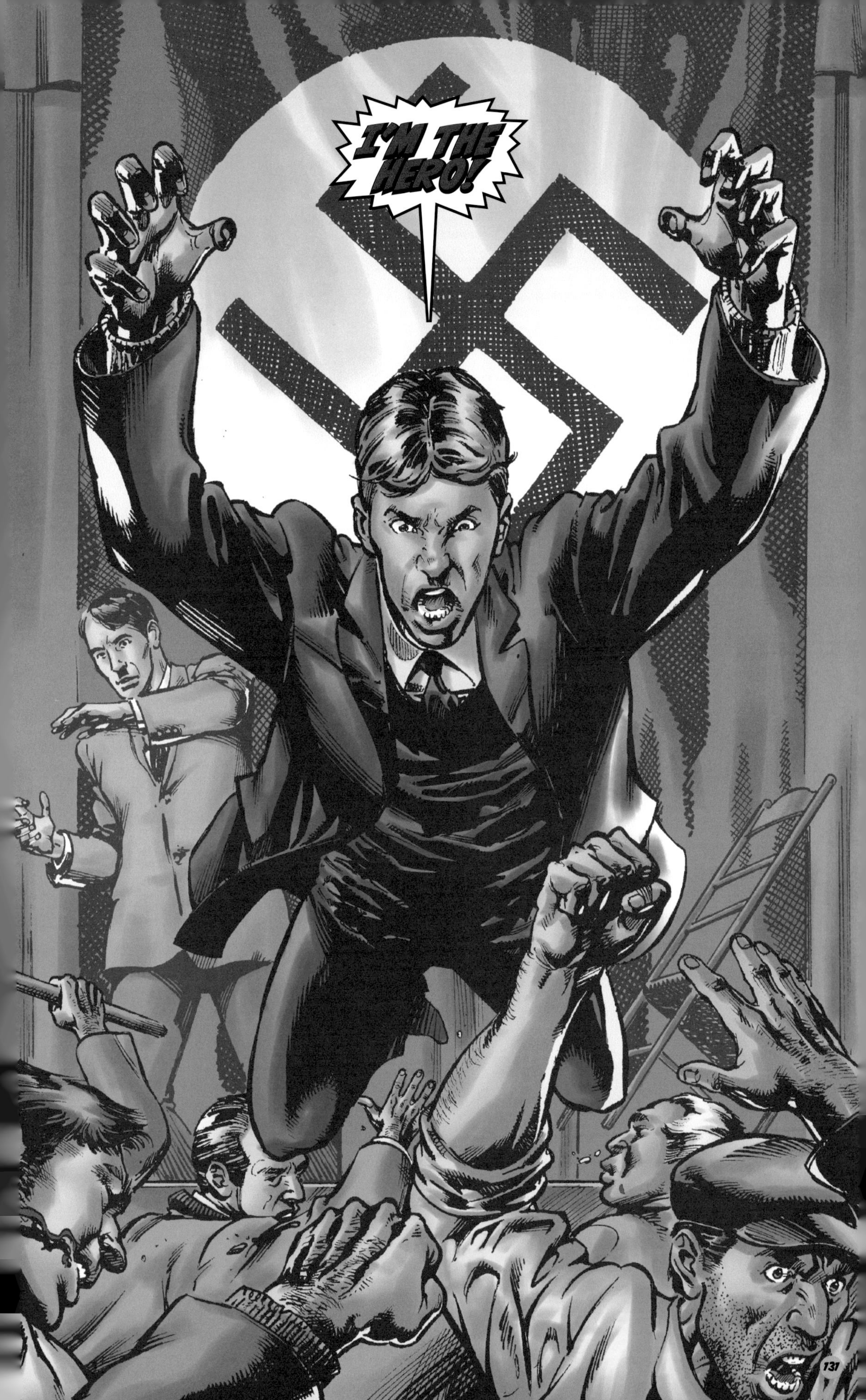
I'M THE HERO!

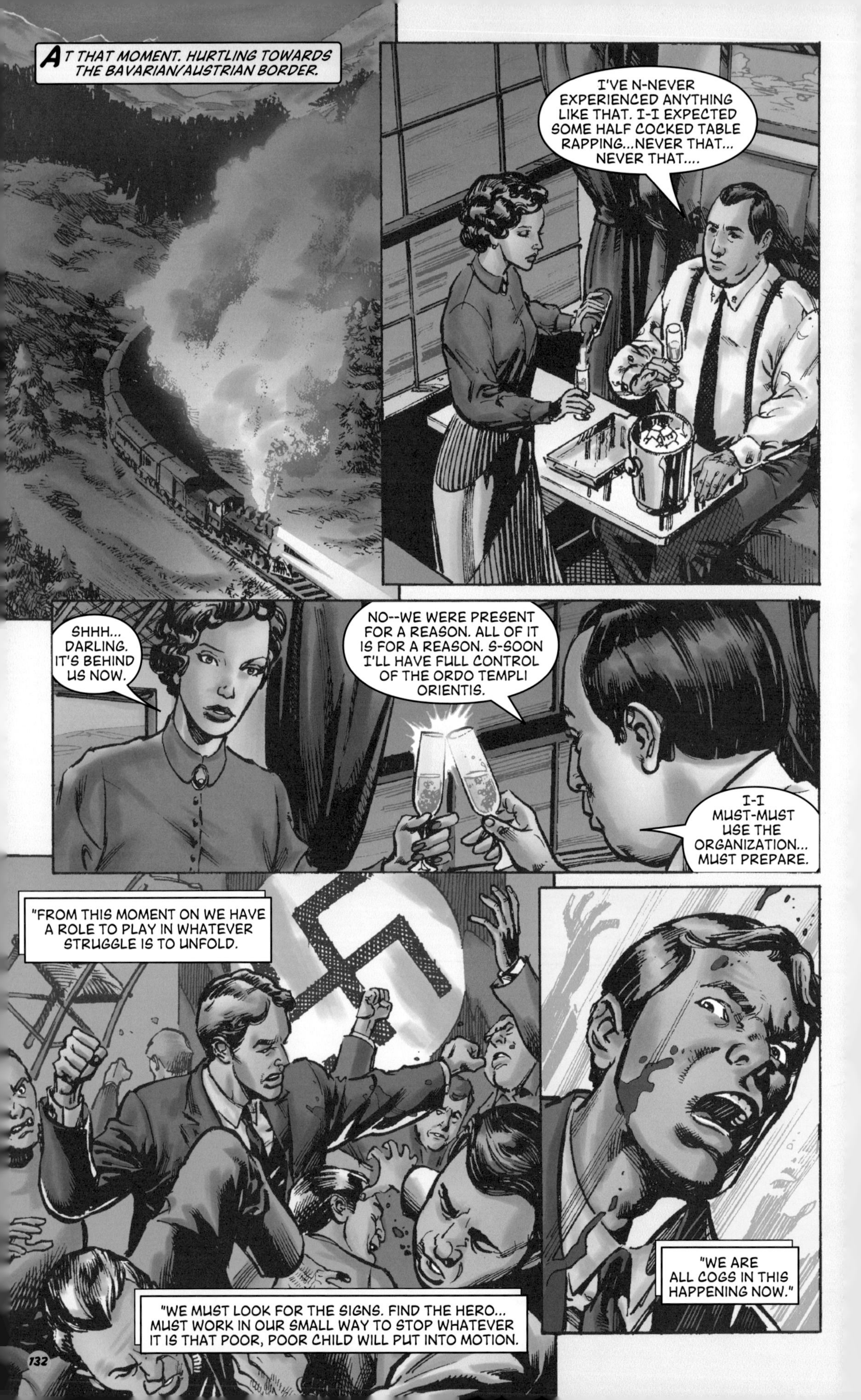
AT THAT MOMENT. HURTLING TOWARDS THE BAVARIAN/AUSTRIAN BORDER.
I'VE N-NEVER EXPERIENCED ANYTHING LIKE THAT. I-I EXPECTED SOME HALF COCKED TABLE RAPPING...NEVER THAT... NEVER THAT....
SHHH... DARLING. IT'S BEHIND US NOW.
NO--WE WERE PRESENT FOR A REASON. ALL OF IT IS FOR A REASON. S-SOON I'LL HAVE FULL CONTROL OF THE ORDO TEMPLI ORIENTIS.
I-I MUST-MUST USE THE ORGANIZATION... MUST PREPARE.
"FROM THIS MOMENT ON WE HAVE A ROLE TO PLAY IN WHATEVER STRUGGLE IS TO UNFOLD.
"WE ARE ALL COGS IN THIS HAPPENING NOW."
"WE MUST LOOK FOR THE SIGNS. FIND THE HERO... MUST WORK IN OUR SMALL WAY TO STOP WHATEVER IT IS THAT POOR, POOR CHILD WILL PUT INTO MOTION.

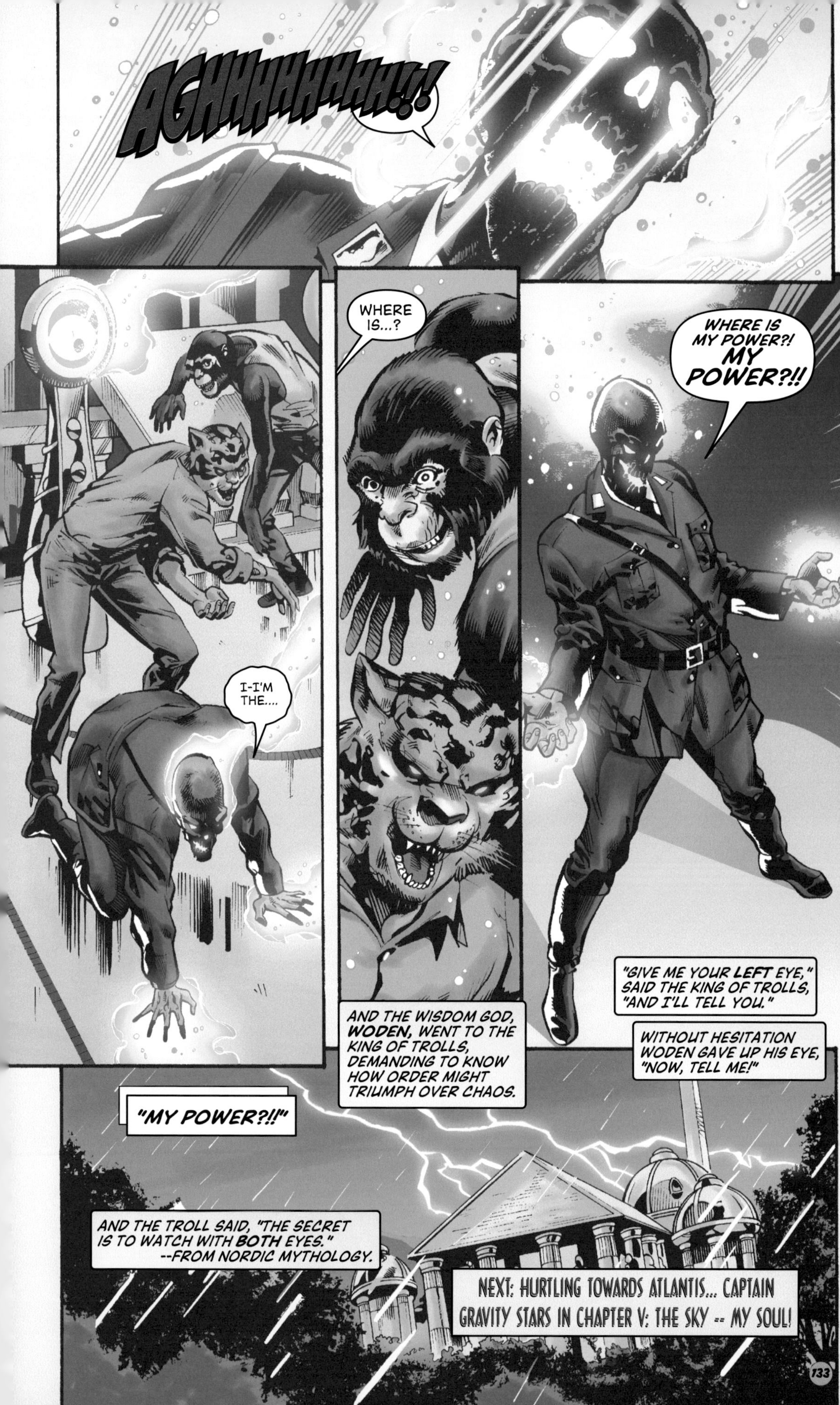
AGHHHHHHHH!!!
WHERE IS...?
WHERE IS MY POWER?! MY POWER?!!
I-I'M THE....
AND THE WISDOM GOD, WODEN, WENT TO THE KING OF TROLLS, DEMANDING TO KNOW HOW ORDER MIGHT TRIUMPH OVER CHAOS.
"GIVE ME YOUR LEFT EYE," SAID THE KING OF TROLLS, "AND I'LL TELL YOU."
WITHOUT HESITATION WODEN GAVE UP HIS EYE, "NOW, TELL ME!"
"MY POWER?!!"
AND THE TROLL SAID, "THE SECRET IS TO WATCH WITH BOTH EYES."
--FROM NORDIC MYTHOLOGY.
NEXT: HURTLING TOWARDS ATLANTIS... CAPTAIN GRAVITY STARS IN CHAPTER V: THE SKY -- MY SOUL!

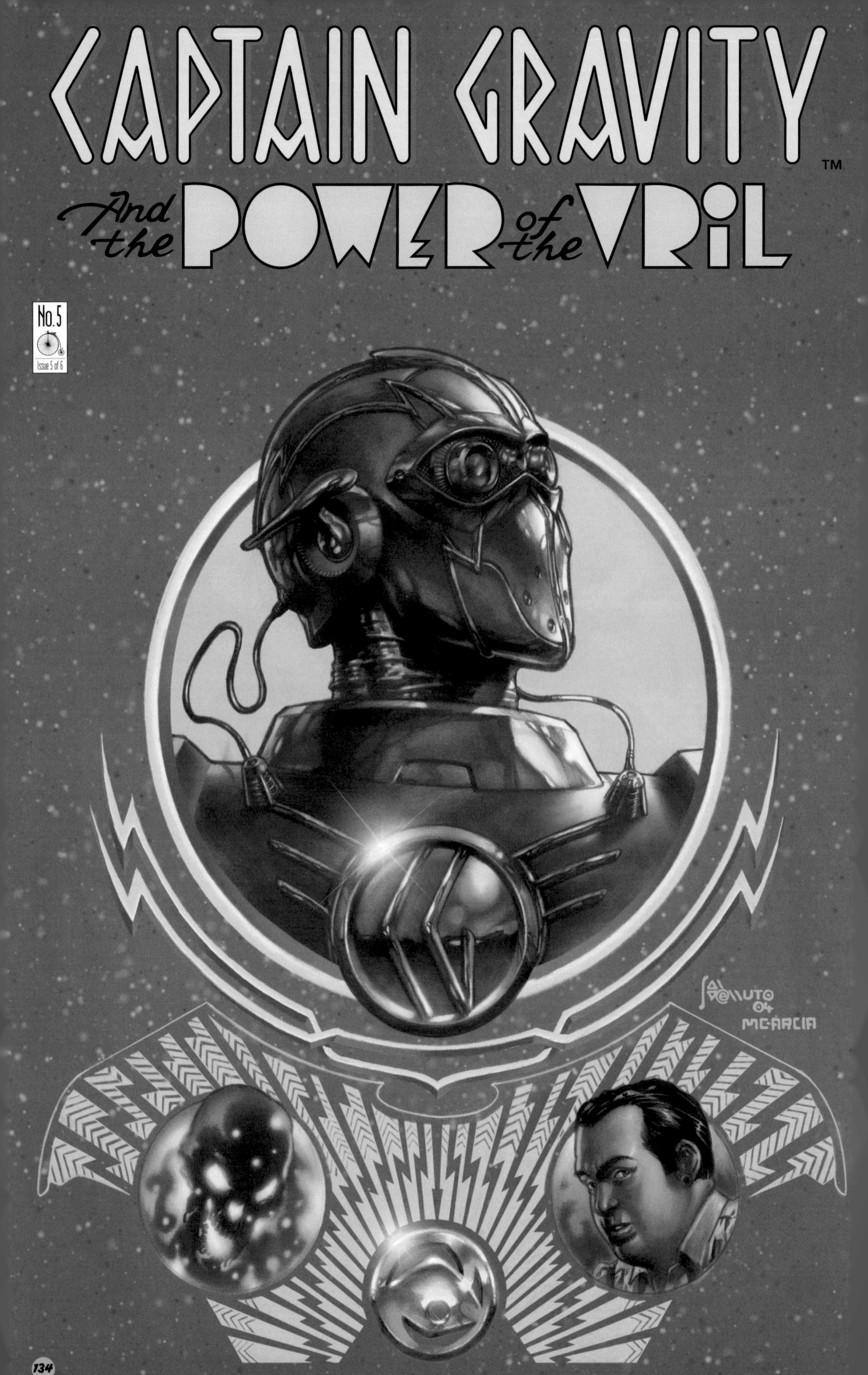
CAPTAIN GRAVITY
TM
And the POWER of the VRIL
No.5
Issue 5 of 6

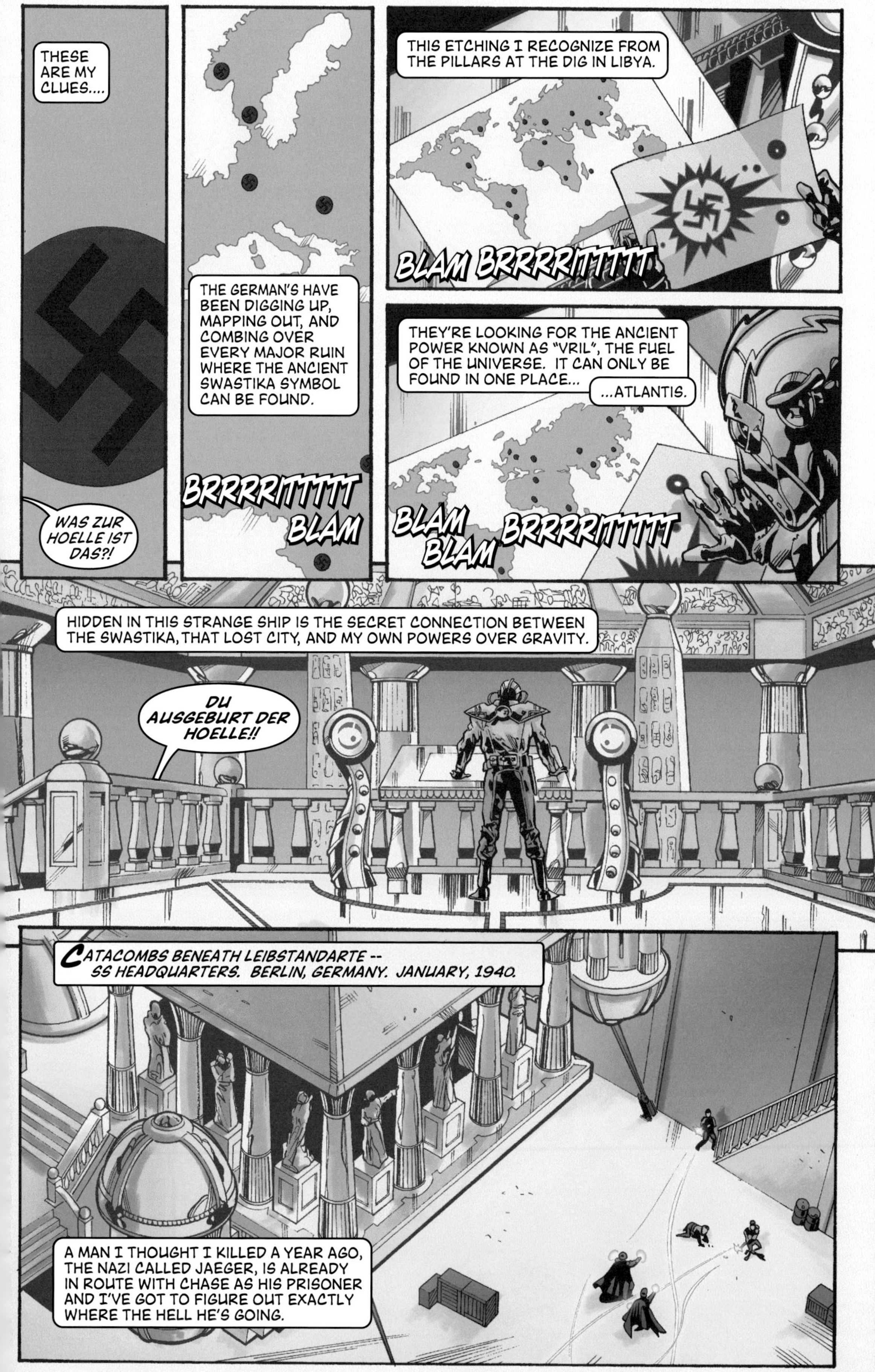

THESE ARE MY CLUES....
THE GERMAN'S HAVE BEEN DIGGING UP, MAPPING OUT, AND COMBING OVER EVERY MAJOR RUIN WHERE THE ANCIENT SWASTIKA SYMBOL CAN BE FOUND.
THIS ETCHING I RECOGNIZE FROM THE PILLARS AT THE DIG IN LIBYA.
BLAM BRRRRITTTTT
WAS ZUR HOELLE IST DAS?!
BRRRRITTTTT
BLAM
THEY'RE LOOKING FOR THE ANCIENT POWER KNOWN AS "VRIL", THE FUEL OF THE UNIVERSE. IT CAN ONLY BE FOUND IN ONE PLACE...
...ATLANTIS.
BLAM BLAM
BRRRRITTTTT
HIDDEN IN THIS STRANGE SHIP IS THE SECRET CONNECTION BETWEEN THE SWASTIKA, THAT LOST CITY, AND MY OWN POWERS OVER GRAVITY.
DU AUSGEBURT DER HOELLE!!
CATACOMBS BENEATH LEIBSTANDARTE -- SS HEADQUARTERS. BERLIN, GERMANY. JANUARY, 1940.
A MAN I THOUGHT I KILLED A YEAR AGO, THE NAZI CALLED JAEGER, IS ALREADY IN ROUTE WITH CHASE AS HIS PRISONER AND I'VE GOT TO FIGURE OUT EXACTLY WHERE THE HELL HE'S GOING.

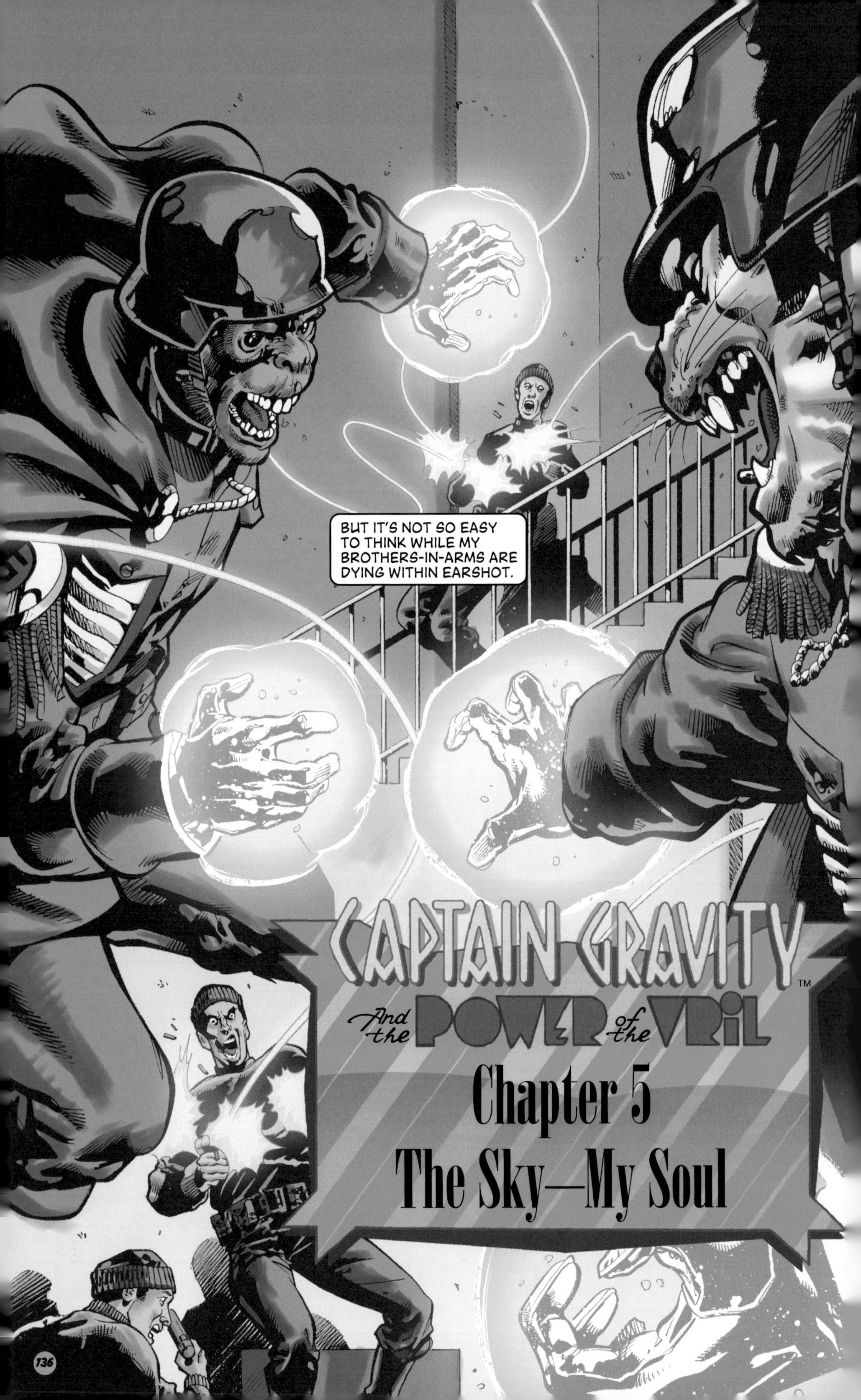
BUT IT'S NOT SO EASY TO THINK WHILE MY BROTHERS-IN-ARMS ARE DYING WITHIN EARSHOT.
CAPTAIN GRAVITY™
And the POWER of the VRIL
Chapter 5
The Sky—My Soul

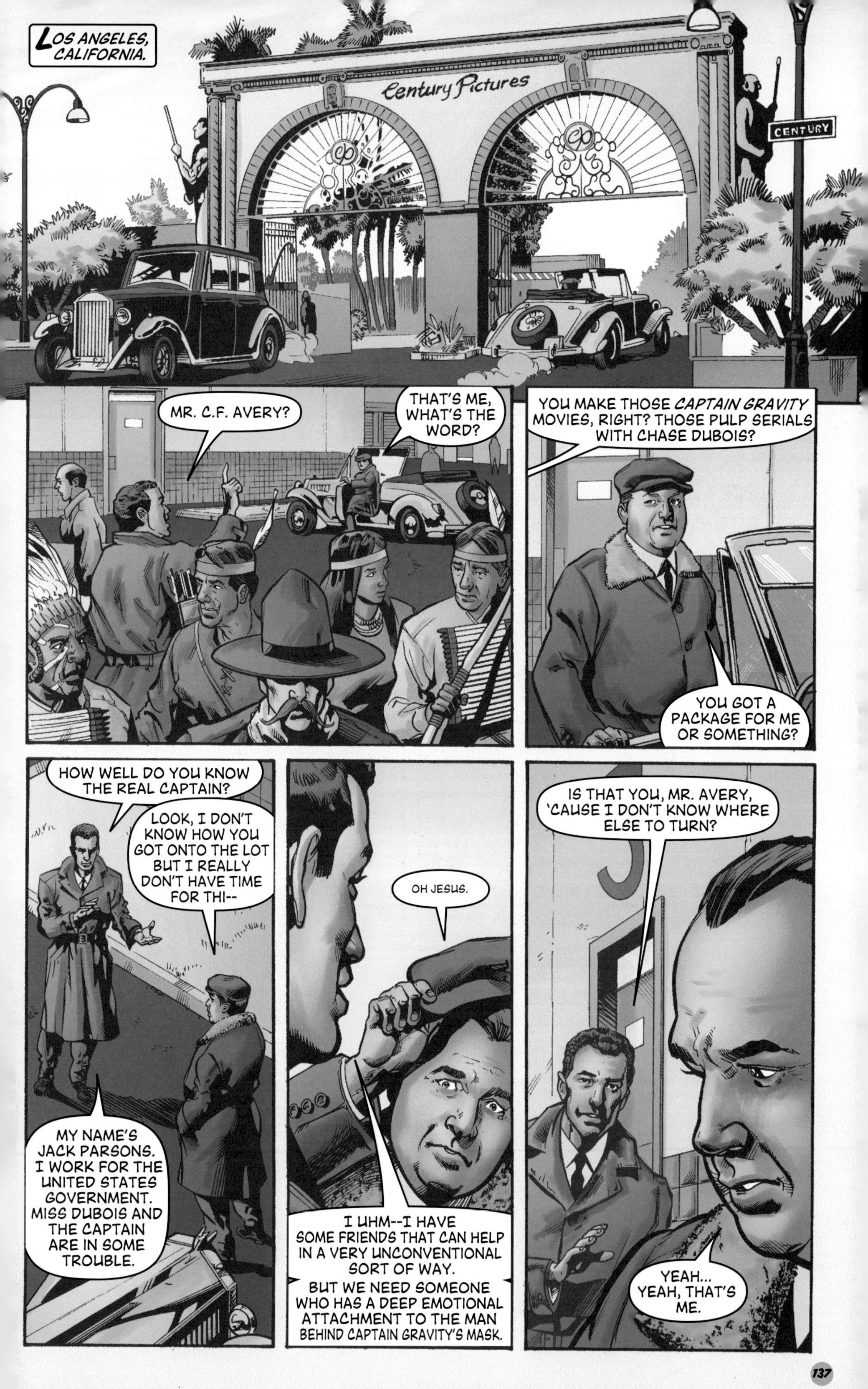

LOS ANGELES, CALIFORNIA.
Century Pictures
CENTURY
MR. C.F. AVERY?
THAT'S ME, WHAT'S THE WORD?
YOU MAKE THOSE CAPTAIN GRAVITY MOVIES, RIGHT? THOSE PULP SERIALS WITH CHASE DUBOIS?
YOU GOT A PACKAGE FOR ME OR SOMETHING?
HOW WELL DO YOU KNOW THE REAL CAPTAIN?
LOOK, I DON'T KNOW HOW YOU GOT ONTO THE LOT BUT I REALLY DON'T HAVE TIME FOR THI--
MY NAME'S JACK PARSONS. I WORK FOR THE UNITED STATES GOVERNMENT. MISS DUBOIS AND THE CAPTAIN ARE IN SOME TROUBLE.
OH JESUS.
I UHM--I HAVE SOME FRIENDS THAT CAN HELP IN A VERY UNCONVENTIONAL SORT OF WAY.
BUT WE NEED SOMEONE WHO HAS A DEEP EMOTIONAL ATTACHMENT TO THE MAN BEHIND CAPTAIN GRAVITY'S MASK.
IS THAT YOU, MR. AVERY, 'CAUSE I DON'T KNOW WHERE ELSE TO TURN?
YEAH... YEAH, THAT'S ME.

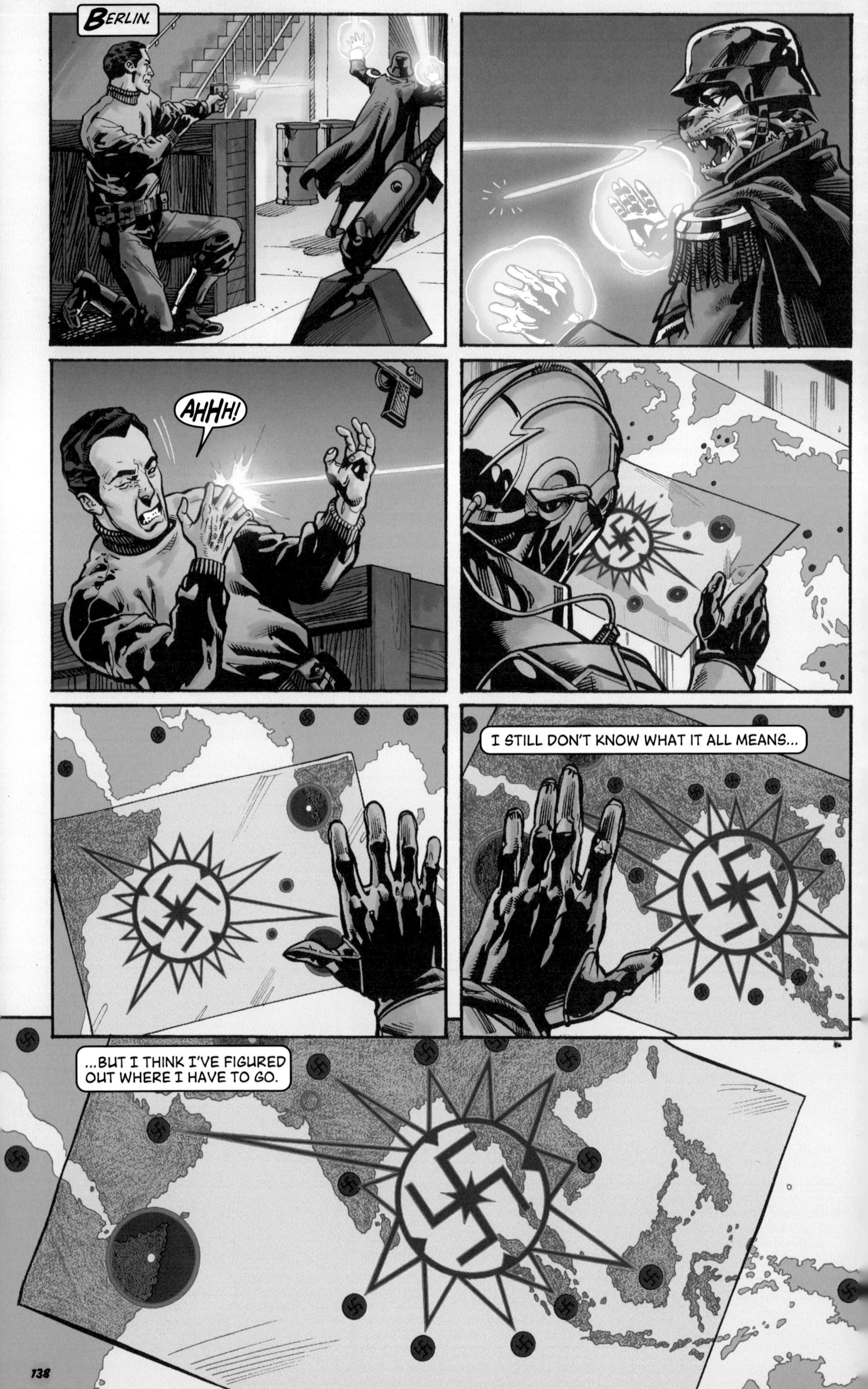
BERLIN.
AHHH!
I STILL DON'T KNOW WHAT IT ALL MEANS...
...BUT I THINK I'VE FIGURED OUT WHERE I HAVE TO GO.

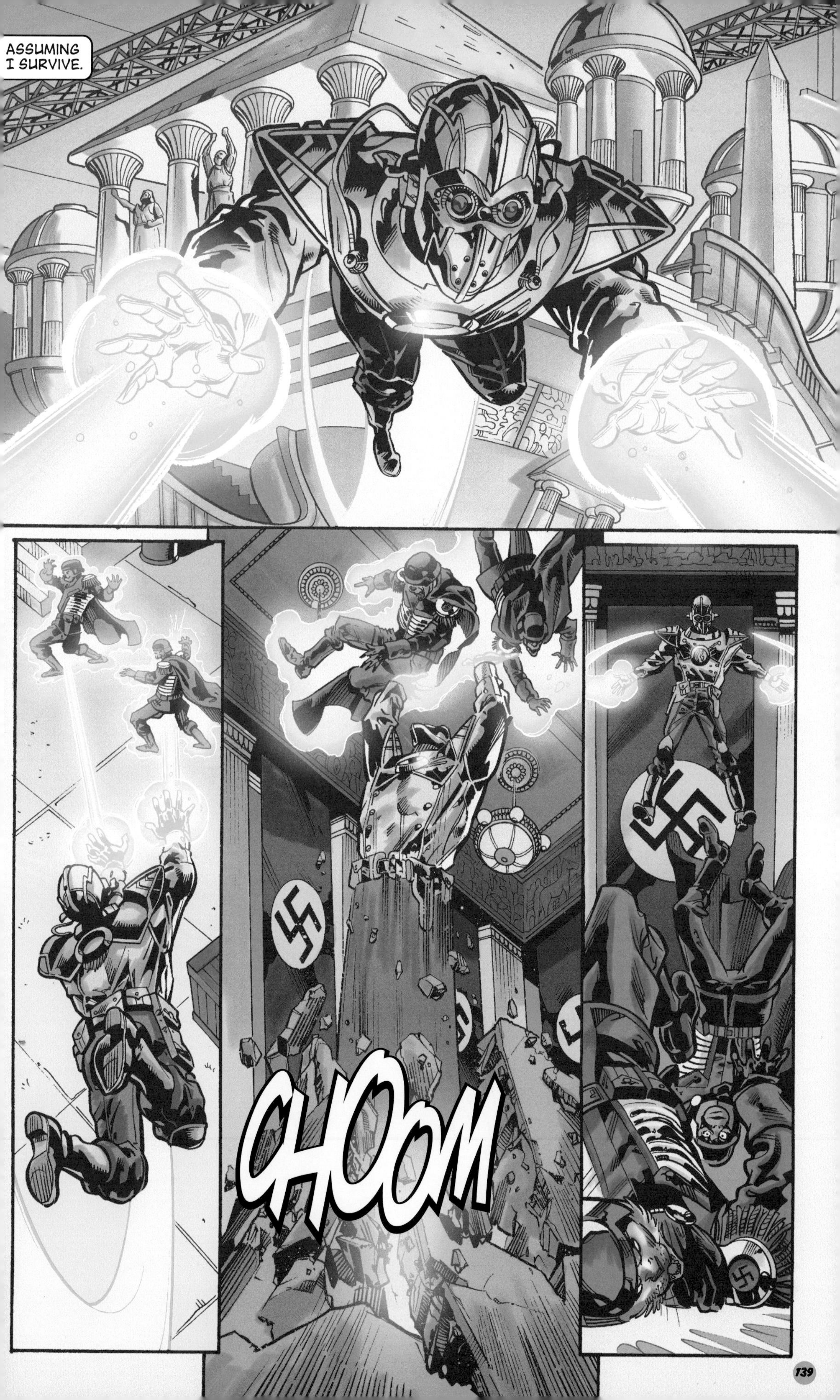
ASSUMING I SURVIVE.
CHOOM

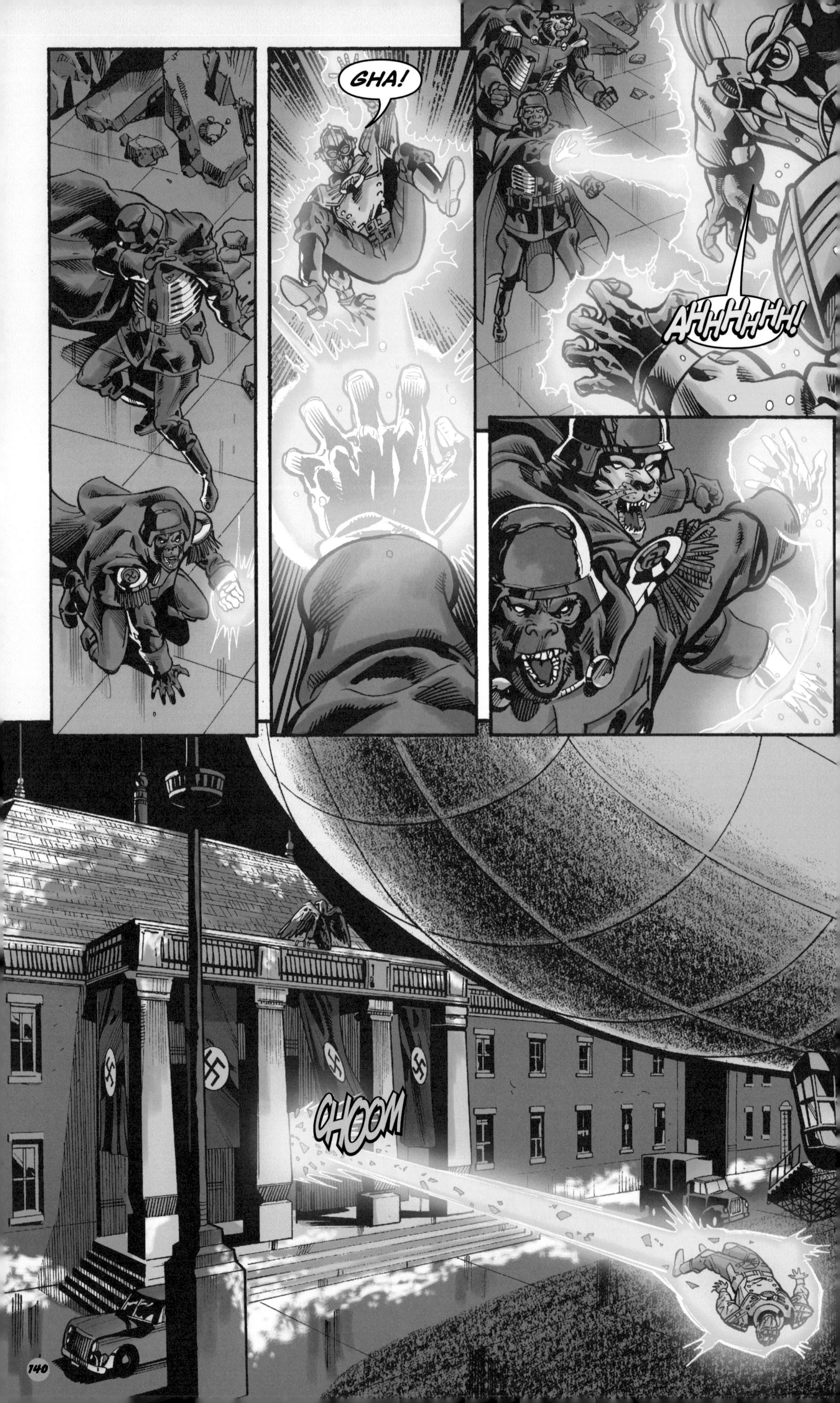
GHA!
AHHHHHH!
CHOOM

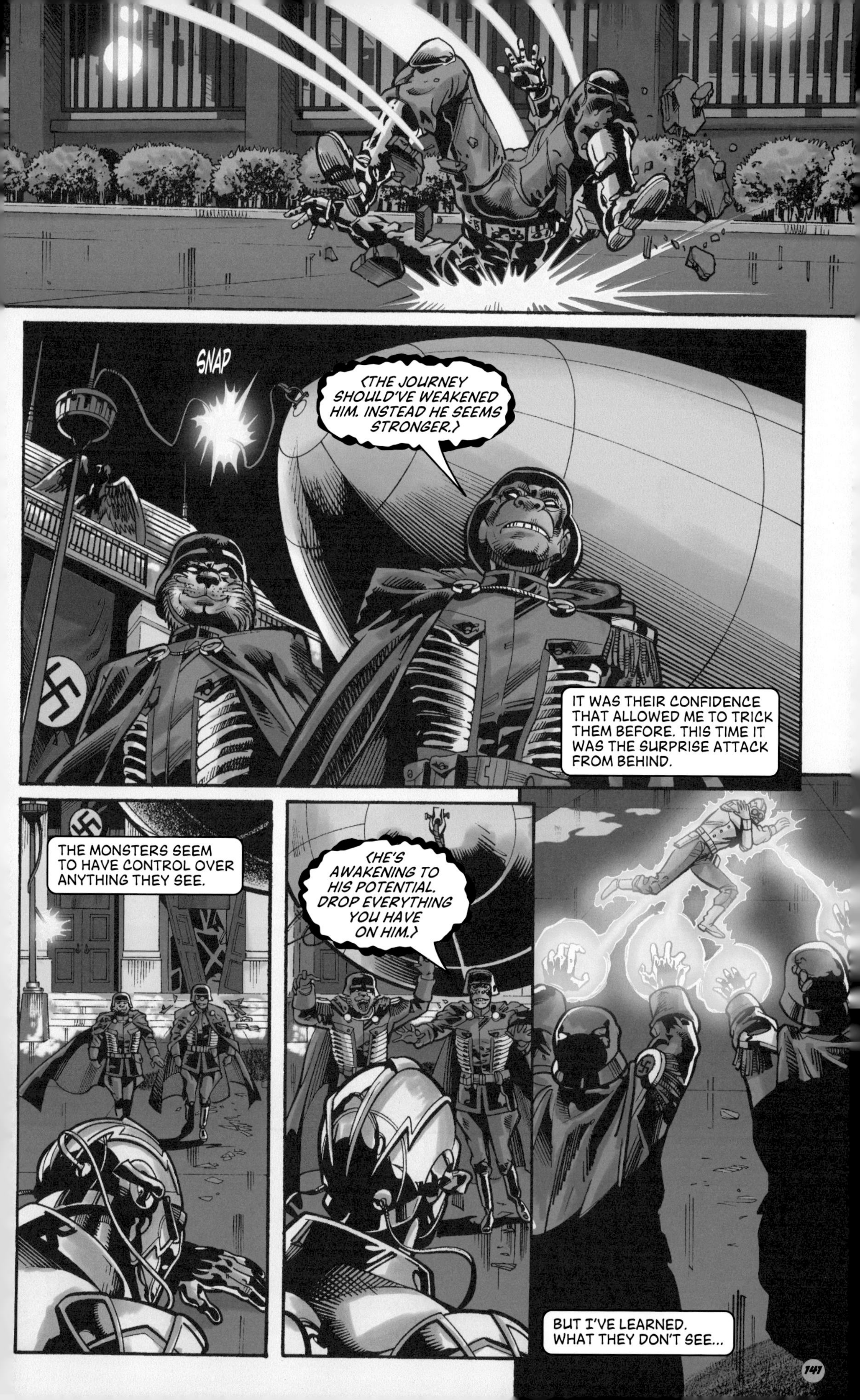

SNAP
<THE JOURNEY SHOULD'VE WEAKENED HIM. INSTEAD HE SEEMS STRONGER.>
IT WAS THEIR CONFIDENCE THAT ALLOWED ME TO TRICK THEM BEFORE. THIS TIME IT WAS THE SURPRISE ATTACK FROM BEHIND.
THE MONSTERS SEEM TO HAVE CONTROL OVER ANYTHING THEY SEE.
<HE'S AWAKENING TO HIS POTENTIAL. DROP EVERYTHING YOU HAVE ON HIM.>
BUT I'VE LEARNED. WHAT THEY DON'T SEE...

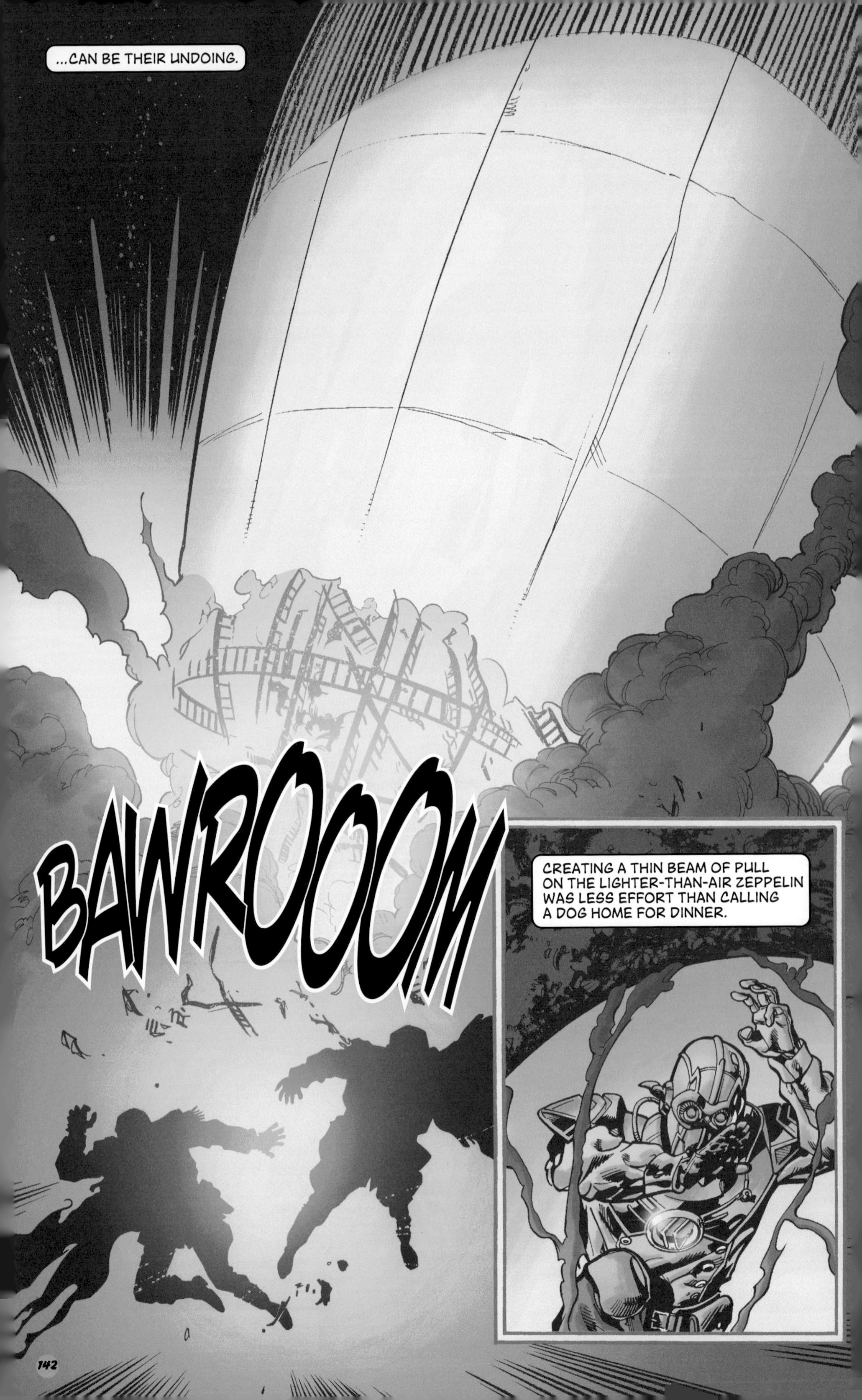
...CAN BE THEIR UNDOING.
BAWROOOM
CREATING A THIN BEAM OF PULL ON THE LIGHTER-THAN-AIR ZEPPELIN WAS LESS EFFORT THAN CALLING A DOG HOME FOR DINNER.

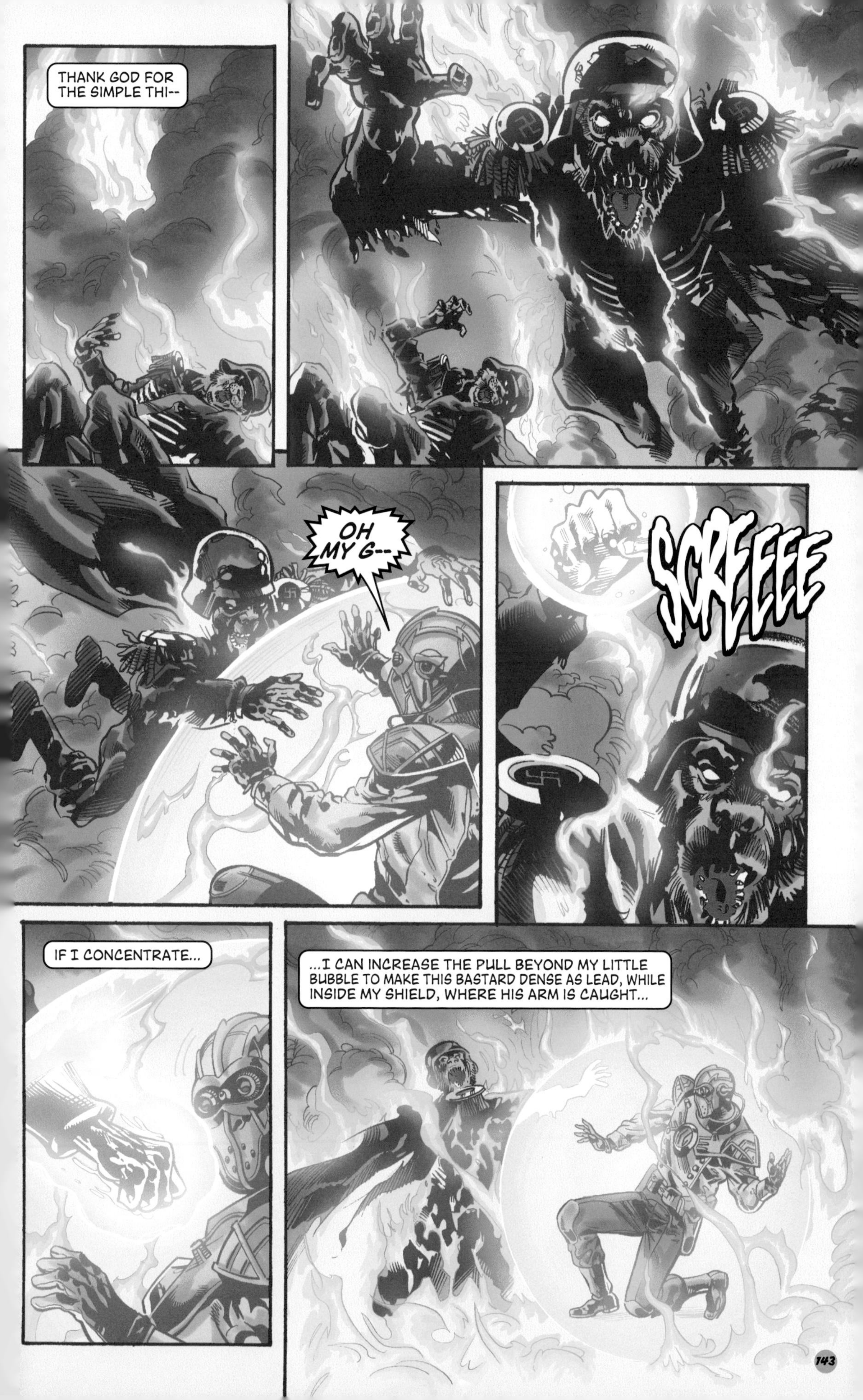
THANK GOD FOR THE SIMPLE THI--
OH MY G--
SCREEEE
IF I CONCENTRATE...
...I CAN INCREASE THE PULL BEYOND MY LITTLE BUBBLE TO MAKE THIS BASTARD DENSE AS LEAD, WHILE INSIDE MY SHIELD, WHERE HIS ARM IS CAUGHT...

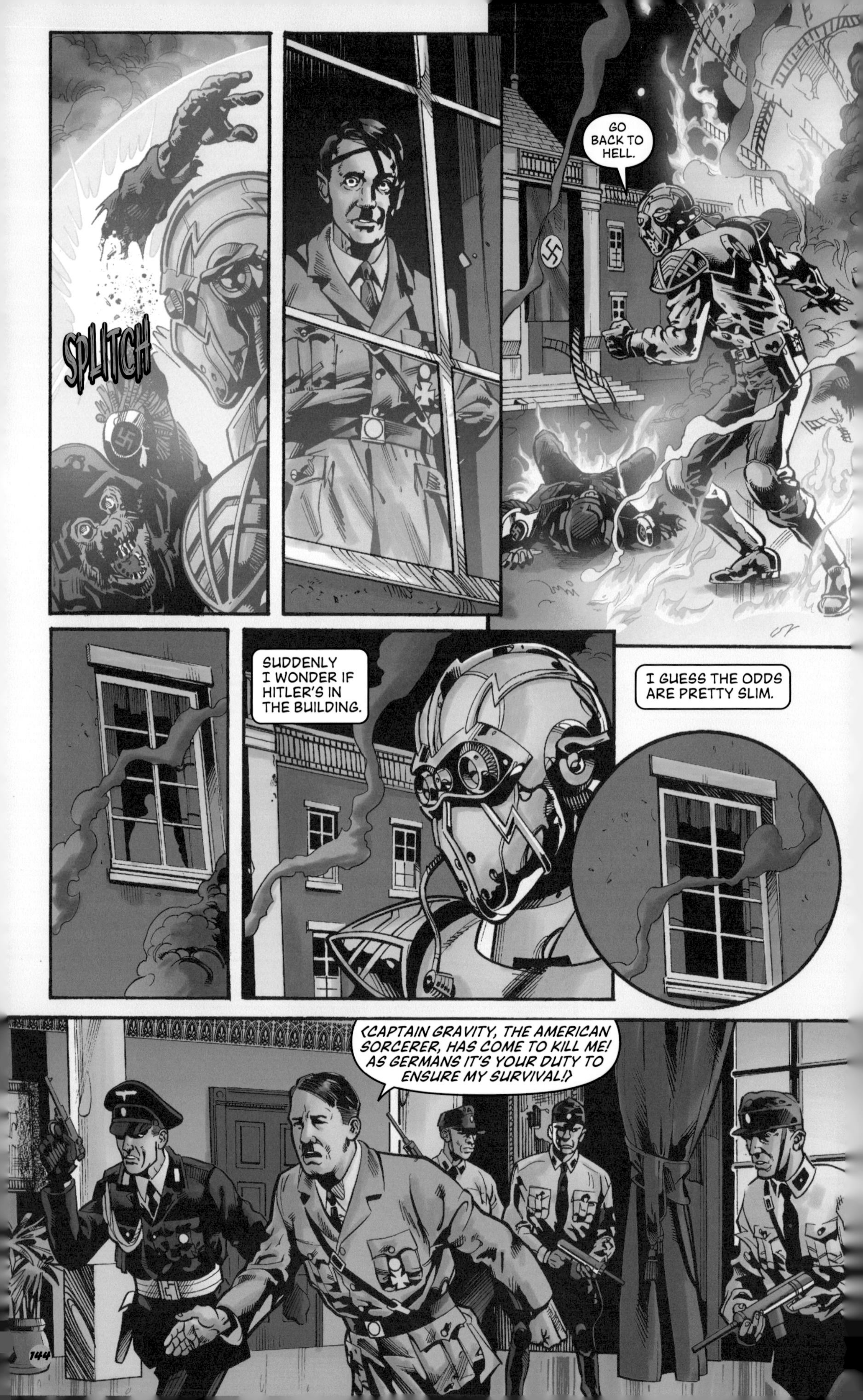
SPLITCH
GO BACK TO HELL.
SUDDENLY I WONDER IF HITLER'S IN THE BUILDING.
I GUESS THE ODDS ARE PRETTY SLIM.
<CAPTAIN GRAVITY, THE AMERICAN SORCERER, HAS COME TO KILL ME! AS GERMANS IT'S YOUR DUTY TO ENSURE MY SURVIVAL!>

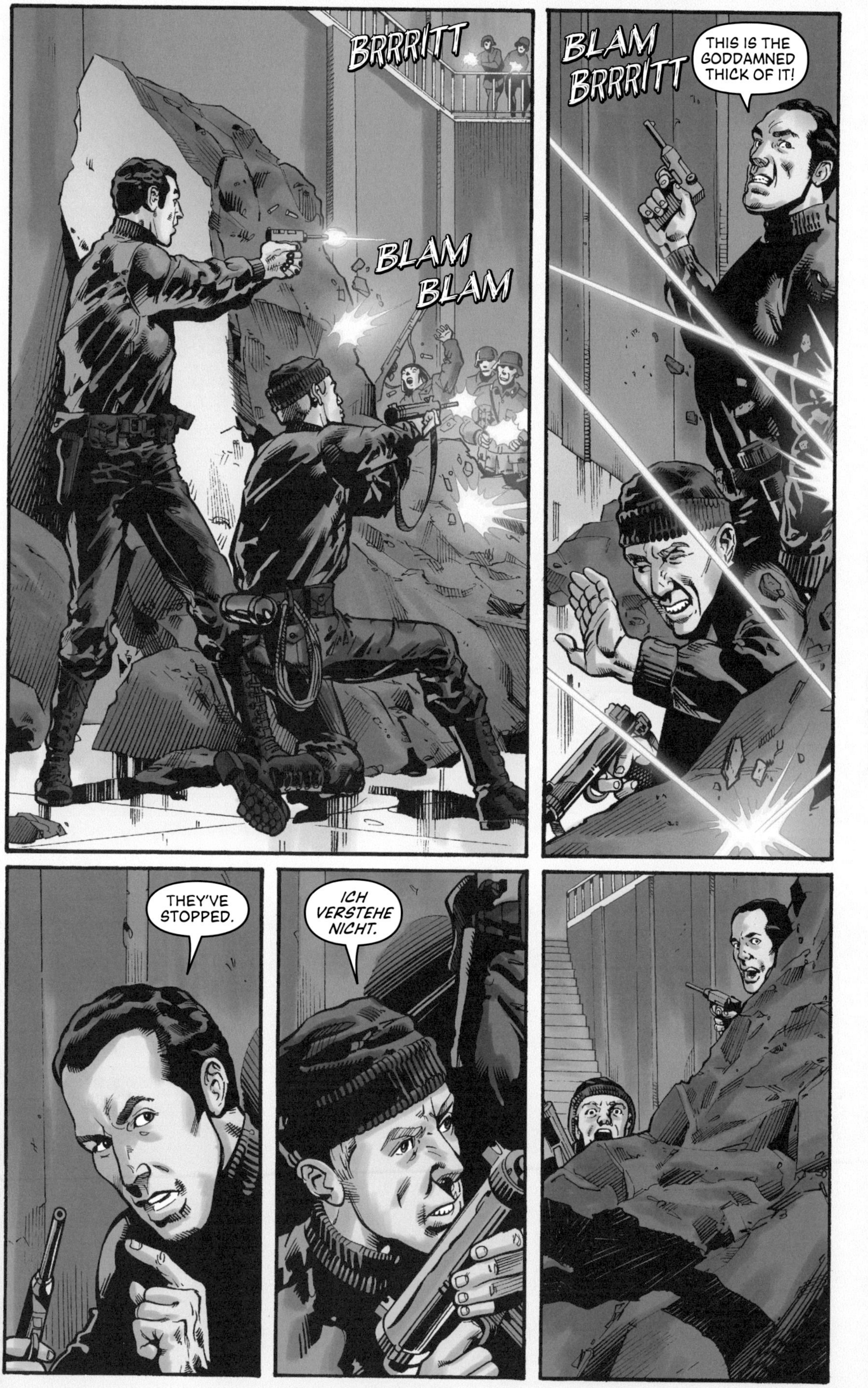
BRRRITT
BLAM
BLAM
BLAM
BRRRITT
THIS IS THE GODDAMNED THICK OF IT!
THEY'VE STOPPED.
ICH VERSTEHE NICHT.

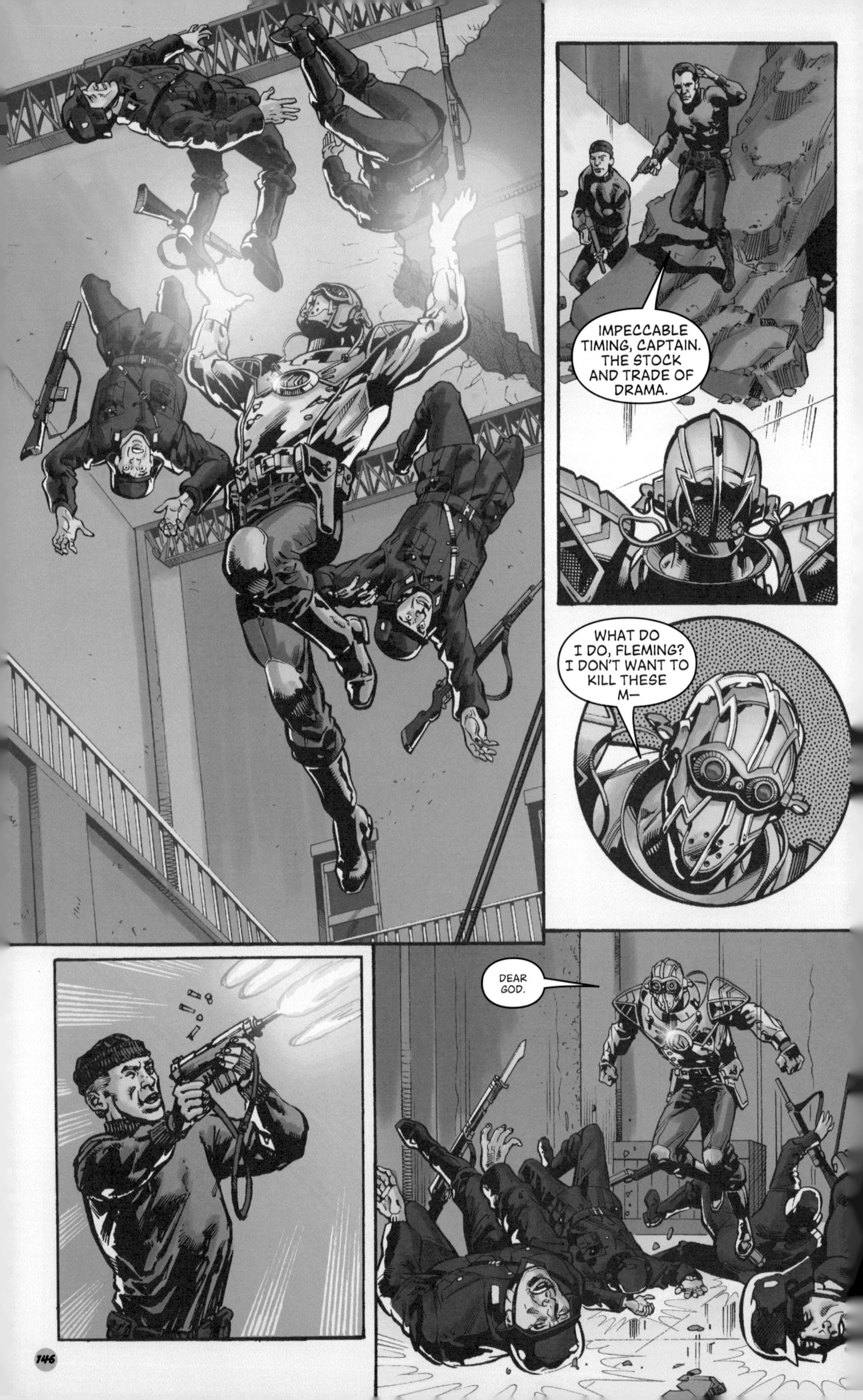
IMPECCABLE TIMING, CAPTAIN. THE STOCK AND TRADE OF DRAMA.
WHAT DO I DO, FLEMING? I DON'T WANT TO KILL THESE M—
DEAR GOD.

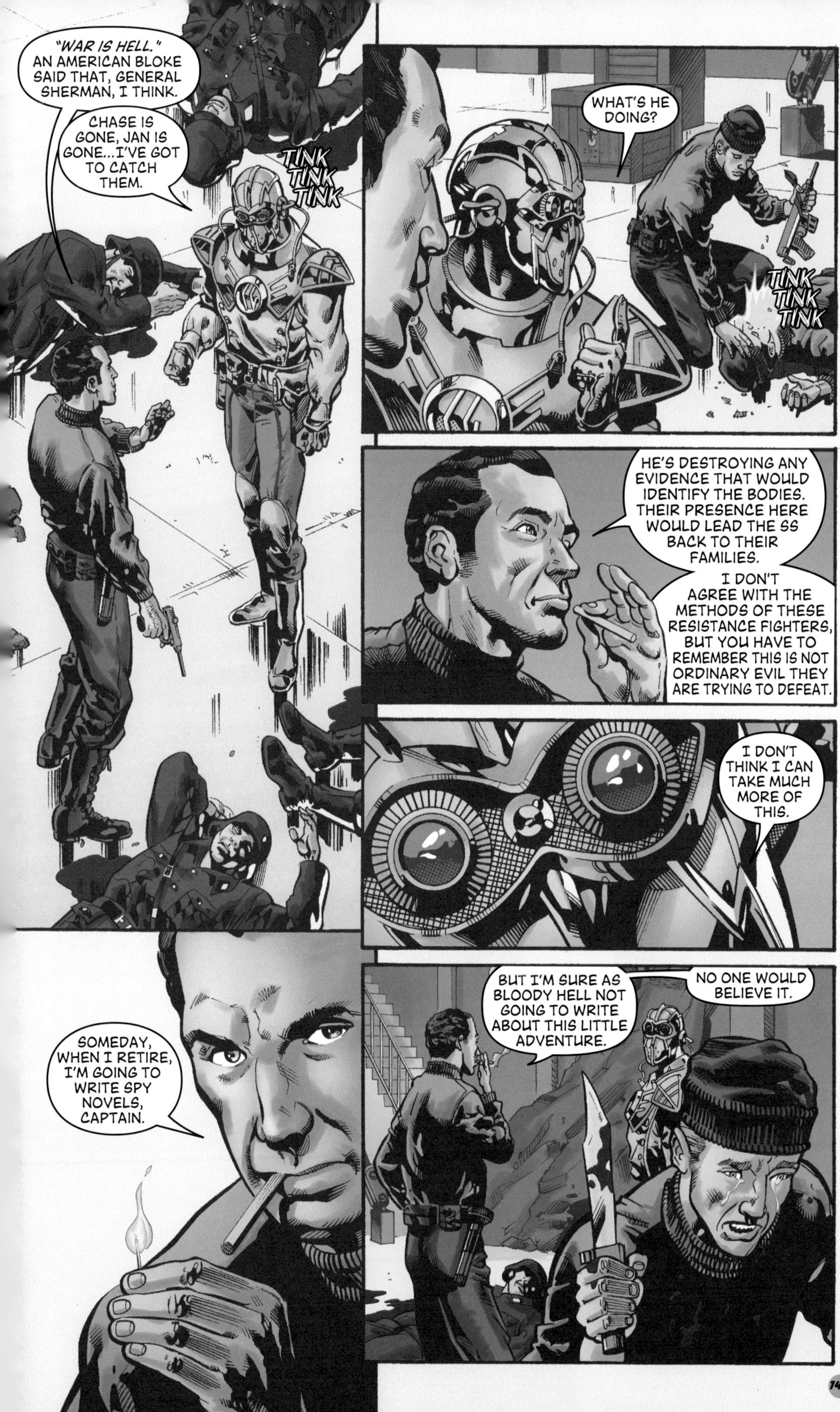
"WAR IS HELL." AN AMERICAN BLOKE SAID THAT, GENERAL SHERMAN, I THINK.
CHASE IS GONE, JAN IS GONE...I'VE GOT TO CATCH THEM.
TINK TINK TINK
WHAT'S HE DOING?
TINK TINK TINK
HE'S DESTROYING ANY EVIDENCE THAT WOULD IDENTIFY THE BODIES. THEIR PRESENCE HERE WOULD LEAD THE SS BACK TO THEIR FAMILIES.
I DON'T AGREE WITH THE METHODS OF THESE RESISTANCE FIGHTERS, BUT YOU HAVE TO REMEMBER THIS IS NOT ORDINARY EVIL THEY ARE TRYING TO DEFEAT.
I DON'T THINK I CAN TAKE MUCH MORE OF THIS.
SOMEDAY, WHEN I RETIRE, I'M GOING TO WRITE SPY NOVELS, CAPTAIN.
BUT I'M SURE AS BLOODY HELL NOT GOING TO WRITE ABOUT THIS LITTLE ADVENTURE.
NO ONE WOULD BELIEVE IT.

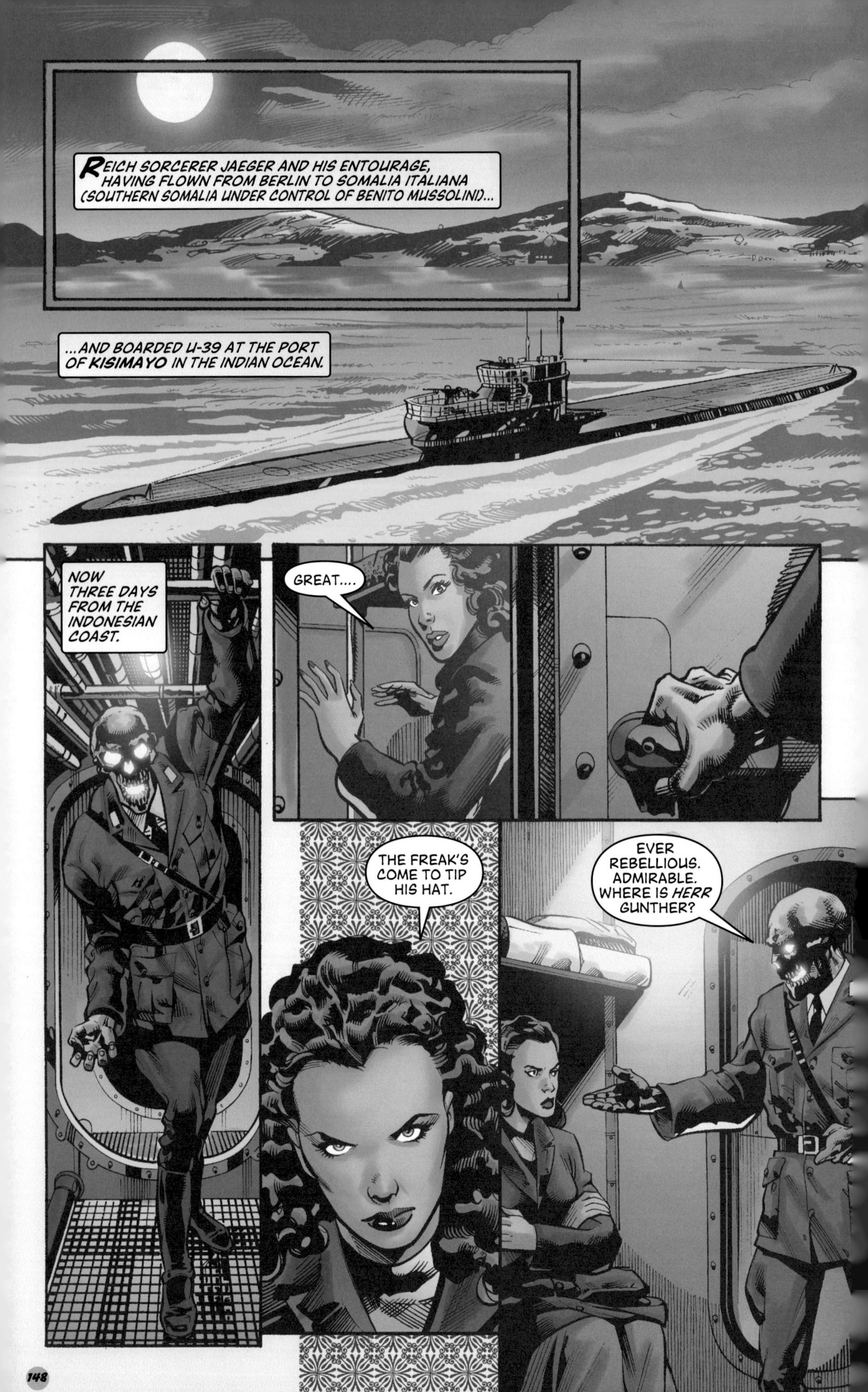
REICH SORCERER JAEGER AND HIS ENTOURAGE, HAVING FLOWN FROM BERLIN TO SOMALIA ITALIANA (SOUTHERN SOMALIA UNDER CONTROL OF BENITO MUSSOLINI)...
...AND BOARDED U-39 AT THE PORT OF KISIMAYO IN THE INDIAN OCEAN.
NOW THREE DAYS FROM THE INDONESIAN COAST.
GREAT....
THE FREAK'S COME TO TIP HIS HAT.
EVER REBELLIOUS. ADMIRABLE. WHERE IS HERR GUNTHER?

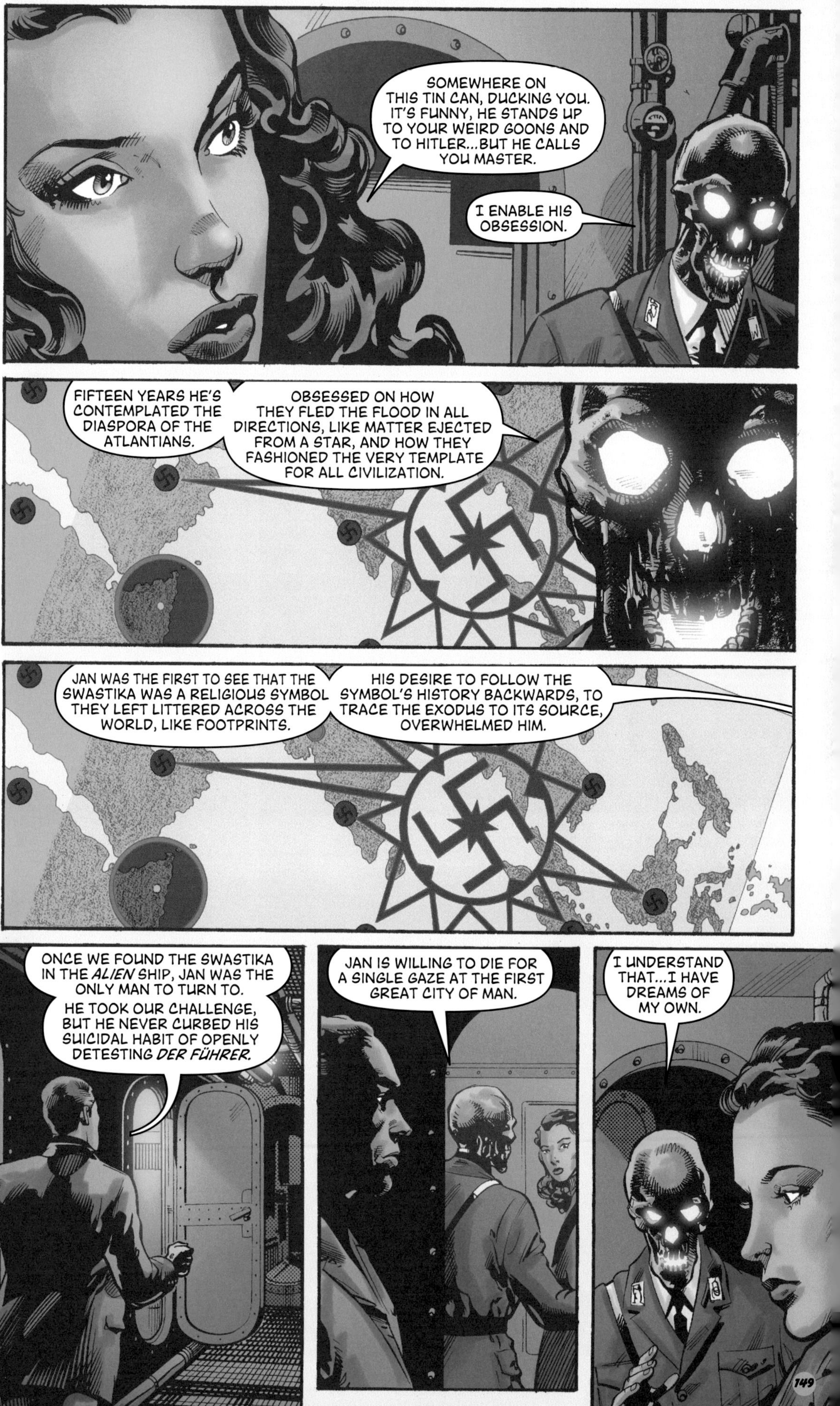
SOMEWHERE ON THIS TIN CAN, DUCKING YOU. IT'S FUNNY, HE STANDS UP TO YOUR WEIRD GOONS AND TO HITLER...BUT HE CALLS YOU MASTER.
I ENABLE HIS OBSESSION.
FIFTEEN YEARS HE'S CONTEMPLATED THE DIASPORA OF THE ATLANTIANS.
OBSESSED ON HOW THEY FLED THE FLOOD IN ALL DIRECTIONS, LIKE MATTER EJECTED FROM A STAR, AND HOW THEY FASHIONED THE VERY TEMPLATE FOR ALL CIVILIZATION.
JAN WAS THE FIRST TO SEE THAT THE SWASTIKA WAS A RELIGIOUS SYMBOL THEY LEFT LITTERED ACROSS THE WORLD, LIKE FOOTPRINTS.
HIS DESIRE TO FOLLOW THE SYMBOL'S HISTORY BACKWARDS, TO TRACE THE EXODUS TO ITS SOURCE, OVERWHELMED HIM.
ONCE WE FOUND THE SWASTIKA IN THE *ALIEN* SHIP, JAN WAS THE ONLY MAN TO TURN TO.
HE TOOK OUR CHALLENGE, BUT HE NEVER CURBED HIS SUICIDAL HABIT OF OPENLY DETESTING *DER FÜHRER.*
JAN IS WILLING TO DIE FOR A SINGLE GAZE AT THE FIRST GREAT CITY OF MAN.
I UNDERSTAND THAT...I HAVE DREAMS OF MY OWN.

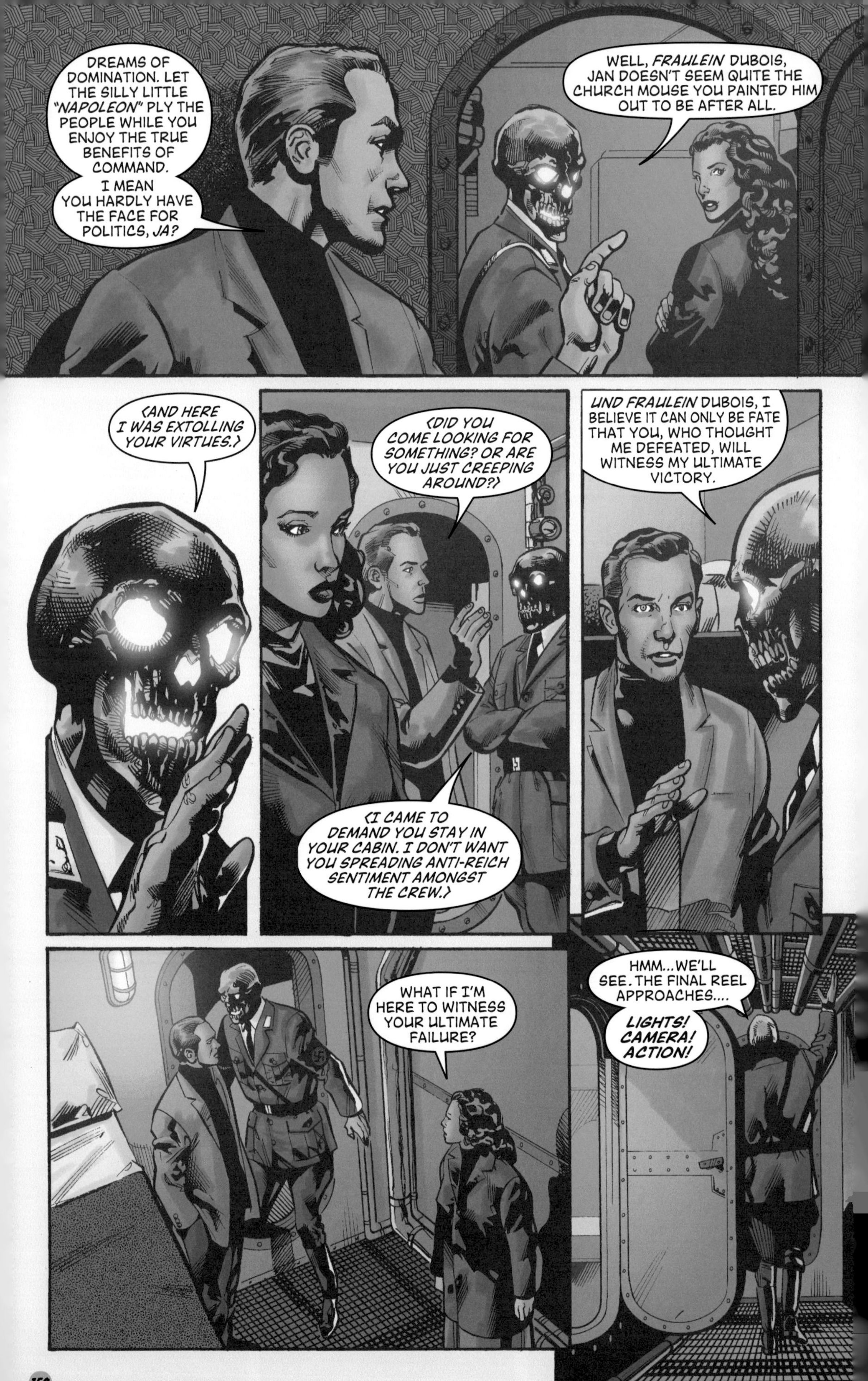
DREAMS OF DOMINATION. LET THE SILLY LITTLE "NAPOLEON" PLY THE PEOPLE WHILE YOU ENJOY THE TRUE BENEFITS OF COMMAND.
I MEAN YOU HARDLY HAVE THE FACE FOR POLITICS, JA?
WELL, FRAULEIN DUBOIS, JAN DOESN'T SEEM QUITE THE CHURCH MOUSE YOU PAINTED HIM OUT TO BE AFTER ALL.
<AND HERE I WAS EXTOLLING YOUR VIRTUES.>
<DID YOU COME LOOKING FOR SOMETHING? OR ARE YOU JUST CREEPING AROUND?>
<I CAME TO DEMAND YOU STAY IN YOUR CABIN. I DON'T WANT YOU SPREADING ANTI-REICH SENTIMENT AMONGST THE CREW.>
UND FRAULEIN DUBOIS, I BELIEVE IT CAN ONLY BE FATE THAT YOU, WHO THOUGHT ME DEFEATED, WILL WITNESS MY ULTIMATE VICTORY.
WHAT IF I'M HERE TO WITNESS YOUR ULTIMATE FAILURE?
HMM...WE'LL SEE. THE FINAL REEL APPROACHES....
LIGHTS! CAMERA! ACTION!

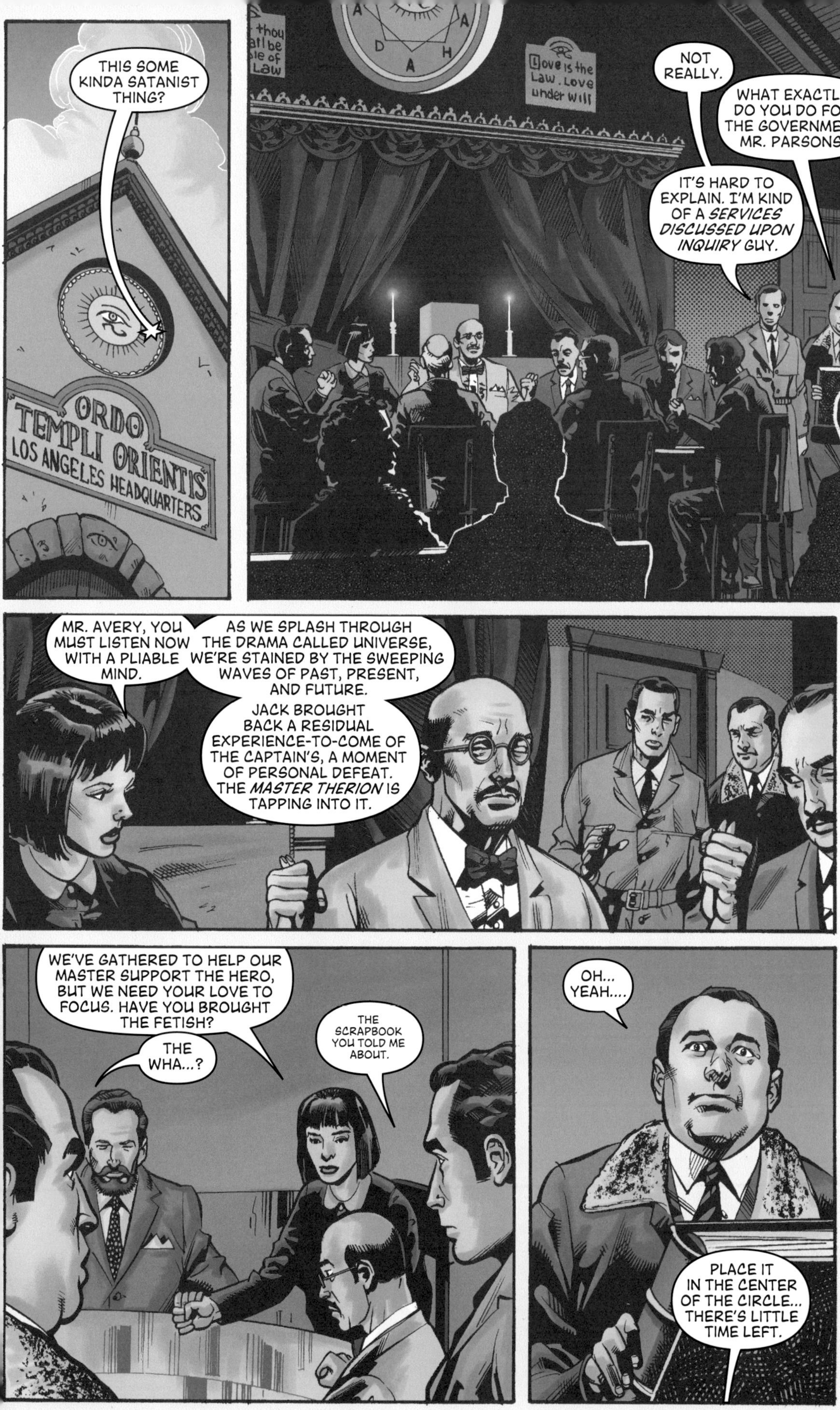
THIS SOME KINDA SATANIST THING?
ORDO TEMPLI ORIENTIS LOS ANGELES HEADQUARTERS
Love is the Law. Love under will
NOT REALLY.
WHAT EXACTLY DO YOU DO FOR THE GOVERNMENT, MR. PARSONS?
IT'S HARD TO EXPLAIN. I'M KIND OF A *SERVICES DISCUSSED UPON INQUIRY* GUY.
MR. AVERY, YOU MUST LISTEN NOW WITH A PLIABLE MIND.
AS WE SPLASH THROUGH THE DRAMA CALLED UNIVERSE, WE'RE STAINED BY THE SWEEPING WAVES OF PAST, PRESENT, AND FUTURE.
JACK BROUGHT BACK A RESIDUAL EXPERIENCE-TO-COME OF THE CAPTAIN'S, A MOMENT OF PERSONAL DEFEAT. THE *MASTER THERION* IS TAPPING INTO IT.
WE'VE GATHERED TO HELP OUR MASTER SUPPORT THE HERO, BUT WE NEED YOUR LOVE TO FOCUS. HAVE YOU BROUGHT THE FETISH?
THE WHA...?
THE SCRAPBOOK YOU TOLD ME ABOUT.
OH... YEAH....
PLACE IT IN THE CENTER OF THE CIRCLE... THERE'S LITTLE TIME LEFT.

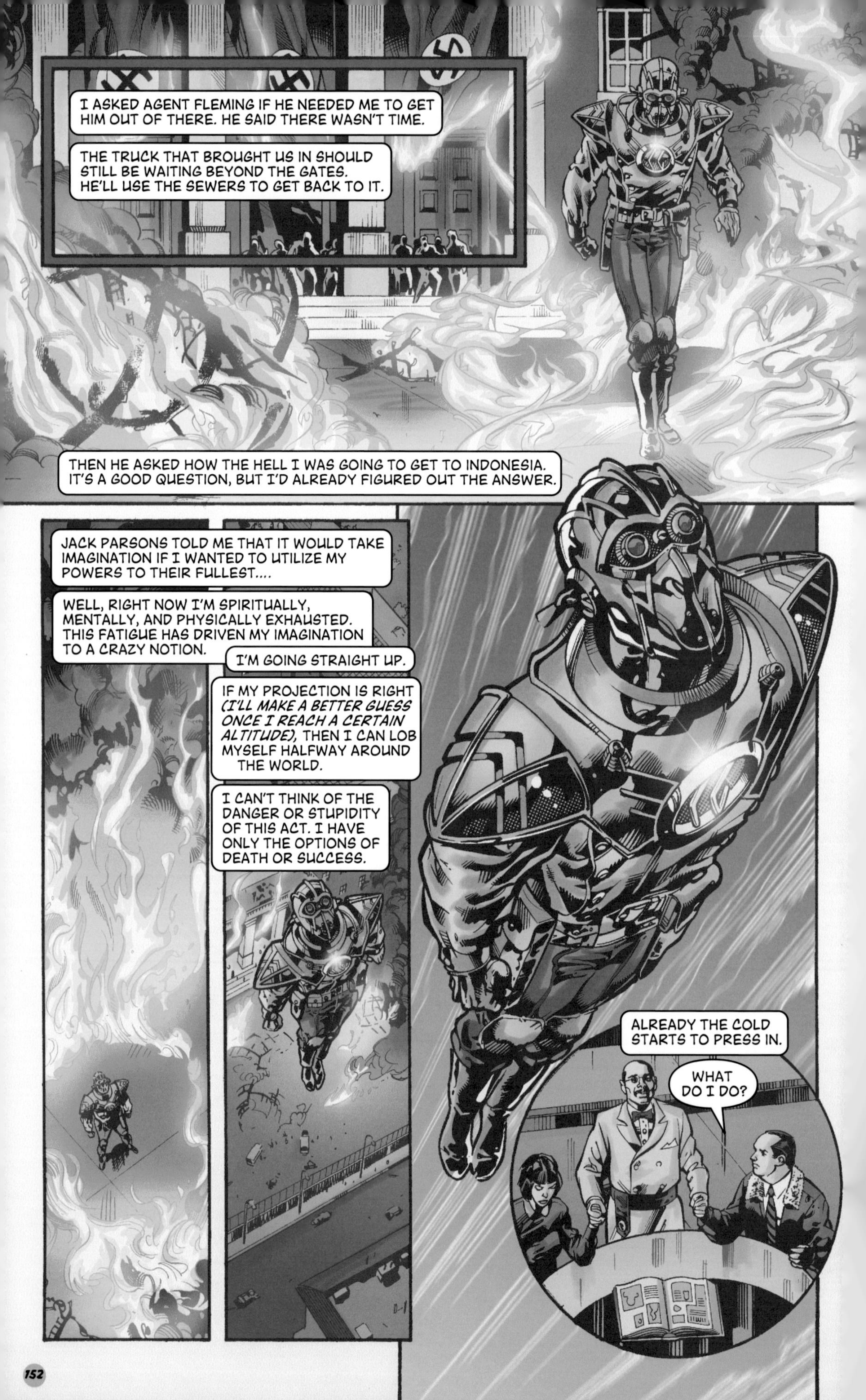
I ASKED AGENT FLEMING IF HE NEEDED ME TO GET HIM OUT OF THERE. HE SAID THERE WASN'T TIME.
THE TRUCK THAT BROUGHT US IN SHOULD STILL BE WAITING BEYOND THE GATES. HE'LL USE THE SEWERS TO GET BACK TO IT.
THEN HE ASKED HOW THE HELL I WAS GOING TO GET TO INDONESIA. IT'S A GOOD QUESTION, BUT I'D ALREADY FIGURED OUT THE ANSWER.
JACK PARSONS TOLD ME THAT IT WOULD TAKE IMAGINATION IF I WANTED TO UTILIZE MY POWERS TO THEIR FULLEST....
WELL, RIGHT NOW I'M SPIRITUALLY, MENTALLY, AND PHYSICALLY EXHAUSTED. THIS FATIGUE HAS DRIVEN MY IMAGINATION TO A CRAZY NOTION.
I'M GOING STRAIGHT UP.
IF MY PROJECTION IS RIGHT *(I'LL MAKE A BETTER GUESS ONCE I REACH A CERTAIN ALTITUDE),* THEN I CAN LOB MYSELF HALFWAY AROUND THE WORLD.
I CAN'T THINK OF THE DANGER OR STUPIDITY OF THIS ACT. I HAVE ONLY THE OPTIONS OF DEATH OR SUCCESS.
ALREADY THE COLD STARTS TO PRESS IN.
WHAT DO I DO?

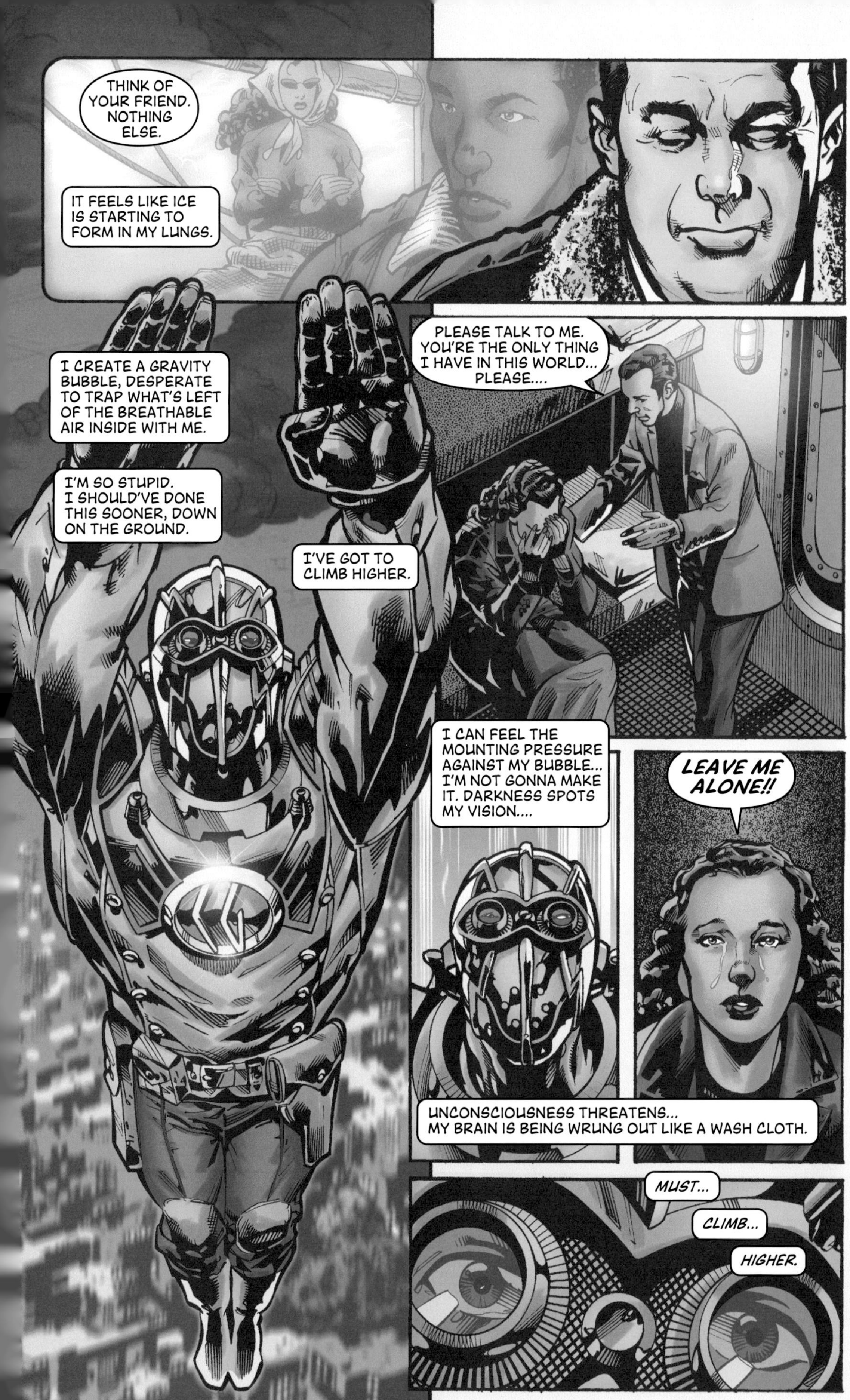
THINK OF YOUR FRIEND. NOTHING ELSE.
IT FEELS LIKE ICE IS STARTING TO FORM IN MY LUNGS.
I CREATE A GRAVITY BUBBLE, DESPERATE TO TRAP WHAT'S LEFT OF THE BREATHABLE AIR INSIDE WITH ME.
I'M SO STUPID. I SHOULD'VE DONE THIS SOONER, DOWN ON THE GROUND.
I'VE GOT TO CLIMB HIGHER.
PLEASE TALK TO ME. YOU'RE THE ONLY THING I HAVE IN THIS WORLD... PLEASE....
I CAN FEEL THE MOUNTING PRESSURE AGAINST MY BUBBLE... I'M NOT GONNA MAKE IT. DARKNESS SPOTS MY VISION....
LEAVE ME ALONE!!
UNCONSCIOUSNESS THREATENS...
MY BRAIN IS BEING WRUNG OUT LIKE A WASH CLOTH.
MUST...
CLIMB...
HIGHER.

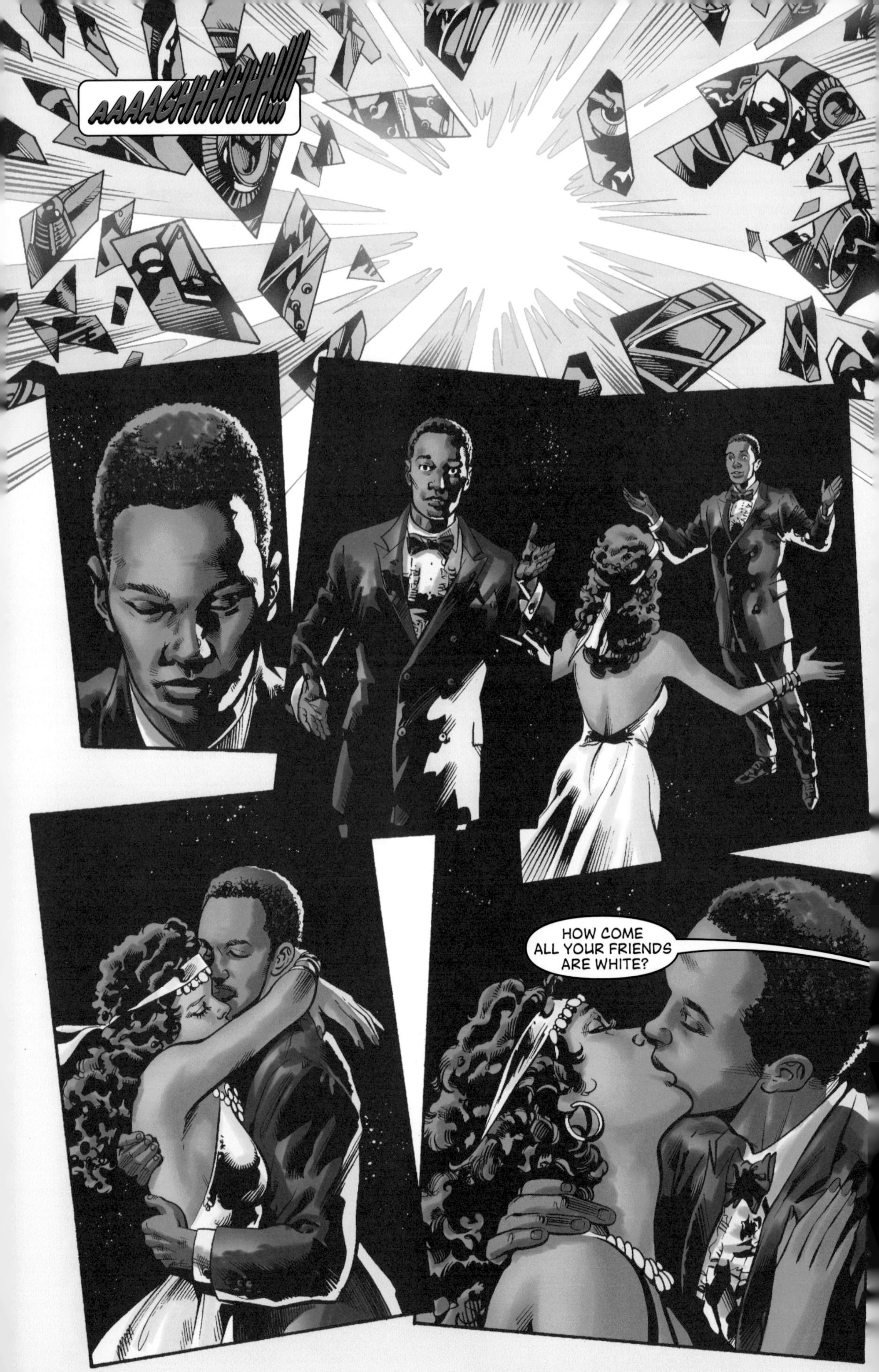
AAAAGHHHHHH!!!!
HOW COME ALL YOUR FRIENDS ARE WHITE?

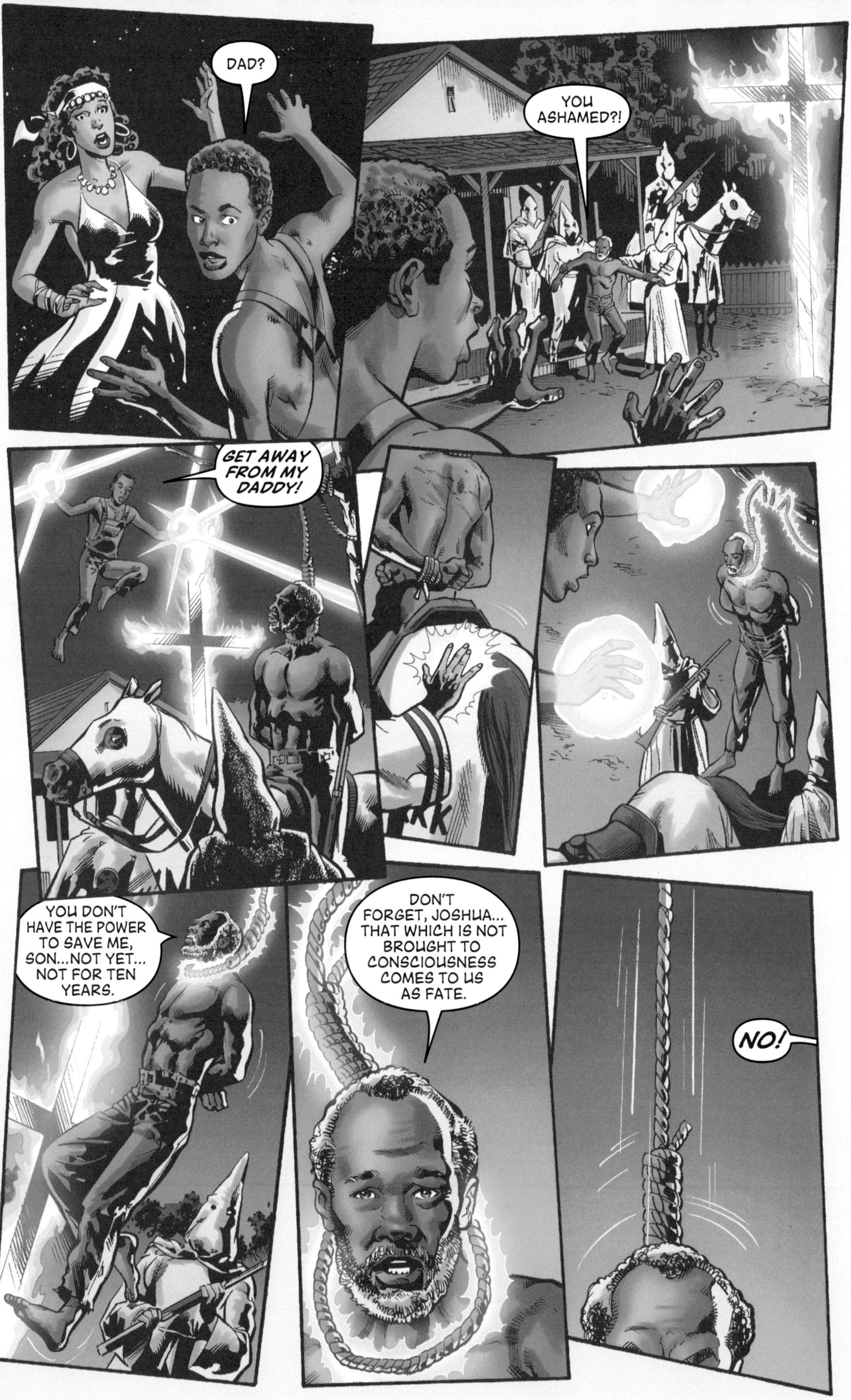
DAD?
YOU ASHAMED?!
GET AWAY FROM MY DADDY!
KKK
YOU DON'T HAVE THE POWER TO SAVE ME, SON...NOT YET... NOT FOR TEN YEARS.
DON'T FORGET, JOSHUA... THAT WHICH IS NOT BROUGHT TO CONSCIOUSNESS COMES TO US AS FATE.
NO!

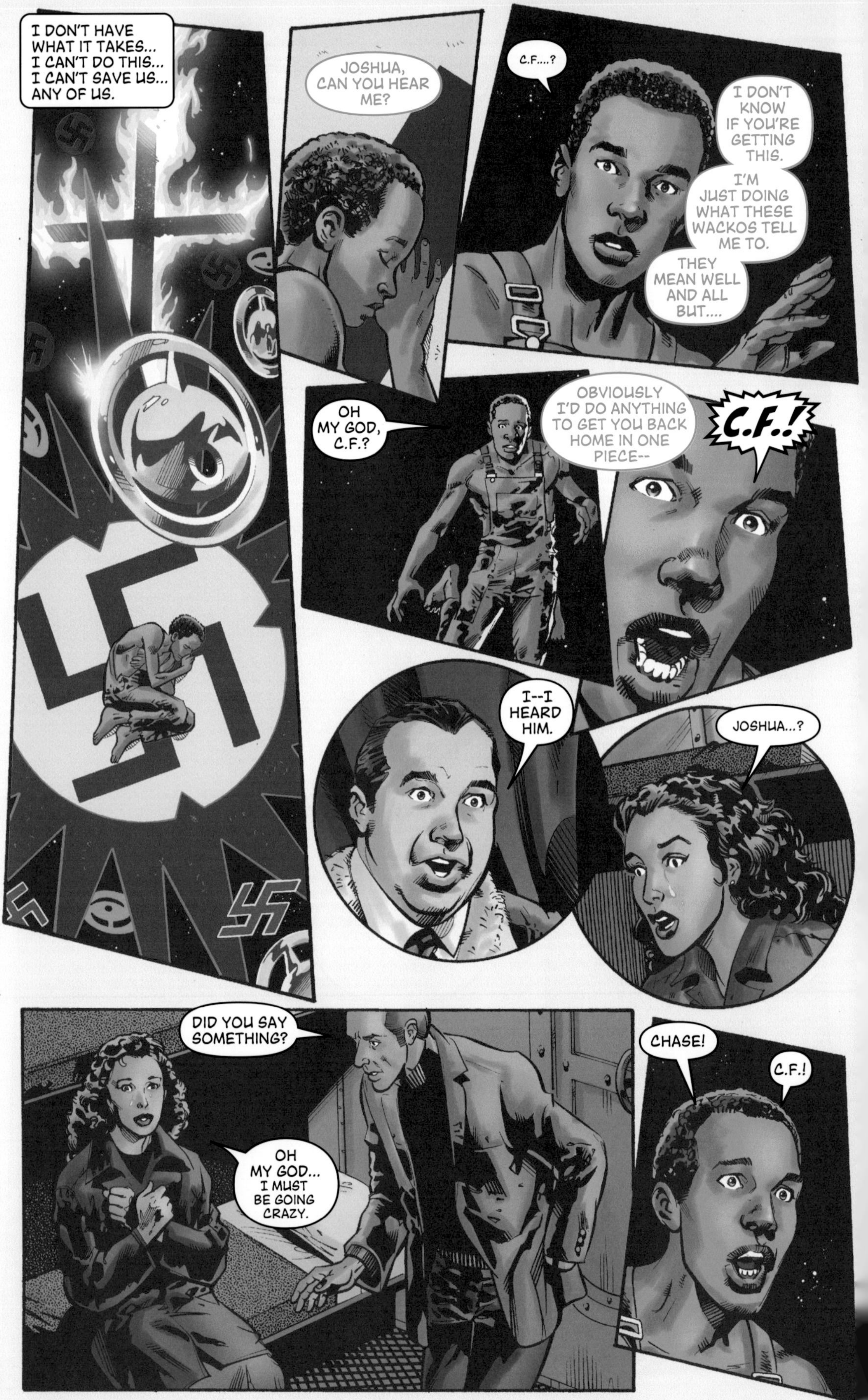
I DON'T HAVE WHAT IT TAKES... I CAN'T DO THIS... I CAN'T SAVE US... ANY OF US.
JOSHUA, CAN YOU HEAR ME?
C.F....?
I DON'T KNOW IF YOU'RE GETTING THIS.
I'M JUST DOING WHAT THESE WACKOS TELL ME TO.
THEY MEAN WELL AND ALL BUT....
OH MY GOD, C.F.?
OBVIOUSLY I'D DO ANYTHING TO GET YOU BACK HOME IN ONE PIECE--
C.F.!
I--I HEARD HIM.
JOSHUA...?
DID YOU SAY SOMETHING?
OH MY GOD... I MUST BE GOING CRAZY.
CHASE!
C.F.!

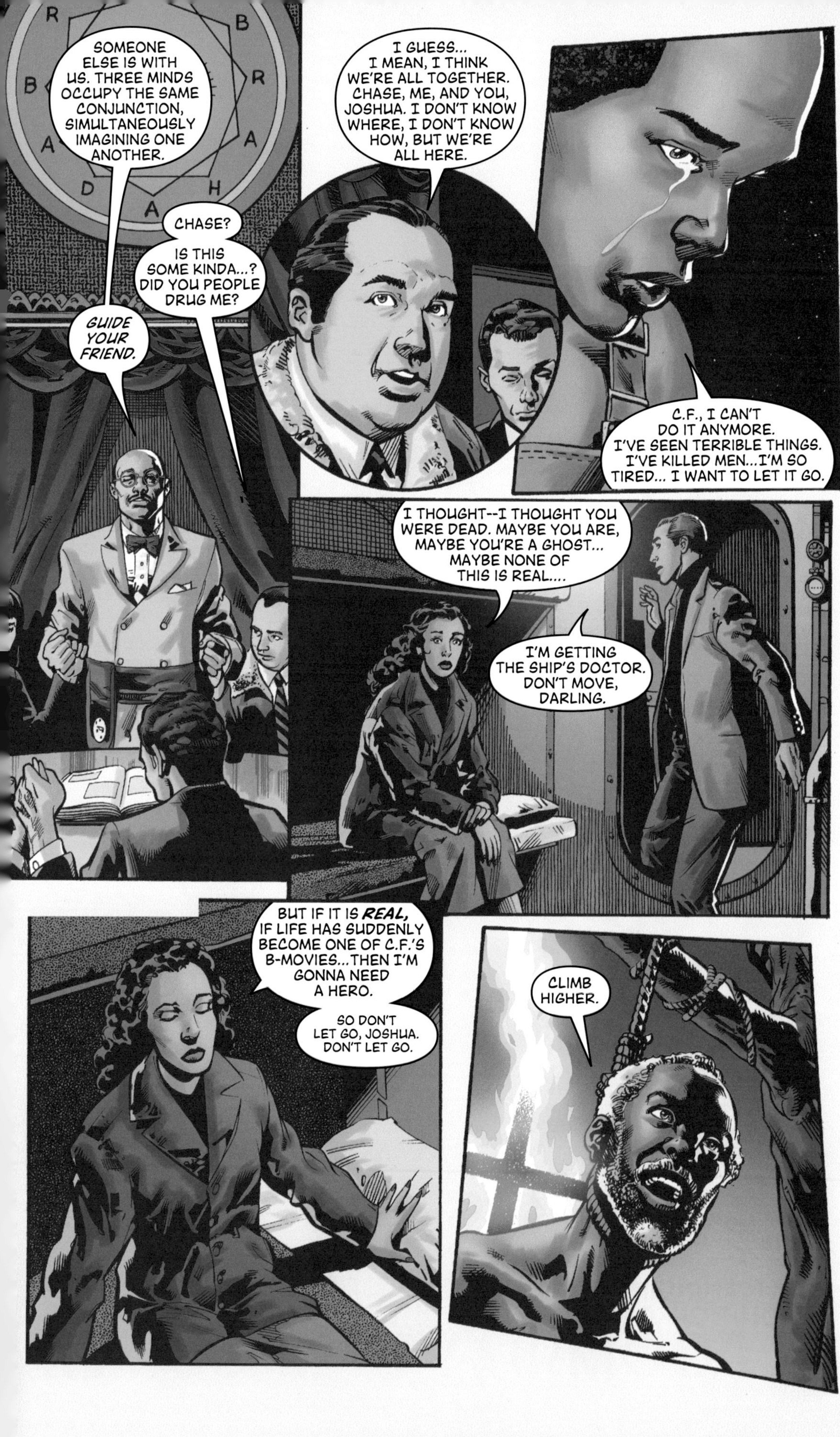
B
R
B
R
A
A
D
A
H
SOMEONE ELSE IS WITH US. THREE MINDS OCCUPY THE SAME CONJUNCTION, SIMULTANEOUSLY IMAGINING ONE ANOTHER.
GUIDE YOUR FRIEND.
CHASE?
IS THIS SOME KINDA...? DID YOU PEOPLE DRUG ME?
I GUESS... I MEAN, I THINK WE'RE ALL TOGETHER. CHASE, ME, AND YOU, JOSHUA. I DON'T KNOW WHERE, I DON'T KNOW HOW, BUT WE'RE ALL HERE.
C.F., I CAN'T DO IT ANYMORE. I'VE SEEN TERRIBLE THINGS. I'VE KILLED MEN...I'M SO TIRED... I WANT TO LET IT GO.
I THOUGHT--I THOUGHT YOU WERE DEAD. MAYBE YOU ARE, MAYBE YOU'RE A GHOST... MAYBE NONE OF THIS IS REAL....
I'M GETTING THE SHIP'S DOCTOR. DON'T MOVE, DARLING.
BUT IF IT IS *REAL,* IF LIFE HAS SUDDENLY BECOME ONE OF C.F.'S B-MOVIES...THEN I'M GONNA NEED A HERO.
SO DON'T LET GO, JOSHUA. DON'T LET GO.
CLIMB HIGHER.

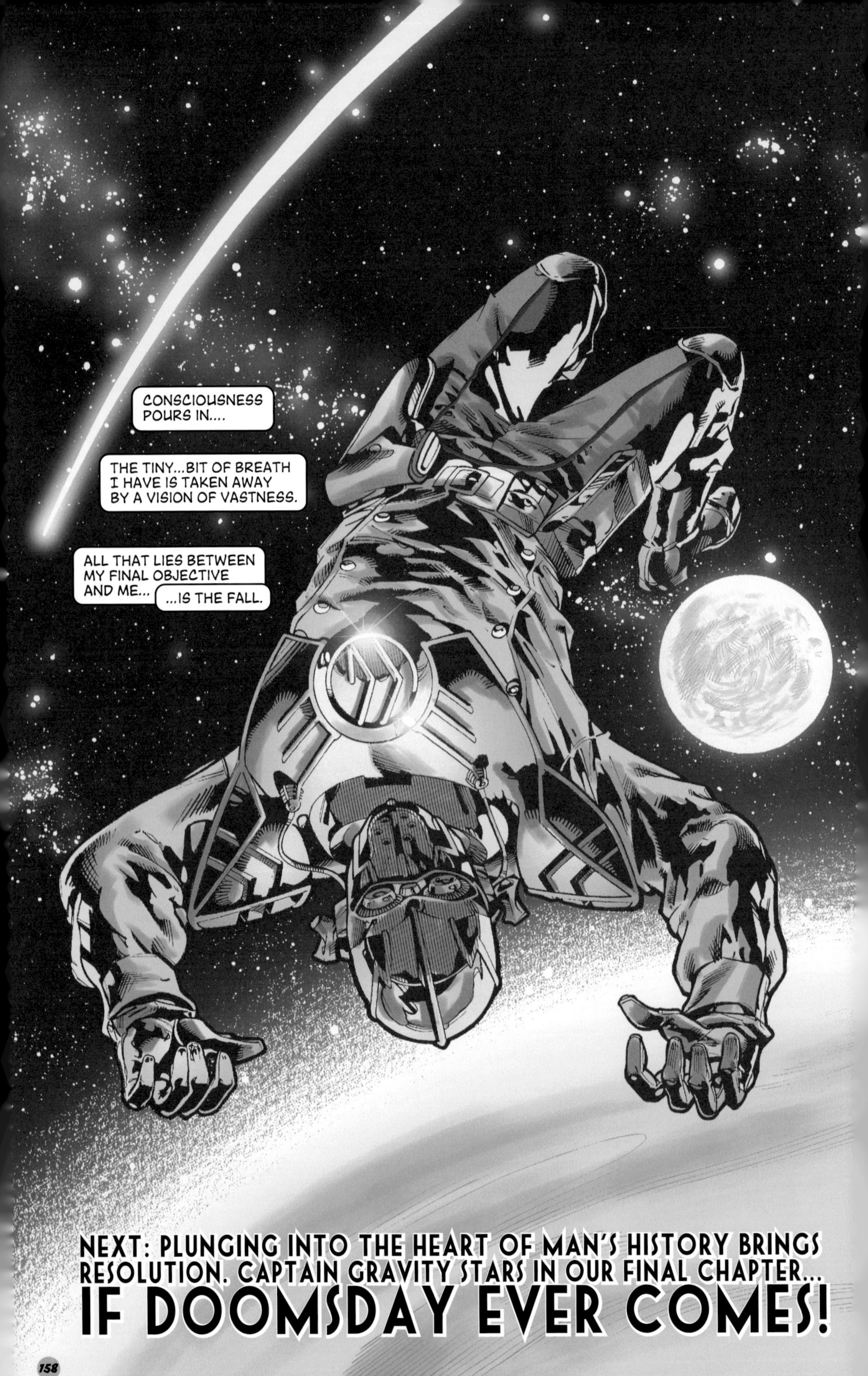
CONSCIOUSNESS POURS IN....
THE TINY...BIT OF BREATH I HAVE IS TAKEN AWAY BY A VISION OF VASTNESS.
ALL THAT LIES BETWEEN MY FINAL OBJECTIVE AND ME...
...IS THE FALL.
NEXT: PLUNGING INTO THE HEART OF MAN'S HISTORY BRINGS RESOLUTION. CAPTAIN GRAVITY STARS IN OUR FINAL CHAPTER...
IF DOOMSDAY EVER COMES!

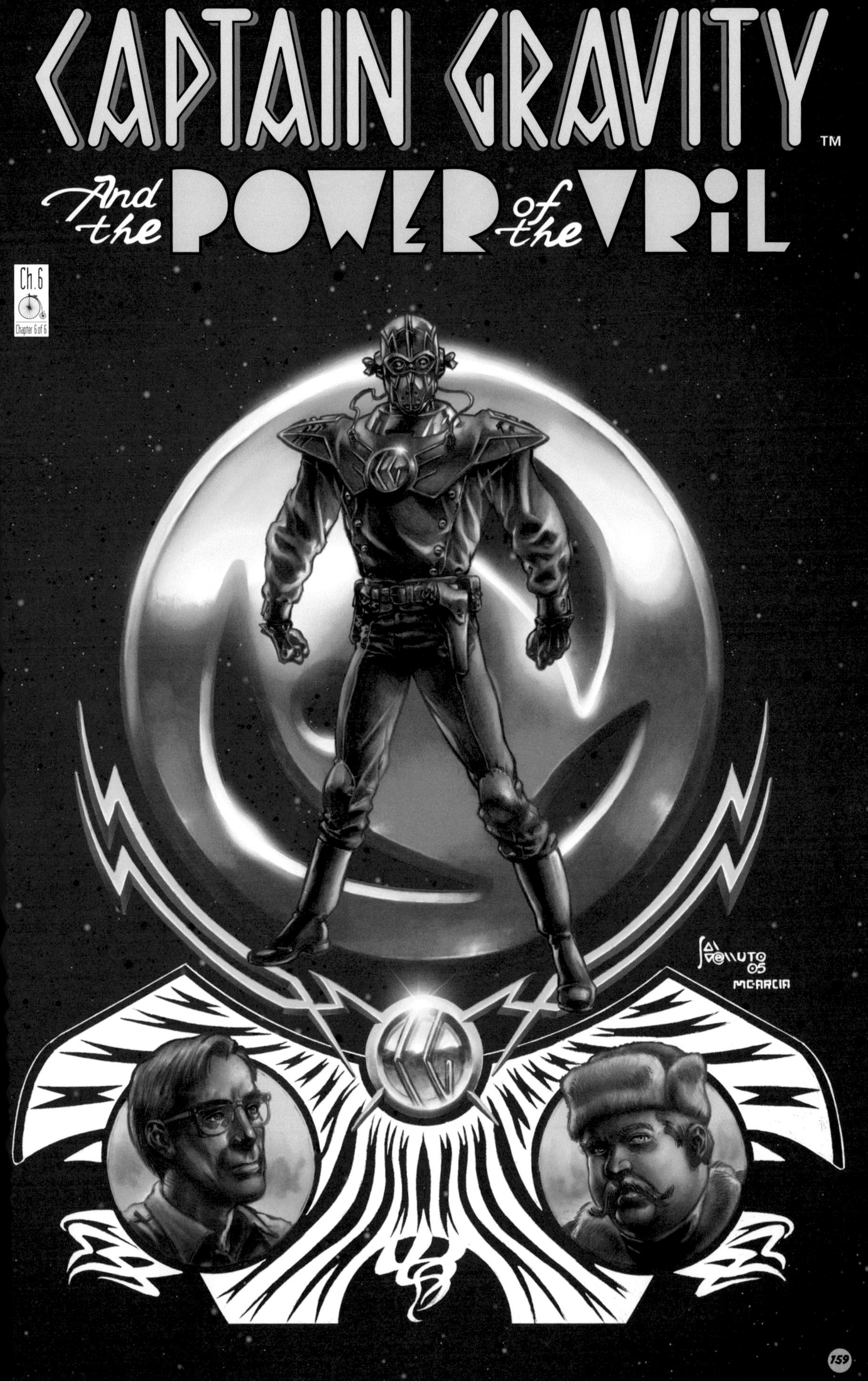
CAPTAIN GRAVITY™
And the POWER of the VRIL
Ch. 6
Chapter 6 of 6
MCGARCIA

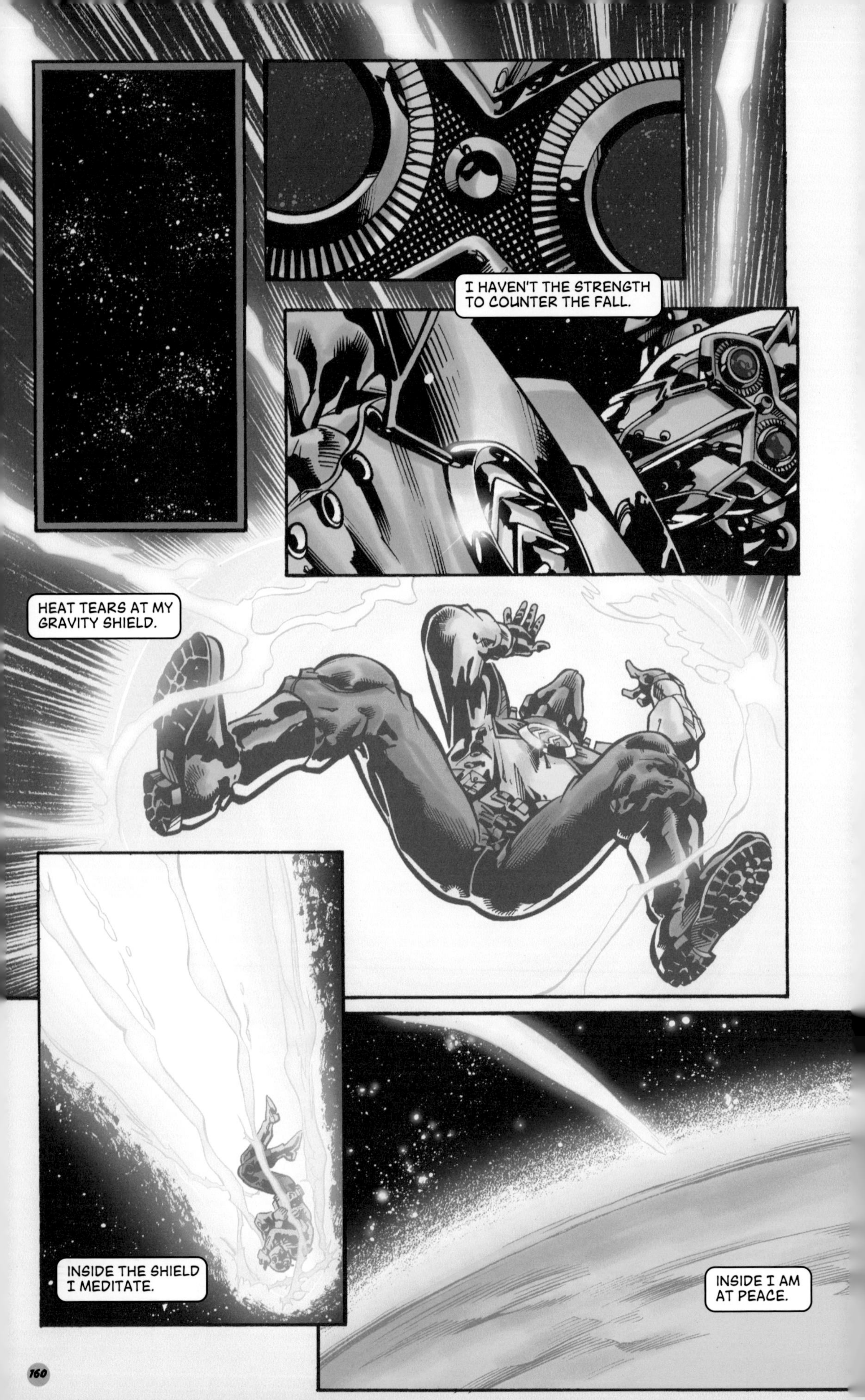
I HAVEN'T THE STRENGTH TO COUNTER THE FALL.
HEAT TEARS AT MY GRAVITY SHIELD.
INSIDE THE SHIELD I MEDITATE.
INSIDE I AM AT PEACE.

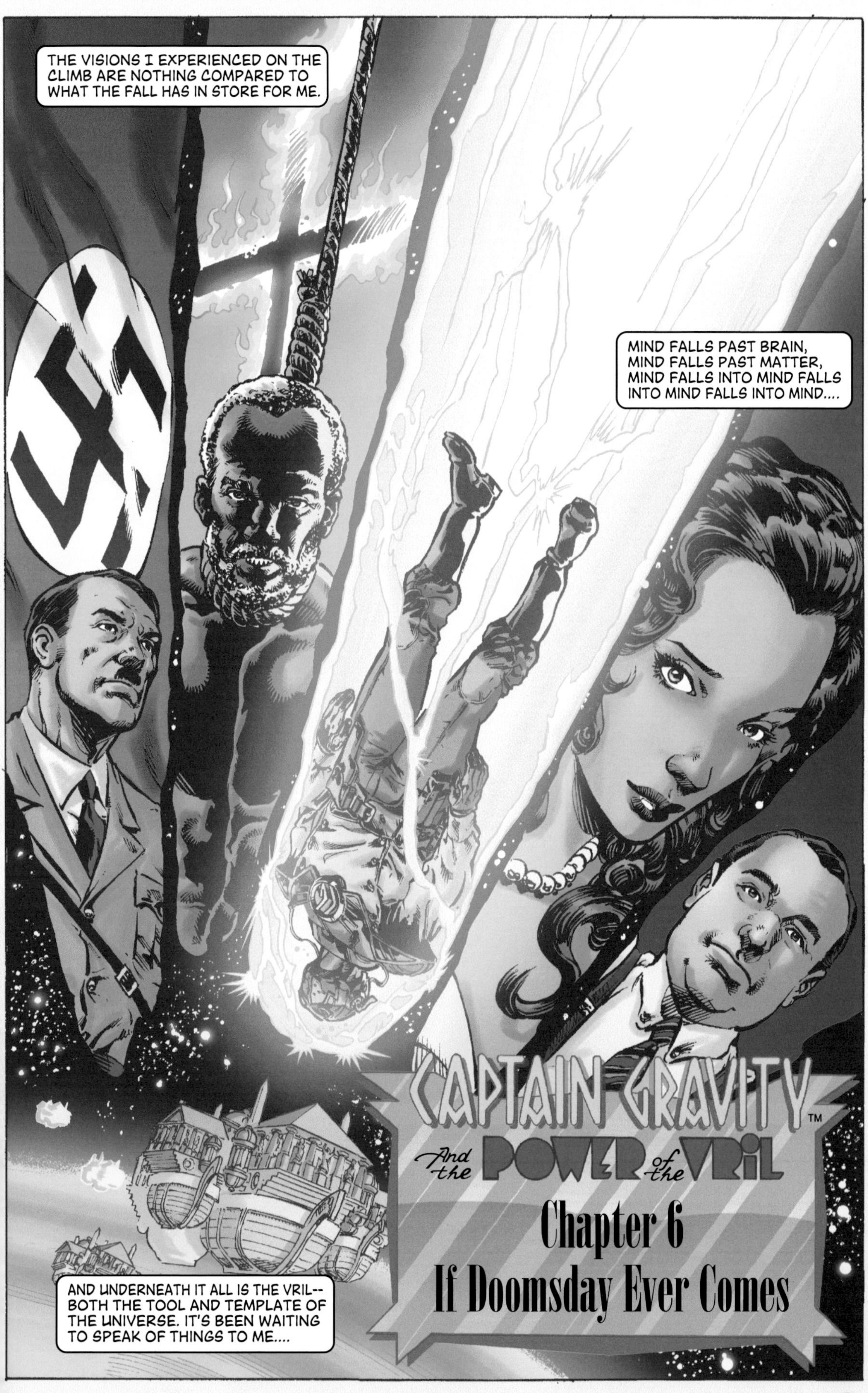

THE VISIONS I EXPERIENCED ON THE CLIMB ARE NOTHING COMPARED TO WHAT THE FALL HAS IN STORE FOR ME.
MIND FALLS PAST BRAIN, MIND FALLS PAST MATTER, MIND FALLS INTO MIND FALLS INTO MIND FALLS INTO MIND....
CAPTAIN GRAVITY™
And the POWER of the VRIL
Chapter 6
If Doomsday Ever Comes
AND UNDERNEATH IT ALL IS THE VRIL-- BOTH THE TOOL AND TEMPLATE OF THE UNIVERSE. IT'S BEEN WAITING TO SPEAK OF THINGS TO ME....

IT'S IN THESE DEPTHS OF MYSELF THAT I LEARN HOW PROFESSOR GOETHALS (DISCOVERER OF MY POWER OVER GRAVITY) GOT SO MUCH RIGHT, BUT A FEW THINGS WRONG.

HE THEORIZED THAT IT WAS ALIENS WHO HAD VISITED THE MAYANS.

WHEN IN FACT IT WAS HUMANS. THE LAST DIRECT DESCENDENTS OF THE ATLANTIAN DIASPORA, DESPERATE TO ESCAPE THE ABUNDANT CIVILIZATIONS THAT HAD SPRUNG UP IN THEIR WAKE.

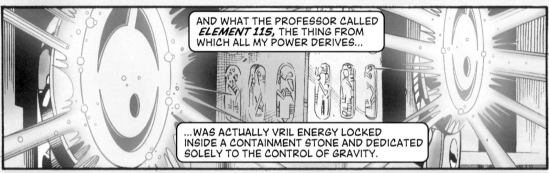

AND WHAT THE PROFESSOR CALLED *ELEMENT 115*, THE THING FROM WHICH ALL MY POWER DERIVES...

...WAS ACTUALLY VRIL ENERGY LOCKED INSIDE A CONTAINMENT STONE AND DEDICATED SOLELY TO THE CONTROL OF GRAVITY.

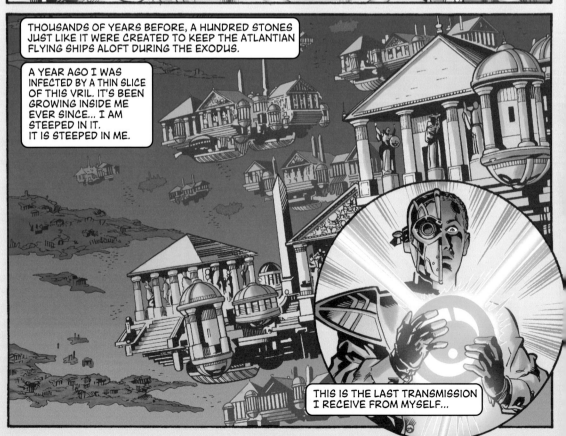

THOUSANDS OF YEARS BEFORE, A HUNDRED STONES JUST LIKE IT WERE CREATED TO KEEP THE ATLANTIAN FLYING SHIPS ALOFT DURING THE EXODUS.

A YEAR AGO I WAS INFECTED BY A THIN SLICE OF THIS VRIL. IT'S BEEN GROWING INSIDE ME EVER SINCE... I AM STEEPED IN IT. IT IS STEEPED IN ME.

THIS IS THE LAST TRANSMISSION I RECEIVE FROM MYSELF...

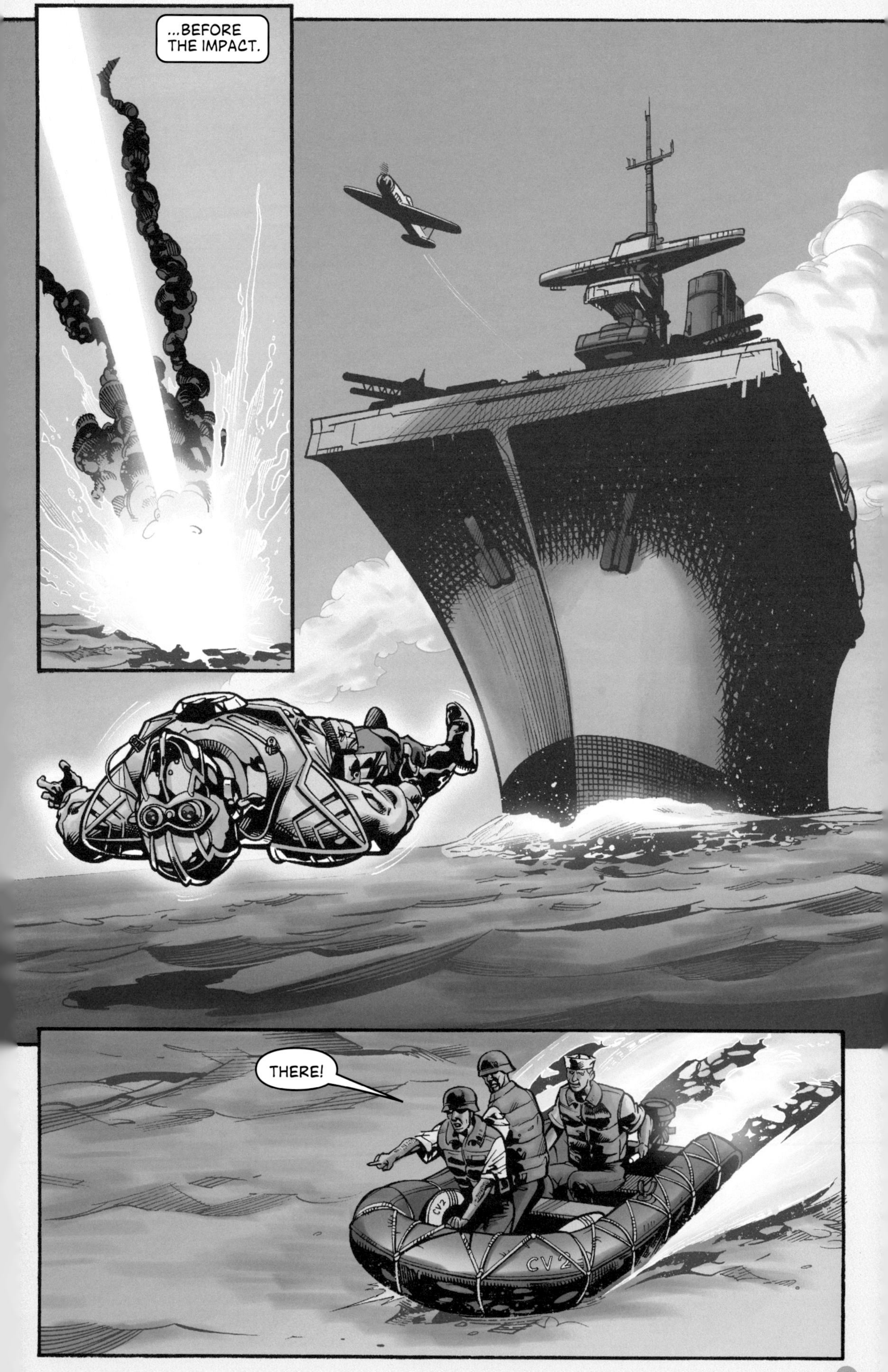
...BEFORE THE IMPACT.
THERE!

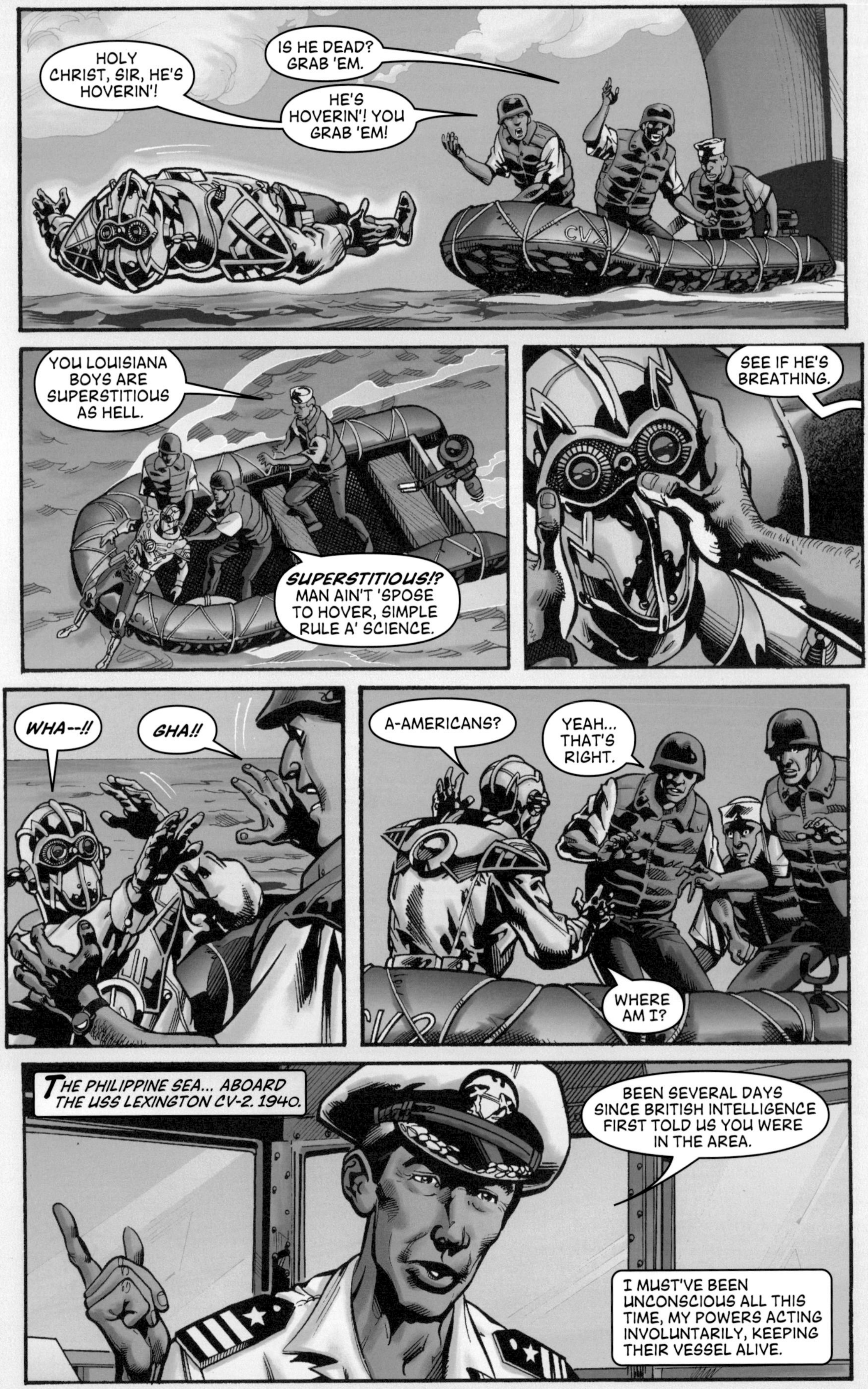
HOLY CHRIST, SIR, HE'S HOVERIN'!
IS HE DEAD? GRAB 'EM.
HE'S HOVERIN'! YOU GRAB 'EM!
YOU LOUISIANA BOYS ARE SUPERSTITIOUS AS HELL.
SUPERSTITIOUS!? MAN AIN'T 'SPOSE TO HOVER, SIMPLE RULE A' SCIENCE.
SEE IF HE'S BREATHING.
WHA--!!
GHA!!
A-AMERICANS?
YEAH... THAT'S RIGHT.
WHERE AM I?
THE PHILIPPINE SEA... ABOARD THE USS LEXINGTON CV-2. 1940.
BEEN SEVERAL DAYS SINCE BRITISH INTELLIGENCE FIRST TOLD US YOU WERE IN THE AREA.
I MUST'VE BEEN UNCONSCIOUS ALL THIS TIME, MY POWERS ACTING INVOLUNTARILY, KEEPING THEIR VESSEL ALIVE.

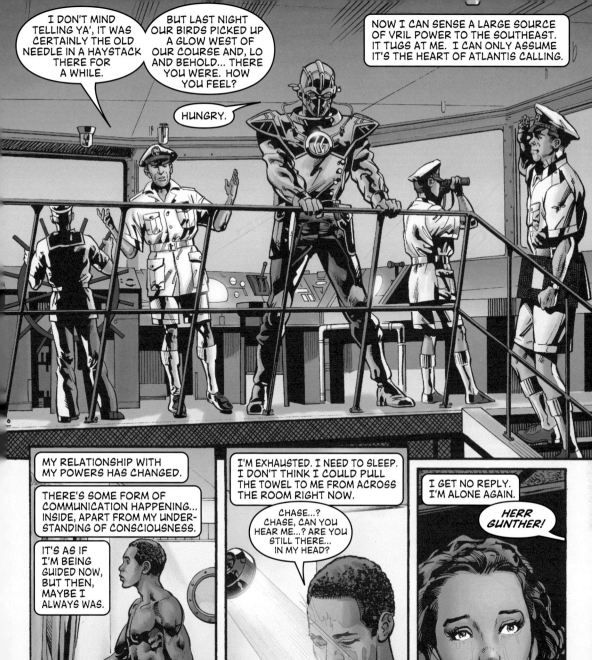

I DON'T MIND TELLING YA', IT WAS CERTAINLY THE OLD NEEDLE IN A HAYSTACK THERE FOR A WHILE.

BUT LAST NIGHT OUR BIRDS PICKED UP A GLOW WEST OF OUR COURSE AND, LO AND BEHOLD... THERE YOU WERE. HOW YOU FEEL?

HUNGRY.

NOW I CAN SENSE A LARGE SOURCE OF VRIL POWER TO THE SOUTHEAST. IT TUGS AT ME. I CAN ONLY ASSUME IT'S THE HEART OF ATLANTIS CALLING.

MY RELATIONSHIP WITH MY POWERS HAS CHANGED.

THERE'S SOME FORM OF COMMUNICATION HAPPENING... INSIDE, APART FROM MY UNDER-STANDING OF CONSCIOUSNESS.

IT'S AS IF I'M BEING GUIDED NOW, BUT THEN, MAYBE I ALWAYS WAS.

I'M EXHAUSTED. I NEED TO SLEEP. I DON'T THINK I COULD PULL THE TOWEL TO ME FROM ACROSS THE ROOM RIGHT NOW.

CHASE...? CHASE, CAN YOU HEAR ME...? ARE YOU STILL THERE... IN MY HEAD?

I GET NO REPLY. I'M ALONE AGAIN.

HERR GUNTHER!

ABOARD U-39.

165

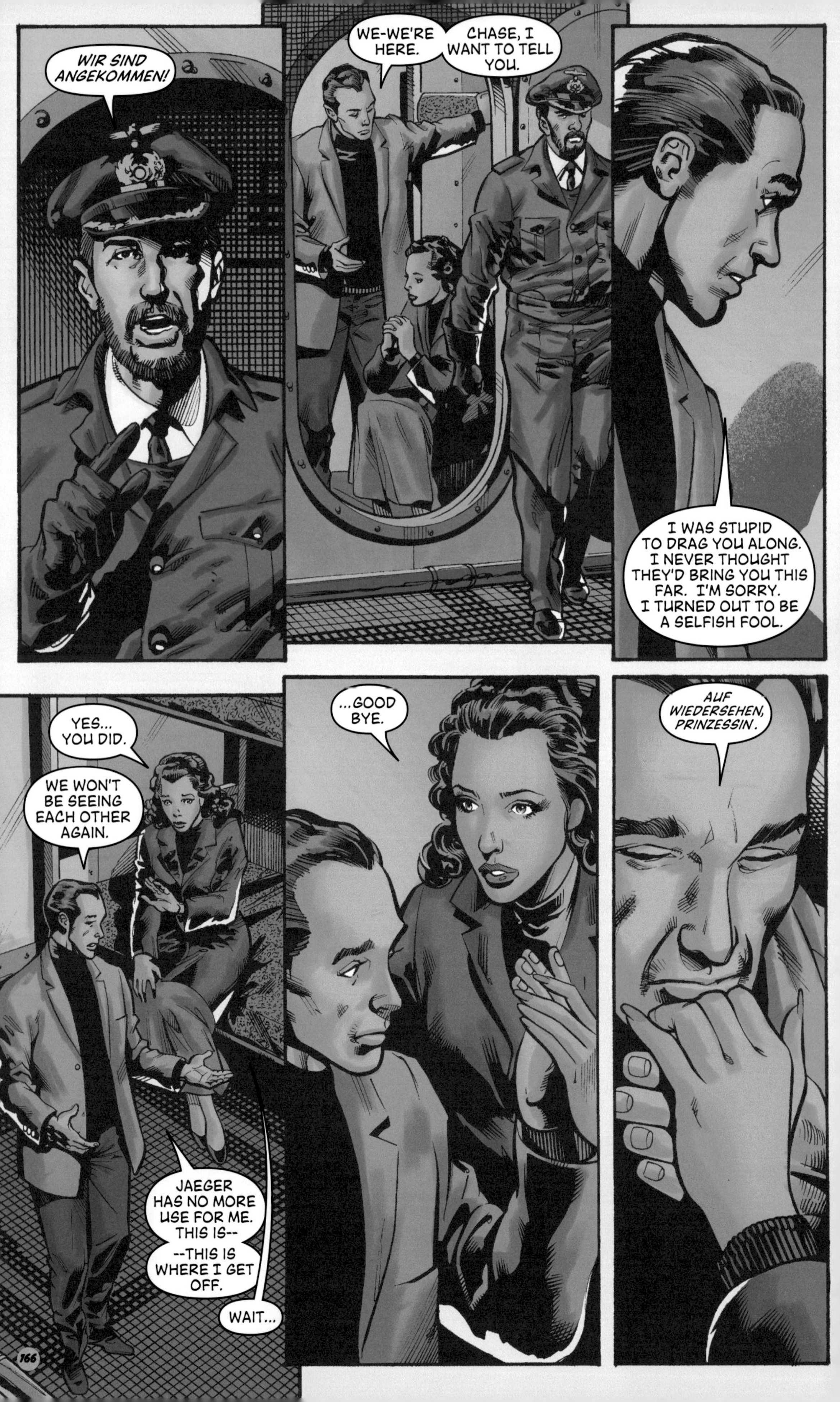
WIR SIND ANGEKOMMEN!
WE-WE'RE HERE.
CHASE, I WANT TO TELL YOU.
I WAS STUPID TO DRAG YOU ALONG. I NEVER THOUGHT THEY'D BRING YOU THIS FAR. I'M SORRY. I TURNED OUT TO BE A SELFISH FOOL.
YES... YOU DID.
WE WON'T BE SEEING EACH OTHER AGAIN.
JAEGER HAS NO MORE USE FOR ME. THIS IS--
--THIS IS WHERE I GET OFF.
WAIT...
...GOOD BYE.
AUF WIEDERSEHEN, PRINZESSIN.

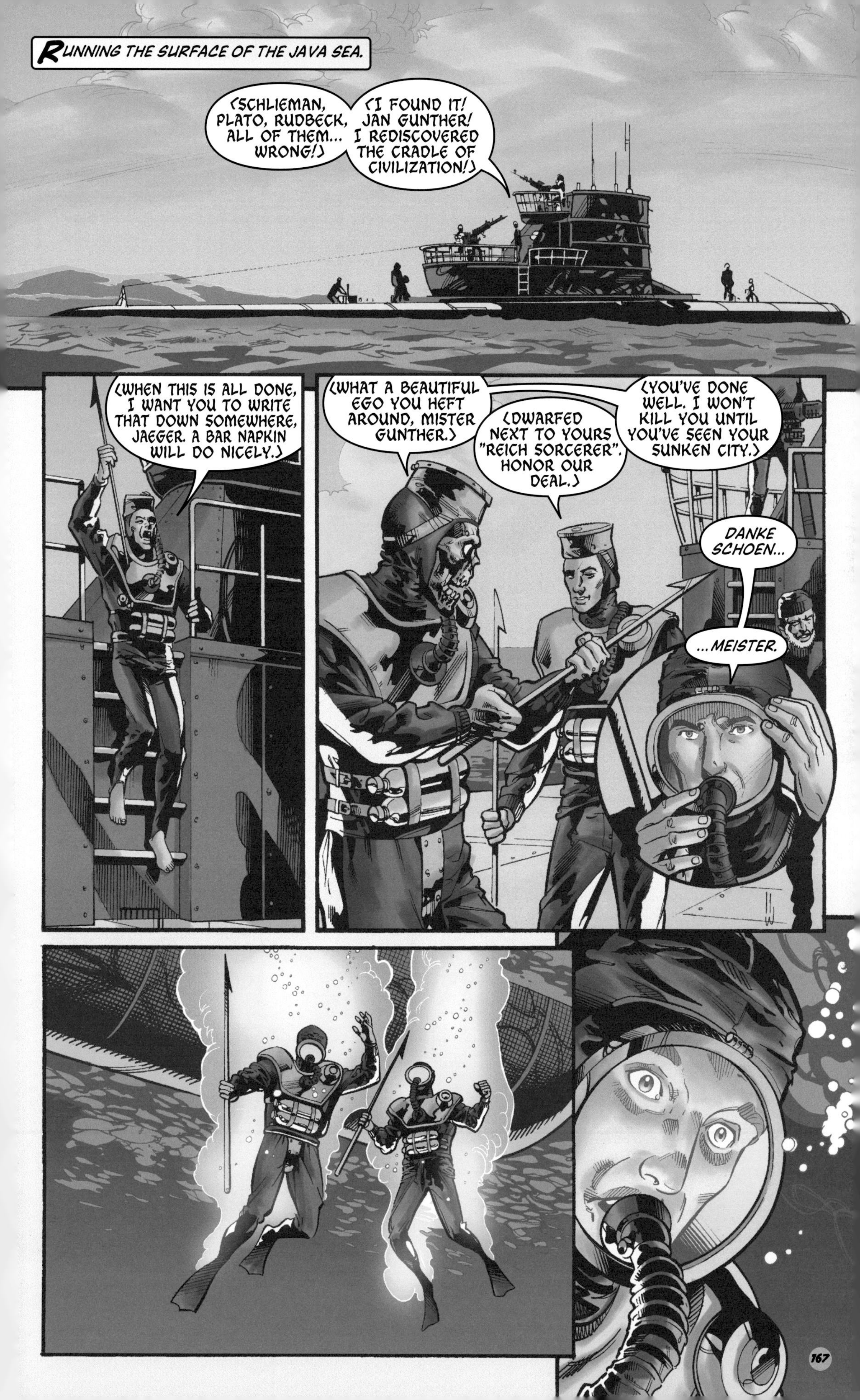
RUNNING THE SURFACE OF THE JAVA SEA.
(SCHLIEMAN, PLATO, RUDBECK, ALL OF THEM... WRONG!)
(I FOUND IT! JAN GUNTHER! I REDISCOVERED THE CRADLE OF CIVILIZATION!)
(WHEN THIS IS ALL DONE, I WANT YOU TO WRITE THAT DOWN SOMEWHERE, JAEGER. A BAR NAPKIN WILL DO NICELY.)
(WHAT A BEAUTIFUL EGO YOU HEFT AROUND, MISTER GUNTHER.)
(DWARFED NEXT TO YOURS "REICH SORCERER". HONOR OUR DEAL.)
(YOU'VE DONE WELL. I WON'T KILL YOU UNTIL YOU'VE SEEN YOUR SUNKEN CITY.)
DANKE SCHOEN...
...MEISTER.

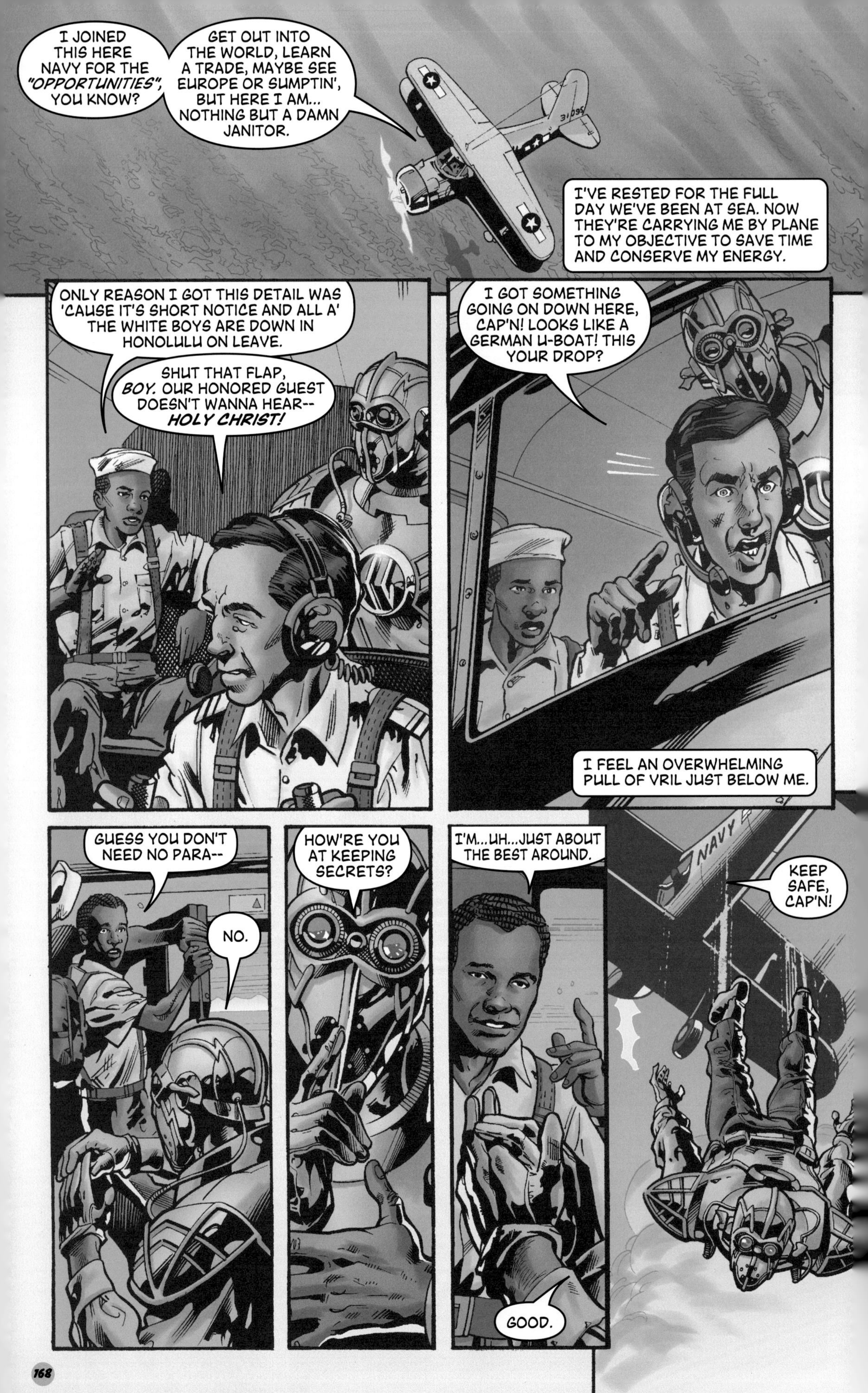

I JOINED THIS HERE NAVY FOR THE "OPPORTUNITIES", YOU KNOW?
GET OUT INTO THE WORLD, LEARN A TRADE, MAYBE SEE EUROPE OR SUMPTIN', BUT HERE I AM... NOTHING BUT A DAMN JANITOR.
I'VE RESTED FOR THE FULL DAY WE'VE BEEN AT SEA. NOW THEY'RE CARRYING ME BY PLANE TO MY OBJECTIVE TO SAVE TIME AND CONSERVE MY ENERGY.
ONLY REASON I GOT THIS DETAIL WAS 'CAUSE IT'S SHORT NOTICE AND ALL A' THE WHITE BOYS ARE DOWN IN HONOLULU ON LEAVE.
SHUT THAT FLAP, BOY. OUR HONORED GUEST DOESN'T WANNA HEAR-- HOLY CHRIST!
I GOT SOMETHING GOING ON DOWN HERE, CAP'N! LOOKS LIKE A GERMAN U-BOAT! THIS YOUR DROP?
I FEEL AN OVERWHELMING PULL OF VRIL JUST BELOW ME.
GUESS YOU DON'T NEED NO PARA--
NO.
HOW'RE YOU AT KEEPING SECRETS?
I'M...UH...JUST ABOUT THE BEST AROUND.
GOOD.
KEEP SAFE, CAP'N!

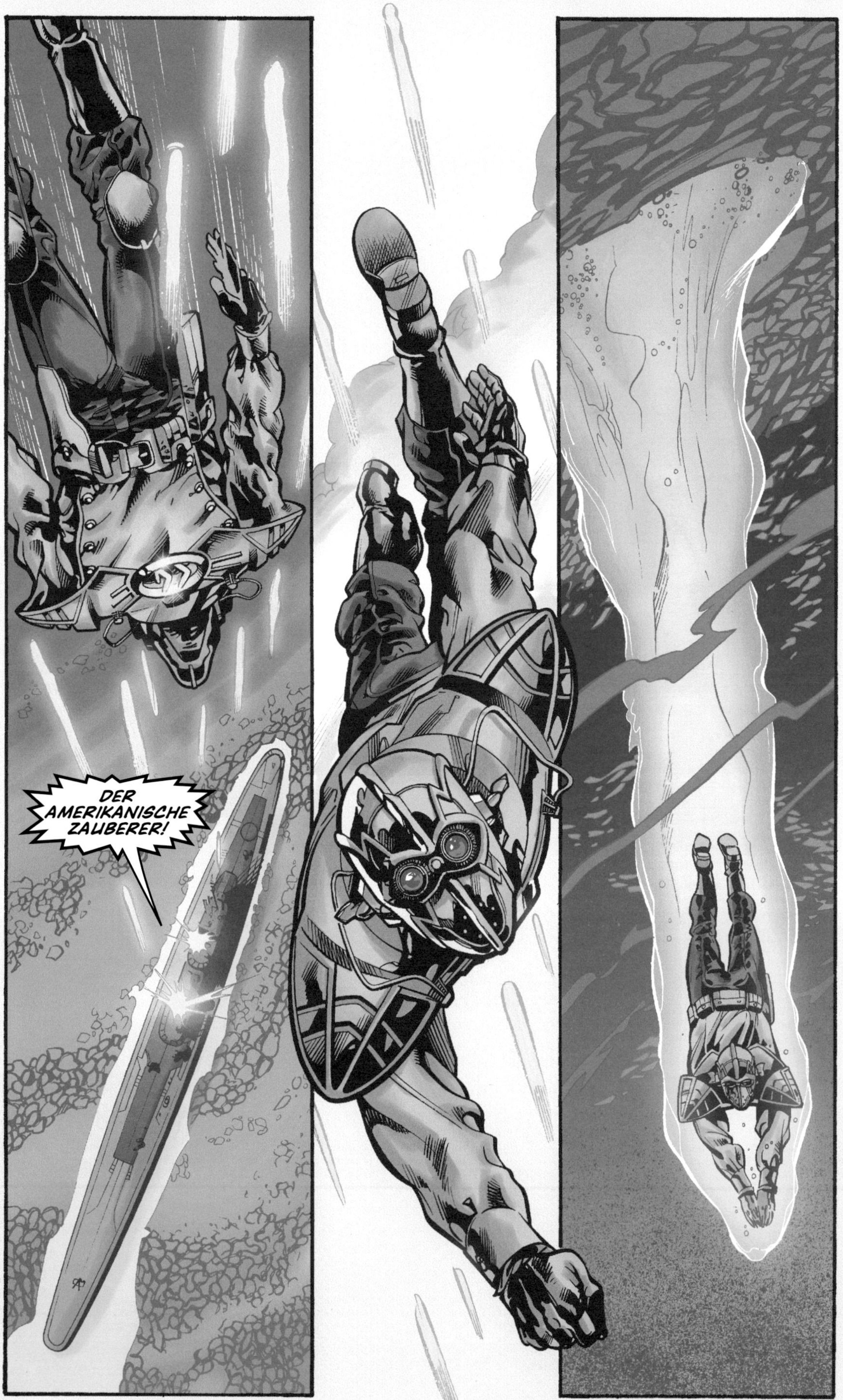
DER AMERIKANISCHE ZAUBERER!

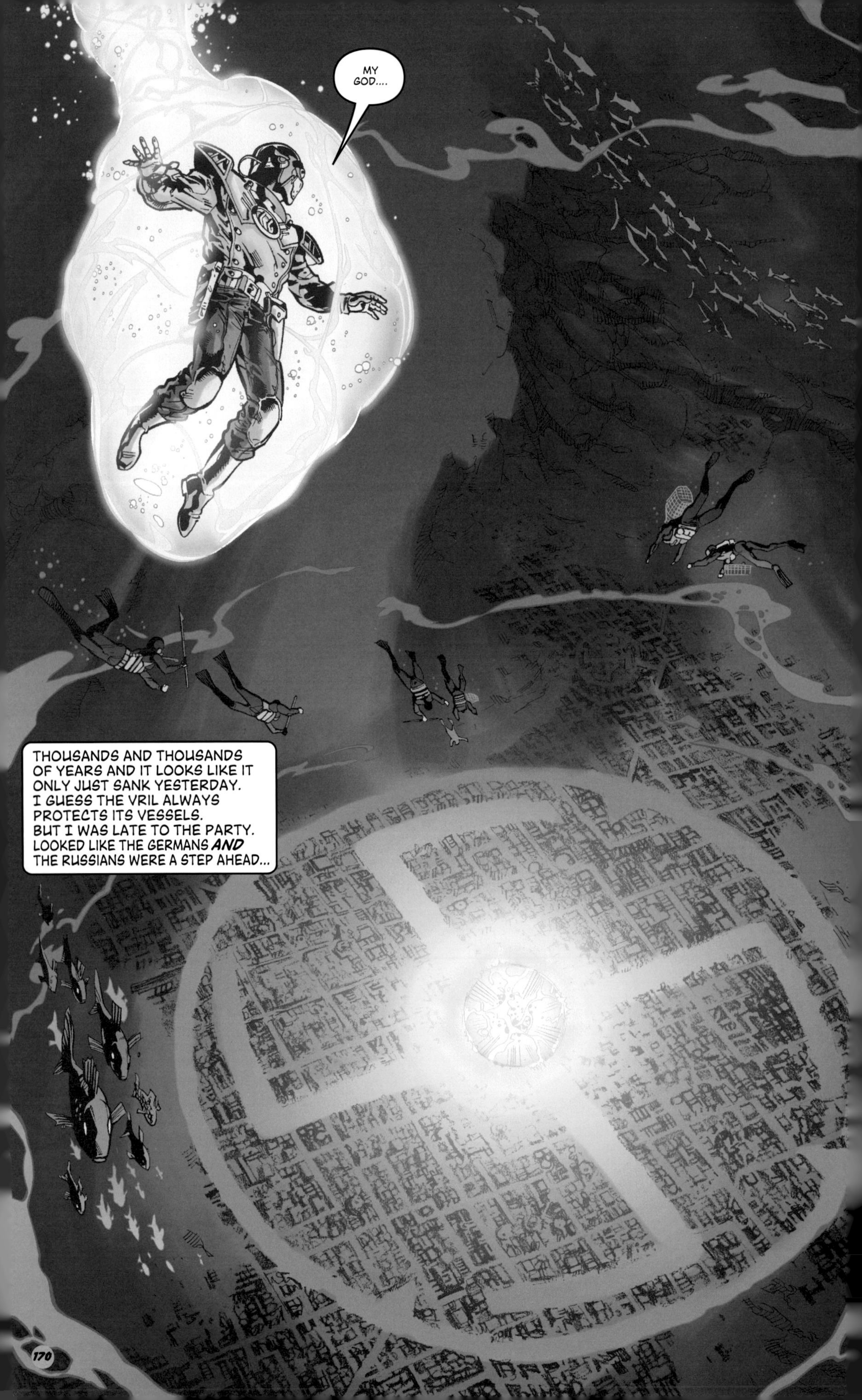
MY GOD....
THOUSANDS AND THOUSANDS OF YEARS AND IT LOOKS LIKE IT ONLY JUST SANK YESTERDAY. I GUESS THE VRIL ALWAYS PROTECTS ITS VESSELS. BUT I WAS LATE TO THE PARTY. LOOKED LIKE THE GERMANS ***AND*** THE RUSSIANS WERE A STEP AHEAD...

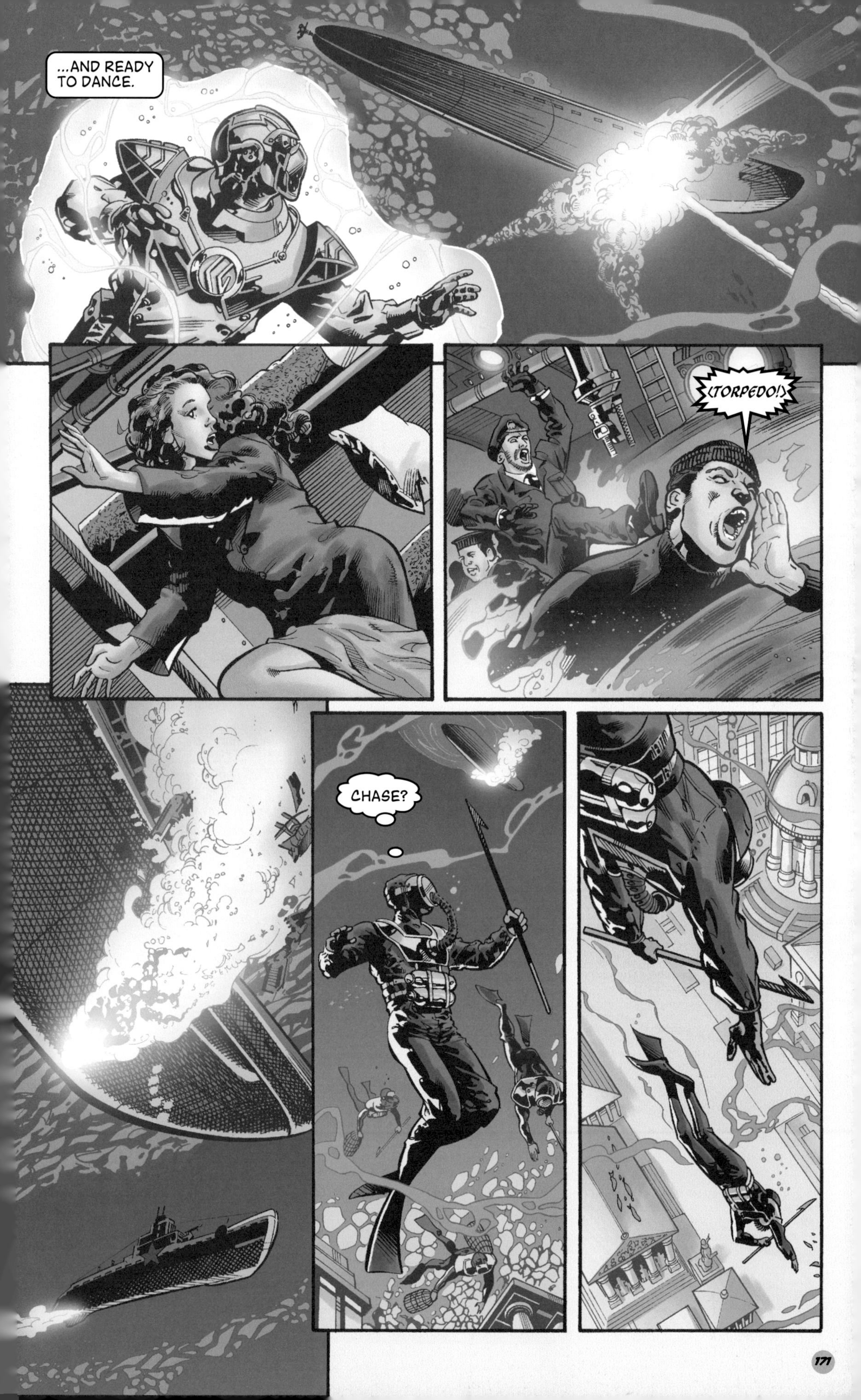
...AND READY TO DANCE.
‹TORPEDO!›
CHASE?

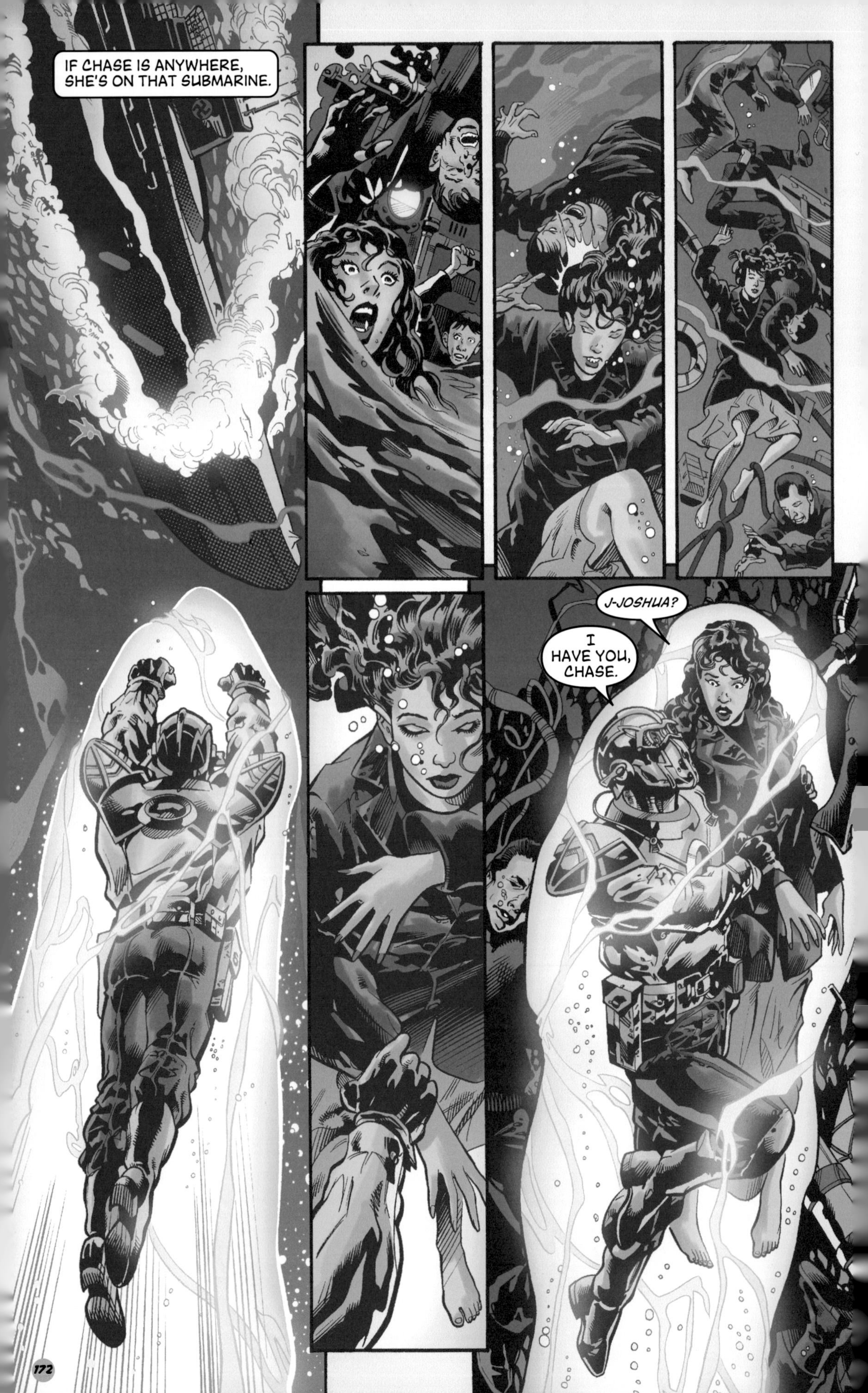
IF CHASE IS ANYWHERE, SHE'S ON THAT SUBMARINE.
J-JOSHUA?
I HAVE YOU, CHASE.

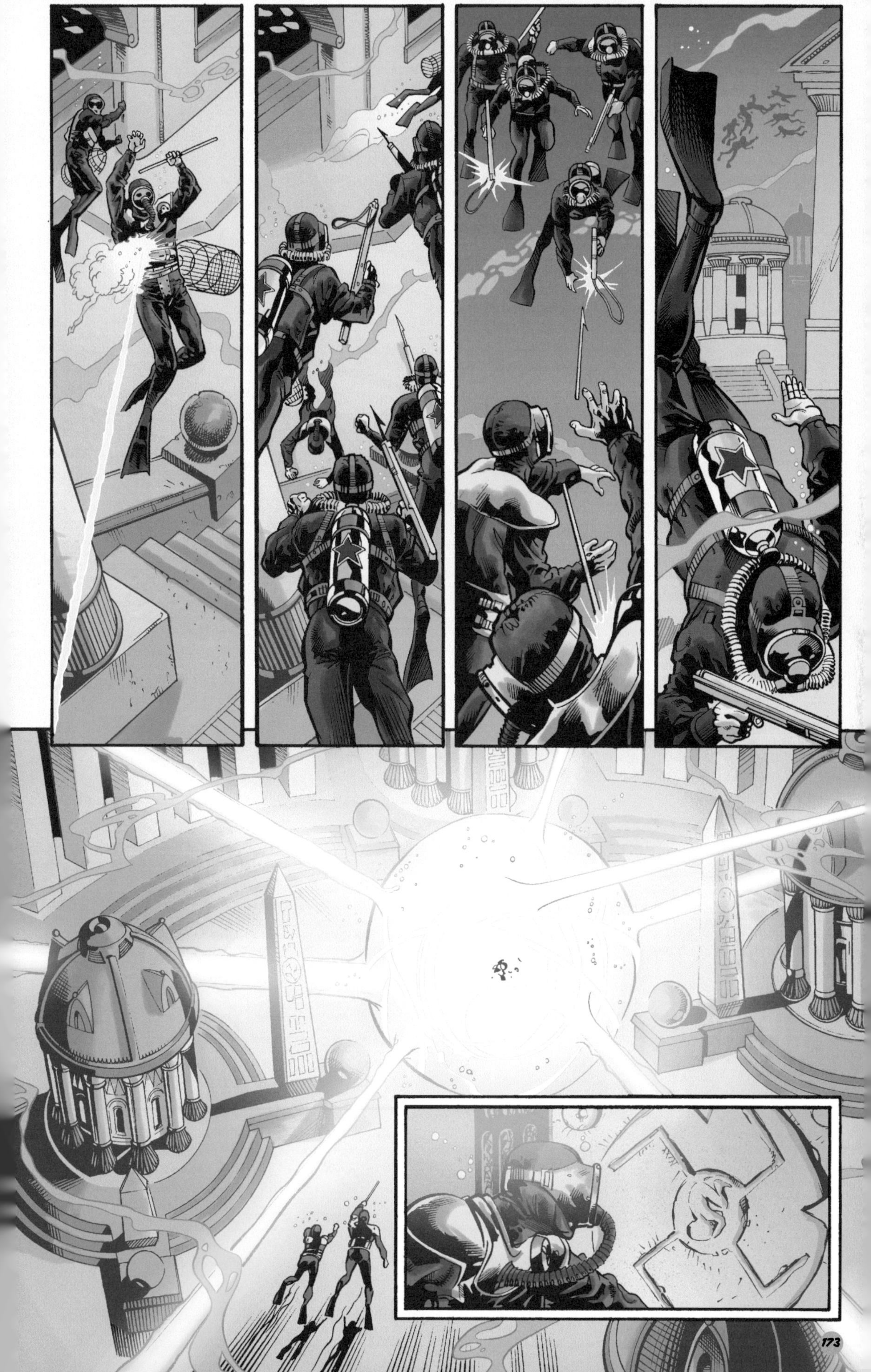

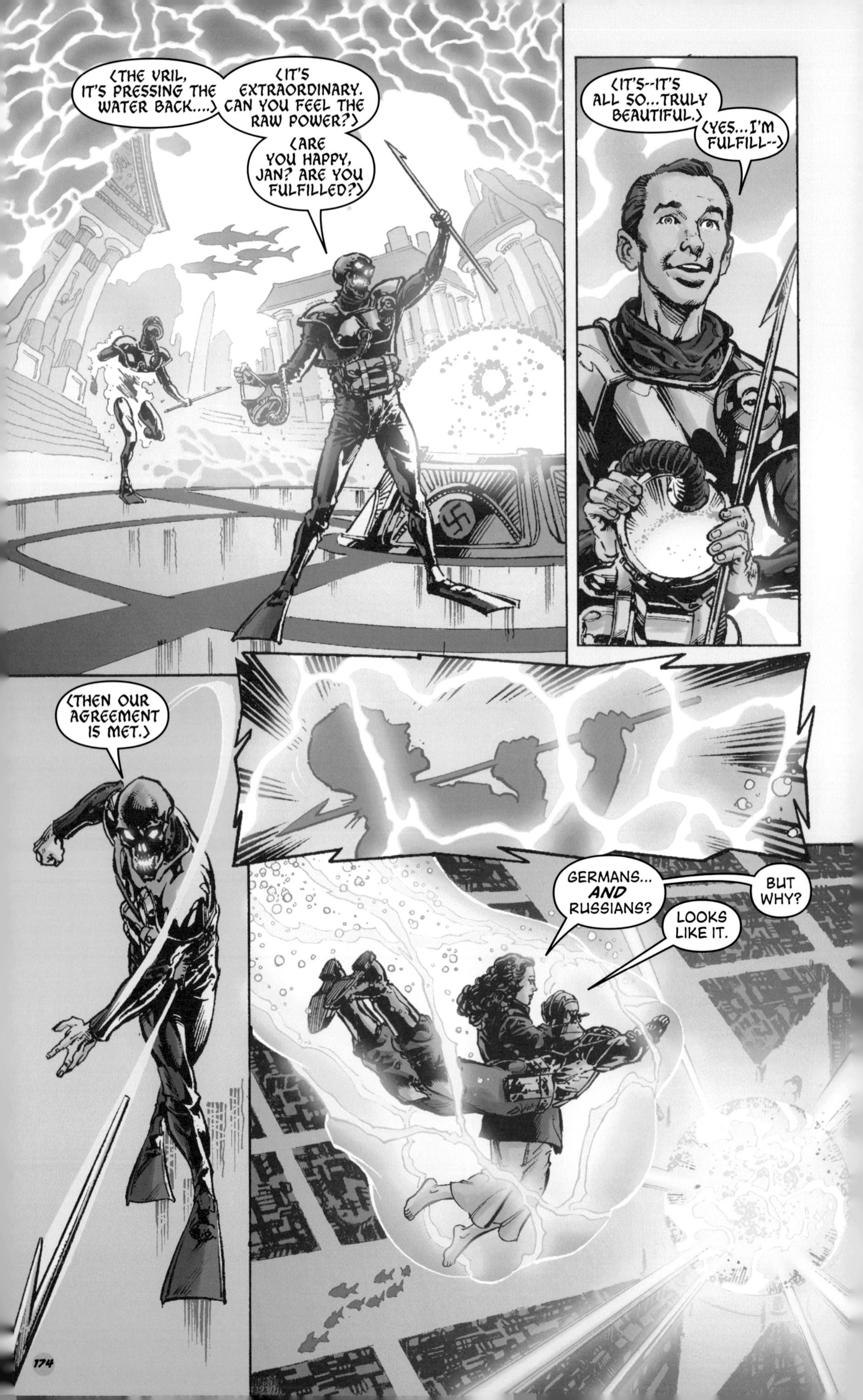
<THE VRIL, IT'S PRESSING THE WATER BACK....>
<IT'S EXTRAORDINARY. CAN YOU FEEL THE RAW POWER?>
<ARE YOU HAPPY, JAN? ARE YOU FULFILLED?>
<IT'S--IT'S ALL SO...TRULY BEAUTIFUL.>
<YES...I'M FULFILL-->
<THEN OUR AGREEMENT IS MET.>
GERMANS... **AND** RUSSIANS?
LOOKS LIKE IT.
BUT WHY?

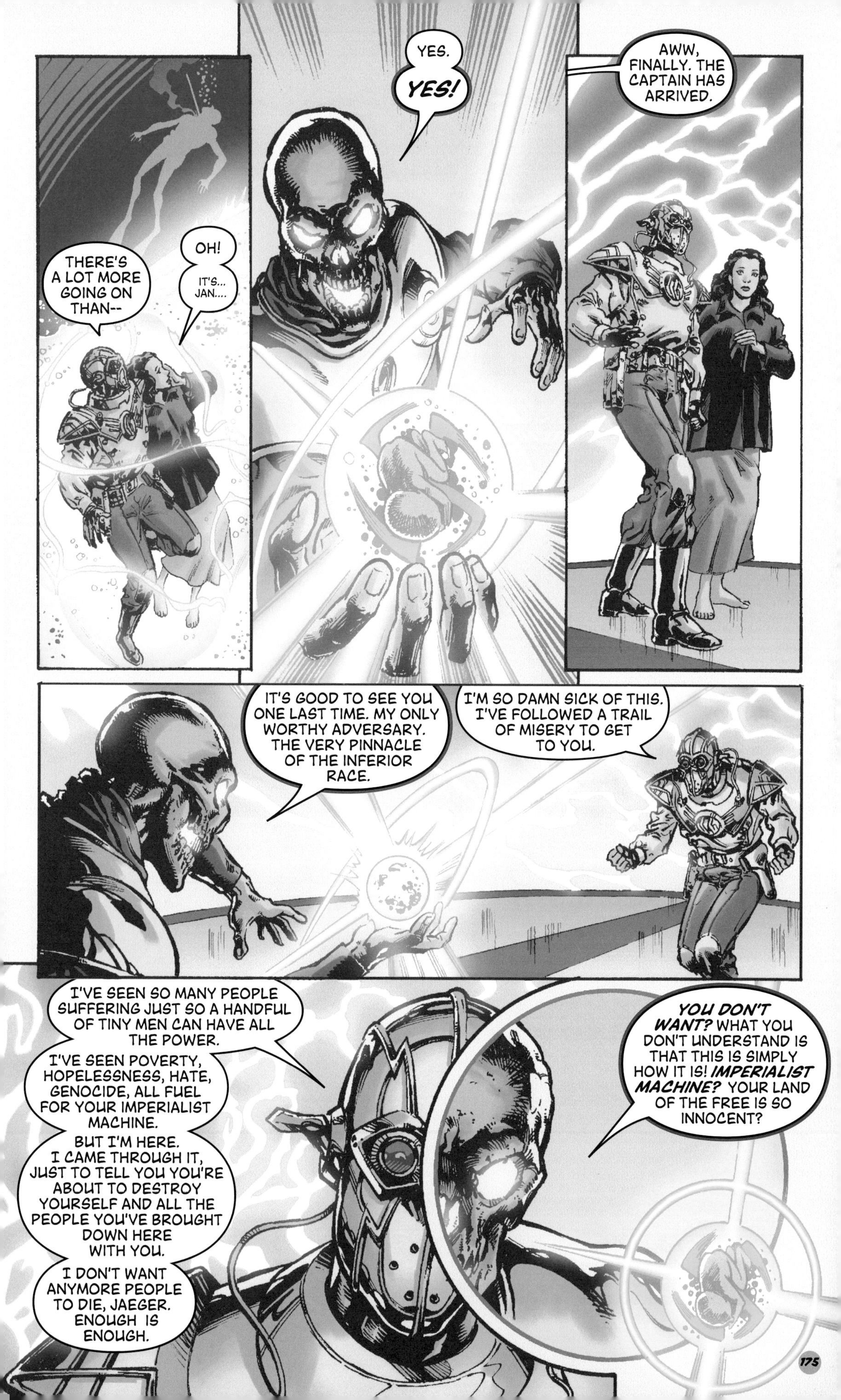
THERE'S A LOT MORE GOING ON THAN--
OH!
IT'S... JAN....
YES.
YES!
AWW, FINALLY. THE CAPTAIN HAS ARRIVED.
IT'S GOOD TO SEE YOU ONE LAST TIME. MY ONLY WORTHY ADVERSARY. THE VERY PINNACLE OF THE INFERIOR RACE.
I'M SO DAMN SICK OF THIS. I'VE FOLLOWED A TRAIL OF MISERY TO GET TO YOU.
I'VE SEEN SO MANY PEOPLE SUFFERING JUST SO A HANDFUL OF TINY MEN CAN HAVE ALL THE POWER.
I'VE SEEN POVERTY, HOPELESSNESS, HATE, GENOCIDE, ALL FUEL FOR YOUR IMPERIALIST MACHINE.
BUT I'M HERE. I CAME THROUGH IT, JUST TO TELL YOU YOU'RE ABOUT TO DESTROY YOURSELF AND ALL THE PEOPLE YOU'VE BROUGHT DOWN HERE WITH YOU.
I DON'T WANT ANYMORE PEOPLE TO DIE, JAEGER. ENOUGH IS ENOUGH.
YOU DON'T WANT? WHAT YOU DON'T UNDERSTAND IS THAT THIS IS SIMPLY HOW IT IS! IMPERIALIST MACHINE? YOUR LAND OF THE FREE IS SO INNOCENT?

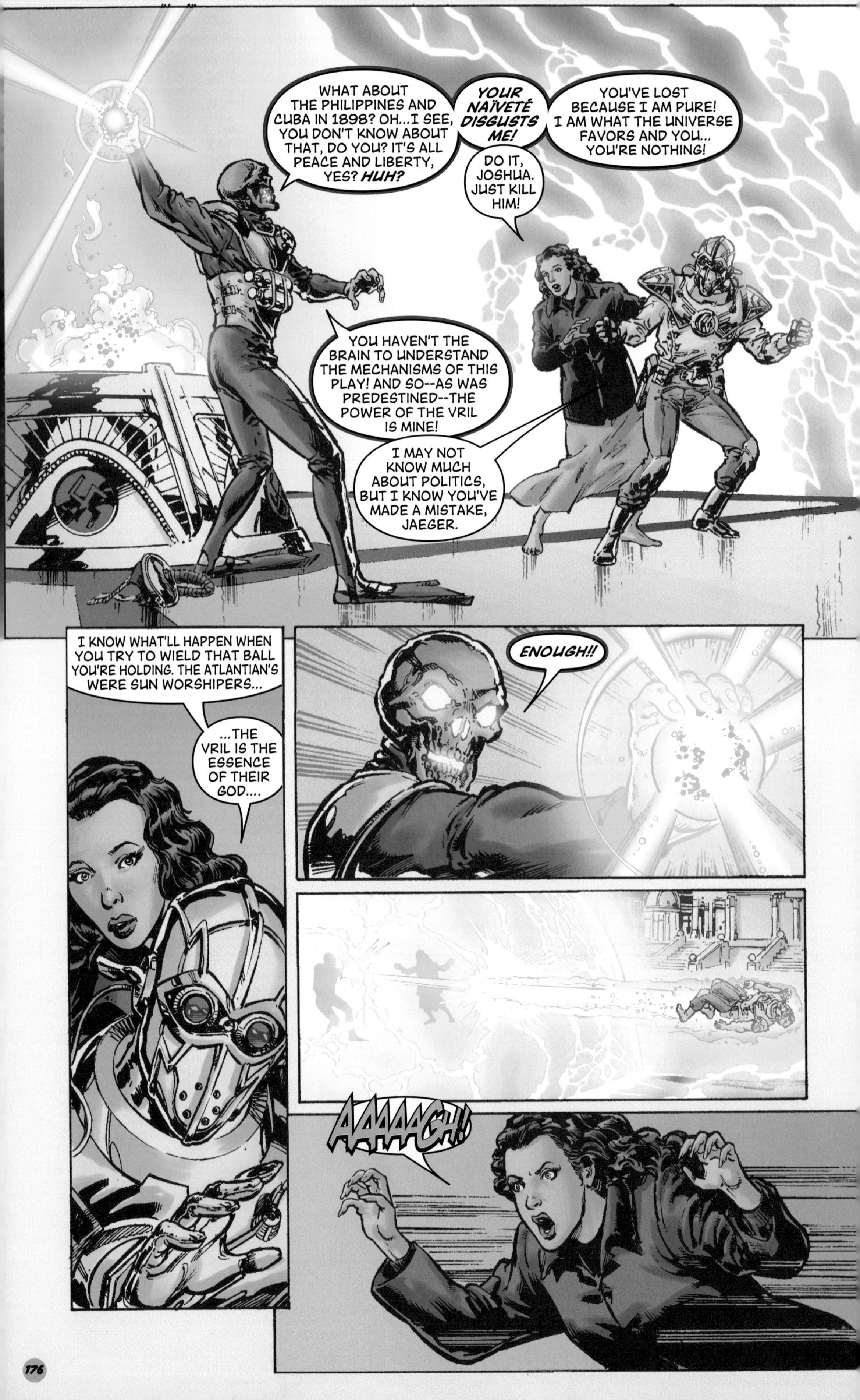
WHAT ABOUT THE PHILIPPINES AND CUBA IN 1898? OH...I SEE, YOU DON'T KNOW ABOUT THAT, DO YOU? IT'S ALL PEACE AND LIBERTY, YES? HUH?
YOUR NAÏVETÉ DISGUSTS ME!
YOU'VE LOST BECAUSE I AM PURE! I AM WHAT THE UNIVERSE FAVORS AND YOU... YOU'RE NOTHING!
DO IT, JOSHUA. JUST KILL HIM!
YOU HAVEN'T THE BRAIN TO UNDERSTAND THE MECHANISMS OF THIS PLAY! AND SO--AS WAS PREDESTINED--THE POWER OF THE VRIL IS MINE!
I MAY NOT KNOW MUCH ABOUT POLITICS, BUT I KNOW YOU'VE MADE A MISTAKE, JAEGER.
I KNOW WHAT'LL HAPPEN WHEN YOU TRY TO WIELD THAT BALL YOU'RE HOLDING. THE ATLANTIAN'S WERE SUN WORSHIPERS...
...THE VRIL IS THE ESSENCE OF THEIR GOD....
ENOUGH!!
AAAAAGH!!

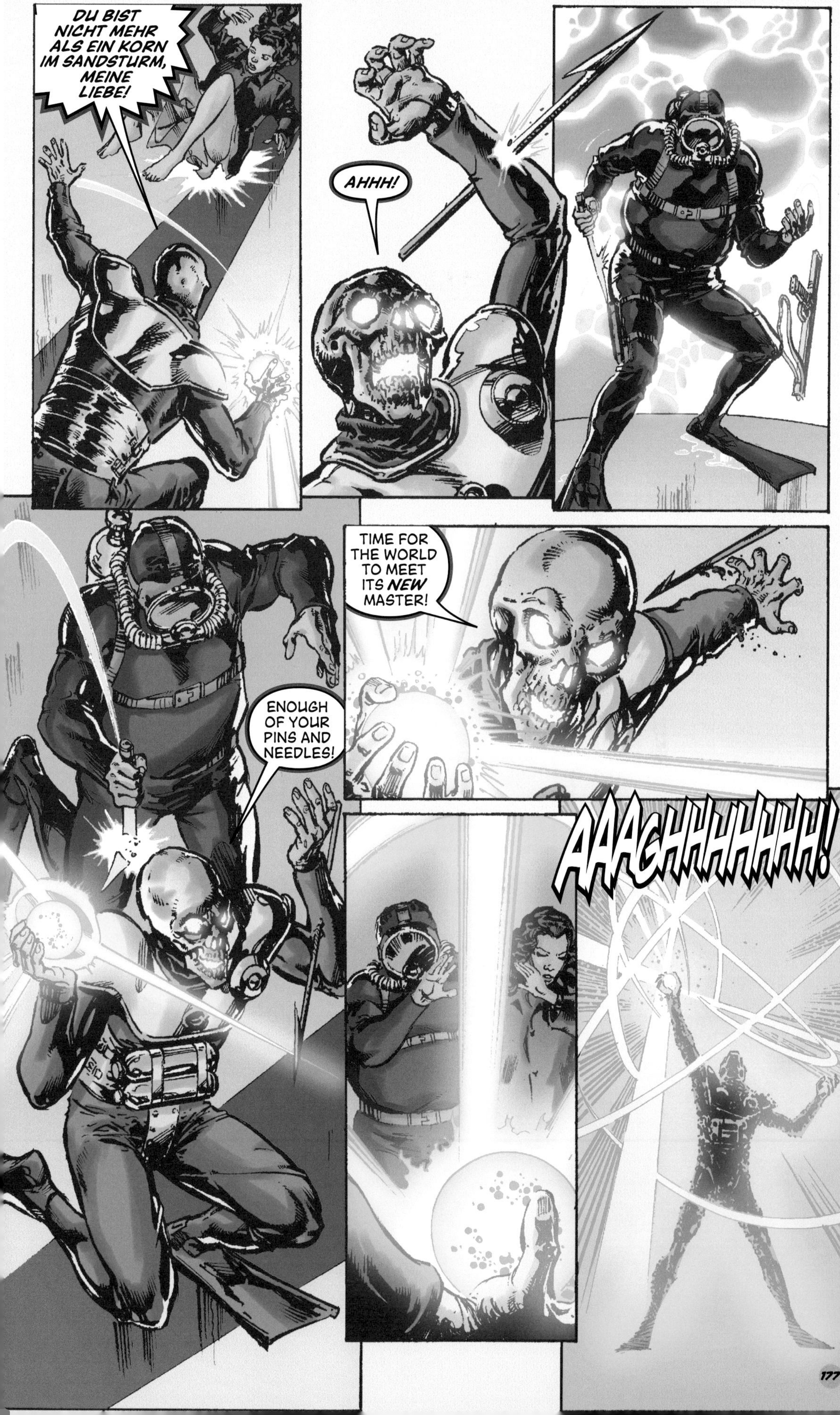
DU BIST NICHT MEHR ALS EIN KORN IM SANDSTURM, MEINE LIEBE!
AHHH!
TIME FOR THE WORLD TO MEET ITS NEW MASTER!
ENOUGH OF YOUR PINS AND NEEDLES!
AAAGHHHHHHH!

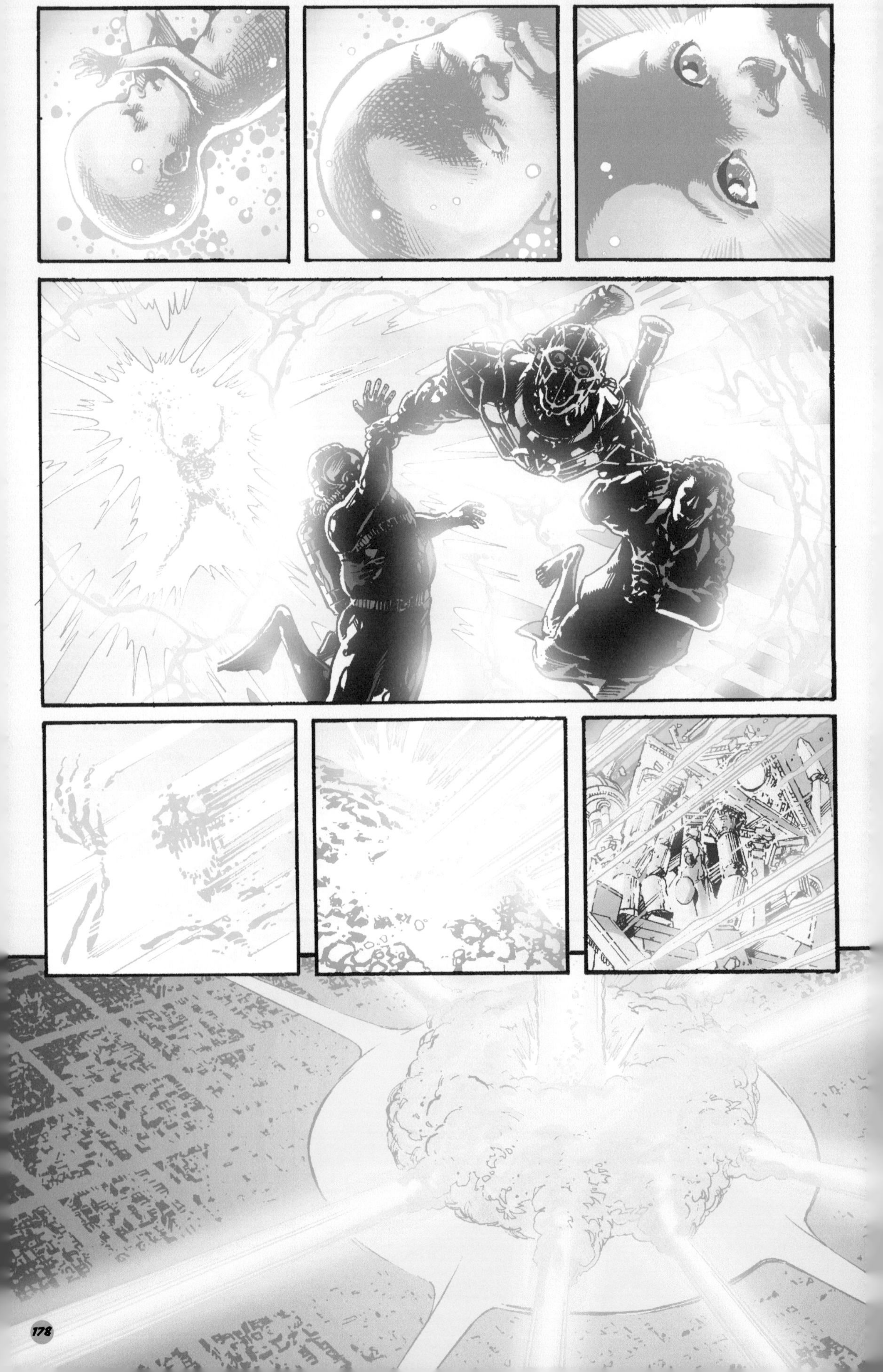

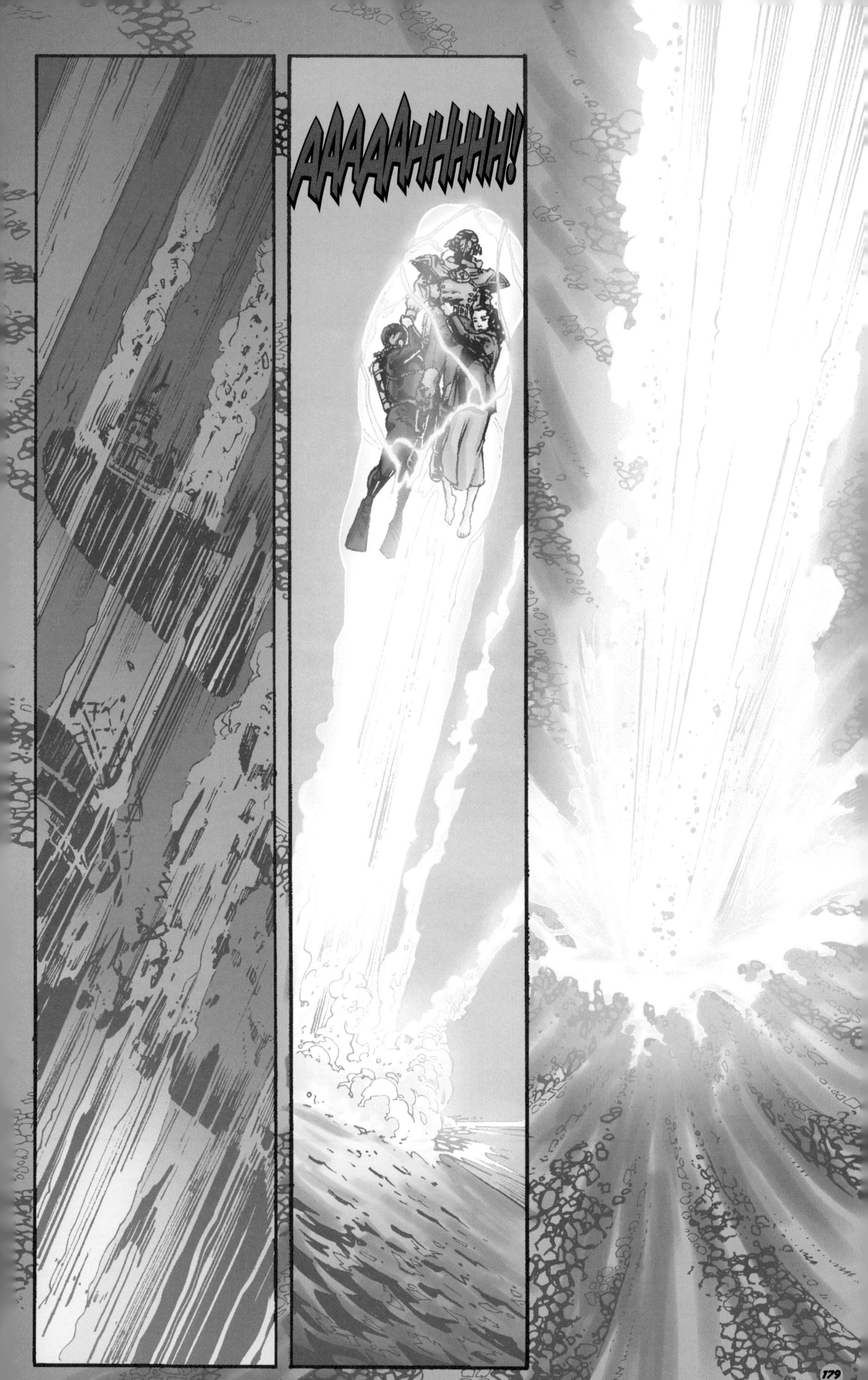
AAAAAHHHHH!

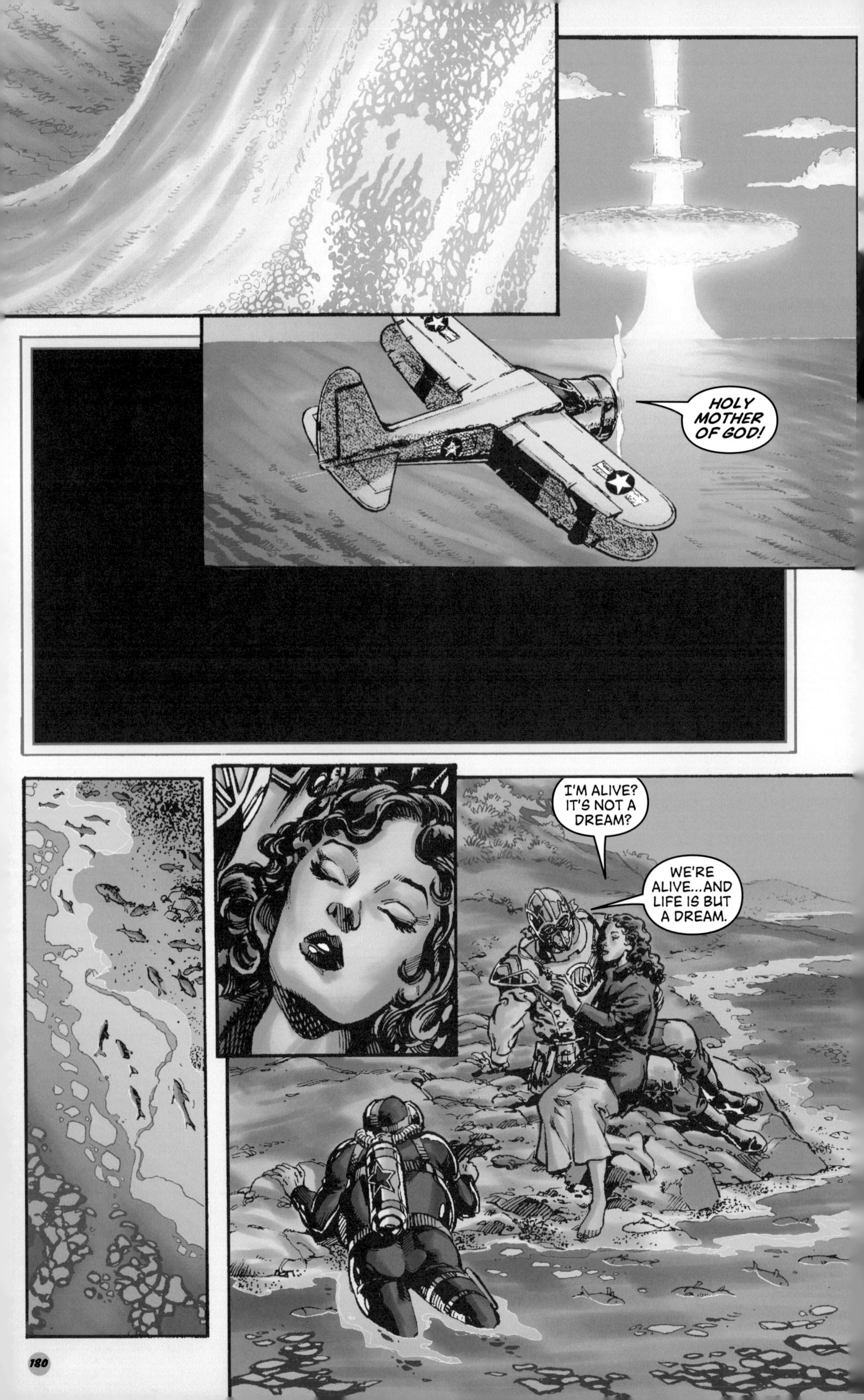
HOLY MOTHER OF GOD!
I'M ALIVE? IT'S NOT A DREAM?
WE'RE ALIVE...AND LIFE IS BUT A DREAM.

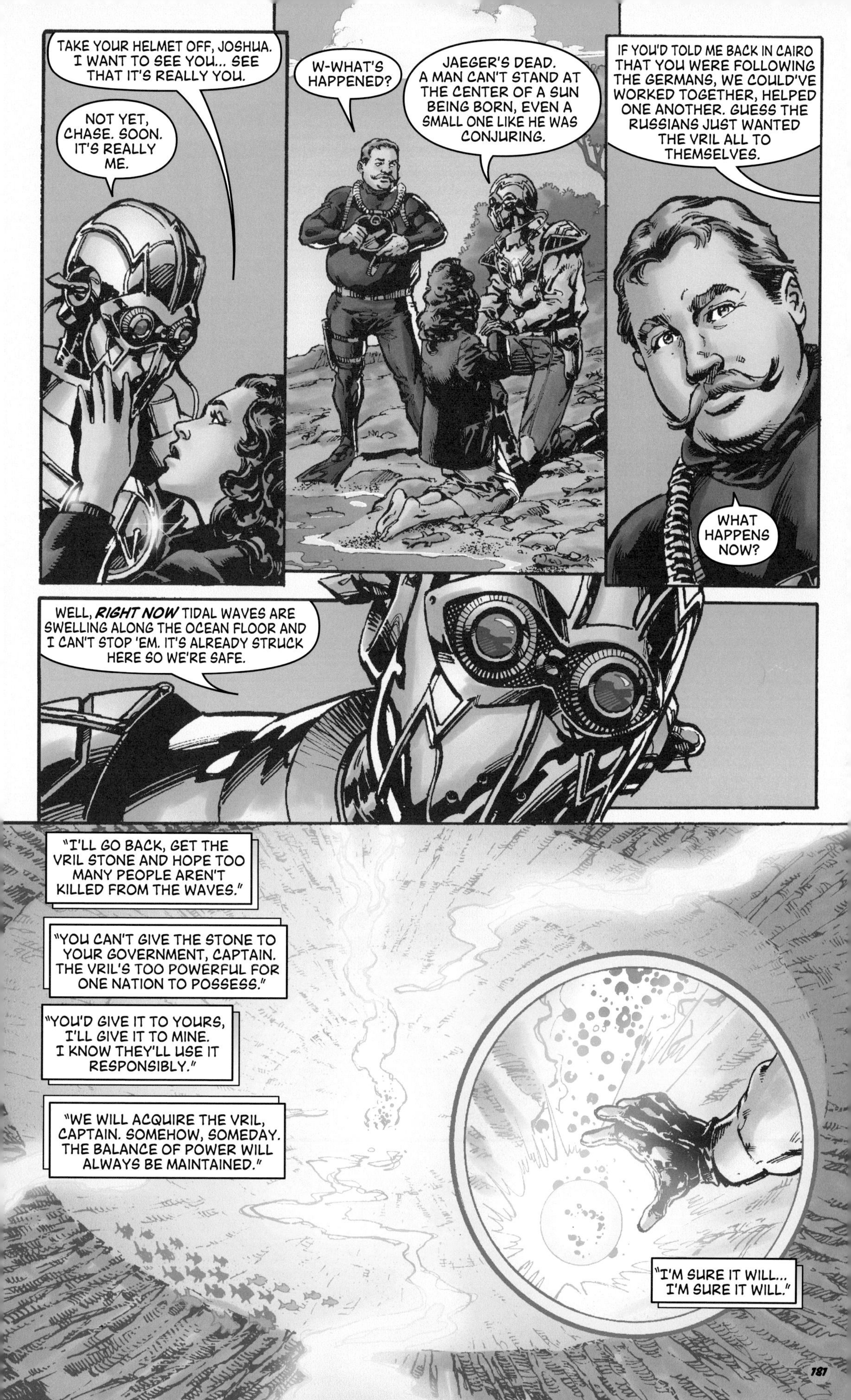
TAKE YOUR HELMET OFF, JOSHUA. I WANT TO SEE YOU... SEE THAT IT'S REALLY YOU.
NOT YET, CHASE. SOON. IT'S REALLY ME.
W-WHAT'S HAPPENED?
JAEGER'S DEAD. A MAN CAN'T STAND AT THE CENTER OF A SUN BEING BORN, EVEN A SMALL ONE LIKE HE WAS CONJURING.
IF YOU'D TOLD ME BACK IN CAIRO THAT YOU WERE FOLLOWING THE GERMANS, WE COULD'VE WORKED TOGETHER, HELPED ONE ANOTHER. GUESS THE RUSSIANS JUST WANTED THE VRIL ALL TO THEMSELVES.
WHAT HAPPENS NOW?
WELL, ***RIGHT NOW*** TIDAL WAVES ARE SWELLING ALONG THE OCEAN FLOOR AND I CAN'T STOP 'EM. IT'S ALREADY STRUCK HERE SO WE'RE SAFE.
"I'LL GO BACK, GET THE VRIL STONE AND HOPE TOO MANY PEOPLE AREN'T KILLED FROM THE WAVES."
"YOU CAN'T GIVE THE STONE TO YOUR GOVERNMENT, CAPTAIN. THE VRIL'S TOO POWERFUL FOR ONE NATION TO POSSESS."
"YOU'D GIVE IT TO YOURS, I'LL GIVE IT TO MINE. I KNOW THEY'LL USE IT RESPONSIBLY."
"WE WILL ACQUIRE THE VRIL, CAPTAIN. SOMEHOW, SOMEDAY. THE BALANCE OF POWER WILL ALWAYS BE MAINTAINED."
"I'M SURE IT WILL... I'M SURE IT WILL."

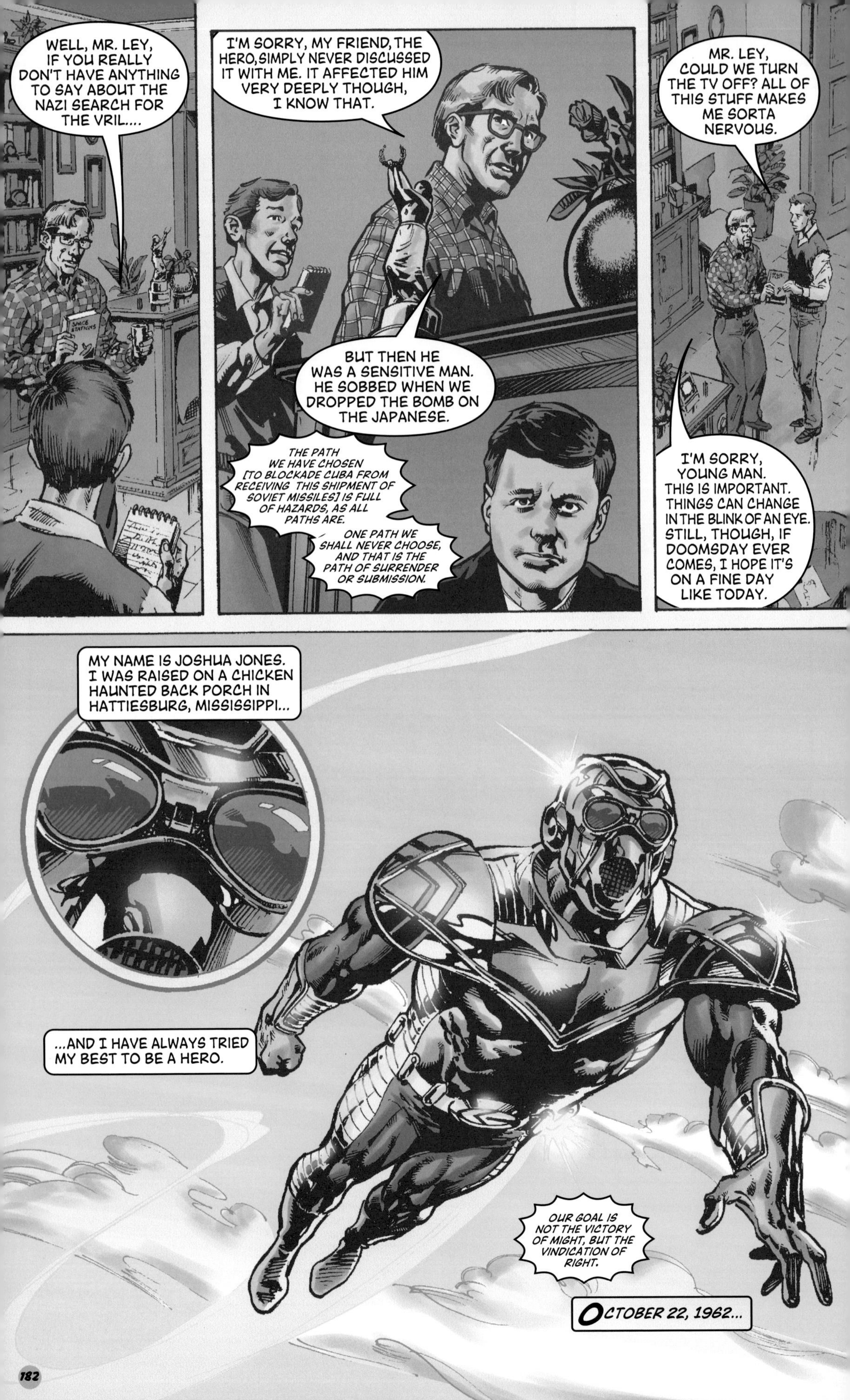
WELL, MR. LEY, IF YOU REALLY DON'T HAVE ANYTHING TO SAY ABOUT THE NAZI SEARCH FOR THE VRIL....
SPACE STATIONS
I'M SORRY, MY FRIEND, THE HERO, SIMPLY NEVER DISCUSSED IT WITH ME. IT AFFECTED HIM VERY DEEPLY THOUGH, I KNOW THAT.
BUT THEN HE WAS A SENSITIVE MAN. HE SOBBED WHEN WE DROPPED THE BOMB ON THE JAPANESE.
THE PATH WE HAVE CHOSEN [TO BLOCKADE CUBA FROM RECEIVING THIS SHIPMENT OF SOVIET MISSILES] IS FULL OF HAZARDS, AS ALL PATHS ARE.
ONE PATH WE SHALL NEVER CHOOSE, AND THAT IS THE PATH OF SURRENDER OR SUBMISSION.
MR. LEY, COULD WE TURN THE TV OFF? ALL OF THIS STUFF MAKES ME SORTA NERVOUS.
I'M SORRY, YOUNG MAN. THIS IS IMPORTANT. THINGS CAN CHANGE IN THE BLINK OF AN EYE. STILL, THOUGH, IF DOOMSDAY EVER COMES, I HOPE IT'S ON A FINE DAY LIKE TODAY.
MY NAME IS JOSHUA JONES. I WAS RAISED ON A CHICKEN HAUNTED BACK PORCH IN HATTIESBURG, MISSISSIPPI...
...AND I HAVE ALWAYS TRIED MY BEST TO BE A HERO.
OUR GOAL IS NOT THE VICTORY OF MIGHT, BUT THE VINDICATION OF RIGHT.
OCTOBER 22, 1962...

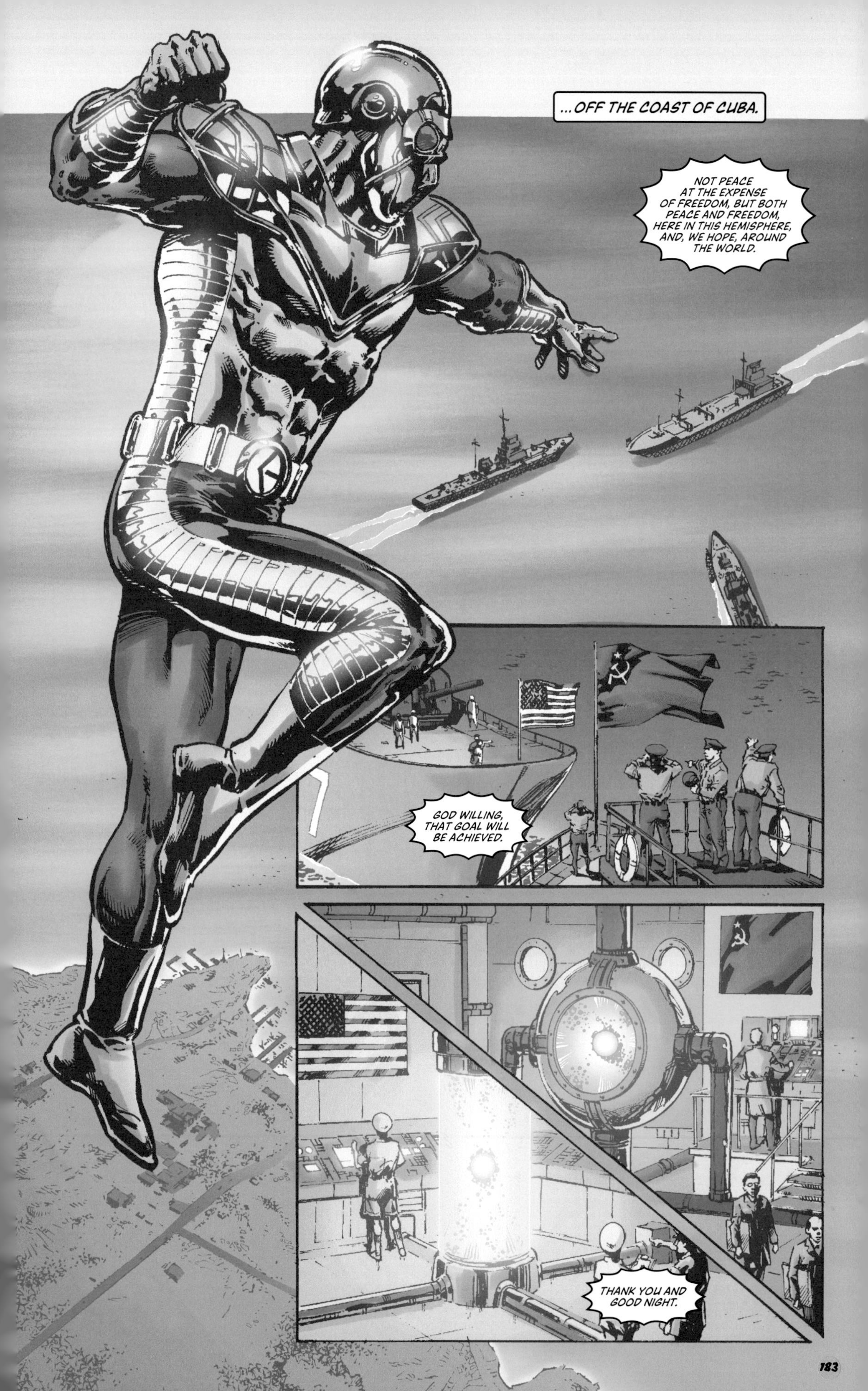
...OFF THE COAST OF CUBA.
NOT PEACE AT THE EXPENSE OF FREEDOM, BUT BOTH PEACE AND FREEDOM, HERE IN THIS HEMISPHERE, AND, WE HOPE, AROUND THE WORLD.
GOD WILLING, THAT GOAL WILL BE ACHIEVED.
THANK YOU AND GOOD NIGHT.

BOB ALMOND, comics fan from straight out of the womb, began his career as an ink artist in 199? with Marvel Comics. He spent a decade collaborating on various assignments like WARLOCK & TH? INFINITY WATCH, STARMASTERS, ULTRAGIRL, STAR TREK: DS9, SILVER SURFER, but he's probably most rec? ognized for his work alongside Priest and Sal Velluto on their critically-acclaimed three-year wor? on BLACK PANTHER. Besides inking for numerous publishers such as Malibu, DC, and Acclaim on title? ike JSA, AQUAMAN, and BLOODSHOT, Bob was among the group of original creators that helpe? introduce Penny-Farthing Press to comicdom through his collaboration with creator Courtne? Huddleston on the original DECOY series. Initially turning down the offer to ink CAPTAIN GRAVIT? & THE POWER OF THE VRIL due to a schedule conflict, fate would again come calling as Bob wa? ater reoffered the series and reunited with his oft-partner Sal. Bob's most recent project wa? embellishing the art on VAMPIRELLA: REVELATIONS for Harris Comics.

He lives in Massachusetts with his precious family, wife Diane, son Nathan, and cat Tux. He dab? bles in space exploration and time travel but spends most of his spare time on patrol for the? Big Peanutt.

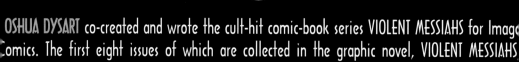

JOSHUA DYSART co-created and wrote the cult-hit comic-book series VIOLENT MESSIAHS for Image? Comics. The first eight issues of which are collected in the graphic novel, VIOLENT MESSIAHS? Volume I: Book of Job.

More recently his comic projects have included the DC six-issue mini-series THE DEMON: DRIVEN OU? and the Dark Horse one-shot VAN HELSING: BENEATH THE RUE MORGUE. He's currently the monthl? writer on Vertigo's SWAMP THING.

He lives by the beach. He loves his mother. He's trying to learn how to hold himself in the palm? of his own hand, but has yet to figure it out. I think he's afraid, and that's what's holding him back? He really digs writing for a living. He recommends it over almost all other forms of slavery.

Josh Dysart never learned to play Jazz on any instrument, but then...it's not too late, is it?

MIKE GARCIA The colorist formally know as Mike Garcia, now going under the alias The Big? Peanutt or just a symbol of a nut, is said to be hiding out in gloomy, Southern California. Thi? alty hooligan is so brash, one "T" just wasn't enough. With Mrs. Nutt and The Little Peanutt b? his side, The Big Peanutt sets out to destroy all comic art that crosses his path. This Nutt is said? to be "un" armed but dangerous. We have three of his powder-puffed cronies, J.T-bone Steak? Stinky-Cheese Huddlestoned, and Raunchy Jam Woody in custody, but we need your help to find?

the Big Guy. Beneath his ridiculous shell hides a nutcase who takes himself much too seriously.

We believe The Big P is devising a plot for creative world domination as we speak and could be hidden in plain sight. Several people, animals, and...things including elephants, baseball park vendors, and angry artists will not rest until he is caught.

At thirteen, JOE RUBINSTEIN worked as an assistant to the legendary inker/artist Dick Giordino. Now over thirty years later, he has worked with just about every well-known artist on just about every well-known title.

SAL VELLUTO broke into comics as a professional in 1988, drawing POWER PACK (fill-ins and a Graphic Novel) for Marvel. Since then, his work has appeared on hundreds of publications both in the U.S. and Europe.

Sal has been the regular artist on many series and mini-series: MOON KNIGHT, SILVER SURFER, LOFTIER THAN MORTAL, BLACK PANTHER (Marvel), JUSTICE LEAGUE TASK FORCE, FIREBRAND, JSA, ALL-STARS, (DC) X-O MANOWAR, BLOODSHOT (Valiant/Acclaim), ARMOR (Acclaim) plus many more.

He has also worked on several Saturday morning cartoons, (layout and storyboards), video games (production art) magazine, book and commercial illustrations, web interactive games, and trading cards.

Sal lives in Utah with his wife of 20 years, Sharon, and their four children.

STEPHEN VRATTOS has written articles for the *New York Post*, *Comics Buyer's Guide* and *Marvel Age* to name a few. His first published comic story appeared in SPIDER-MAN Unlimited #7. He can be seen as Stephan the Waiter in SPECTACULAR SPIDER-MAN (first series) #158 and walking a dog in AVENGERS (first series) #313. He's probably signed more autographs and had his picture taken with more fans than most people in comicdom, though they will never realize it (cue ominous music). He's thrown out first pitches for the Toronto Blue Jays and Montreal Expos; participated in six Macy's Thanksgiving Day parades; bungee jumped; sky dived; waited on Johnny Depp and Winona Ryder; acted with Marisa Tomei, Brad Oscar and Michael Chiklis; dined with Stan Lee, John Byrne and Alan Moore; and created CAPTAIN GRAVITY for Penny-Farthing Press, but considers the greatest moment in his life as the day he met his wife Audrey.

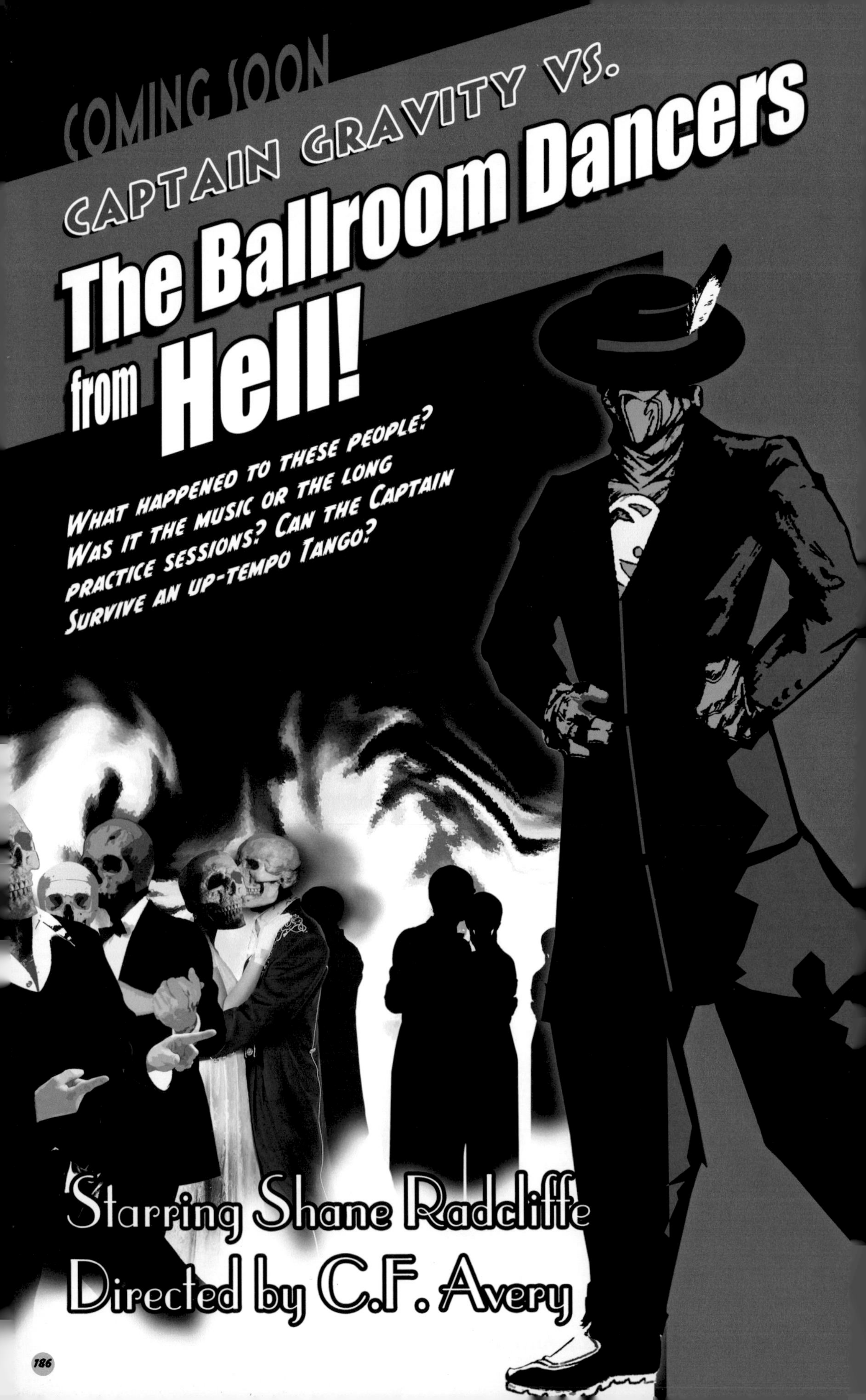
COMING SOON
CAPTAIN GRAVITY VS.
The Ballroom Dancers from Hell!
WHAT HAPPENED TO THESE PEOPLE? WAS IT THE MUSIC OR THE LONG PRACTICE SESSIONS? CAN THE CAPTAIN SURVIVE AN UP-TEMPO TANGO?
Starring Shane Radcliffe
Directed by C.F. Avery

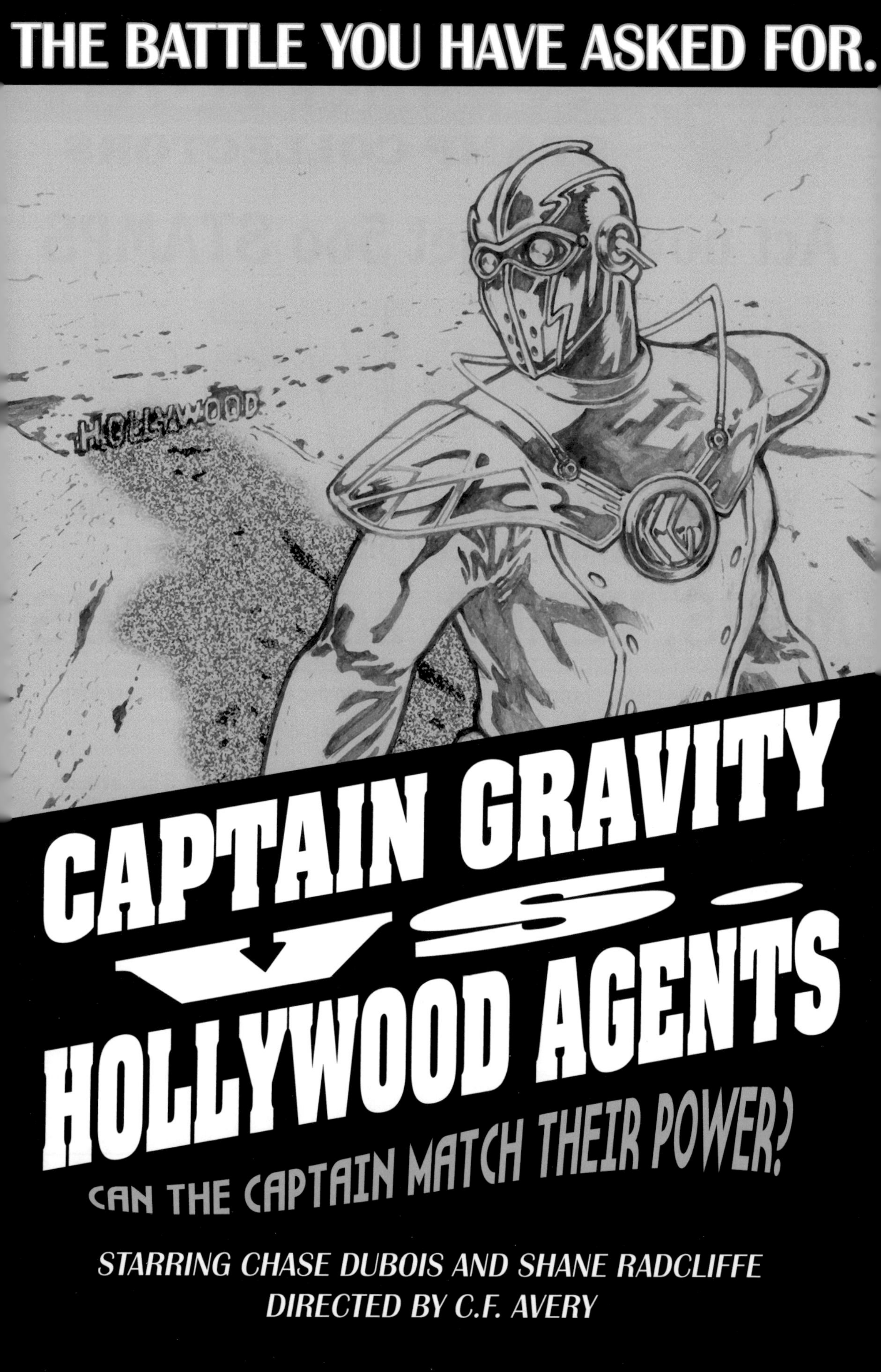
THE BATTLE YOU HAVE ASKED FOR.
HOLLYWOOD
CAPTAIN GRAVITY
VS.
HOLLYWOOD AGENTS
CAN THE CAPTAIN MATCH THEIR POWER?
STARRING CHASE DUBOIS AND SHANE RADCLIFFE
DIRECTED BY C.F. AVERY

ATTENTION:
STAMP COLLECTORS

Act now and get 500 STAMPS for only 5¢!

You will receive stamps from the U.S., foreign countries, and several planets including

MARS, VENUS, and URANUS

Not only are the planet stamps excellent collector items, they can also be used for postage on all your letters to other planets in our solar system—WOW!

Now get this, you will also receive 25 of our *Taste-N-Stick* stamps. They actually taste like the picture on the stamp. Try the famous steak and potatoes stamp, and for you vegetarians—a broccoli stamp. Lastly, we will include 10 non-food Taste-N-Stick stamps including such tasty treats as sweaty gym clothes, a rubber tire, and our current best seller, the colon biopsy triangle stamp.

Can you believe it?!

¢5
PIZZA CRUST
Mexico
5
5
Visit Earth
G HEAD
¢5
POTTED HAM

*Not responsible for side effects caused from **Taste-N-Stick** stamps, including tongue sores, blindness, fatigue, loss of hair, Lyme Disease, Scarlet Fever, fever blisters, mange, lice, gingivitis, gangrene or loss of limbs.

—PARODY OF AN EARLY COMIC BOOK AD—

Create AN INVISIBLE FRIEND

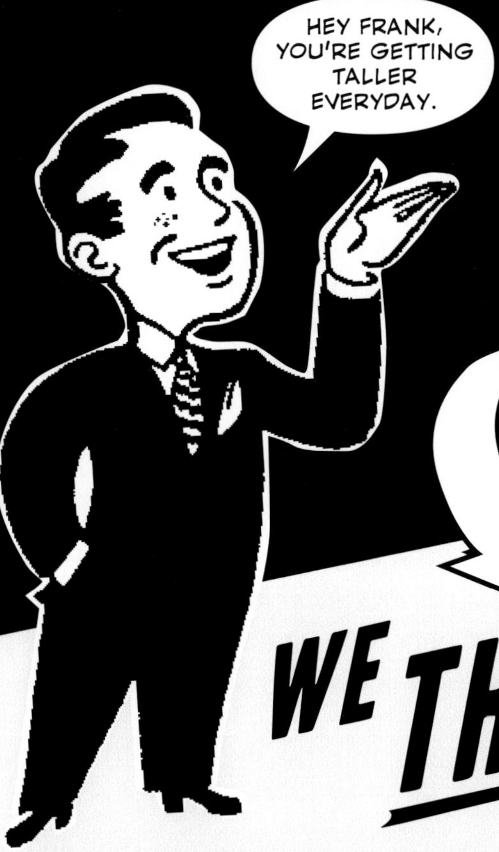

HEY FRANK, YOU'RE GETTING TALLER EVERYDAY.

ARE YOU SHY AROUND PEOPLE?

DO CROWDS MAKE YOU NERVOUS?

HAVE TROUBLE STARTING CONVERSATIONS?

WE THOUGHT SO!

Contact us RIGHT NOW and we will send you our special book titled, *HOW TO CREATE YOUR NEW BEST FRIEND*.

The possibilities are endless—someone to go to the movies with, or take bowling, and best of all, he or she never has bad breath!

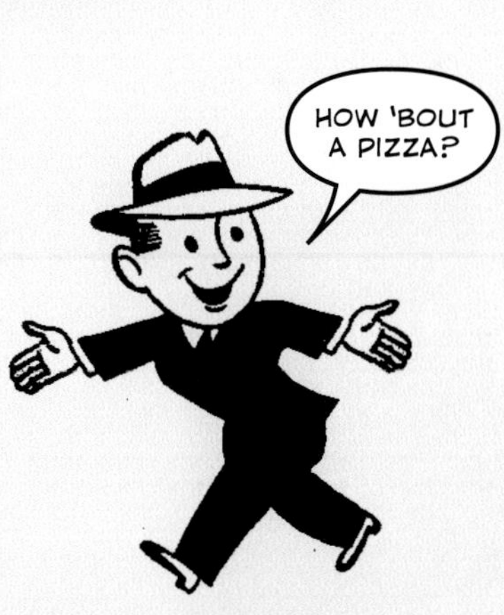

HOW 'BOUT A PIZZA?

Send us $29.99 and we will also send you a companion book — *WHAT TO DO WHEN YOUR INVISIBLE FRIEND GETS SICK.*

LEARN TO *Repair* ALL CARS

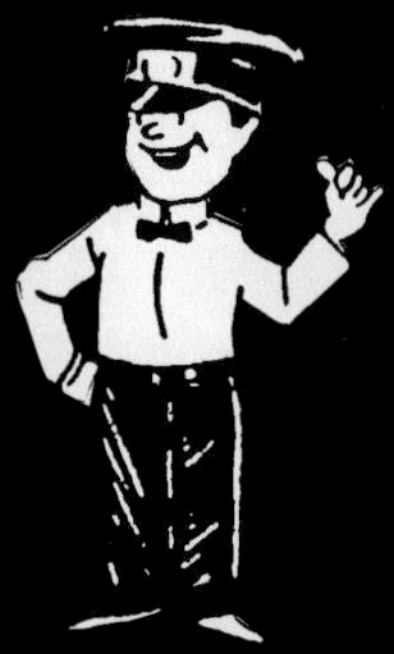

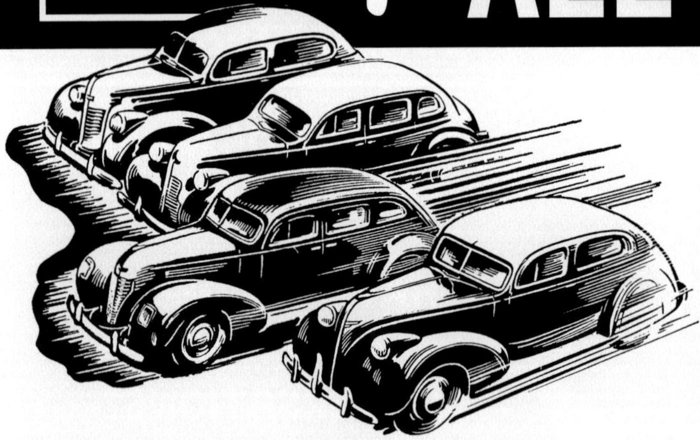

Do you love the satisfaction of REPAIRING your own car and saving the high labor charges of auto mechanics?

We have a deal for you– Turn this labor of love into a new and rewarding career.

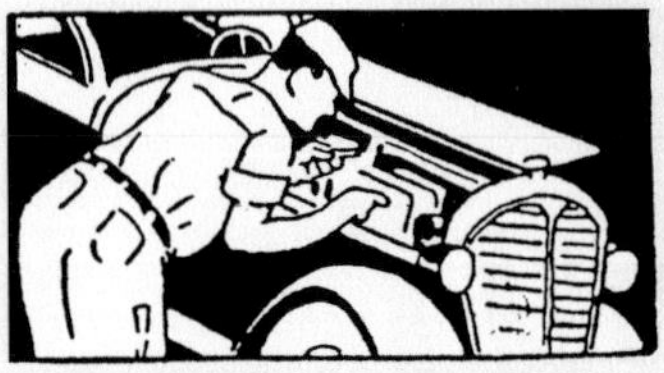

STEP 1: Locate the black circle thing above the metal doo-hickey.

Easy-to-follow detailed instructions.

Our staff has compiled **THE COMPLETE AUTO ENCYCLOPEDIA**. This large book provides specific instructions on how to repair ***all automobiles***–yes, every car that has ***ever been built*** in the United States, France and Costa Rica–and includes every type of repair that can be performed on these vehicles.

This book is available for the next 30 days at the reasonable price of $50. However, due to its size (over 5,000 pages), the shipping cost is an additional $200, which must be paid in advance to us. Cash only, please.

But, get this–if you order now, we will send you (at NO additional cost) our new companion book–which explains how to repair ***all*** of the new car models that will be **introduced during the next 10 years**. Think about it! You will have a head start on everybody.

* Note: the companion book does not include cars produced in Costa Rica.

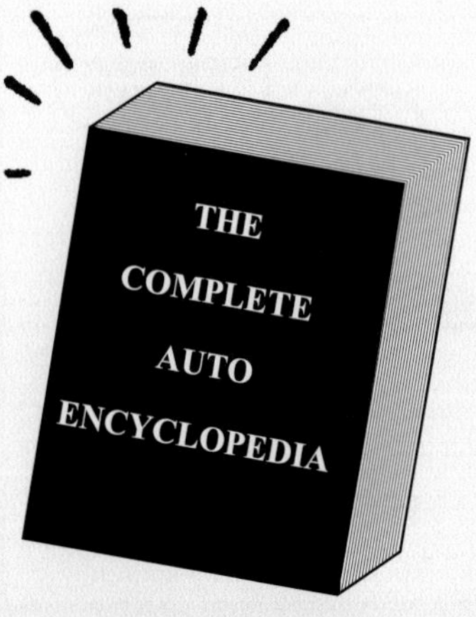
THE
COMPLETE
AUTO
ENCYCLOPEDIA

***Book shown actual size.**

PARODY OF EARLY COMIC AD

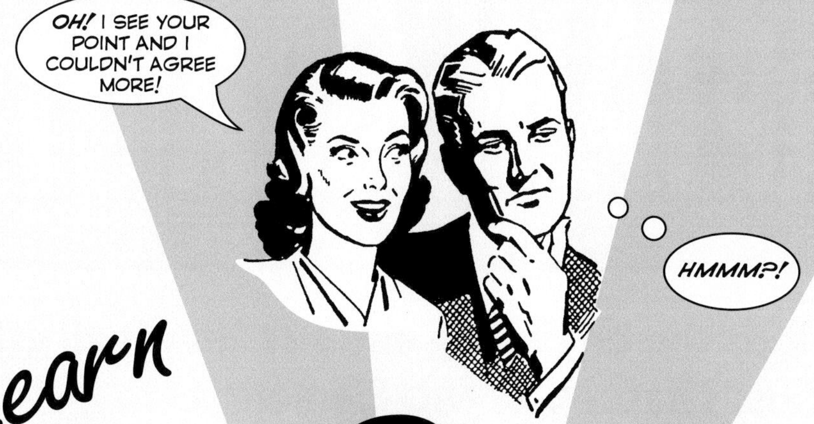
OH! I SEE YOUR POINT AND I COULDN'T AGREE MORE!
HMMM?!

Learn E.S.P.

EXTRA SENSORY PERSUASION

ESP is a skill that can be learned and can CHANGE YOUR LIFE.

Our head of research went deep into the Himalayan mountains where he studied Tibetan techniques which have been used for centuries. These techniques will allow YOU to persuade others to your way of thinking.

Imagine this! You go to your boss and ask for a raise and in less than 10 minutes you leave with the biggest salary increase of your life. You race home to celebrate by taking your wife to dinner – you want a pizza, she wants a vegetable casserole. In less time than it takes to straighten your tie, she is dragging you to the car begging for a pepperoni pizza.

This secret will be limited to the first 5,000 individuals who contact us, and, of course, pay the very reasonable fee of $100 in cash – send today to LET'S DO IT MY WAY, INC.

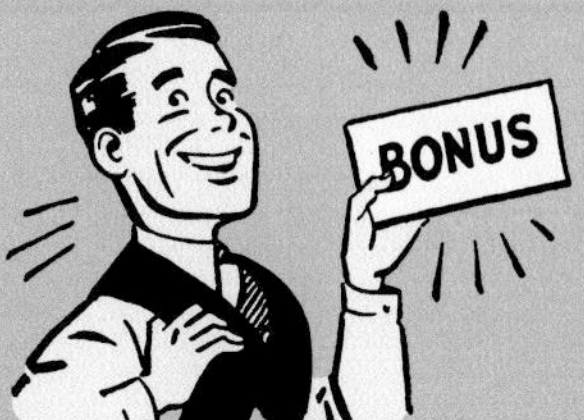
BONUS

PARODY OF AN EARLY COMIC BOOK AD

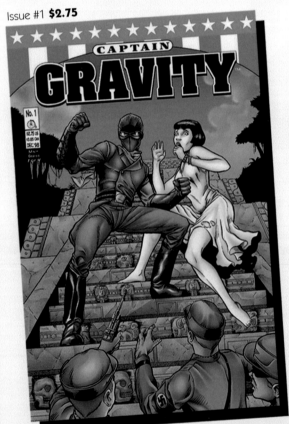

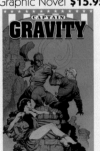